GOVERNMENT AND CAPITALISM

GOVERNMENT AND CAPITALISM

Public and Private Choice in Twentieth Century Australia

N.G. BUTLIN   A. BARNARD   J.J. PINCUS

Sydney
GEORGE ALLEN & UNWIN
London   Boston

First published in 1982 by
George Allen & Unwin Australia Pty Ltd
8 Napier Street
North Sydney NSW 2060

National Library of Australia
Cataloguing-in-Publication entry:

Butlin, N.G. (Noel George).
    Government and capitalism.

    Includes index.
    ISBN 0 86861 187 5.
    ISBN 0 86861 195 6 (pbk.).

    1. Australia — Economic policy — 20th century.
    I. Title.

330.994'04

Library of Congress Catalog Card Number:
81-52288

Set in 10 on 11 pt times by Press Etching Pty Ltd,
Brisbane

Printed in Singapore by the Singapore National Printers (Pte) Ltd.

Contents

Tables

Figures

Preface

This book is the first major outcome of a collaborative research project upon which we and colleagues in the Department of Economic History, Institute of Advanced Studies, Australian National University are engaged. Our interest is in the evolution of the interactions between the Australian public and private sectors since 1901, partly as a matter of historical concern, partly as background to contemporary issues of today.

In publishing this preliminary study, we might have incorporated a great deal of quantitative data. In fact, very few statistics are included. This is because a major task undertaken by the Department was the preparation of a massive data base, fully computerised, on public expenditures and revenues of all levels of government and on related private activity. This data base is being developed for selected years over the period 1901-75 and we intend that it will be readily available once completed. For our purposes, it will provide essential material for quantitative research in the future and it is intended to develop further and more detailed studies from this base. In the meantime, this historical outline and assessment helps to raise questions and suggest tentative explanations that can be tested more carefully in due course.

Part of these statistics have already been exploited, particularly in an article by the present authors on public and private employment and by Barnard and Butlin on public and private investment throughout 1901-75. The present historical treatment and these statistical efforts need to be seen in the context of other work completed and in hand in the Department - theoretical writing by Pincus on regulation and other Departmental research projects on the evolution of Australian taxation, the development of major statutory undertakings in communications and the history of important policies, particularly environmental and energy policy.

We have therefore produced the present volume in a milieu in which a good deal of related activity is occurring. We have also been fortunate in the fact that other relevant but independent work has been carried out in the Research School of Social Sciences within the Institute - particularly on the politics of manufacturing development and the philosophical problems raised by the concepts of 'public' and 'private'.

The choice of three areas of public sector activity - regulation and allocative policy, social policy, public enterprise - for inclusion in this introductory book was made on grounds of contemporary as well as historical interest. Increases in public outlays since the 1950s on health, education and welfare programs (Part 3) have been subject to considerable recent comment in the press, government reports and academic writings. Regulation of private economic activity and allocative policies (Part 2) have had profound effects on Australian economic and social life and on the course and prospects of Australian development. Here, too, regulation is increasingly being questioned. The public enterprises (Part 4) are less important within the public sector now than in 1901 and, on most measures, less substantial relative to the rest of the economy. But in their dealings with these enterprises, Australians still have their most frequent contact with public employees. And the future ownership and mode of operation of some of these enterprises are matters of active policy consideration.

All three authors are responsible for the overall design of the current book, and each has made considerable contribution towards the contents in every section. Nonetheless, each Part has its primary author with final say as to what went in: Butlin for Parts 1, 2 and 5; Barnard for Part 3, and Pincus for Part 4. The issues covered in Parts 1 and 2 formed part of lectures given by Butlin as Professor of Australian Studies at Harvard University during 1979-80. He wishes to acknowledge the help of Mrs Betty McIsaac, Administrative Assistant in the Australian Studies Program, in the preparation of early scripts. Nevertheless, the research for the work was carried out and the writing done at the Australian National University.

Readers will see that there are very few footnotes in this book. We could have cluttered the pages with references. Instead we have provided at the end of Part 5 a fairly carefully structured bibliography. In this reference list, we have grouped sources for quite small sections of each chapter. Hence those who wish to check our statements or to carry any part of the discussion further may do so. To assist in this, we have listed a good many sources that we believe would be of value for further research in relation to the sub-sections of the chapters. Inevitably, qualifications to some generalisations made in our discussion will be found in these sources.

We benefited from the comments and help of other members of our Department, the members of the Economic History Seminar and colleagues elsewhere. Special thanks go to N. Cain, F. Gruen, I. McLean,

R. Scott, R. Shlomowitz and W. Sinclair. Drafts were skilfully typed by E. Jackson, J. Hicks and C. Cromwell; W. Naughton and J. Larocque oversaw the computer word-setting. Miss Kyra Suthern prepared the index.

N.G. Butlin
A. Barnard
J.J. Pincus

Part One

Introduction

1

Methods and Themes

The growth of 'big government' and the appropriate 'limits to government' are leading issues in contemporary society, at both popular and academic levels. This book has taken some of the issues in this debate to provide a springboard into historical investigation. As historians, we are interested in such matters as these: government today intervenes widely, deeply and in detail in private decision-making; private pressures are exerted on government to act to discriminate in favour of special groups, at times intensifying conflict and at other times constraining it; by no means paradoxically, government now seems less and less able to solve many of the problems that it purports to deal with or which private interests seek to have solved by public (government) action; yet private interests often appear to be dependent on government to 'solve' their problems by non-market means without full consideration of market possibilities. All these relate to the interplay between public and private choice.

No doubt, there are several ways of investigating some or all of these questions. One mode is to ask by what route and for what reasons did the present relationships between public and private decision-making develop. We have approached this question as economic historians. Whether there are any lessons to be learnt by attempting to retrace the path is a matter on which readers are almost certain to disagree. We leave the 'lessons of history' to be drawn out by others in debate. We believe that the various protagonists in the popular debate on 'big government' will find little or at most partial comfort in what we have to say. Certainly, we have not sought to take sides. We hope that academic discussion and more particularly theoretical consideration of the issues involved may receive some stimulus and some real grounding from our investigation.

There is very little theory of the interactions of public and private groups on which we may draw - except that, in various ways and places, a great deal of economic theory and some political theory have found their way into the book. Some of the recent literature on public

2

choice has been of particular value though we have found it much less useful in a study of Australian experience than it appears to be in the case, for example, of the United States chiefly because of the scope and scale of government intervention in Australian history (intervention that appears to have been made at times with a considerable degree of government autonomy). In using this and other theoretical approaches we have generally preferred theory to remain implicit in our investigation. The fourth section is to some extent an exception.

It is important to make clear some of the matters with which we are *not* concerned. Although government intervention figures strongly, we are *not* concerned with a traditional study of the 'role of government' in society or the economy. Our focus is on the historical experience of the interaction between public and private decision-making, essentially over this century (with some reference to experience before 1900). A primary interest is in the way in which, the extent to which and to what degree of detail private decision-making has been increasingly altered by government action or by the private use of government. We take it as an essential characteristic that substantially every act of government or every private use of government alters the allocation of resources and the distribution of income and wealth. In other words, through these two processes it alters the bases on which market decisions are made and the outcomes of market decisions. The wider the scope of public action or private dependence on government, the greater is likely to be the alteration of market decision-making. There is, however, a third phenomenon (strictly an extreme form of market alteration) which we have chosen to call 'displacement'. In some given area, government may substitute its decision making *wholly* for private. Most obviously, by replacing private with public enterprise, part of the production decisions of the private sector of the economy is 'displaced' - in this case, market and other decision-making structures are altered. Accordingly, allocative, distributive and displacing issues (each of which often overlap with the others) run through our study as motives for public and private action and as outcomes of government policy. In the Australian case, there is a fourth question of general economic and social management through and by government in the pursuit of very broad structural or developmental ends; attempts to explain this matter will often depend on combining many of the features arising in the three preceding approaches.

'Displacement' introduces, however, an additional question. If public enterprises are substituted for private, how do the resulting public businesses behave? Do they differ significantly from the mode of private operation? If so, what peculiar policies do they pursue or to what peculiar influences are they subject? Is there anything inherent in public enterprises that leads them to differ from private market behaviour?

We have attempted to trace these issues through the various parts of this volume. We begin, as is appropriate in Australia, with a form of general economic management (nineteenth-century 'colonial socialism' as it was known) and move into allocative and regulatory policies. Redistributive problems are examined most directly in the context of social policies relating to welfare. Taxation provisions have a most direct implication for distribution. Some of these provisions are taken up throughout this book. Unfortunately, we have had to defer any thorough-going discussion on the implications of tax arrangements until further detailed research has been carried out. In this context, we have concentrated, instead, on tracing a long-term shift from concern with poverty to an essentially non-redistributive system of 'welfare for all'. The fourth section of the volume deals with the conduct and performance of public enterprise. Throughout all these chapters, we have attempted to bring the interaction of public and private decision-making to the forefront. In doing so, we have had to recognise that much Western historical experience (and its related theory) has only limited value to Australia because of the prominence of governments throughout virtually the whole of Australian history *in all decision-making processes*. Hence 'government' must figure, in our story, as a much more significant (and in some periods autonomous) 'actor' than is the case in Europe or North America. Perhaps for this reason, Australian history may have a special value in illuminating the larger story.

By 'government' we mean the ultimate coercive authority of the nation-state and the institutions constitutionally derived from it. Five levels of government accordingly are relevant - colonial governments, Federal, State and local governments and statutory authorities. This is an institutional delimitation that is blurred at the edges. We have to live with some obscurity in setting our boundaries. Where we refer to 'public' action or the 'public sector' throughout the book, we mean 'government' in this institutional sense. What we have attempted to portray is an evolving map or network: a progressively widening and deepening intervention by or dependence on government in private choice; a shifting public intervention from the special (and very important) forms of general economic management in the nineteenth century to a different style from the beginning of the present century, emphasising allocative and redistributive influences on or pressuies from private bodies; the progressive extension of these allocative and distributive influences in the course of this century in both economic and social (welfare) policy; the significance of public supportive or private dependent behaviour and the evolution of eventually *constraining* action by government arising from the commitments to full employment, anti-inflation and macro-economic policies. In these sequences, tendencies to centralisation are prominent. In the account of the changing conduct and performance of the public enterprises in Australia, we have attempted to display the major shifts in investment criteria, pricing and output policies and the politicising of public decision-making leading to cross-subsidisation or discriminatory benefits to particular private groups. At the end of the book we have included a chapter presenting a summary interpretative sketch.

Some writers have proposed (Peacock and Wiseman 1961, Buchanan and Flowers 1975) that the growing 'size of government' can be measured by relating some measures of government activity to economy-wide or private counterparts. Implicitly, the design of social accounts provides such a measure by estimates of public capital outlays, public current consumption, public cash transfers and so on. More specifically ratios of public expenditures to gross domestic product or public employment to total employment or workforce have been suggested.

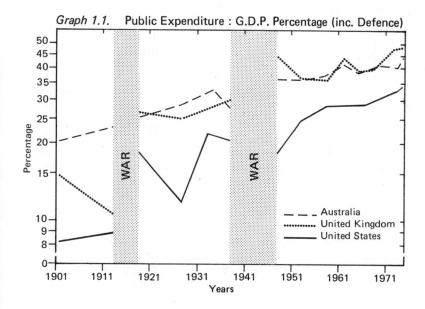

Graph 1.1. Public Expenditure : G.D.P. Percentage (inc. Defence)

Graphs 1.1 and 1.2 illustrate the type of evidence some writers have used, presenting ratios of public expenditures and employment to gross domestic product and total employment respectively. The graphs show this Australian behaviour between 1901 and 1975 in comparison with the United States and Britain, using readily available statistics. Generally, public employment (excluding defence) has grown much more rapidly than the total civilian workforce in all three

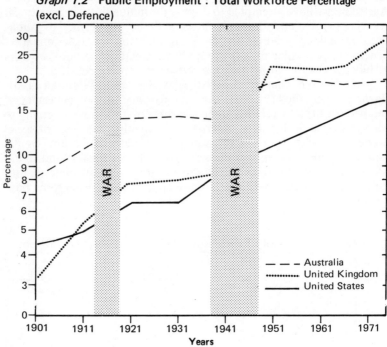

Graph 1.2 **Public Employment : Total Workforce Percentage (excl. Defence)**

countries. So, too, has government expenditure relative to gross domestic product. Recent estimates by OECD (1978, Table 2) indicate that these three countries now bear a close family resemblance to many Western economies.

Undoubtedly, these figures suggest a marked structural shift towards a greater presence of government in these economies. Australia seems interesting, however, in that the ratios have grown much more slowly than they have in Britain and USA.

But, interesting as they are, these figures do not measure the 'size of government' and the trends do not measure the 'growth of government' relative to the rest of the economy. Certainly, the increase of employment or expenditure by government relative to total workforce or gross domestic product has interesting and important implications. But as measures they are seriously flawed. They do not provide us with even a starting point for analysing the trends in the influences altering the bases or outcomes of market decision-making which are the focuses of this book.

Patently, government policy could, in theory, be carried out by hiring private persons instead of directly employing bureaucrats. Public influence may be exerted by raising revenues rather than spending them. Private behaviour may be significantly adapted by concessional allowances in the tax structures, reducing both revenues and expenditures or as alternatives to raising and spending 'public' moneys. Most obviously, perhaps regulatory processes are not mirrored in public expenditures and employment. And so on. We can tell very little about the influence - even the nature, let alone the dimension - of government from the statistics used in these graphs. *Once one becomes concerned, as we are, with the adaptation of decision-making processes*, there is little point in investigating these conventional measures. Hence this book contains few of them.

Social accounting measures are even more confused and confusing. It is a remarkable fact that measures of public outlays, for example, including in particular public current consumption and capital expenditures, conceal rather than reveal the operations of government and, particularly, government activity relative to private. Thus current consumption is measured as gross current expenditure minus recoupments from revenue from government services. It is a net figure. The larger the revenue offsets, the more the gross government purchases are concealed and the more the potential influence on private activity is confused. For many questions, such as preference in procurement that government gives to private Australian activity, we need the *gross* current expenditures. Similar problems arise in other areas such as the broader question of the external benefits or costs of public action. Adopted widely as instruments of Keynesian policies, social accounting measures have led us down a blind alley. What we need, in so far as statistics are useful, are *gross* measures of public and private counterparts. These are not yet available and one important extension of this investigation would be to develop these *gross* measures for both public and private activity. In the meantime, it is disastrous that much contemporary Australian data, not merely processed official estimates, are being presented within the confines of social accounting systems. It is curious that governments that reject Keynesian solutions are deceiving themselves and their constituencies.

The matter becomes worse when one moves into the component activities of public and private behaviour. Most obviously, in Australia, government was a major influence on private activity at the beginning of the century (and before). One of the central features of Australian experience has been the differences in trends followed in different areas of the economy, in different markets and in different policies. Some modes of interaction e.g. the high share of public investment in total Australian investment appear, in the long run, to have declined by 1975 compared to 1901. Partly in substitution, however, there appears to have been a very extensive growth of more direct and specific allocative or regulatory influence in private decision-making. Thus we seem to have 'opposing trends'. Alternatively, we might perceive this adaptation as representing a consistent pattern of public intervention or private dependence, in which public policy or private pressures for public action are responsive to changing economic, political and social circumstances. Similar conflicts emerge in the investigation of social policy and in the conduct and performance of public enterprise.

These issues take us out of the arena of public budgets and social accounting statistics. We need to follow a complex network of interactive processes in which the condition and size of the economy, changing productive opportunities and changing relations with the trading world form essential parts of the story. But the process cannot be studied exclusively in economic terms. The nature of private interests, the influences to which they are subject and the modes of their response, the strength and formal or informal organisation of private interest groups and their relationship to the political and governing process must also be prominent. So, too, must changes in the structure and personnel of government. Together, these provide us with the beginnings of a picture of public and private interaction in decision making and of the alterations that have occurred in the conditions and outcomes of market decision-making. Our object has been to provide a preliminary outline of this process as it evolved in Australia.

Part Two

Economic Management

2

The Decline of Colonial Socialism
1901 to 1975

In economic management, the relationship between the public and private sectors in twentieth-century Australia developed through three distinct forms. In the first, there was at the beginning of the century, a strongly supportive relationship, almost a partnership, of government towards major private business interests and a private acceptance (and use of) this supportive partnership. The partnership relationship was manifested most obviously in the variety of forms of *direct* market participation by government. From the beginning of the century, however, more indirect modes of intervention developed, particularly through regulatory and allocative action, a change that attained greatest prominence in the period of severe development problems in the inter-war years. In this second form, direct forms of intervention gave ground to indirect; but both remained, except in the depression of the nineteen-thirties, predominantly supportive of major private interests. The third style of relationship may be seen as clearly initiated in the depression of the nineteen-thirties but attained prominence after the Second World War: the emergence of public constraint on and even some antagonism towards private business arising out of the requirements of macro-economic management in the preservation of price stability, full employment and the stabilisation of external balances.

It is with this broad sweep that Chapters 2-5 are concerned. The general trend picture contains a number of conflicting tendencies so that from some points of view the scope, scale and detail of government intervention in the market increased while from other points of view they diminished. The present chapter deals with one important area in which, in a variety of ways, government tended to withdraw from intervention. Essentially, this withdrawal represented a reduction in direct market participation or as it might be perceived through nineteenth-century eyes, the 'decline of colonial socialism' (Butlin 1959). As landowners, land sellers, investors, borrowers, business operators, employers and managers of immigration programs,

Australian governments were prominent in the late nineteenth century as direct actors in all the implied markets. Expressed in terms of market structure, they accounted for a large share of the transactions in these markets. In development terms, these direct actions of governments made them important - perhaps vital - contributors to the process of economic expansion and growth. Whereas, in the United States, private enterprise has been traditionally regarded as the primary 'engine' of growth, in Australia that role was shared between public and private actors. Private interests accepted this position the more readily, or pressed government to assume, direct activity in the market because this direct intervention was perceived as predominantly (there were some short-term qualifications) supportive of rather than displacing or impeding major private interests.

The early years of the twentieth century appeared to confirm this nineteenth-century relationship - virtually a partnership one - between government and private business. Nevertheless, by the beginning of the nineteen-thirties a 'retreat' from many of these forms of direct market participation is visible. Here, again, some contrast with the United States may be suggested in that it was in the nineteen-thirties that the United States government became much more intrusive.

The 'decline of colonial socialism' is in itself a complex set of changes - an absolute fall in public overseas borrowing, a decline in the public share of the investment and employment 'markets', a much more belated decline in public management of immigration programs and, partly through changed pricing policies, an actual rise in the share of the public sector in gross domestic production. A good deal of this 'retreat' is therefore to be seen in ratio terms of the scale of public activity relative to private counterparts.

It is with this 'decline' of direct market participation that this chapter deals. In discussing it, it must be stressed that other, indirect types of public intervention increased - through regulatory and allocative measures and, eventually, through macro-management. These are issues reserved to Chapters 3-5, seeking to trace increasingly interactive allocative and regulatory intervention, widening in scope, increasing in detail and centralising in national government, altering the circumstances of private decision-making. Although these direct and indirect modes of intervention are separated in this manner, it is also to be stressed that at least for half a century after 1900, public intervention of both types was essentially supportive of private business interests.

Why was direct market participation adopted on a large scale and why was there a retreat from it? A common explanation of direct government action runs in terms of public efforts to deal with imperfections in the market. Undoubtedly, there were substantial imperfections in product, capital, labour, and other markets in Australia in the nineteenth century. This style of explanation is in some cases, helpful. However, the opposite hypothesis seems at least if not more relevant. This is that direct government interaction in markets occurred because government or private interests perceived that it was possible for government actually to increase the imperfections of the market to the advantage of some private interests (though not necessarily in a growth situation to the disadvantage of others). This seems to have been most relevant through the ability of nineteenth-century governments to distribute costs of public action to widely dispersed groups while concentrating the benefits on a more limited range of private interests.

The common explanation of direct government intervention might suggest on grounds of symmetry that public withdrawal from direct intervention in the market from the early nineteen-thirties may have been prompted by reduced market imperfections. Symmetry is not necessarily implied in the conventional hypothesis. Certainly, the public 'withdrawal' in Australia occurred in circumstances of mass market failure during the early nineteen-thirties. It appears that the loss of faith in government as an engine of growth through direct market participation can reasonably be dated from the depression. Government in Australia was or appeared to be so deeply implicated in the onset and severity of the depression that it was compelled, to a considerable degree by private pressure, to retreat. In incremental terms, at least, it was displaced by the private sector. In this case, too, there is a sharp contrast with the opposite American experience in which private enterprise appeared as most obviously implicated in market failure and yielded ground to government.

It is not implied that the depression was the determining factor in subsequent trend experience. Opportunities for private Australian expansion were enlarged during the nineteen-thirties and more definitely after 1945. Moreover, the nature of this private growth was such as to be less dependent on public supportive intervention through direct market participation. Indeed, to some extent, private activity crowded out the public sector particularly during the nineteen-fifties and sixties. Nevertheless, the beginnings of this relative 'withering away' of public direct intervention can reasonably be dated from the beginning of the depression.

The relative displacement of public by private activity continued until 1972. It was only briefly reversed in the Whitlam years - and with one major qualification was quickly resumed. It is by no means clear how the market share of public and private sectors will behave in the long-term future. Despite the attempts to counter-act the Whitlam efforts of 1972-75, public investment in particular has risen throughout the second half of the seventies relative to private investment. Whether this is due to laggard private investment in the short-run or to deeper and more sustained influences remains to be seen.

The nature of colonial socialism

By 1900, a basic pattern of relationship between public and major private interests had been long established. This late nineteenth-century pattern of public and private relations depended first on large-scale public action to attract resources of capital and labour into the economy from outside (essentially Britain), enhancing rates of increase beyond those that the private market was capable of delivering, and second on the direct participation by public institutions in investment and the delivery of marketed output on a scale that was rare in the Western world. Combined with these activities, governments were the landlords of most of the Australian continent. A central motif in this pattern was that governments became highly market-oriented and their revenues were predominantly from government enterprise, land and customs receipts.

The coercive potential of government was not strongly revealed and governments were to a very substantial degree constrained within market rules. Admittedly, governments could internalise benefits from added inputs not readily captured by individuals in the market partly because of public land ownership, partly because of certain limited coercive elements, most notably in powers to levy customs taxation as a major source of revenue. But the latter represented limited qualifications to the predominantly market orientation of public action in these areas. The outcome was the widespread public and private acceptance of a strongly supportive role of government *vis-a-vis* major private interests through direct market participation by government.

One of the consequences of this mode of direct government intervention was the development of large-scale public business undertakings, most importantly in transport and communications but also in urban amenities of water and sewerage. These all had significant elements of natural or artificial monopoly. In the course of the nineteenth century, the presence of similar enterprises, conducted privately in other countries, had raised problems of conflict of different private interests, particularly between producers and consumers. In these circumstances, the alternatives to resolve or limit these conflicts were whether to convert them to public ownership or to subject private business to regulation. The choice, in Australia, of public ownership and operation limited the growth of the specific and detailed regulation of private activity of private business that emerged, for example, in the United States under the Interstate Commerce Commission and the Sherman Anti-Trust Act and ensuing discriminatory regulations. Those American efforts to constrain private 'monopolies' led American public policy along one stream of public-private relations: the increasing adversary relationship between populist Federal government and large-scale business. In opting for public ownership and operation, Australians limited greatly the sources of adversary relationships. The outcome may have been 'inefficient' allocation relative to some ideal standard. But these arrangements succeeded, given the special limitations on the type and range of public enterprises, in introducing a strong sense of partnership between government and important business interests. This sense is fundamental to the understanding of nineteenth-century and much of twentieth-century public and private choice in Australia.

This relationship between private business and government undertakings was heavily reinforced by the dependence of private economic development on access to overseas resources and specifically on the transfer of factors from overseas to Australia. The extremely low ratio of capital and labour to Australian natural resources made this external dependence a fundamental one. The transfer of capital and labour implied the transfer of embodied technology. The limitations of the private market in achieving a desired rate of transfer of capital, labour and technology was established early in the nineteenth century. Accordingly, except for brief episodes, chiefly during the 1850s, private business interests looked to and pressed on government to assume the role of accelerating these transfers. So long as these transfers were not predominantly absorbed into the public sector, there were substantial benefits to private activity from public intervention. The success of pressures for the abandonment of transportation implied the release of labour increments from the public sector; the price paid by the private sector was the commitment of land revenue (i.e. private outlays for purchase and lease of Crown land) to subsidies for immigration, a procedure formalised in the 1830s. The net benefit was presumed to be substantial. Briefly, during the 1830s, some private interests sought to be free-riders in such an arrangement, 'squatting' without legal basis on virgin lands. By 1847, these extra-legal arrangements were codified into leasehold payments; by the 1860s a combination of leasehold and freehold tenure implied the private payment of land revenues to government partly supporting large-scale assisted migration over long periods.

The accession of migrants at a rate much greater than that achievable by private choice became and remained until recently a tenet of both public and private faith. This belief might be briefly challenged by wage earners in the slight and short recessions that occurred before 1890. As a sustained, long-term ambition of public and private interests, it became and remained until the nineteen-sixties an unchallenged object of long-term Australian policy, basic to both public and private behaviour.

That the private market could not deliver the desired rate of immigration (except in brief recession) was widely accepted. That government should intervene to accelerate population inflow was similarly widely accepted. In part, this acceptance rested in the prevalent private view that enlarged population was needed for defence reasons. Almost as generally, interference with the market was accepted as a means of altering the sex ratio from the high proportion of males in the mid-nineteenth century. More specifically and variously, major rural business interests sought public intervention to provide service, construction and farm labour. In the last cases, the dominant business interests could seek to secure benefits whose costs might be transferred, in substantial part, to a larger local community. Across the board of different private interests there was general approval of artificial arrangement to migration and there was stronger pressure from major business interests, particularly pastoralists, that, in any event, dominated the Australian political scene and acted with a strong sense of community of interest.

At a different remove, even given high real earnings in Australia, non-market attraction to migrants themselves was vital. Transfer costs were very high; information costs were large; and relocation costs were substantial. Relocation costs tended to encourage concentration in towns. But this, in turn, induced Australian non-urban, especially pastoral, interests to press for higher rates of assisted migration, recognising their persistent losses through urban settlement.

The absence of formal infrastructure and the massive capital commitments of rural producers in generating rural activities in individual enterprises provided the essential conditions for major private support of public foreign borrowing and public capital formation. No doubt there were imperfections in the relevant capital markets. But the conditions existed for specific private support of public foreign borrowing and public capital formation, as a means of limiting the capital commitments of private business, predominantly private rural interests. To this extent, therefore, the growth of public intervention in foreign borrowing and in domestic capital formation may be seen as a means of limiting capital commitments of pastoralists. Most importantly, public access to customs revenue implied that private rural interests and some urban business could pass to non-rural groups part of the costs of funding the infrastructure needed to support rural economic development. Customs revenue provided a device for transfering to public hands a portion of the foreign exchange earnings of rural export industries, and for imposing part of the costs of foreign borrowing and related infrastructure development on non-rural Australians. On the other hand, with access to customs and land revenues, public authorities were able to tolerate lower direct yields on public enterprise assets than private enterprise might have sought. Major consumers of public enterprise services were, therefore, able to secure these services at a lower price or on a larger scale than the private market could deliver.

The matter, however, went further in the preferential position established by public authorities in access to foreign (British) capital. With the security of colonial revenues as a whole, Australian governments were able to offer highly attractive public securities in London at yields well below those demanded by British investors in Australian private activity. Not for nothing did Australian government securities become defined as 'Colonial Consols' taken up at rates fractionally higher than British Consols. Private borrowers could not compete, and private producers had a substantial advantage to gain both by low costs of public capital and the relatively low direct yields that public business could accept.

The compatibility of public and major private interests might be disturbed in the short run. It depended more fundamentally on a consistency of intent between a limited but powerful array of private interests - particularly pastoralists, import merchants and financial intermediaries - that were dominant in terms of economic activity and politics until the last years of the nineteenth century. But efforts by such interests to secure benefits of public policy entailed the creation not merely of a substantial bureaucracy but a highly skilled bureaucracy, much of it made up of 'foreign' experts. Unfortunately, limited attention has been given to the work of these public servants and one cannot offer very confident interpretation or assessment of their roles or their significance in introducing some independent initiative in public action. It appears reasonably clear, through the relatively 'open government' that prevailed in the nineteenth century, that they were highly influential in determining the levels and composition of public capital and business inputs into the economy. As the scale of economy grew in the second half of the nineteenthth century it appears that this influence increased substantially. It would be inappropriate to approach Australian public-private relations primarily through private interests or the collective interests of private groups. But a great deal more research is needed on top-level bureaucrats before much further can be said.

In the period 1860 to 1900, public intervention in the areas specified attained such a scale that

- government had subsidised the inflow of some 350 000 migrants, compared to a total net immigration of 750 000 and a total net population increase of 2 600 000;

- government had been directly responsible for securing the inflow of half the total foreign capital imports;

- government had accounted for approximately 40 per cent of total domestic capital formation, essentially in the areas of transport and communications;

- government, by 1900, owned approximately half the total fixed capital (excluding land) of Australia;

- government, by 1900, conducted the largest enterprises in the economy primarily in transport and communications and in water and sewerage, thereby absorbing approximately 5 per cent of the total workforce in the economy and generating some 6 per cent of gross domestic product.

We are not concerned here to attempt in any detail the counterfactual assessment of whether any of these inputs would have occurred without government intervention. It is possible, for example, that some assisted migrants would have come without subsidies. It is also possible that some unassisted migrants were attracted (information costs reduced?) by the knowledge of public programs. All we seek to do with the specification of public action is to provide some evidence of the scale of public activity and the market shares of the public and private sectors.

The end of sustained and rapid economic expansion after 1889 and the long-drawn-out depression and hesitant recovery until after the turn of the century introduced vital changes in the significance of different private interests and in their relationships with and attitudes towards government. Foreign investors sought to recover private capital in private business (and some public securities) and there was a substantial capital outflow until as late as 1908. Net immigration was reversed and there was a net outflow substantially until 1907. Private capital formation fell sharply in the nineties. Private business suffered severely, not least in the areas of pastoral, merchant and financial interests that had dominated Australian development from 1860.

In these circumstances, the private dependence on public action to minimise these losses of assets and factors increased sharply. The role of government in encouraging immigration, labour and (less firmly) capital inflow and delivering service output became relatively a great deal more important. At the same time, the major private interests of the second half of the nineteenth century suffered severely in terms of both economic and political significance. All private groups became much more dependent on public action to sustain, or minimise the decline in, the economy. It would appear that the scope for independent initiative of government was, for a time, considerably enhanced, and that the private interest groups inducing public action became more diverse and less cohesive while private efforts to encourage public action increased. It was in this context of sustained private losses and disturbances and of public initiative that the twentieth century began. It appears that this finale of the nineteenth century served to emphasise the assumption of a strongly supportive role of government in relation to private activity, and to induce private interests to look to public action with a much more explicit allocative purpose in influencing the flows of inputs into the economy. The simple nineteenth-century concept of 'developing the country' was gradually replaced by a more complex strategy of economic growth in which the allocative conditions of aggregate expansion objectives came increasingly to the fore.

Accessing foreign resources and public capital formation 1901 to 1914

The federation of the Australian colonies into the Commonwealth of Australia, with a new Federal government, had comparatively little direct significance for the respective roles of public and private decision-making in factor inflows into Australia. Nor did it mean much for the process of public and private capital formation and the public delivery of marketed services (note that we exclude throughout all public non-marketed services). Apart from the operation of the Post Office, transferred to Federal responsibility, the State Governments were the public authorities that dominated in public decision-making. Rather, it was the relative weakness of private interests in coping with the successive influences of depression and drought and in countering the problems of Australian external dependence that was important. This dependence showed most obviously in the outflow of both capital and labour from Australia during much of the first decade. Economic recovery began after 1905 and moved to boom conditions by 1913. In this recovery process, the private sector, with limited exceptions, was heavily dependent on public action. The supportive role of government shows up most prominently in the first fifteen years of the century.

Depression in the decade to 1900, exogenous drought problems, the British withdrawal of capital and the outflows of people from Australia appear as major factors in determining the relations between public and private choice. Capital outflow continued until 1908, net emigration (with slight qualifications) until 1907. Public action to stem and reverse these flows became a matter of the first importance.

Capital flows were confused. There was substantial new British (and some other foreign) investment in Australian mining. This was the one private activity that continued to attract private overseas funds. The implication is that the dominant areas of British private investment other than mining - pastoral, financial and urban real estate - suffered more severely from the repatriation of private British funds. But this repatriation implied domestic monetary constraint on other private areas, particularly the 'new' growing points in the economy, manufacturing and non-pastoral rural industries. Private interest in public action to stem and reverse this outflow would appear to be widespread. Pastoral, financial and real estate interests were concerned to soften and finalise reconstruction processes; manufacturing and non-pastoral rural interests to secure less domestic monetary constraint, particularly as recovery began after 1905.

Apart from mining, private activity could offer few attractive possibilities to foreign investment. Similarly, in migration, Australian market and labour conditions offered little inducement to unassisted immigration until well into the first decade of the century. It would be idle to suggest that an adequate explanation can be offered as to the respective roles of private or public decision-making in achieving such public intervention in capital, labour and other population inflows that occurred in the early years. The elementary problem is that for the first seven or eight years, the flows of public borrowing from abroad (and of publicly assisted immigration) were so small as to make any systematic explanation suspect. Indeed, Australian public issues were not attractive in London and there was a significant public debt repatriation. It was not until the recovery of Australian activity was well under way that public borrowing overseas could be restored. What we do not know - and future research may reveal - is the presence or otherwise of public initiative in the process. As will be suggested below, there appear to be several considerations suggesting incentive for distinct public interest, *but in the form of encouraging the recovery of private activity.*

So far as migration is concerned, a net outflow of 30 000 occurred between 1901 and 1906. This was constrained by a contrary inflow of publicly assisted migrants of some 10 000. Small though these figures are, they reflect the still flickering ambitions to sustain Australian population increase through public action to reduce transfer costs of immigrants. This ambition was quickly restored to full flame after economic recovery began. Between 1907 and 1913, net immigration, both assisted and unassisted, rose rapidly to achieve a total for the period of some 260 000. Publicly assisted migration, however, totalled approximately 182 000 for the same period - a figure equal to almost 70 per cent of the total net inflow.

This implied either or both of a massive commitment or response to public rather than free market choice in influencing the flow of immigrants (and hence additions to the Australian workforce and population). It is not, of course, suggested that none of these assisted migrants would have arrived without aid. On the other hand, it should be appreciated (see Chapter 3) that more than merely transfer costs were altered by public action. Large-scale public assistance to rural settlement, a floor set under wage incomes (the basic wage) and under post-retirement incomes (old age pensions) illustrate other modes of public alteration of the market affecting private migration decisions.

A network of public intervention for strategic development purposes was in process of emerging.

The role of public action in immigration markets was central to the efforts to increase population just as the acceleration of population increase beyond that achievable by the 'free' market was a - perhaps *the* - basic plank in Australian development objectives after 1906. Some comments on private and public interests in this objective are appropriate.

First, it should be appreciated that there were few opportunities, even after 1906, for private agencies to intervene in migrant flows (though private 'nomination' of particular immigrants played some part). The nature of Australian economic development, the restricted opportunities for self-advancement of new migrants compared with circumstances in other 'new world' countries, the transfer costs of migration to Australia and the isolation of Australia largely ruled these private possibilities out just as they limited independent unassisted immigration. Secondly, unassisted migrant flows were, after 1900, constrained by the changed circumstances of the Australian economy as compared with those before 1890. Real income per head in Australia, relative to Britain, though still superior had now fallen significantly. The long-established pattern of public supportive intervention, and of private acceptance of it, was to that extent reinforced after 1900. For the new recruits to Australian population, the role of public action in facilitating their passages and assisting their settlement was one of their first perceptions of Australian society.

Some of the particular sources of private pressure for this post-1900 public support may be fairly readily appreciated. The old defence objective remained. But it was now firmly enshrined as a 'White Australia' policy - to establish a population capable of defending the continent and to restrict immigration of non-whites. Defence and 'racial purity' became joint public goods. By contrast, the imbalance of the sexes had lost most of its force. More generally, Australians continued to seek British immigrants, partly to sustain a homeland connection, partly to re-create in Australia the type of society with which they had been familiar. The common objective of increasing the domestic market had wide appeal and appeared as a much more significant matter as the economy moved away from its pastoral exporting stance. The growth of non-pastoral rural activity and of manufacturing implied greater private market dependence on local consumption. Hence these two private activities provided new sources of private pressures for public assistance to immigration. From manufacturing, in particular, came a new demand - encouragement of the immigration of skilled workers.

Beside such private pressures needs to be set a range of public interests in enhanced immigration. As large employers engaged in increasingly complex operations, government agencies were concerned, with private business, in the attraction of skilled labour. Committed to the delivery of marketed services in transport and communication, government institutions shared with private interests the general objective of increasing the domestic market by assisted immigration. In the government case, the importance of distributing overheads in large-scale operations was more impelling. Clearly related to this public interest in transport enterprises was the fact that revenue from land sales and leases was a substantial item. Public agencies had, accordingly, an interest in the recovery of farming and particularly of the rural real estate market. This was a matter of some significance to the State Government landlords of, still, some 90 per cent of the Australian continent. Immigration was particularly relevant in so far as the farming recovery was looked to as relatively labour-intensive settlement. In this prospect, government, pastoralists and financial agencies shared a common interest. Once export demands increased after 1905, the accelerated inflow of immigrants through public intervention became important as one major factor to increase the elasticity of supply of exports and to raise the demand for land.

The efforts to increase population in this manner were nevertheless made in a society in which, in reality, the majority of people sought urban locations and in which rural development, even after greater diversification beyond pastoral activity, remained relatively non-labour-intensive. Development was expected to be concentrated on rural activity, but labour tended to flow to manufacturing. From this contrast partly competitive and partly complementary claims arose for public attention in servicing rural and urban development through the public supply of capital assets and related services.

The developing farming after 1905, emphasising growth of non-wool production, was much more location-bound and more transport-dependent, particularly in meat, grain, dairy and orchard products. These farmers faced high-risk undertakings because of seasonal variations and perishable products which were also low-value products relative to their bulk. Financially constrained pastoralists converting to mixed farming (including meat), new wheat farmers and orchardists faced much tighter constraints on their ability to fund farming assets than had nineteenth-century pastoralists. Moreover, most operated in smaller enterprises. Their ability to supply their own transport was accordingly more restricted and their dependence on public provision of transport assets and communication facilities correspondingly enlarged. It was not until after the First World War, effectively, that the internal combustion engine opened an efficient prospect for small-scale transport enterprise. Even so, the provision of road facilities represented a major task for which private business looked to government and essentially to State Government. In the meantime, private pressures on government to provide assets and services in roads and railways and rural communications (post and telephone) increased. In the nature of post-1905 development, these facilities and services were designed to meet the demands of (on Australian standards) relatively close rural settlement. Accordingly a great deal of rail and road building was in the form of branch networks, built largely under the direction of State Public Works Departments and operated by State Railway Authorities.

At the same time, rising urban and especially city populations, exerted increasing pressure for the provision of amenities of water and sewerage, urban rail, tram and road services and some additional energy supplies. These were, to a significant degree, consumer demands and implied widespread private pressures. But these services were also directly and indirectly significant inputs into urban business activity - to facilitate the movement of shoppers, of labour and the intracity transfer of materials and goods. Real estate values could also be enhanced for private owners, subject to location. In meeting these pressures, private business could effectively compete with public action in two areas: gas and electricity generation and supply. For the rest, public coercive powers of taxation and public creditworthiness in the capital market made public action a preferred mode. In some areas, most obviously water and sewerage, public action had become traditional in Australia (and other countries) as a means of coping with the externalities of individuals living in concentrated communities. Even in the case of electricity, however, public enterprise had a competitive advantage or, in some cases, could disregard market tests. Electricity generation by railways could attain relatively large scale with surplus energy sold off. The question of scale became increasingly important in the years immediately before the war as technological change opened the opportunity for long-distance transmission of electricity.

Rural and urban growth was supported by and demanded rising public investment in rail, tram, road, water and sewerage, port and harbour and energy services. Substantially throughout the first decade and a half of the century, public capital formation as a whole ran (see Table 2.1) above the aggregate of private capital formation which was concentrated in urban industrial and service structures and equipment and in farm and mining assets. The large-scale public provision of infrastructure served as a powerful support to private enterprise and personal amenity. It may appear, therefore, that over half the total capital formation in Australia was exposed to miscalculation and misallocation in so as far market tests were muted. This is a matter to be considered in the fourth section of this volume.

At the moment, one important point should be noted. The increas-

TABLE 2.1 **Public and private gross capital formation 1900-01 to 1912-13**

	Post Office A $m	Civil Aviation B $m	Broad-casting C $m	Railways D $m	Urban Transit E $m	Ports* etc. F $m	Elect. & Gas G $m	Water & Sewerage H $m	Total Capital Formation Business Under-takings I $m	Total Capital Formation Public J $m	Total Capital Formation Private K $m	G.D.C.F. Public & Private L $m	Ratio I to J %	Ratio J to L %
1900-01	0.00	0.00	0.00	10.51	0.51	0.00	0.05	3.67	14.74	26.87	27.00	53.87	54.86	49.88
02	0.07	0.00	0.00	12.25	1.33	0.00	0.08	3.73	17.46	32.06	40.00	72.06	54.46	44.49
03	0.27	0.00	0.00	14.82	0.45	0.00	0.09	3.28	18.91	32.53	44.00	76.53	58.13	42.51
04	0.38	0.00	0.00	9.70	0.39	0.00	0.22	2.55	13.24	21.58	29.00	50.58	61.35	42.67
05	0.26	0.00	0.00	6.19	0.63	0.00	0.35	1.87	9.30	16.89	29.00	45.89	55.06	36.81
06	0.29	0.00	0.00	7.44	0.39	0.00	0.27	2.12	10.51	19.79	32.00	51.79	53.11	38.21
07	0.55	0.00	0.00	8.42	0.32	0.00	0.35	2.39	12.03	22.93	48.00	70.93	52.46	32.33
08	0.85	0.00	0.00	11.78	0.83	0.00	0.50	3.97	17.93	28.55	45.00	73.55	62.80	38.82
09	1.08	0.00	0.00	14.66	2.05	0.00	0.41	3.76	21.96	35.57	38.00	73.57	61.74	48.35
10	1.11	0.00	0.00	16.97	1.86	0.00	0.51	4.33	24.78	39.32	40.00	79.32	63.02	49.57
11	1.56	0.00	0.00	21.06	1.89	0.00	0.81	4.96	30.28	49.42	45.00	94.42	61.27	52.34
12	3.37	0.00	0.00	27.15	1.91	0.00	1.05	6.68	40.16	61.46	58.00	119.46	65.34	51.45
13	3.22	0.00	0.00	31.06	2.51	0.00	1.17	8.99	46.95	68.50	72.00	140.50	68.54	48.75

*not separately estimated

ed share of public capital formation *as compared with pre-1890 experience* did not necessarily mean a displacement of private by public investment or even increased competitive pressure by public authorities in labour, equipment or capital markets. In part, any such competition was reduced by assistance to immigration. But most importantly, the capital intensity of private activity had been considerably reduced as a result of the constraints on pastoral investment and the rationalisation of pastoral activity. Already, by 1890, the essential physical assets required to support Australian flock populations until the middle of the twentieth century had been installed. The relationship between public and private investment after 1900 needs to be perceived in the light of the greatly reduced demands for capital in pastoral activity. But, in addition, service and manufacturing development also required significantly less enterprise capital per unit of output. Private pressures could more successfully seek public additions to infrastructure, or public authorities could, with little sense of competitive conflict, seek to guide private development through the influence of infrastructure. We do not, as yet, suggest on which side the priority of influence lay. What is basic at the moment, however, is that the circumstances of growth permitted this public development with little if any recognition of conflict and predominantly as a supportive intervention. This limitation of conflict was reinforced by the mode of operation of public enterprises - neither seeking monopoly profits nor, generally, imposing heavy claims for budget subsidies.

Partly, but not entirely, arising from the massive public capital inputs into the economy, an array of large-scale public enterprises expanded or emerged, implying a very large public supply of marketed services. In the main, these were enterprises that were 'traditionally' public in nineteenth-century Australia. The chief exceptions to the tradition were in electricity and, to some extent, in banking. In the years immediately before the war a novel element entered with the establishment of a large number of small State enterprises in many areas of activity. A complete list of all the public enterprises would be a very long one. But such a list would quickly degenerate into minor and insignificant items.

All levels of government were represented - Federal, State, semi-government and local authority. The enterprises or types of enterprises that were substantial were, in highly generalised terms:

(a) Post Office, including telephone and telegraph (Federal);

(b) Railways and Tramways commonly but not invariably operated together (State Governments);

(c) Port and Harbour Authorities in each capital city (State Government Statutory Authorities, sometimes part of State Government Departments)

(d) Regional Water and Sewerage Authorities in each State, most commonly as State Government Statutory Bodies, together with small urban systems under local bodies;

(e) State Irrigation and Water Supply Authorities (under State Governments);

(f) State Savings and in some cases Agricultural Banks as Statutory Bodies under State Governments; to these the Commonwealth Bank was added in 1911 as a Savings Bank (under Federal control).

Not yet of great significance but subsequently to become so were emergent electricity bodies gradually developing partly in association with rail and tram, partly by the absorption into State systems of small private and local organisations. In addition to these came a multitude of small State enterprises in a large variety of areas in most States, primarily in the half decade before the war. Then an array of State businesses began to take shape and survived for varying periods into the inter-war years - in coal mines, brick and pipe works, pastoral properties, some sugar mills, and down to butchers' shops and even, at the last resort, tobacconists!

This last array represented a flurry of Labor Governments' attempts in the States to establish a special form of socialist State enterprises. In certain respects they reflected, in minor key, an adversary attitude toward business by (populist) labour interests. They offered, it was thought, a source of information to government on the operations of corresponding private business, and hence a source of advice to governments on alleged 'profiteering' of business as inflationary pressures developed from around 1910. But, in addition, there was a strongly pragmatic and businesslike issue behind these concerns. All State Governments were large purchasers of almost every type of finished goods, materials and equipment. One object was to test the private tenders for government contracts. In that respect, these enterprises may be at least partially viewed as an extension of the State Government practice of public power generation, public maintenance and repair shops for railway rolling stock and the public construction of new rolling stock as ancillary to large railway enterprises.

Of all these enterprises, the Post Office was by far the largest, once the State systems were amalgamated into one Federal concern. Table 2.2 gives some indication of relative dimensions of some of the concerns in terms of labour employed.

Certainly the Post Office and the separate railway systems in all but the smallest States represented very large concerns, much larger than any private business in Australia. To that extent, therefore, public

TABLE 2.2 Public sector employment 1900-01 to 1912-13 ('000s)

	Land Trans- port A	Other Trans- port B	Commun- ication C	Banking D	Elect. & Gas E	Water & Sewer- age F	Other (Misc.) G	Total Public Business Under- takings H	Public Sector Employ I	Total Civilian Workforce J	Total Workforce K	Ratio H to I "%	Ratio H to J "%	Ratio H to K "%
1900-01	46.00	0.90	15.50	0.20	1.50	3.30	2.90	70.30	133.80	1542.30	1543.70	52.54	4.56	4.55
02	46.80	1.00	17.80	0.20	1.50	3.10	3.10	73.50	134.00	1565.40	1567.10	54.85	4.70	4.69
03	45.70	1.00	20.30	0.20	1.30	3.00	3.20	74.70	133.00	1584.40	1586.60	56.17	4.71	4.71
04	46.10	1.00	21.20	0.20	2.50	3.00	3.00	77.00	135.90	1610.30	1612.90	56.66	4.78	4.77
05	46.70	0.80	21.20	0.20	1.50	3.00	3.10	76.50	134.90	1634.10	1637.20	56.71	4.68	4.67
06	46.80	0.90	21.20	0.30	2.10	3.10	3.20	77.60	137.20	1653.20	1657.00	56.56	4.69	4.68
07	51.60	0.90	23.00	0.30	2.30	3.20	3.40	84.70	148.90	1683.90	1688.00	56.88	5.03	5.02
08	55.80	1.00	26.30	0.30	2.30	3.80	3.60	93.10	159.50	1712.50	1716.80	58.37	5.44	5.42
09	60.80	1.10	28.10	0.30	2.50	5.40	4.10	102.30	171.00	1759.00	1763.50	59.82	5.82	5.80
10	68.30	1.30	30.00	0.30	2.90	5.00	5.70	113.50	184.90	1809.30	1813.90	61.38	6.27	6.26
11	78.90	1.50	27.80	0.40	2.50	5.40	6.20	122.70	202.60	1879.30	1884.20	60.56	6.53	6.51
12	90.40	1.70	26.40	0.40	2.70	7.00	8.10	136.70	227.80	1956.70	1961.60	60.01	6.99	6.97
13	97.30	1.80	23.30	0.60	2.70	8.80	8.20	147.70	245.10	2054.90	2062.40	60.26	7.19	7.16

business undertakings were highly visible as managers and consumers of capital and as employers and not simply as suppliers of marketed services. The degree of expertise and of administrative ability demanded were considerably higher than in most private concerns. In the years before 1914, public employment in these businesses rose considerably faster than the total workforce, increasing its share from approximately 4.5 per cent to over 7 per cent between 1901 and 1913. This increase in share was due almost entirely to rail and tram and the Post Office, the former more than doubling from 46 000 to 97 000, the latter not quite doubling from 15 500 to 28 000. At the same time the share of total public employment absorbed by public enterprises as a whole rose from 52 per cent to 60 per cent. Australian governments had, in terms of employment, become primarily the operators of large business undertakings.

A very similar change occurred in terms of capital formation. First, public capital formation lifted from approximately 40 per cent of total capital formation in the early years of the century, on an average, to just over 50 per cent by 1911. In this process, the share of public investment due to public business undertakings rose from about 55 per cent to approximately two thirds. In contrast with employment experience, the Post Office contributed little: the increased share of investment was dominated by the State railway systems.

In these circumstances, it is appropriate to concentrate attention on railways and, to a less extent, on the Post Office. In the former case, public officials had a strong incentive, on technical grounds, to attempt to amplify the predominantly trunk line system laid down in the nineteenth century: the twentieth-century task was partly to 'complete' the trunk line system but chiefly to amplify it with branch line construction (associated closely with feeder roads). Given the overhead assets of long-distance rail lines, the marginal cost of cheap branch lines to spread capital overheads was relatively small. But this public attitude to transport development conformed to private interests in the growth of closer settlement for purposes of non-pastoral farming.

Railways grew from some 19 000 kilometres opened in 1901 to approximately 28 000 kilometres (compare private railways of about 2400 kilometres). Freight tonne kilometres increased considerably faster (only three States have data), almost exactly doubling, a reflection of bulky and heavy commodities carried to major ports over long distances. Freight earnings of the railways more than doubled, from $11.2m in 1901 to $24.9m in 1913, a growth that did not keep pace with the rate of inflation by 1913. Passenger kilometres are very difficult to estimate; deflated passenger receipts imply an increase of the order of 2.5 times in passenger kilometres - a growth significantly faster than in the case of freight tonne kilometres.

These indicators reflect a strong emphasis in public policy in responding to the developing rural pressures. In the absence of private transport means other than animal power, railways were the great carriers, particularly as high capacity transport agents over long distance. To travellers and freight consignors (and consignees) they were a vital means of movement. But their significance was not confined to rural interests. Railway authorities were already responding to urban and metropolitan claims in amplifying urban transit systems, both through rail development and the expansion of tram services. In doing so, public action served the interests of travellers as final consumers of transport services and of factory and shop enterprises in the transfer of goods, materials and labour. As will be seen in Chapter 9, these functions were carried out without exercising strong monopoly powers and without making substantial inroads into public budgets.

Before the First World War, the Post Office was still regarded as a provider of social services rather than a business undertaking. This reflected British attitudes which were, however, reinforced in the conditions of a continent of vast distances and uneven population density. The transfer of postal and telegraph services to the Commonwealth had important implications for the conduct of the Post Office throughout much of the pre-war years. There was the organisational task of amalgamating and federating the staff and service system. This tended to hold expansion of services in check. More important in constraining capital expansion were the financial arrangements that the Constitution provided between the States and the Federal Government, limiting Federal revenues and, in particular, Federal loan-raising.

Nevertheless, between 1901 and 1913 the number of postal articles rose by some 80 per cent and the number of telephones to over four times. Services continued to be heavily subsidised, the more so when penny postage was introduced in 1911, thereby extending to all States the subsidy that some had granted to rural letters. Rural interests were further served by cheap carriage of newspapers. Nevertheless, the foundations were being laid, in the growth of telephone services, for the rise of telecommunications and the public provision of the type of service of particular significance also to urban business.

Private interests, public capital formation and enterprises 1920 to 1939

The circumstances of Australian public and private choice were considerably altered during the inter-war years by changes in intergovernmental relations, in the conditions of economic growth and structure and in international economic relations. The Federal

Government acquired, relative to the position before 1914, increased significance in particular through its role in the war, the subsequent retention of Federal income tax, the co-ordination of State borrowing and the influence, through the Premiers' Conference, on expenditure constraints during the depression. Other sources of increased prominence are referred to in Chapters 4 and 7. This structural change represented a movement towards centralisation which is a central theme of this book, a process accelerated by private reaction to the market failure in the depression. Centralisation did not become dominant before 1939; the States remained the main spenders, particularly in capital formation. Nevertheless, in providing for capital outlays and marketed services in the economy, the Australian government structure became definitely a federal system, with the Federal Government an important component. That centralisation was not carried further reflects, in part, the Australian public and private responses to depression that left the Australian governments still in an essentially supportive relationship towards private business. Unlike the events in the United States, where the Federal Government assumed a much more intrusive role than it had, Australian governments were forced, by private pressures and some self-constraint, to limit rather than expand expenditure. Other devices to stimulate private activity were adopted, perhaps above all in tariffs and other related allocative influences (see Chapter 4).

The development of a federal structure in part reflected and in part encouraged the emergence of an integrated national economy, accompanied by the formation of interest groups more closely and separately associated with organised political parties at both State and Federal levels. The old Lib-Lab coalitions and associations were effectively broken (except for intermittent resurgence at the State level) from the early 1920s as farm representation, backed by national and State producer organisations, led to the establishment of organised Country Parties. The coalition of these with other 'anti-labour' parties, largely representing urban interests, in large measure derived from the now well-defined structure of the economy into manufacturing and farming sectors. Public policy was now accommodated to the interests of three distinct groups: farm, manufacturing and labour (largely urban labour) interests.

In turn, these three interest groups were deeply affected by external dependence and by domestic growth prospects. For manufacturing and much of farm activity (other than wool) the preservation and development of the domestic market was a prime consideration. This placed greatest importance on Federal action not merely in the allocative influence of the tariff but also on the sustained encouragement of immigration. But immigration depended more closely on public intervention in so far as Australian economic growth slowed down from the mid-twenties and as any differential advantage in real income per head in Australia relative to Britain became much narrower. This loss of attraction to migrant labour, combined with unemployment at quite high rates, implied a greater sensitivity of labour interests, especially trade unions and their mouthpiece, the political Labor Parties, to the rate of inflow of immigrants. A response to this sensitivity was the clarification of migration objectives: to sustain population increase subject now to maintaining the level of real wages.

In part, both public and private aims sought to achieve some established ends: a secure, defensible continent and a White Australia. The public good of an expanded local market was pressed most strongly by manufacturing interests, as an ingredient in an ambition for Australian manufacturing, behind a tariff wall, to attain sufficient economies of scale to counter and replace foreign imports. This will-o'-the-wisp persisted throughout the inter-war years. But it was, to a considerable extent, shared by farmers whose domestic sales remained a substantial fraction of output and were taken to offer a springboard into export markets (but subject to other forms of public support - see Chapter 4).

A basic problem in the ability of the free market to deliver a high rate of immigration was not merely the relatively stagnant economy but also the persistent feature of Australian farming - its low labour intensity. Indeed farm populations and many rural towns were, by the twenties, growing very slowly and, by the thirties, actually declining. Nevertheless, the pressure for farm immigrants remained throughout the twenties. That it did appears as partly a misjudgment of Australian farm prospects. In part, it derived from public decision to offer a particular mode of compensation to war veterans (soldier settlement). It was partly explicable also by intervention of the British government in seeking to contribute to a redistribution of Empire population and resources (as in the 'Thirty Millions Agreement'). But it was also a reflection of a form of oligopolistic competition between State Governments, especially the least populous and developed ones of Queensland and Western Australia, to expand farm settlement and publicly assisted immigration (and other related assistance - see Chapter 4).

Many of these public efforts were disastrous failures, only reluctantly and belatedly recognised as such. Ostensibly, a different 'failure' of public action occurred: the failure to attract farm immigrants at high target levels. In fact, had greater 'success' been attained, a far more serious farm problem would have emerged in lower efficiency and lower farm living standards. In practice, Western Australia and Queensland made substantial farming gains, aided not merely by Federal immigration subsidies but also by detailed measures of State support. But the main outcome was to swell the populations of the towns and, most importantly, the main cities, contributing an impetus to expansion of services and manufacturing.

Major public efforts to support immigration and to intervene more closely than before 1914 in settlement processes occurred in the twenties. The figures of the early inter-war years are distorted particularly by repatriated servicemen. But from 1920 to 1929, total net immigration of some 320 000 accounted for approximately 40 per cent of population increase; in the process public passage assistance was provided for a little over 210 000 or slightly more than two thirds the number of net immigrants. It should be appreciated that governments, in this period, went considerably beyond mere passage assistance in the case of farm immigrants but (especially the States) entered into the determination of farm size and location, settlement costs and subsidised purchase and equipping of farms. In this process lay a more intimate penetration of public decision-making into private choice - still in a supportive role, but also symptomatic of one form of emergent 'big' government.

The depression terminated large-scale migrant flows whether assisted or unassisted. Some 20 000 only were received as net immigrants during the thirties; of these only 7000 were publicly assisted. Until the Second World War changed the relative attractiveness of Australia and until public intervention developed in a highly organised form, the objective of publicly accelerated population growth was largely abandoned.

The central position of the depression in forcing a retreat from population ambitions appears in other areas of public intervention to alter the rate of growth of capital inputs into the economy, particularly in foreign borrowing and in capital formation, and it appears to have strongly influenced the long-run conditions of public output of services. This is the turning point in the decline of colonial socialism.

Public debt due overseas rose rapidly following the First World War - far more rapidly than it had between 1900 and 1913. Until 1927, at least, this increase was largely due to (separate and often competitive) State government borrowing. From 1920 to 1929, public overseas debt rose from approximately $360m to $595m (cf. 1901 to 1913, when it rose from $180m to $210m). Thereafter public debt overseas grew very slowly to reach only $680m by 1939. This slackening represented a far more drastic revision of public policy towards foreign public borrowing than may appear on the surface. In fact the peak of Australian public indebtedness abroad, up to 1975, was reached in 1943. Thereafter it fell to reach miniscule levels by 1975. The experience of the depression had produced a strong public and private revulsion against public fixed interest obligations overseas. The retreat from this indebtedness began after 1932.

We do not have any very useful statistics of inflow of overseas capital into the private sector. Balance of payments calculations imply, however, that public borrowing was a large fraction of total inflow at least between 1920 and 1932. In the circumstances of Australian economic development in the twenties, Australian public borrowing abroad appears to have been competitive with private capital acquisitions. Much of foreign capital inflow into the private sector was directed towards metropolitan activity, particularly manufacturing. A great deal represented the flows arising from direct British investment in Australian manufacturing, with implied direct or indirect competition with Australian public authorities in the British capital market.

This matter cannot be pressed very far. In any event, a different problem arose for the Australian private sector from the magnitude of public borrowing and the attached fixed interest commitments. While private export earnings and import replacement rose to the mid-twenties (supported by public infrastructure and allocative public intervention) the problem of a rising overseas interest commitment did not obviously lead to contention between public and private action within Australia. As export earnings and import replacement slackened and in some major industries fell, in the second half of the decade, fixed public interest commitments overseas became a large claim on overseas earnings. As public borrowing continued to rise, the increasing interest bill bit more deeply into foreign earnings. By 1929, a crisis was reached. Severe public constraint on private activity was imposed progressively and foreign resources mobilised to meet public obligations, with serious consequences for the private sector. Yet it was largely the private sector, especially financial intermediaries, that imposed these conditions. One alternative, of default on public debt or rearranging interest commitments was rejected, despite attempts in New South Wales. Australia preserved its quite rare reputation of not defaulting, in part thereby placing the burden of adjustment on the private sector, not merely in levels of activity and unemployment but also in the reduction of overseas remittances from private indebtedness through reduced dividends, debt adjustment and outright bankruptcies. In the depth of the depression, in 1931, the 'Premiers' Plan' under private pressures achieved some co-ordinated reduction of public expenditures, particularly by the States; and exchange depreciation had actually been initiated by the private banks. By then the main cost had been imposed on private activity and thereafter public foreign borrowing overseas was kept at very low levels until it dwindled and was largely reversed in debt repatriation after 1940.

This public borrowing was designed in the traditional supportive public approach in the provision, essentially, of infrastructure. In the inter-war years, the composition of this capital formation changed considerably as compared with that before 1914.

Until the mid-thirties, public and private investment each ran at close to half total Australian capital formation (the public sector moved above during the depression). Private investment concentrated on urban assets of dwellings, manufacturing plant and equipment and commercial and office structures. Rural private investment remained a relatively small figure, supported by the increasing mechanisation (and labour displacement) of Australian agriculture. Public investment responded to and reinforced this orientation of private capital formation. It is true that, in the early twenties, significant rural branch railways and roads were constructed by government, that considerable public capital outlays were directed to irrigation and water development schemes and to farm improvement. This reflected essentially public pressures still to press forward with the farm settlement of artificially expanded population. With hindsight one may judge much of these outlays to have been misdirected.

But the concentration of public investment was increasingly towards urban assets and misdirected rural investment was the minor part of capital outlays. Capital formation in public business undertakings are indicated in Table 2.3, generally accounting for between 50 and 60 per cent of total public capital outlays (compared with 55 to 65 per cent before 1914). The relative decline of investment by public undertakings mainly reflected the increasing demand for roads as the motor vehicle claimed a greater share of public capital resources in both country and town. But there was a marked drop in the enterprise share in public investment during the thirties, matching the decline in public use of overseas funds for investment purposes. During the twenties, five types of public business undertakings became significant consumers of capital resources - in order, railways, water and sewerage, Post Office, electricity and urban transit. Taking all levels of governments and types of undertakings, over thirty major public bodies competed strongly for available funding (compared with, at most, seven before 1914) confusing the public allocative process. They also enlarged their public share of total Australian employment (Table 2.4).

In all these activities, the interests of urban and especially metropolitan activities were the primary beneficiaries. The urban claims to public infrastructure support became most clearly marked in the thirties as, in particular, the impetus to the main traditional area, railways, slackened greatly. Capital outlays on water and sewerage moved upwards to vie with railways for first rank, and electricity, telephone systems and urban transit investment all rose relatively rapidly after the depression. Public investment in infrastructure came progressively to accommodate to rather than lead the basic tendencies of population location and of urban concentration of activity.

This adaptation emerged gradually. During the twenties it appears

TABLE 2.3 Public and private gross capital formation 1919-20 to 1938-39

	Post Office A $m	Civil Aviation B $m	Broad-casting C $m	Railways D $m	Urban Transit E $m	Ports* etc. F $m	Elect. & Gas G $m	Water & Sewerage H $m	Total Capital Formation Business Under-takings I $m	Total Capital Formation Public J $m	Total Capital Formation Private K $m	G.D.C.F. Public & Private L $m	Ratio I to J %	Ratio J to L %
1919-20	2.49	0.00	0.00	23.63	1.36	0.00	2.19	10.50	40.17	101.48	100.00	201.48	39.58	50.37
21	3.84	0.00	0.00	30.04	1.93	0.00	5.56	13.61	54.98	131.28	108.00	239.28	41.88	54.86
22	5.06	0.00	0.00	36.21	2.59	0.00	8.75	16.01	68.62	123.34	131.00	254.34	55.63	48.49
23	6.55	0.00	0.00	30.83	3.05	0.00	14.12	17.87	72.42	121.72	147.00	268.72	59.50	45.30
24	11.40	0.00	0.00	32.26	3.22	0.00	8.85	18.80	74.53	129.84	156.00	285.84	57.40	45.42
25	11.88	0.00	0.00	37.75	2.40	0.00	12.67	19.57	84.27	144.22	153.00	297.22	58.43	48.52
26	12.53	0.00	0.00	49.21	2.35	0.00	8.13	14.66	86.88	147.66	151.00	298.66	58.84	49.44
27	11.31	0.00	0.00	52.32	1.97	0.00	10.98	16.00	92.58	159.71	155.00	314.71	57.97	50.75
28	10.63	0.00	0.00	50.21	2.11	0.00	11.59	17.01	91.55	162.56	153.00	315.56	56.32	51.51
29	9.52	0.00	0.00	45.34	2.85	0.00	11.56	15.42	84.69	152.49	165.00	317.49	55.54	48.03
30	8.93	0.00	0.02	35.63	2.37	0.00	10.90	13.96	71.81	131.72	98.00	229.72	54.52	57.34
31	4.46	0.00	0.00	17.35	1.62	0.00	15.89	14.02	53.34	95.84	72.00	167.84	55.66	57.10
32	3.34	0.00	0.07	14.96	1.10	0.00	4.77	10.66	34.90	66.57	50.00	116.57	52.43	57.11
33	3.27	0.00	0.06	14.24	1.05	0.00	3.05	12.32	33.99	69.53	60.00	129.53	48.89	53.68
34	3.82	0.00	0.03	15.02	1.70	0.00	3.54	11.69	35.80	71.69	77.00	148.69	49.94	48.21
35	5.14	0.00	0.22	19.06	1.92	0.00	5.60	17.51	49.45	93.68	107.00	200.68	52.79	46.68
36	6.70	0.00	0.07	21.04	1.76	0.00	7.45	16.85	53.87	101.89	117.00	218.89	52.87	46.55
37	7.59	0.00	0.18	21.27	1.76	0.00	8.31	19.45	58.56	110.23	130.00	240.23	53.13	45.89
38	9.70	0.00	0.16	22.54	2.51	0.00	10.66	20.78	66.35	124.89	162.00	286.89	53.13	43.53
39	10.87	0.00	0.00	20.93	1.79	0.00	13.03	15.44	62.06	119.87	161.00	280.87	51.77	42.68

*not separately estimated

TABLE 2.4 Public sector employment 1919–20 to 1938–39 ('000s)

	Land Transport A	Other Transport B	Commun- ication C	Banking D	Elect. & Gas E	Water & Sewerage F	Other (Misc.) G	Total Public Business Under- takings H	Public Sector Employ I	Total Civilian Workforce J	Total Workforce K	Ratio H to I '%	Ratio H to J '%	Ratio H to K '%
1919–20	111.40	2.70	30.00	1.80	6.60	7.50	15.80	175.80	279.80	2072.80	2100.20	62.83	8.48	8.37
21	116.20	2.30	30.70	2.20	7.80	7.30	14.30	180.80	289.40	2162.40	2171.10	62.47	8.36	8.33
22	123.00	2.30	32.10	2.30	10.20	8.00	14.60	192.50	302.10	2242.00	2249.80	63.72	8.59	8.56
23	124.50	2.30	33.50	2.20	11.30	7.80	14.70	196.30	306.40	2302.50	2310.00	64.07	8.53	8.50
24	128.50	2.10	34.50	2.10	12.30	7.80	16.20	203.50	326.90	2338.80	2345.80	62.25	8.70	8.68
25	134.00	2.30	36.00	2.20	12.10	9.30	17.40	213.30	345.80	2419.60	2426.00	61.68	8.82	8.79
26	138.60	2.40	37.30	2.40	12.50	10.00	18.50	221.70	358.00	2448.20	2454.80	61.93	9.06	9.03
27	139.30	2.40	39.20	2.40	12.50	10.90	19.30	226.00	363.10	2490.60	2497.00	62.24	9.07	9.05
28	135.00	2.40	36.90	2.80	13.10	12.10	19.10	221.40	372.10	2536.20	2541.90	59.50	8.73	8.71
29	133.70	2.80	30.80	2.90	12.50	12.50	18.50	213.70	373.40	2567.60	2573.50	57.23	8.32	8.30
30	122.80	1.70	29.20	3.00	13.10	9.30	18.70	197.80	356.30	2577.50	2583.80	55.52	7.67	7.66
31	113.10	1.20	25.00	3.00	11.00	5.70	12.80	171.80	322.60	2577.10	2582.80	53.25	6.67	6.65
32	109.80	1.10	24.90	3.20	8.80	5.00	12.00	164.80	312.00	2610.70	2616.20	52.82	6.31	6.30
33	108.60	0.80	25.00	3.20	10.20	5.10	10.50	163.40	318.10	2665.80	2671.10	51.34	6.13	6.12
34	111.40	1.00	26.50	3.30	10.70	6.50	10.10	169.50	336.50	2693.10	2699.70	50.37	6.29	6.28
35	116.60	1.00	27.80	3.50	10.70	6.40	11.10	177.10	354.30	2741.30	2748.60	49.99	6.46	6.44
36	118.00	1.50	29.50	4.60	12.70	6.50	11.00	183.80	356.60	2762.70	2770.70	51.54	6.65	6.63
37	120.80	1.60	31.30	4.80	12.20	13.50	13.30	197.50	374.00	2796.20	2805.10	52.81	7.06	7.04
38	124.00	1.70	33.70	5.20	11.80	10.80	14.50	201.70	384.50	2842.70	2852.20	52.46	7.10	7.07
39	123.80	2.00	34.90	5.50	11.60	13.20	16.10	207.10	398.00	2896.60	2907.90	52.04	7.15	7.12

to have been largely government determination to push growth ahead, supporting population growth and the twin objects of urban manufacturing and farm expansion, accepting considerable costs in real income per head. This appears as the central object of government policy and a deliberate growth path sought both by government and private interests. Public calculus was increasingly dictated by several influences, in addition to the absence of market tests. The great increase in access to income tax reduced the restraints on performance criteria, allowing the possibility of greater budget subsidies to public undertakings. Competition for development capital between States considerably aggravated the difficulties of achieving a rational calculus. A variety of private interests, most importantly farmers and some particular urban consumers, sought discriminatory benefits from public undertakings, eroding the earlier performance rules. As the growth of private activity slackened after 1925, public investment sought to sustain prosperity.

The persistence of public investment at high levels to the end of the twenties, based on foreign borrowing and with declining attention to yields on public capital, accentuated the crisis problems in the depression. In this fact, more than in any other, lay a revealed conflict between public and private effort. It was not a conflict of interest but the manifestation of a basic problem confronting Australian economic development: public infrastructure and public foreign borrowing could no longer be regarded as traditionally they had been, as one of the essential engines of accelerated growth. This issue appeared more clearly as the problems confronting the farm sector emerged during and after the depression and as manufacturing, located in cities, led Australian recovery out of the slump. From that perspective, the need was recognised for a fundamental reappraisal of the role of public intervention in influencing the rate of flow and allocation of developmental inputs into the economy.

In the thirties, this reappraisal was partly checked by a quite extensive substitution of public for private enterprise during and following the depression. In electricity, gas and urban transit undertakings, public business grew rapidly, partly as a result of inter-sectoral transfer of ownership and operation. But, in addition, the private pressures of motor vehicle users were gathering strength in opposition to the adversary policies of railway undertakings. So, in the thirties, public investment in roads to meet vehicle needs represented the (belated) success of private interests in achieving a major reallocation of public capital resources. In doing so, these pressures added substantially to the problem of public calculus by enhancing (through road investment) the importance of unpriced services of public capital. These problems were aggravated further by the human problem of high unemployment and the attractiveness of road development as a relatively easily organised source of relief work for unemployment.

Retreat from public infrastructure 1945 to 1975

The tendency to a retreat, in relation to the scale of private activity, from public provision of infrastructure and the conduct of public enterprises after the Second World War is confused and partially concealed by three different questions. First, the immediate post-war difficulties required some priority of attention to the restoration of infrastructure as a precondition of the recovery of private business. In particular, the production of key materials, particularly coal and steel, depended on the restoration of public transport, and manufacturing production was severely constrained by energy shortages, of which electricity in particular was mainly generated by public authorities. This last question merged in the longer run into the second matter, the relatively very rapid growth of certain types of public capital formation and public enterprises (see Table 2.5). Of these, electricity generation and distribution were major growth areas rising rapidly into the early 1950s and remaining high and rising thereafter so that they were, from 1950 to 1971, the main area of public capital formation. In part associated with this, public capital outlays on telecommunications (with some supplement from ordinary Post Office outlays) rose very rapidly from 1954, representing generally the fastest growing segment of public capital formation. Less costly but still substantial, some new activities were incorporated, most importantly government airlines, along with an expansion of civil aviation. But these expanding or new areas are to be set against a long lag in public provision of water and sewerage and, most importantly, the loss of impetus to capital outlays in the traditionally dominant area of railways. Railway investment remained a substantial claimant for capital funds - for re-equipment, for electrification and conversion to diesel power and for gauge unification. But it fell behind in growth terms and by the mid-sixties ranked only fourth behind (in order) electricity, post and telecommunications and water and sewerage. It is worth noting, for future reference, that in the first two, post and telecommunications and electricity, the Federal Government was deeply implicated; in the two important areas tending to lag behind, the States were the main bodies responsible for capital outlays.

One needs therefore to observe some conflicting tendencies. However, the aggregate is also important. The aggregation of public capital outlays implies a relative decline (a) of public enterprise outlays in total public capital formation and (b) of public capital formation as a whole in total Australian capital formation. This is the

TABLE 2.5 Public and private gross capital formation 1944-45 to 1974-75

	Post Office A $m	Civil Aviation B $m	Broad-casting C $m	Railways D $m	Urban Transit E $m	Ports etc. F $m	Elect. & Gas G $m	Water & Sewerage H $m	Total Capital Formation Business Under-takings I $m	Total Capital Formation Public J $m	Total Capital Formation Private K $m	G.D.C.F. Public & Private L $m	Ratio I to J %	Ratio J to L %
1944-45	12.67	2.90	0.10	34.24	2.18	2.98	6.32	3.28	64.67	118.03	118.00	236.03	54.79	50.01
46	15.60	2.14	0.14	30.68	2.80	3.94	9.52	4.28	69.10	143.77	198.00	341.77	48.06	42.07
47	19.78	9.20	0.36	41.88	3.22	9.22	12.06	13.22	108.94	223.55	288.00	511.55	48.73	43.70
48	26.22	15.98	0.36	48.10	4.82	8.22	19.78	18.20	141.68	292.12	368.00	660.12	48.50	44.25
49	37.28	9.42	0.36	57.38	6.98	17.38	42.12	20.70	191.62	360.64	365.00	725.64	53.13	49.70
50	49.73	9.00	0.32	73.66	5.42	18.32	84.46	23.42	264.33	473.72	496.00	969.72	55.80	48.85
51	68.04	11.00	0.42	118.84	6.58	27.56	156.56	45.80	434.80	722.61	646.00	1368.61	60.17	52.80
52	81.70	14.00	0.50	148.52	7.66	30.20	206.46	64.06	553.10	922.25	924.00	1846.25	59.97	49.95
53	78.58	11.00	0.40	155.96	10.40	26.82	222.10	59.08	564.34	919.26	1135.00	2054.26	61.39	44.75
54	86.85	8.00	0.56	142.60	7.78	31.00	199.76	65.70	542.25	953.81	1143.00	2096.81	56.85	45.49
55	91.53	21.00	0.54	147.70	9.34	31.74	194.30	80.10	576.25	1013.50	1321.00	2334.50	56.86	43.41
56	100.25	22.00	1.64	155.98	11.06	34.02	201.24	89.60	615.79	1094.77	1502.00	2596.77	56.25	42.16
57	96.15	16.00	5.30	145.94	11.06	43.78	220.00	94.04	632.27	1123.83	1641.00	2764.83	56.26	40.65
58	106.24	15.00	3.12	152.22	11.74	43.16	220.88	106.30	658.66	1177.58	1717.00	2894.58	55.93	40.68
59	113.89	38.00	2.74	156.20	9.34	46.66	238.24	119.40	724.47	1289.53	1859.00	3148.53	56.18	40.96

TABLE 2.5 Public and private gross capital formation 1944-45 to 1974-75 (Contd.)

	Post Office A $m	Civil Aviation B $m	Broad-casting C $m	Railways D $m	Urban Transit E $m	Ports etc. F $m	Elect. & Gas G $m	Water & Sewerage H $m	Total Capital Formation Business Under-takings I $m	Total Capital Formation Public J $m	Total Capital Formation Private K $m	G.D.C.F. Public & Private L $m	Ratio I to J %	Ratio J to L %
1959-60	128.80	63.00	7.00	164.38	8.52	44.04	241.48	130.16	787.38	1412.26	1906.00	3318.26	55.75	42.56
61	136.97	20.00	2.76	160.24	9.02	50.84	226.32	150.66	756.81	1448.32	2401.00	3849.32	52.25	37.63
62	145.25	44.00	5.64	177.86	6.68	44.80	255.38	169.02	848.63	1628.33	2369.00	3997.33	52.12	40.74
63	141.34	16.00	7.58	175.28	6.76	45.92	265.04	159.54	817.46	1659.82	2559.00	4218.82	49.25	39.34
64	157.20	14.00	7.00	188.06	7.46	48.50	285.40	169.40	877.02	1790.94	2913.00	4703.94	48.97	38.07
65	182.96	66.00	9.00	189.84	8.48	53.60	333.80	182.40	1026.08	2030.90	3412.00	5442.90	50.52	37.31
66	206.98	66.00	8.00	208.92	7.30	55.70	359.50	187.90	1100.30	2219.34	3635.00	5854.34	49.58	37.91
67	235.32	53.00	6.00	217.58	7.92	53.10	408.20	206.02	1187.14	2368.49	3799.00	6167.49	50.12	38.40
68	270.92	100.00	8.00	226.88	10.18	56.20	414.50	217.40	1304.08	2551.34	4122.00	6673.34	51.11	38.23
69	305.46	59.00	7.00	233.54	10.10	68.70	421.50	246.70	1352.00	2719.37	4723.00	7442.37	49.72	36.54
70	345.14	66.00	5.00	253.76	14.26	86.30	447.40	275.90	1493.76	2959.39	5150.00	8109.39	50.48	36.49
71	363.94	96.00	10.00	257.20	16.00	61.10	428.80	310.30	1543.34	3151.57	5831.00	8982.57	48.97	35.09
72	418.26	176.00	12.00	289.34	17.20	90.10	416.60	374.20	1793.70	3527.55	6267.00	9794.55	50.85	36.02
73	469.24	59.00	10.00	299.72	13.50	85.30	423.10	472.00	1831.86	3738.39	6483.00	10221.39	49.00	36.57
74	570.58	85.00	15.00	318.96	14.60	75.10	442.70	505.10	2027.04	4259.49	7996.00	12255.49	47.59	34.76
75	687.62	99.00	23.00	435.14	29.00	139.00	555.30	624.60	2592.66	5858.33	8802.00	14660.33	44.26	39.96

third issue referred to above. The extent of this relative decline is, however, contrary to official estimates which show a more constant and lower ratio of public to private investment as a trend experience. These official estimates were seriously misleading. Major estimation problems arise in the official *Social Accounts* from the late 1940s, declining in significance up to 1972 (and then briefly becoming more important). These problems cannot be fully discussed here but they are too important to leave aside. Basically, they derive from the official omission of very large outlays through internal funding by public enterprise, of other capital expenditures in telecommunications and from an official confusion in the case of housing between actual capital formation and transactions in existing assets. Partial corrections were made in official estimates and revisions eventually made extended back at the end of the sixties. A more complete adjustment for these omissions, however, alters substantially the ratio of public to private capital formation into a more significant decline in that ratio between 1946 and 1972 and radically changes the composition of public capital formation. Revision of past estimates by the Bureau of Statistics does not alter the fact that throughout the 1950s and 1960s, the public sector provided seriously misleading information to both the public and private sectors.

Post-war pressures tended to lift the ratio of public to private investment until 1952, though still at a level corresponding to the reduced public sector performance in the late 1930s. After 1952, there was a relatively sharp decline and then a tendency to gradual drift downwards until 1968 when a further sharp decline occurred until 1972. The Whitlam years witnessed a brief restoration which was as quickly reversed after 1975.

In this long-run relative decline, the capital outlays by public business undertakings as a proportion of total public capital formation fell considerably faster. Public enterprise investment accounted for most of the immediate post-war lift in public investment until 1953; and then they became the most slowly growing segment, not recovering even in the Whitlam years. That this relative decline occurred was predominantly due to the great slackening in railway investment after 1953 despite continued upgrading of assets. The traditional public sector contribution to Australian economic growth was a spent force. Its place was partially taken, but only slowly and after a considerable lapse of time into the sixties, by public investment in roads. Then, belatedly, the private pressures for investment in roads triumphed over the interests in public railways.

This experience of public capital inputs into Australian economic growth was not reflected fully in the (measured) delivery of public marketed services either in terms of employment or of gross product. Public enterprise employment as a fraction of total workforce tended to remain relatively stationary until the late 1950s (Table 2.6). Thereafter it fell quite heavily from some 8.5 per cent down to 6.5 per cent. This decline represented more than the general downward drift of capital outlays. It reflects the increasing capital intensity and the increasing automation of public activity. On the other hand, gross product of public undertakings tended to rise (with some fluctuations) until the late 1960s. The peak was actually reached in 1962 with an ensuing major swing. The implication is that gross surplus of public enterprises tended to rise strongly until about 1970. This rise reflected a basic change in the attitudes to the pricing of public marketed services. Now, in the post-war years, not only was public enterprise investment perceived as a less important engine of growth but the private sector was expected to meet more of the costs of public enterprise services. This appears to have been the case in all areas of public investment but most obviously in those for which Federal authorities had major responsibilities or could exert more direct influence. It might be suggested that, now, in contrast with pre-1939 attitudes, public enterprises were prepared or were forced by 'superior' government to exploit more of their monopolistic powers in both the pricing of services and in their willingness to supply these services in response to private demands - and at a time when their monopoly was, in several ways, being eroded.

This changed attitude may be seen as beginning with the experience of the depression after 1929 and of the special role of government interest obligations overseas. It followed the determination, particularly, of Labor Governments, reflecting trade union attitudes, to avoid fixed overseas commitments. But these attitudes gradually faded. First, in the apparent success of post-war industrialisation until the 1960s, it appeared appropriate to a dominant Federal Government that public enterprises might share in this economic 'success'. But secondly, as industrial growth was partly replaced by mineral discoveries and the growth of mineral exports, a fundamental change of attitude between the public and private sectors occurred during the 1960s. Then government attitudes firmed with the expectation that private developmental projects should bear more of the infrastructure costs of Australian development. In the circumstances of tax concessions for private developmental projects, this may not have represented very strong public resolution. But it applied not only to land transport and housing infrastructure; it extended to concepts of public and private joint ventures also in port development and the provision of facilities. Public attitudes were by no means conclusive. Much of mineral development occurred in geographical isolated conditions. In these circumstances, private enterprise could expect to capture most and perhaps all of any externalities that might flow from infrastructure provisions (including the external benefits of the possession of company towns).

TABLE 2.6 Public sector employment 1946–47 to 1974–75 ('000s)

	Land Trans-port A	Other Trans-port B	Commun-ication C	Banking D	Elect. & Gas E	Water & Sewerage F	Other (Misc.) G	Total Public Business Under-takings H	Public Sector Employ I	Total Civilian Workforce J	Total Workforce K	Ratio H to I '%	Ratio H to J '%	Ratio H to K '%
1946–47	157.70	5.60	80.60	9.70	13.90	6.90	0.00	274.40	564.10	3072.30	3155.70	48.64	8.93	8.70
48	161.80	6.60	84.30	10.40	14.70	7.50	0.00	285.30	588.90	3176.20	3222.20	48.45	8.98	8.85
49	159.80	7.20	92.70	11.00	15.20	7.80	0.00	293.70	618.40	3278.80	3314.50	47.49	8.96	8.86
50	163.10	7.00	99.40	11.40	16.30	9.00	0.00	306.20	656.40	3389.70	3423.30	46.65	9.03	8.94
51	152.20	7.80	96.70	13.70	18.80	9.60	0.00	298.80	678.30	3503.60	3543.10	44.05	8.53	8.43
52	154.00	7.90	94.70	13.50	20.80	11.70	0.00	302.60	687.60	3580.60	3640.50	44.01	8.45	8.31
53	159.70	7.60	95.10	13.20	21.00	9.20	0.00	305.80	672.20	3575.40	3639.60	45.49	8.55	8.40
54	166.50	8.40	97.10	13.40	22.50	9.90	0.00	317.80	702.20	3616.90	3681.20	45.26	8.79	8.63
55	167.20	9.00	97.60	13.90	23.60	11.10	0.00	322.40	729.90	3695.20	3756.80	44.17	8.72	8.58
56	167.40	9.60	103.40	14.40	23.70	11.20	0.00	329.70	741.80	3792.10	3853.10	44.45	8.69	8.56
57	167.70	9.90	107.50	15.00	24.90	10.50	0.00	335.50	747.90	3843.20	3899.40	44.86	8.73	8.60
58	163.10	9.80	109.10	15.60	25.10	10.80	0.00	333.50	765.50	3909.30	3958.00	43.57	8.53	8.43
59	161.10	10.70	110.40	16.80	25.80	11.10	0.00	335.90	784.00	3965.60	4014.90	42.84	8.47	8.37

TABLE 2.6 **Public sector employment 1946–47 to 1974–75 ('000s) (Contd.)**

	Land Transport A	Other Transport B	Communication C	Banking D	Elect. & Gas E	Water & Sewerage F	Other (Misc.) G	Total Public Business Undertakings H	Public Sector Employ I	Total Civilian Workforce J	Total Workforce K	Ratio H to I %	Ratio H to J %	Ratio H to K %
1959–60	157.40	11.10	111.80	15.70	25.50	11.50	0.00	333.00	788.40	4050.10	4098.40	42.24	8.22	8.13
61	154.90	11.40	115.80	17.20	24.80	12.00	0.00	336.10	812.60	4275.40	4321.50	41.36	7.86	7.78
62	154.20	11.60	113.80	17.70	24.70	12.50	0.00	334.50	829.10	4426.90	4474.70	40.34	7.56	7.48
63	149.90	12.20	115.60	19.30	24.70	12.90	0.00	334.60	848.40	4462.40	4511.70	39.44	7.50	7.42
64	147.40	13.50	118.70	20.00	24.40	15.30	0.00	339.30	867.60	4545.60	4597.40	39.11	7.46	7.38
65	143.70	15.80	112.00	21.40	24.80	16.20	0.00	333.90	888.40	4668.50	4723.20	37.58	7.15	7.07
66	143.50	16.40	121.10	22.40	25.00	16.80	0.00	345.20	943.50	4803.00	4869.60	36.59	7.19	7.09
67	141.60	16.90	125.80	23.70	25.90	17.70	0.00	351.60	965.50	4934.40	5011.70	36.42	7.13	7.02
68	140.20	17.70	129.30	25.40	25.70	19.20	0.00	357.50	997.10	5063.70	5144.50	35.85	7.06	6.95
69	138.00	18.70	131.30	26.60	25.60	18.60	0.00	358.80	1021.80	5197.40	5280.90	35.11	6.90	6.79
70	135.40	20.30	135.50	29.00	25.80	19.80	0.00	365.80	1053.20	5385.80	5470.00	34.73	6.79	6.69
71	135.30	19.70	139.10	30.70	26.10	20.70	0.00	371.60	1062.50	5525.10	5608.30	34.97	6.73	6.63
72	133.40	20.10	143.20	32.40	26.50	22.50	0.00	378.10	1098.70	5572.60	5653.70	34.41	6.78	6.69
73	132.90	20.60	142.10	33.40	26.80	25.50	0.00	381.30	1132.90	5701.10	5775.20	33.66	6.69	6.60
74	131.50	20.80	145.90	34.80	26.70	26.90	0.00	386.60	1171.50	5867.70	5935.30	33.00	6.59	6.51
75	130.90	21.20	147.50	36.20	27.50	29.80	0.00	393.10	1295.50	5940.10	6009.30	30.34	6.62	6.54

This evolving change in attitudes to public infrastructure was closely related to basic developments in funding of capital outlays and in the structure of Australian government. First, in funding, the Australian reluctance, both public and private, to depend on foreign fixed obligations on public account persisted beyond the thirties. During the war, indeed, significant amounts of foreign debt were repatriated. Subsequently, much of public capital formation was funded either by current revenues or by domestic loan raisings. It was only during the Whitlam years that efforts to make large overseas loan raisings were made. At first repudiated by the coalition parties, these efforts were subsequently resumed (looking to different purposes and sources) by the Fraser Government.

So far as domestic issues were concerned, the public dependence on domestic loan raisings implied a much more direct conflict between public and private interest than had ever occurred in Australian history. The relative success of Australian industrialisation until the early 1960s made this competition for resources the more pressing. Conservative public policies, backed by Federal authority, made the recognition of this potential funding competition more explicit. At the same time, Federal policies, designed to encourage the private capital market (see Chapter 5), tended to encourage private rather than public capital formation - but, as always in Australian pragmatism, with important qualifications coercively inducing large private holdings of public securities.

Moreover, public policies were increasingly designed to attract foreign capital into private ventures after 1949 (until 1972 and after 1975). The Federally orchestrated foreign investment in and takeover of much of Australian manufacturing during the 1950s and of Australian mining in the late 1960s (and second half of the 1970s) represented a major public intervention in the attraction of foreign private capital, foreign technology and foreign managerial expertise. Until the mining boom, these policies appear to have reaped considerable benefits for Australian residents to a considerable degree because foreign manufacturers could be more readily 'captured'. The advantages appear to have been less obvious with mining, partly because of State competition and the extremely generous tax concessions accorded to foreign mining enterprises outside the Whitlam years, and partly because of the horizontal integration of relevant multinationals, reducing Australian bargaining power.

Advantages apart, public action in capital formation and in the funding of public investment may be perceived as fitting into the supportive Australian tradition. In the years after 1945, after immediate post-war scarcities were dealt with, the public sector tended to withdraw relatively, leaving more of the field to private business. So far as public action was concerned, public attention shifted from the provision of physical capital towards a greater emphasis on human capital. So developed, in part, the public concentration on education during the fifties and, more particularly, in the sixties. It was not until the inflation and unemployment problems of the 1970s that serious doubt was cast on the value of public support to accretion of human capital through education.

In the meantime, however, more fundamental though possibly temporary doubts about human capital had arisen. These doubts focused on the wisdom of the traditional approach to Australian growth: publicly assisted immigration and accelerated population growth. In the post-war years from 1946 to 1975 more than 2 000 000 migrants (net) arrived in Australia. This massive injection of population surpassed by far all previous accessions, over comparable periods, of population and of labour from outside. Similarly, publicly assisted migration far exceeded any other Australian program of intervention: some 1 750 000 persons were publicly assisted immigrants.

Australia, in 1945 and subsequently, was not, in market terms, a particularly attractive prospect for immigration. Any advantage relative to Britain in real income per head had largely, if not entirely, disappeared. The Second World War appeared, from this point of view, as an enormous benefit to Australia. Large numbers of displaced persons in Europe were available for transplantation, and it was on displaced persons, initially, that Australian (Federal) policy concentrated. To these persons, ordinary market comparisons had, for long, little relevance. Their attraction to and eventual location in Australia, however, led Australian Government into far more detailed intervention in private decision-making than had ever previously occurred. Not merely passage assistance but the public organisation and chartering of transport (sea and air), the public provision of accommodation of families, public intervention in teaching English, in public health and school care, and public efforts to locate jobs for breadwinners all meant deep intrusion, for supportive purposes, in private decision-making. This was 'big government' operation in almost every sense. Once the main supplies of displaced persons were exhausted, attention shifted to other national groups. Though British immigrants received attention, one outstanding consequence of public intervention was a basic alteration in the ethnic composition of the Australian population, a change that would not have been comprehensible in terms of free market operation.

Doubts about the wisdom of this program were being hinted during the 1960s. They became more effective at the end of the decade. Then both doubts about the absorptive capacity of the Australian economy and the fashion of zero population growth led to a drastic scaling down of net immigration and of public assistance. Stagflation reinforced this reaction. By 1975, public assistance to immigration had fallen heavily. Any consideration of resumption appeared to depend to a large degree on selective skill requirements of Australian development, particularly in and linked to the mineral boom.

This is not the place to explore 'push' versus 'pull' factors in immigration. Specifically public initiative in the introduction of this post-1945 program appear to be reasonably clear cut, both in terms of international relief agencies and of Federal immigration policies. Nevertheless, the continuation of massive immigration must be partly (and significantly) explicable in terms of Australian private interests. First, post-war Australian labour supply was affected by the lagged effects of low birth rates in the depression period 1930 to 1934. Abnormally low rates of entry into the workforce followed during the late 1940s and early 1950s. Boom conditions enhanced the demand for labour. In particular, manufacturing expansion accompanied by foreign investment in and takeover of Australian industry enhanced the demand for industrially skilled labour. The 'success' of Australian manufacturing development throughout the 1950s sustained a high demand for immigrant labour which provided, in fact, a large part of the labour increment sought for this expansion.

But the continuation of the immigration program must be sought in other private reactions to post-war economic growth. In the years 1945 to 1965 lay one of the exceptional periods of improvements in Australian per capita real income, improvements closely related to the increased use of human skills and enhanced human capital. One of the consequences of higher standards and of the demands experienced for skills was a greatly increased demand, by Australians, for more advanced education. Greatly increased school participation rates, to more advanced ages, followed, and so, too, did the demand for postschool education (see Chapter 8). This implied that a very considerable proportion of the population deferred entry into the workforce, leading to demand for substitute - i.e. migrant (and local female) - labour. This response appears to have been important until the end of the sixties and perhaps into the beginning of the seventies when stagflation reversed these expectations of the benefits of higher education. Then unemployment and the capital costs of immigration weighed much more strongly in private and public assessment of the advantages of immigration. The basic nineteenth- and twentieth-century tenet of Australian growth was at last, in the early 1970s, challenged and, at least for a time, appeared to be abandoned. This shift of values was accentuated as the 'mineral boom' developed with its strong message in population terms: perhaps more than any other Australian development, it was non-labour-intensive though it might require special skills. Moreover, the mineral boom tended to erode the other prop of Australian population ambitions: the viability of labour-intensive manufacturing. Nevertheless, there remained another issue: whether Australia could or would supply from its own resources sufficient skilled labour to service the mining boom.

These basic changes in the relationship between public and private action - relatively declining public capital formation, declining public borrowing overseas, an eventually declining share of public enterprise product in gross domestic product and a long-sustained but eventually dwindling program of assisted immigration - represented a fundamental shift in the priorities of public versus private choice. But the shift was a complicated one. It was not merely that private choice acquired increasing priority. A radically new element emerged. It appeared that it was foreign private interest that acquired a much stronger representation in both public and private motivation and decision making. It was a matter of Australian public action more and more in relation to foreign private interests, not domestic Australian interests.

In this shift and in the thirty years experience after 1945, it was central (i.e. Federal) government that played the dominant role. In this respect 'big government', in the sense of centralised Federal Government, came much more to the forefront as, in several important respects, public choice gave way to private choice in providing inputs into the economy. This was not the prospect in the years immediately after the war. But it was, to a significant degree, the product of structural changes within government during and immediately after the war and of the nature of private institutional (especially foreign business) development.

The essential point is the fiscal and policy-making pre-eminence attained by the Federal Government over State and local and semi-government bodies. This pre-eminence flowed from the adoption of Uniform Income Tax in 1942 and the consequential limitation of State-revenue raising powers; the co-ordinating control of the Loan Council and the Premiers' Conference in determining levels and allocation of current and capital spending; and from the constitutional authority of the Federal Government with respect to immigration, banking and trade (including the management of the conditions of capital inflow and foreign business entry). Combined with these features was the Federal responsibilities for the maintenance of full employment until the early 1970s, giving the Federal Government authority to constrain and not merely to support both the private sector and the nonFederal public sector.

Given this centralisation of authority, the political successes of 'anti-Labor' governments at the Federal level over almost a quarter century set Australia on a path radically different from that pursued before the Second World War. How firmly this path is defined remains to be seen. Its course does not imply an abdication of government. On the contrary. Until the early 1970s, the characteristics of public choice in relation to private interest were not radically different from experience between 1920 and 1939. It is the implication of the mineral boom and the entry of foreign multinationals that blurred the prospect of the immediate, let alone the long-run, future.

Despite this uncertainty, centralised authority, exercised for the first time in Australian history, has led since the early 1950s to a gradual retreat from public capital formation, public dependence on foreign capital, public enterprise as a substantial producer of services and, much more recently, public assistance in hastening population growth. In this sense, Australia has witnessed a decline of big government. But, as a contradiction, it has taken big government to achieve this redirection, and the withdrawal in terms of the public provision of infrastructure and its services has tended, through Federal constraint, to be concentrated on State activities. Those specific areas in which Federal interest is strong have maintained and increased their presence.

3

Managing Diversified Recovery 1900 to 1914

Introduction

It was not the process of decline in colonial socialism that brought allocative and regulatory[1] intervention to the fore. Indeed, in the historical circumstances of the decades immediately after 1900, the growth of this style of public action was a necessary concomitant of the continuation of policies of 'colonial socialism': the artificial, government efforts to push the rate of increase of factor inputs ahead of that which the private market would deliver.

Some, but very limited, regulatory intervention occurred in Australia in the second half of the nineteenth century. With a relatively specialised economy engaged in rapid and geographically expansive growth in pastoral activity, the pressures for micro-intervention were constrained. The depression of the nineties presented government with the task of restorative and ameliorative action. But by 1900 the weaknesses in the late nineteenth-century economic structure had been brought home forcefully by depression losses which provided strong inducements to government action or private pressures on government to intervene in particular private markets and to alter the conditions and activities of private decision-making.

As recovery proceeded, with continued ambitions above all to accelerate population growth through government action, the nature of the Australian economy and of its relations with the outside world largely forced attention to allocative policy and regulation on a scope and with a degree of detail that contrasted sharply with late nineteenth-century experience.

---

[1] Although all or substantially all public policies are allocative, they are not necessarily regulatory. The concept of regulation is included within but not synonymous with allocation.

The strategic influence appears to have been the population ambitions in an economy with reduced growth horizons and dependent on more diversified resource use. From this flowed the conscious government efforts and private pressures on government to divert resources into particular markets as a means of assisting private expansion and to intervene in a variety of ways in the operation of those markets. Accordingly this and the two succeeding chapters are to a large extent structured around related markets and the evolving government intervention in them.

Until 1914, the system of intervention was still inchoate though already the scope and detail of measures had greatly increased. The emphasis was still on largely experimental efforts to support private recovery in those markets through reduced competition, the encouragement of monopoly organisation and practices, and to arrange in a very detailed way the conditions of access and entry into those markets. After the war, with severely constrained growth prospects, the dependence on this style of intervention increased greatly but was then subject to much more prominent private interest, with an emphasis on the restraint of competition and the accommodation of conflict. Arising out of the depression in the 1930s, this allocative and regulatory intervention became the dominant mode of public support of private activity and of private dependence on government. It was not until after 1945 that the commitment to full employment and macro-economic policy introduced general characteristics of constraint and a high degree of centralisation in government intervention. Until then, public allocative policy might properly be perceived as a commitment to deliver, as a public good, a growth strategy for the private sector.

Given the hypothesis of population ambitions with limited growth horizons as strategic factors and given the consequential treatment of separate markets, a brief outline of the main factors of economic and political change is necessary.

Economic and political change

At the beginning of the century, the six Australian colonies were approaching the end of a long-drawn-out depression beginning in 1889. They were on the point of encountering, during 1902-03, perhaps the most severe drought experienced throughout the whole period of white settlement, a drought that decimated livestock populations. The key export industry, woolgrowing, had ceased to be the centre of growth, the rationale of land occupation, the underlying attraction for foreign investment and the impetus to the public provision of overhead transport capital and to the operation of public transport enterprises.

Depression, debts, the withdrawal of British investment, the drastic revaluation of assets and widespread foreclosures had radically altered the wealth, social status and political influence of large-scale pastoralists. Major changes in relative profitability had induced significant alterations in the composition of the economy, with shifts towards manufacturing, mining and services and towards non-wool land use. Financial institutions that had dominated growth to 1890 were still in some disarray, their numbers severely reduced, their activities curtailed and the managements of several still preoccupied with financial readjustment. Unemployment was still high, real wages lowered and trade union membership greatly reduced. Depression losses encouraged strong pressure for the restoration of unionism and for the Australia-wide formation of political Labor Parties. Reduced job opportunities had reversed the flow of migration and a net emigrattion of population, particularly of the workforce, had occurred and continued into the first five years of the twentieth century.

Australian policy was still preoccupied with artificially increasing population. But efforts to push population ahead of the flows that the private market could deliver were now set in a development context much less favourable than had existed in the nineteenth century. Above all else, population expansion, central to Australian aims, now required increasing attention to allocative measures, in contrast with the nineteenth century. What had then been a matter essentially of aggregative or general economic management (different from the modern macro concepts) now became one of public allocative and regulatory intervention that dominates much of public and private relations in this century.

The Commonwealth Constitution adopted in 1901 provided for a range of specific powers by the new Federal Government, including, in particular, defence, international trade, immigration control, banking and finance (except State Government bodies) and certain issues such as industrial disputes extending beyond the limits of any one State. State sovereignty for matters not dealt with - all residual powers - was preserved by each State.

The constitutional and related administrative transition occupied several years. Before it was completed, the Australian economy was embarked on a phase of rapid recovery, growth and structural change, particularly from 1904-05 to 1913-14. The First World War marks a very clear division in allocative and regulatory principles and methods and in their implications for private sector behaviour. Between 1901 and 1914, substantially novel and often experimental regulations and allocative measures were introduced, designed to encourage private expansion in particular directions, essentially by altering conditions of entry and by limiting competition. The emphasis was on easing entry into rural enterprise and on limiting risks of rural activity; other private business decisions were only slightly affected, if at all. Restraint of competition was directed (with qualified effectiveness) towards reducing competition of foreigners and towards the public encouragement of monopoly organisations and practices. In the latter case, though some business organisations gained, the primary beneficiaries were trade unions. By 1914, these allocative measures represented a still inchoate system in which individual State governments were the main (and often competitive) actors. One fundamental nineteenth-century characteristic remained, however: public intervention was designed to be supportive and protective of private business.

The severe drought of 1902 and 1903 checked an incipient recovery and led to a flurry of short-term measures, essentially of relief, by all government levels. But once the drought was over, net emigration and capital outflow slackened rapidly and a powerful export-led boom developed. In these circumstances, government regulation was directed towards the encouragement of the boom rather than towards other regulatory constraints; and for a variety of reasons, governments acted primarily to aid and support the major growing points in the economy without, in general, being required or encouraged to exercise detailed and inhibiting intervention.

TABLE 3.1 **Simple annual average growth rates 1900-01 to 1913-14 (%)**
             (current prices)

Gross Wool Proceeds	4.2
Agric. Gross Product	11.2
Dairy Gross Product	6.6
Manuf. Gross Value Added	11.2
Banking and Finance	6.3
Professional and Domestic Service	5.0
Distribution Factor Earnings	9.5
Public Bus. Undertakings	8.0
Public Services	9.1
Public Construction	13.4
Mining	1.4
Exports (current)	5.0
Imports (current)	7.5
Current GDP	8.9
Constant GDP	5.9
Wage and Salary Earners	3.3

Table 3.1 shows differences in growth rates and the nature of major restructuring of the economy. Between 1905 and 1914, the economy expanded relatively quickly if not as rapidly as between 1860 and 1890 and real income per head rose considerably, after fifteen years of stagnation. Of the export industries, mining increased very slowly, partly because gold production had expanded earlier in the nineties.

Much more importantly, wool output expanded at the second slowest rate of product components. Even this low rate may be somewhat exaggerated by the effects of the drought of 1902-03. In the rural sector, meat production, agriculture, dairying and miscellaneous rural production grew significantly more rapidly, indicating a substantial diversification of rural activity. Though not displayed in this tabulation, a similar diversification of rural exports also occurred. This diversification represented a significant withdrawal from Australian natural resource advantage - the diversion from fine wool production to crossbred meat-producing sheep, the extension of grain, especially wheat farming, and the growth of regionally constrained dairying and other miscellaneous rural products such as sugar, rice, fresh and dried fruit, wine etc. Of these, the major items were meat and wheat, the expansion of one occurring within the pastoral industry, and of the other due to large-scale geographical extension into dry areas opened up by a combination of technical development in wheat-breeding, clearing, ploughing and cultivating and in fertiliser use. In the nineteenth century, Victoria and South Australia had become wheat exporters; now New South Wales entered as a major producer for export, followed by Western Australia and Queensland. Together these States achieved a highly unstable production and exporting performance. Distance, climatic variability and the quality of products made these 'new' rural exports relatively insecure and inferior export products still dependent on domestic markets. But they were taken to offer the chief prospects for continued settlement and absorption of rural population. Some supplementary products, such as sugar and rice, did not attain significant export capability. Although they offered greater prospects of closer settlement than did wool, most of these additional rural activities still left sparse settlement often dependent on family farming and casual, seasonal labour.

Manufacturing far outpaced the growth of rural activity. More importantly, in terms of Australian population ambitions, this growth was highly labour intensive. There is an over-ready tendency to assume that Australian comparative advantage lay only in rural production. In fact, however, this manufacturing expansion revolved closely round Australian rural products - foodstuffs, textiles, leather, stone products, timber products, wagon making etc. - in general subject to comparatively limited processing. The availability of local primary materials made this array of manufacturing capable of effective import competition without high protection. It was this array that grew most rapidly until the First World War, outpacing the less competitive and more complex manufacturing activities. Increasingly, too, both types of activities moved towards metropolitan locations, helping to depopulate the country towns.

Closely related to rural and manufacturing developments, construction activity was by far the most rapid growth area in the economy. Construction for private purposes expanded significantly more slowly than that for public authorities and enterprises. Essentially, this minor private role was due to the reduced construction demands of the pastoral industry and the limited construction requirements of the supplementary rural activities. Construction for public purposes, rising very rapidly, was directed both to rural infrastructure and metropolitan expansion. Branch railways and rural roads were to service particularly the growth of grain production, much more sensitive to transport costs than wool had been. Urban roads, water and sewerage, ports and electricity were designed to cope with a backlog of city and suburban services and to provide for more efficient conditions of expanding populations, manufacturing and commercial activities in the cities.

The relatively rapid growth of imports at an average 13 per cent per annum compared to exports (4.2 per cent) was indicative of the strong domestic growth and dependence of that growth on imports supported by a resumption of borrowing by Australian State governments to fund public works. Similarly, net immigration, most assisted publicly, was restored to be some 25 per cent of total population increase. These substantial contributions of both capital and migrant inflow occurred despite net outflow in the early part of the century.

By 1913-14, this expansion had become unstable and was slackening. Export growth had slowed down after 1910 and gold production had fallen heavily. The level of importing was at risk with world prices rising rapidly immediately before the war. The ability of governments to service the foreign borrowing became more doubtful. The outbreak of war led, however, to radically different problems and a sharp break in the relationships between the public and private sectors.

A significant factor in the behaviour of government was the emergence of Labor Parties in the Commonwealth and State parliaments. Although at the beginning of the twentieth century, conservative governments occupied the Treasury benches, the new force of Labor politics was quickly felt. Despite shifting fortunes of parties in attaining government power, Labor Parties soon acquired, at least, the ability to exercise the balance of power in the various parliaments and through that power to have a great deal of their policies embodied in legislation. In fact, some of these legislative successes turned out to be hollow victories as judicial interpretations disallowed some important legislation.

Nevertheless, from the very early years of the century, the political pattern made it extremely difficult if not impossible to view Australian governments as predominantly the handmaidens of business interests; governments were now able and expected to act much more autonomously. A much wider, but still weakly organised, array of pressure group interests acquired, particularly in the case of wage earners, political and governing prominence far beyond that achieved in the nineteenth century or, it would seem, in other British countries or the United States. (It is also possible that, with the Australian tradition of employing British administrative experts in the nineteenth century, opportunities for public sector initiative and independence in framing policy with respect to regulation were enhanced.)

Labor Party electoral successes extended beyond the achievement of balance of power to actual formation of independent government. A brief Labor reign in 1904 in the Commonwealth led to a reversion to several years of balance of power politics. Then in 1910 Labor entered a substantial period of continuous government; only briefly were conservatives able to regain government and in 1914 Labor resumed power at the Commonwealth level.

The behaviour of State politics is more obscure but in all States, even in Victoria, Labor had become a power to be accommodated. In New South Wales, conservatives depended on active Labor support for much of the second half of the first decade, and then Labor governed from 1910 to 1916. Comparable 'successes' by Labor occurred in Queensland and, with less clarity, in South Australia. Only in Victoria did Labor have to depend on a balance-of-power role. Given the nature of the constitutional division of powers, this political experience of the States was, perhaps, a good deal more important than Federal experience, though, as we shall suggest, key national provisions at the Federal level (in tariffs and wage regulation and in some rural marketing regulations) came soon to be leading elements in allocative and regulatory measures.

Allocative intervention 1901 to 1914

Broad thrust of intervention

Despite Commonwealth powers with respect to foreign trade and notwithstanding the importance of exports - and diversified exports - in the boom to the First World War, governments played only a minute role in export markets. Gold production was acquired under Mint purchase conditions, an intervention of some significance given the scale of gold production. But under fixed price terms of the international gold standard, this controlled market made gold mining progressively less attractive throughout the boom as other prices rose. Much of the rural expansion and substantially all of the manufacturing growth depended on domestic markets, the prevalent attitude seeing exporting (other than wool) as a means of 'surplus' disposal.

Nevertheless, a key object of government policy was to encourage the allocation of resources to rural expansion and to enlarge rural export earnings, and at the same time to provide an expanding domestic market through assisted immigration. The almost exclusive emphasis on expansionary policies gave a particular orientation to government policy, to enhance opportunity for entry and expansion in a wide range of activities *and not to constrain.*

This government-supported expansion concentrated, to 1914 (and perhaps a little beyond the First World War), on rural settlement and diversification, but this concentration could and did accommodate the encouragement of a large range of rural-related manufacturing. Moreover, Australian real income per head, though less exceptional, was still high relative to the rest of the world. The importance of restored migration made the attraction of labour from Britain (and hence in part the restoration of employment *and* real wages) central to public and private objectives. Labour and manufacturers' views, the distribution of the cake apart, were broadly similar on many issues of encouraging activity. With some unease in the relationship, employers and employees could and did join together in the State-managed effort to provide opportunities as an invitation to new migrants. In the most general terms, one may approach pre-1914 labour regulation in part as a process determining the conditions to be accorded new (migrant) additions to the existing Australian population. Nevertheless, this approach did not preclude discrimination against a number of less important sectional interests. It is convenient to look at the emerging process in terms of a number of separate markets in rural, manufacturing and some service activities and the labour market.

Regulation of rural producers

The Commonwealth Constitution essentially left Crown land title and control over land transfers to the States (the Northern Territory came under Federal responsibility). The States retained considerable power to regulate access to and conditions of land occupation. Less than 6 per cent of the entire continent was alienated or in process of alienation into private ownership. Almost half the continent was unoccupied. And a great many Crown leaseholds, the total accounting for 40 per cent of the continent, were available at low prices or were being abandoned, many of them former large pastoral holdings (general statistics are given in Table 3.2).

Regulatory reforms to encourage farm entry and the expansion of settlement varied greatly from State to State, depending on the availability of land and credit and the extent of development of non-wool land use. Through all ran a central theme: the positive encouragement of private 'closer' settlement and the support of private non-wool land activities. To this end, provisions for acquisition of both freehold and leasehold multiplied with highly variable tenure

TABLE 3.2 **Australian land tenure 1901 (million acres)**

	Private Lands		Public Lands		Total
	Alienated	In process of Alienation	Leased or Licensed	Other	Area
N.S.W.	26.4	21.6	127.1	127.1	198.6
Qld.	13.5	2.8	280.0	132.8	429.1
S.A.	7.5	0.6	85.6	93.7	149.6
Tas.	4.9[a]	n.a.	6.4	10.4	16.8
Vic.	20.1	3.5	20.4	12.2	56.2
W.A.	3.5	6.1	97.5	517.5	624.6
N.T.	0.5	—	112.7	222.0	335.1
Australia	76.4	34.6	729.7	1012.1	1852.8[b]

[a] Inc. land in process of alienation.
[b] Because of rounding, items do not sum exactly.
Source: *Commonwealth Year Book No. 1*, 1907.

provisions suited to specific land conditions (King n.d., p.138). In the period to 1914, in sharp contrast with the nineteenth-century approach, some 150 different types of tenure emerged defining a wide variety of access conditions. Discrimination against large holdings was tightened as governments used compulsion to resume Crown leases and to acquire some freehold. There was considerable reluctance by States to abandon Crown landlord status, even to the lengths of legislating in New South Wales against further alienation of Crown leases. In south eastern Australia, bureaucratic attention was given increasingly, area by area and case by case, to defining an adequate 'living' farm size. The public sector was moving progressively further into private decision-making.

In all States, credit facilities were developed to assist entry into the industry, to fund improvements, to purchase machinery and to meet any capital charges on acquisition of tenure rights. Western Australia had led the way in 1894 with an Agricultural Bank to make advances to settlers and, indeed, added a large number of aids down to the details of free transport of settlers and their effects to farm locations (but as one-way tickets!). Generally, these credits to farmers were provided as Treasury advances. All States offered very low deposits, long payment terms and low mortgage rates. From 1901 to 1912, these forms of capital assistance totalled annually between 0.3 and 0.5 per cent of Australian gross domestic product, representing a substantial financial discrimination in favour of private non-wool rural farming.

By no means all the intended effects were achieved. Easy access conditions allowed profitable easy exit in boom years for farming and, in part, these attempts at State regulation ended in enlarging rather than breaking up existing holdings. But the process did significantly increase the number of small and medium-scale farmers, particularly in grain and fruit production; and directly contributed to the speed of growth of non-wool production. (Counterfactually, the option of the market may have been share farming development on a larger scale. Traditionally this had been strongly resisted by pastoralists.)

Whether this growth significantly retarded the recovery of wool production is a moot question. Market conditions for meat, especially overseas prices, following the drought at the beginning of the century, encouraged strictly pastoral diversification mainly on properties without merino sheep. Perhaps the main regulatory restraint on fine wool production was the positive discouragement to extension into dry lands - as in the New South Wales declaration against restocking the Western Division of the State given the destruction of natural herbaige. But for the 'new' industries, a great deal of continuing support and direction was given in education, advice and extension services by State instrumentalities. In Victoria, land fertilised was said to have risen from only 12 per cent of that cultivated in 1900 to 70 per cent in 1911 thanks primarily to these services, and in South Australia (Dunsdorfs, 1956, p.210) a similar (slightly larger) increase occurred.

Very little intervention in marketing regulation by the States occurred before 1914. The chief (but indicative) exception was in Queensland where the protection of sugar growing was a condition of Queensland acquiescence in Federation. Then a tariff was combined with an excise on manufactured sugar to initiate a regulatory technique that became basic to later rural support systems. Nominally, the condition of the support payments differentiated between 'black' and 'white' labour in sugar production; in practice an additional regulatory device was added in the form of dictation tests that supported the deportation of part of the Islands labour force. This protection system, preserving the local market for local output, was not exclusive to sugar. Protection of sugar, wheat, butter, cheese and other miscellaneous rural products extended back into the nineteenth century. After 1901, as many (but not yet sugar) moved partly into export markets, this rural style of protection became less and less relevant until the 1920s and 1930s when systematic arrangements were provided for local 'quasi-monopolies' and overseas dumping of 'surpluses'.

Marketing did not, however, escape the assisting influence of government regulation. The most important pre-1914 influence was in the grading of export products. This was most notable in the adoption of 'f.a.q.' standards for wheat as determined by government inspectors, but in other rural products, particularly in fresh and dried fruits, butter and cheese, government intervention was widespread in encouraging quality standards for exports (with consequential spin-off for local consumers) (Smith 1936).

Most directly and expensively acting to encourage rural diversification, the States intervened (see Chapters 2 and 10) to provide important infrastructure and subsidised services based on this capital equipment in the form of branch railways and irrigation. The public provision of branch lines was fundamental, given transport constraints, to the extension of wheat production in New South Wales and Victoria, and irrigation was developed to aid fresh and dried fruits and vineyards in the Murray and Murrumbidgee Valleys. These formed a major component of public sector capital outlays before the war (Butlin 1962) and opened yet another opportunity for flexible government intervention in the market in the form of variably subsidised services. In the case of irrigation, the opportunity for direct constraint on use of water by Water Authorities introduced a hint of production control, rare in Australia during the first half of this century. In the four years before 1914, attempts were made to introduce bulk receipt of several rural products, primarily wheat, at railhead but these possibilities of regulation were uncertain and non-coercive, depending on the willingness of individual farmers to co-operate.

Inconsistencies in government regulation emerged most obviously in respect of rural labour. To begin with, State and Commonwealth Governments not only met transfer costs of migrants; the States (except Tasmania) provided extensive assistance (with subsidised local fares and the requital of settlement costs), to a large proportion (almost half) of all immigrants. To this extent, they attracted both the settlers induced to locate on new farms and the labour needed by new farmers. Marginally, they enlarged the local market for rural produce.

On the other hand, the systems of arbitration initiated in 1892 and strengthened from 1901 provided substantial encouragement to rural labour organisation. So far as they went, the arbitration authorities, at both Commonwealth and State levels, provided a mechanism for establishing uniform wages and working conditions, and for union recognition. From a single rural union registered in the mid-nineties, the number escalated to fourteen by 1912. This was an ambivalent outcome. The multiplication of unions clouded the representativeness of the various union bodies and enhanced the prospects of lowest common denominator awards - as the Australian Workers Union found in confrontation with the Federal Court. Moreover, arbitral proceedings did not exert strong upward pressures on rural wage rates relative to urban rates, despite rural boom conditions. Indeed, it appears possible that the substantial margins of urban over rural award rates that developed (actual earnings are unknown) may have contributed to the shift of labour to the towns and, particularly, the cities. It seems probable that a common result of government allocative and regulatory action had already emerged: what it gave with one hand, it took away with the other. Certainly, by 1913, the inability of the 'new' rural industries to support a large rural population was well established, officially, and attention of policy was being increasingly turned to the other development option, urban manufacturing and services.

Public intervention in manufacturing

The large and *increasing* share of low value-added processing industries in total gross value added and employment in manufacturing until the First World War reflected the close association between the growth and diversification of rural activity and manufacturing at this stage. A great deal of the conventional discussion of allocative intervention in rural activity has been presented as if this public intervention were concerned merely with farming. In fact the intervention in farm production was increasingly dependent on linked regulation of processed (manufactured) farm products. To this extent, therefore, much of the preceding discussion of public support for rural growth and diversification may be read as indirect support for manufacturing in the major processing industries: the supply of rural materials was enhanced. This is particularly relevant given the prevalent attitude to the 'new' rural activity that the domestic market was supplied first and it was a 'surplus' that was exported. This interconnection between primary output and manufacturing input was explicitly used to support both rural and secondary activity. (Indeed, as already suggested, it was vital to overcome the last opposition to Federation by a manipulation of tariffs, excise and bounties in the case of Queensland sugar).

More complex manufacture represented the minor (as measured)[2] and more slowly growing part of secondary industry. These industries supplied products on which Australian development depended heavily, especially products consumed in capital formation. Official attitude to them was ambivalent and wavering, partly reflecting, perhaps, the relatively weak political power of these manufacturing interests. On the one hand the importance of such products in Australian growth induced a more ready desire to allow imports with little tariff constraint; on the other hand the high proportion of local consumption met by imports appeared to point to opportunities for import replacement.

Manufacturing was still not accepted as a dominant growth prospect; yet as highly labour-intensive activity, factory production offered the opportunity for labour absorption, appealing to govern-

---

[2] The problem of government manufacturing activity being largely consumed within the public sector made measurement particularly difficult and official estimates were often based on nominal rules of thumb.

ments committed to an acceleration of population through immigration. Wage-earner and manufacturing representatives had reached an apparent consensus on the desirability of protection, with labour support for protection exchanged for employers' support for compulsory arbitration: the potential conflict in the sharing of the manufacturing cake was obscured for a brief period. The provisional compromise led, through curious paths, to the encouragement of monopolistic organisation both in the labour market and in some manufacturing enterprise, thereby initiating a fundamental tendency of Australian regulation.

The discussion of labour market regulation is deferred to later in this chapter. However, some comments on labour are inescapable here because the ambitions of trade unions and manufacturers were closely related in terms of tariff and arbitration policy. The reduction of competition in manufacturing did not occur immediately through the tariff, except, perhaps, in a small number of commodities. The first Federal tariff of 1902 represented a low level of protection. This was an apparent victory for the mass of farmers and merchants. But the acceptance of the *principle* of a protective tariff was a recognition of the interests of manufacturers (and some farm groups) in reducing competition. The calculus made in setting rates was to concentrate (not quite exclusively) on ad valorem duties and to compute across-the-board rates to yield a given per capita revenue. Some amendments in detail were made to this basic position, including the assurance of bounties to industries found to be not adequately protected. A major objective was the establishment of a customs union between the six States.

The first decade left the role of the tariff and the respective roles of the various governments in a condition of considerable confusion. The achievement of a customs union was already obscured by special concessions to Western Australia which was allowed to impose tariffs on inter-State trade for five years. Quota restrictions, excise charges and high tariffs on sugar made up a special arrangement offered Queensland sugar interests to secure support for Federation. Special measures of tariff adjustment or bounty payments were made after 1902 to meet problems of inadequate protection as represented through the separate State governments. The revenue-sharing arrangements until 1908 made the Commonwealth little more than a customs agent for the States. The obscurity of the arrangements for the first decade would make analysis of the effects of this tariff extremely difficult, in so far as it purported to provide a twofold objective: to restrict foreign competition and to provide local manufacturers a larger continental market for purposes of expansion. Certainly the much more rapid manufacturing growth of Victoria and New South Wales after 1901 cannot be readily ascribed to the tariff and customs union, given the intervention of other major internal influences before 1914.

For the time being, the chief significance of the tariff and the use of Commonwealth trade power lay in a different and possibly unintended direction - public efforts to encourage monopoly organisation. Two closely related measures in 1906 were the Excise Tariff Act and the Australian Industries Preservation Act. The former (the so-called 'New Protection') provided for import duties plus excise on local manufacture, the excise being rebatable on condition that factories paid 'fair and reasonable' wages. The latter Act, substantially the Sherman Anti-Trust Act, was aimed at constraining monopolistic pricing policies (a Labor bogey) and also limiting the entry of foreign non-British enterprise into Australian business (an employers' preoccupation).

Both Acts in their original form were ruled unconstitutional and both eventually rendered inoperative. But in the former case, this was not before the concept of the basic wage was introduced into wage determination; as this basic wage spread, it provided a major rigidity in labour costs and enhanced labour bargaining, limiting competitive options in manufacturing and helping to reduce labour market competition. In the latter case, the ruling stemmed from the conclusive British judgement, declaring 'competition' to be potentially 'ruinous', opening the way for the formal approval by Australian Courts of monopolistic structures and monopolistic practices.

The Labor response, following widespread electoral success at the end of the first decade, was to introduce its version of 'competitive socialism' - the establishment of a large variety of enterprises, particularly in manufacturing, designed to provide the basis of regulating prices in private enterprise through public competition. The proliferation of (mostly) minor State concerns that evolved engendered more political heat than allocative or regulatory consequence and was outside the supportive mainstream of regulation.

The measures adopted were designed to encourage expansion of the major industries processing local materials, to support concentration and, until Labor intervened, to defend or at least permit monopolistic practices. The failure of the New Protection legislation illustrates the defence of practices of near-monopoly in agricultural machinery manufacturing. More positively, the concessions to Queensland sugar production, at Federation, brought government, both Commonwealth and State, into close association and, at times, literal partnership with private enterprise. By a combination of high tariffs, excise duties, quotas on manufactured sugar imports and the payment of bounties on local sugar produced with white labour, the Commonwealth provided an assured local market at prices considerably above world levels. The State government intervened by determining the location of sugar mills, ensuring regional monopolies, and provided public financial support to these mills. As public financial commitment rose, the State participated in mill management. On occasion, when viability of certain mills was threatened, a few mills were taken over for limited periods until they could be returned to private management.

The support of local monopoly was replicated in a variety of other areas: in timber milling, the exclusive leasing of Crown forest areas rather than competitive felling helped to establish, systematically, the pattern of regional lumbering and timber monopolies throughout all the eastern States; the franchising of single producers to supply (coal-based) gas and electricity to country towns was a common practice as an alternative to local government enterprise, though this procedure was frequently varied by local government and private enterprise partnership in these activities; the growth of wheat production and the provision of centralised storage, funded by State and Commonwealth governments, promoted similar, if less complete, regional flour milling monopolies.

The ambiguity of government attitudes before 1914 to more complex industries is underscored by the extensive development of public enterprise in important areas of manufacturing. These were primarily related to public capital formation and to the materials and equipment required in the operation of public transport services. By far the most substantial activity was in repair services - of railway rolling stock, tramway rolling stock, port equipment and shipping. From repair to replacement and to the public construction of new equipment were short steps. A more specialised public concern was in the development of defence factories. Unfortunately, no data are available to provide an adequate measure of the rate of growth or dimension of this range of public activities before the First World War. By 1920, however, these government factories in New South Wales, for example, accounted for over 15 per cent of the entire manufacturing workforce of the State.

This displacement of the private sector was not comparable to the attempts at 'socialist competition' referred to above. It did, however, have two significant implications of relevance to the private sector. First, it enlarged the capital inputs into government services supplied below private rates of return. To the extent that the provision of public transport services was used to influence private allocative decisions, public entry in these manufacturing areas reinforced this allocative influence. A second implication, of more general significance, was that the commitment of public authorities to engineering and repair works brought home directly to the bureaucracy a problem that was acutely important in restraining more complex private manufacture - the shortage of skilled labour. With the extension of railway building and expansion of rolling stock and railway operations in the boom from 1905, the awareness of this problem reached a climax in public investigations into the problems of skill and the greatly increased emphasis, in assisted and nominated immigration schemes, on the attraction of skilled migrant labour for industry. The role of the State governments (other than Tasmania) in this respect was a major supportive act for complex manufacturing generally. Like all migration, it had the added attraction in enlarging the domestic market for all producers, thereby widening support for immigration policy.

Public loan expenditure - and, indeed, public current expenditure - had direct significance for local manufacturing through government demand for goods and services. It was a long-standing practice to give preference to local suppliers of materials and equipment, a preference that was given regardless of tariff levels. Iron and steel manufacture, engineering and furniture works, and timber and quarry products all directly received discriminatory support in this manner. Given the dimension of public investment, this was a powerful influence. In addition, however, it was common practice in government current purchases to order into stock without the advertisement of tenders. Victoria was so preoccupied with this possibility of local discrimination before the First World War as to keep a running published check on the extent of import invasion into this specifically 'public market'. As a result, an extensive range of office products received discriminatory support.

On a more general scale, public investment in transport and roads and in the provision of urban facilities and services began, during the pre-1914 years, to support the location of manufacturing in major city areas. The ability to achieve mass transit of bulky goods and the incentive to locate publicly supplied stacking and storage systems at railhead attracted goods flows to railway systems; the construction of tapered freight rates with substantial long-haul concessions extended the net within which city centres could draw in materials inputs and enlarged the rural market to which city-based goods (and imports) could flow at reduced cost. Within the city centres, themselves, the growing government provision of city roads and urban transit services encouraged a market growth and these services along with the provision of water and sewerage, gas and electricity facilities by government attracted more rapidly a labour supply to city locations. The shift in government investment towards city-located facilities was marked before 1914; the tendency was considerably strengthened after 1918 as manufacturing came to receive greater prominence in government intervention. For the pre-war period, the role of public investment, in accelerating the shift to the cities, accentuated the pattern of separate city markets each substantially the preserve of manufacturing located there. There were many ways in which section 92 of the Australian Constitution - the 'absolutely free' inter-State trade - could be subverted. The inter-war years were to demonstrate a full flowering of this subversive interference.

Regulation of private services to 1914

The miscellany of transactions that make up the activity of services is not capable of integrated discussion. They range from the outputs of large-scale enterprises such as banks and other financial intermediaries through wholesale and retail trade, transport and communications, recreation and leisure, to activities in which services are typically provided on a person-to-person basis whether openly as in hotels and restaurants or in private as in the case of medical or dental services or domestic service. Some are predominantly concerned with final consumer services, others are intermediate inputs, and some are a mixture. Some are highly specialised and complex, requiring a high degree of skill, while others demand little expertise; some affect large numbers and others are confined to very small groups.

Though the aggregate volume of these services increased over the twentieth century, it is important also to appreciate that they already represented, in terms of gross product and employment, a very large fraction of total Australian activity in 1900. Moreover, their composition changed as some services requiring fewer skills and delivered on a person-to-person basis stagnated or even declined absolutely (domestic service) while those more significant as intermediate inputs (financial intermediaries, specialist consultancy or advisory services) and requiring substantial skills grew more rapidly.

Prior to 1913, the dominant services were in retail and wholesale trade, domestic service, banking and insurance, housing and transport. It is appropriate to distinguish these from smaller but more skilled activities such as professional services.

In most respects, government regulation was comparatively slight and typically incoherent. Banks and pastoral and housing finance companies that had been severely affected by the depression in the nineties had been actively supported by government legislation to provide for corporate reconstruction. Substantially this process was completed shortly after 1900, after which the supporting State Governments were excluded from most of the private banking and insurance field by the Commonwealth Constitution. Yet the fledgling Federal Government was not prepared to embark on initiatives in financial regulation beyond 'discussions' with trading banks. Accordingly, until the First World War, most of the regulatory procedures relating to banking and insurance remained frozen in their nineteenth-century provisions, mainly drawn from incorporation conditions in countries of origin, especially Britain, the various Australian States, New Zealand and the United States. These conditions of incorporation had limited regulatory significance.

As a group, the banks, pastoral finance companies and insurance companies were exceptional in representing a powerful coterie of interests over which only slight control was or could effectively be exercised. As the basic source of capital funds and trade and consumer credit, as bankers to governments, as the institutions operating (however inadequately) the rules of the gold standard, and as the source of money supply (other than coins) until 1910, the banks were not only capable of fending off public sector interference but were, in fact, the source of such monetary policy as was consciously framed. Indeed, as bankers to governments, they had a major influence on government budgetary policy.

Despite its insurance powers, the Commonwealth limited the exercise of its constitutional authority by a minor provision for assurance of lives of children and by the appointment of a laggard Royal Commission to inquire into life and non-life insurance. By the time the Commission reported, the First World War was in the offing and soon the Federal Government was diverted to more demanding concerns.

Accordingly insurance remained, de facto, a State field of regulation and one in which the States, for constitutional reasons, had little incentive or ability to act. The regulatory provisions varied widely, a great many remaining ossified in nineteenth-century terms while in others adjustments of the general Companies Act represented the limit of action. Regulatory provisions reflected the suspicions of a more primitive society and a deeply rooted British conservatism with respect to insurance. Formally, company legislation prescribing incorporation terms, registration, articles of association, specification of activities and reports to shareholders and/or policy holders typically applied. In addition, not merely audit but (nominally) close actuarial assessment by government was prescribed. Companies were required to deposit surety funds with government and, in several States, to hold part of their funds in government securities. Provisions generally defined protection of policy holders, constrained the powers of creditors to attach policies and limited the freedom of companies to wind up their businesses.

These were not very strong regulations or very powerful inducements to depart from ordinary market behaviour. A little, though not much, more emerged with respect to banking. The British Government retained control of local Mints and continued the issue of British coinage, essentially gold coins, until 1909 when the Australian Coinage Act was passed by the Commonwealth. An attempt to require more detailed returns from the banks was met with uniform total inaction by the banks. Some greater activity occurred with the Australian

Notes Act (1910) and and the Bank Notes Tax Act (1911). By the former, the Commonwealth Treasurer became empowered to issue notes to be legal tender throughout the Commonwealth; by the latter, State Governments were prohibited from issuing notes and a tax of 10 per cent per annum was placed on outstanding private banknotes, the primary source of Australian notes. Almost immediately, the Commonwealth acquired control over the first component of the money supply.

In 1911, also, the Act to establish the Commonwealth Bank was passed, the Savings Bank Department opening in 1912. This bank was intended to become an ordinary trading bank though with no power of note issue. Initiatives for its establishment came from divergent sources. For Labor representatives it was in the mainstream of contemporary 'socialist' policy, in this case designed to 'curb the money power'; more generally it was conceived as a financial institution to support the banking structure. In practice, both objectives became revealed in its behaviour during the inter-war years.

So far as retail and wholesale trade were concerned, comparatively little regulatory interest developed, either within the public sector or the private sector, with one or two notable exceptions. It is important to appreciate that the many small business institutions of the time were rarely specialised ones. Typically, they combined 'a sort' of manufacturing with retailing and often added in other services, particularly transport (cf. home deliveries). To this extent, the separation of manufacturing from retailing and other services in this discussion deals with functional activities, not with institutions. A small miscellany of specific 'consumer protection' provisions dealt with contaminated milk and with provision for meat and fish inspection. In the early years of the twentieth century, food and drug Acts provided the rudimentary provision for inspections and tests of food purity, relating essentially to a limited range of fresh foods and pharmaceuticals; in practice, most of the regulatory requirements competed against other functions for the time of a small number of local government officials.

Not even Labor preoccupations with monopolies, profiteers and 'excessive' pricing led to many inroads in the direction of price regulation (though increasingly these preoccupations encouraged more and more detailed investigations into pricing, consumption standards and the cost of living). On the contrary, the legal defeat of Australia's attempt to legislate the American Sherman Anti-Trust Act opened the way not merely to monopolistic practices but also to monopolistic organisation. Many retail associations were registered under government legislation supporting their association agreements to conduct such monopolistic practices as they could. It is doubtful if these associations had, prior to 1913, much significance because of the large number of trading enterprises, most of them very small. Thus in Victoria at the outbreak of war some 25 000 retail establishments were registered, with little prospect of any effective collusive practices. In some cases, such as in the more concentrated coal trade and in shipping and hotels, the legal support of monopolistic practices may have been more significant.

Nevertheless, the foundations for legal recognition of these associations were laid: it remained for subsequent economic change, with progressive concentration in commerce, to realise the opportunities for legally supported monopolistic practices. These developments were to proliferate after the Second World War.

Some retail activities aroused more regulatory pressures with corresponding responses from affected interest groups and corresponding formation of stronger trade associations. Of these, perhaps the outstanding was the liquor trade and hotel licensing. Strong temperance movements combined with religious groups to fight the demon drink, to secure local option, to reduce licensed premises, to upgrade quality of hotel living accommodation. In a highly concentrated industry, liquor and beer producers dominated hotel business by a system of tied houses. The actions of their opponents to secure control was, nominally, a seesaw of advance and withdrawal; in practice their pressures were matched by the substantial inaction of the various Licensing Courts. And, in the process, the United Licensed Victuallers' Association was able to reduce competition of free houses and to downgrade the provision of living accommodation. The persistence of the temperance movement created the backdrop for the patriotic wartime appeal to reduce alcohol consumption; so came early closing of hotels and 'the six o'clock swill' during the First World War: a degradation of service that typified Australian hotels until long after the Second World War.

A great many regulatory provisions applying to factories to protect physical working conditions and safety did not apply to most commercial establishments. The limitation of size of establishment exempted most shops before 1914. Accordingly, even in these aspects, many trading concerns escaped established regulation - until they became inadvertently absorbed in the regulatory net by growth in size, not by positive public sector initiative. In the main, however, this was a long-delayed issue, a matter more of post-1945 than pre-1914 and inter-war years.

Even in the case of wage regulation, commercial activity escaped lightly. The lack of effective labour organisation in many areas of commerce limited severely the regulatory impact of arbitration processes and consequential ability to achieve legally enforceable working conditions. Broader social legislation to restrain the employment of children led to general restriction of working hours for children in the beginning of the century, but there was little consequential supervision. The primary consequence appears to have been a partially enforced early closing of shops in the metropolitan areas in the early years of the century yielding a slightly reduced working week for adults rather than substantially increased care for juveniles.

One response of the State Labor Parties to the difficulties that were seen in regulating shops was the adoption of a large miscellany of State enterprises, including butchers' shops, cafeterias, tobacconists, brickyards and sawmills (both producers and sellers) etc. These enterprises proliferated in number if not in size or import in the years before 1914 (and again after 1918). In practice, with rare exceptions, this regulatory process, designed to introduce public business competition with the private sector, did little more than delude some Australian voters into believing that Australian Labor politicians had some potential as dangerous revolutionaries.

Australian professionals, locally trained, emerged as a significant group in the latter part of the nineteenth century and, prior to 1914, increased in importance as successors to retiring British professionals. Their activities encountered competition of less adequately trained or wholly untrained persons, most notably in the medical, dental and pharmaceutical professions. Regulation of shop registration and sale of pharmaceuticals by qualified persons were provided for in State food and drug Acts. In the nineteenth century, doctors and dentists were supported in their training by State subsidies to local universities and the registration of qualifications, restrictions were placed increasingly on foreign (non-British) practitioners, and nominally unqualified persons were restrained from practice. In fact 'quacks' survived and in some cases flourished though the battle for their survival was a losing one. In effect, State regulation acted essentially to restrict competition in these limited professional areas though it also - often only incidentally - implied some consumer protection. It did not invade the delivery or pricing of services to clients. Similarly, the States even-handedly preserved the freedom of the market for personal service at the other end of the scale, without in this case restricting entry.

It is unfortunate that very little historical research has been done on building and more particularly dwelling regulation. Already building and land ratings were well established, by 1900, not simply as a fiscal means but to induce the adoption of or fund the public provision of particular health, fire and safety controls, most importantly in water and sewerage. In the 1870s South Australia and in the 1880s New South Wales had provided for the power to condemn unsafe or insanitary buildings, though this power was little used. This provision was the beginning, however, of new constraints that came in the twentieth century, to restrict progressively the freedom to construct and use buildings. Building permits were introduced into South Australia during the late nineteenth century but do not seem to have spread extensively. Nevertheless contractual provisions in house financing increasingly included the legally enforceable approval of building plans partly to provide protection for owners against builders, partly to satisfy growing interest in town planning. How far the various building codes had been developed by 1900 is obscure. By the end of the First World War, however, it is clear that in several States building permits, approval of plans, specifications of wall types, cavities, building lines, siting, sanitary and water supply provisions, and general zoning provisions were established as a systematic if still fairly rudimentary arrangement. Much of this appears to have been a translation of British practice into a regulated Australian situation, subject to local government enforcement. How rapidly, for what reasons and with what effectiveness these formal controls spread is a major area for further investigation. They came to influence significantly the cost of building construction and to limit the freedom of choice of many individuals both as home owners or as builders for sale or rental.

Labour market regulation

In comparison with other areas of activity, by far the most detailed and nominally protective regulatory provisions were adopted in respect of the labour market, covering types of immigrants, conditions of work, wages and hours, union recognition and union preference, apprenticeship, juvenile and female labour, closing hours, indemnities for wage payments, etc. The framework if not the full effectiveness of these controls was fully established by the First World War. The adoption of this early regulation of the labour market derived from the efforts by trade unions to recover the losses sustained during the depression of the nineties and from the growing power of Labor Parties in all States and the Commonwealth. The formal legislation did not necessarily imply actual regulatory performance. It was not until the political successes of Labor Parties throughout the Commonwealth at the end of the first decade, combined with prosperity and high employment, that the teeth in the multiplicity of legislation were sharpened and used with major effect.

The hostility conveyed in the nineteenth-century regulations under the various Masters and Servants Acts began to recede most obviously in the 1870s. This change was typified by the adoption of the British Trade Union Acts and the collateral Conspiracy and Protection of Property Act, first in South Australia in 1876 and then through the rest of Australia until Western Australia provided a unanimous Australian declaration in 1902. At the same time, Victoria initiated the *legal* recognition of a 48-hour week for women and children and mine workers in 1873, though it was not until the formation after 1900 of arbitral machinery that all States adopted a legal 48-hour week as the common rule. Victoria accompanied this 1873 initiative in the same year with 'The Supervision of Workrooms and Factories Statute', its original six sections being progressively amplified to 163 in 1905 and to 238 sections in 1907. Tasmania followed suit in 1884 and the other States during the nineties except for Western Australia which enacted similar legislation early in 1902.

These enactments applied essentially to factory, not rural workers. The Maritime Strike of 1890 focused on union recognition for pastoral industry workers as well as their pay demands. The defeat of the unions in that strike and the subsequent depression decimated union membership and union organisations and left wage earners in a weak bargaining position. Union and politically organised Labor ambitions were thereafter directed towards the establishment of systems of compulsory arbitration. Victoria adopted a system of Wages Boards under the Factories and Shops Act of 1896, but it was applicable initially only to six limited industry groups. Only in 1900 was the system, having been little used, broadened to cover all factories. South Australia adopted a Conciliation Act in 1894, again a largely irrelevant gesture at the time. Victoria in 1891 and New South Wales in 1892 passed Acts closely related to these, establishing *voluntary* Conciliation Boards, rarely used because their awards had no binding force.

It was not until after the coalition of wage earners and employers was achieved to trade a Federal protective tariff for compulsory arbitration that the twentieth century course of regulation was initiated in the handling of union recognition and preference, wages and hours and apprenticeship conditions. Then, while the Constitution did not allow direct legislative control of wages and hours it provided for Commonwealth powers to deal with inter-State disputes. The Commonwealth Court of Conciliation and Arbitration was legislated in 1904. New South Wales passed its Industrial Conciliation and Arbitration Acts of 1901 and 1905; Western Australia followed in 1902; South Australia continued to use the primitive Act of 1894.

The elementary objective of union recognition was not immediate or easily achieved. Legal precepts, supported by employers' arguments, required that a given labour organisation 'represent' employees. Years elapsed - as many as seven in the extreme case - before a particular union was accepted by industrial courts as representative of claimants. Even when acceptance was conceded, there were long delays in hearing, given the part-time nature of many of the Boards.

By 1913, only the Commonwealth and New South Wales Courts provided awards according union preference. Between 1901 and 1913, wage earners increasingly tended to form inter-State unions in order to obtain access to the Commonwealth Court. These efforts stemmed from the reluctance of many Boards to recognise unions or to expedite claims and the tendency of many Boards to set the lowest common denominator of State standards as awards. A particular stimulus to inter-State organisation was given by the Harvester declaration, defining the terms of a 'basic wage', in 1907 (a determination closely parallelled in New South Wales).

It is important to dispose of the mythology of historians. The 'basic wage' as an actual floor to male wage earners' incomes was not generally established for a long time. It was not until the mid-1920s that the Commonwealth *Labour Bulletin* even recognised the existence of the basic wage as a concept of significance; symptomatically, this recognition coincided with major developments by the Commonwealth and New South Wales in *minimum* wage awards. The Higgins declaration of the basic wage concept in 1907 - the award of wages to support an adult male, wife and three children - became fundamental to Australian trade unions' objectives. The spread of the concept was very slow in pre-war years and it was not until the wartime labour shortages that wage rates approximately attained the 'Harvester' standard (for further discussion see Chapter 6). One important factor perhaps delaying the spread of the Higgins' standard but certainly in promoting the Commonwealth Court to prominence was the absence of Federal powers, under the Constitution, to legislate directly on wages.

The arbitration system, before 1914, was basic to union recognition. This was accepted, in general, in the first two years of the century as a 'common rule'. It laid the foundations for 'bilateral monopolistic' bargaining in the labour market. Yet it is essential to recognise that the Courts, in the first decade, were almost equally relevant in declaring wage *awards* and *registering* the bargaining outcome of direct agreements between employers and organised employees; nevertheless, even in the latter cases, the arbitration system was an important instrument in ensuring the enforceability of contracts.

The recognition of unionism, combined with growing prosperity, transformed the unionisation of the Australian workforce. In 1901, the proportion of wage and salary earners who were members of unions was 5.1 per cent. By 1906, this had escalated to 15.7 per cent; by 1911 to 27.1 per cent; and by 1914 to 34.3 per cent. (The Commonwealth *Labour Reports* record higher proportions unionised. It is difficult to reconcile these official estimates with calculations of wage and salary earners from available statistics. The present estimates are based on official union membership and recent estimates of the workforce.)

The very limited success of union pressures led to increasing numbers of disputes after 1910. This had a key consequence for the arbitration system reflecting the growing power of trade unions. Conciliation, the preservation of industrial peace, became a less overt objective of the regulatory system and, by contrast, the judicial determination of wage rates (and hours) became more prominent. This attitude became the dominant characteristic of post-war wage determination. In the meantime, however, by 1914, over 500 boards of various types, authorised to make wage awards, had been established, and almost 600 awards were in force, ranging over the whole area of manufacturing. It is symptomatic of the ambivalence of unions - and perhaps also the prosperity-induced opportunities - that over 400 bargaining agreements, not awards, were also registered at that time. No adequate data are currently available to assess the impact of the relatively inchoate arbitration system of the time. Average award rates rose by slightly more than 25 per cent in current terms between 1901 and 1913; average earnings rose by more than 60 per cent. Money income per member of the total workforce (including self-employed and defence workers) rose by approximately 50 per cent. This might have represented a shift in the share of gross product to wage earners. Whether any shift that may have occurred was due to any significant degree to the regulatory system rather than to the movement from semi-depression to relatively high prosperity is an issue that needs thorough exploration. An important question would be the extent to which regulation raised actual rates by extension of awards to below-award groups without necessarily increasing the level of awards. This exploration is beyond the bounds of this discussion.

One issue appears reasonably definite: that wage rates (including imputed rent allowances) awarded in manufacturing (urban occupations) were significantly higher, even where little if any skills were required, than those in rural activities. To this extent regulation (if it was responsible) provided a cost advantage to rural activities, but it would also have encouraged the shift of labour to urban activities, particularly manufacturing, and hence to urban locations. A major research task lies in examining the failure of wage rates to keep pace with a rural boom, whether this reflects the declining labour-intensity of rural activity or the traditional antagonism of rural employers to wage earners. Whatever the explanation, the differential that developed appears to be a significant candidate as an explanation of the 'drift to the cities' that became a major social phenomenon before the First World War. The tendency to support, through arbitration, the claims of manufacturing employees was to become a major confrontation problem of the inter-war years.

4

Protection all Round 1914 to 1939

Introduction

Superficially, the 'capture' theory of public regulation might help in explaining the course of government allocative and regulatory intervention during the inter-war years. Certainly, regulatory institutions appear to have come very much more under the influence and control of some private interest groups, and private initiative in the use of public means became much more prominent than before 1914. Nevertheless, the core of public intervention appears to have been in the accommodation of conflicting interests rather than merely the permissive use of regulatory agencies for the benefit of special affected interests. Whether this accommodation was illusion or reality is a matter that invites further research. In conditions of greatly reduced growth prospects, severely restricted rates of increase of productivity and real income per head and an increasingly unsympathetic international economic environment, gains by any interest group became more obviously losses for others. Attitudes derived from qualified prosperity continued into depression intervention with the appeal for 'equality of sacrifice'.

Public intervention remained concentrated on the three main markets of manufacturing, farming and labour. Efforts to interfere with the market became much more detailed and covered larger areas of each market; within any given area a larger range of private decision-making was subjected to government intervention; and there was a significant shift towards the centralisation of intervention at the national level. The institutions adopted and the measures applied remained essentially supportive of the actors in the three markets, and the evolving administration of measures applied tended progressively to interconnect the artificial adjustments in each market. Population expansion and growth remained the basic object. But in the inter-war years, the emphasis on restraint of competition greatly increased.

In each major market, different modes of encouraging restraint of competition developed with different procedures of representation and influence by private interest groups. If large common-interest groups are, theoretically, hard to form, Australian farmers showed a remarkable ability to pluck 'monopoly' out of the air. The instrument was the statutory marketing authority as a 'quasi-monopoly' supported at all levels of government and under close producer control backed by formal interest organisation; central to their operations was the active subversion of section 92 of the Australian Constitution, a subversion largely unchallenged until 1936. For manufacturers, the Tariff Board provided the opportunity for sharing interventionist action between manufacturers and the bureaucracy; the Board accentuated opportunities, through case by case procedures, for business to press for special advantage without strong organisational support. In the case of labour, the arbitration systems introduced organised wage earners and manufacturers, competing for shares in a very slowly growing cake, as appellants before largely bureaucratic tribunals. At least implicit coalitions emerged particularly in the mutual support for wage and tariff adjustments.

Protection for all or 'protection all round' appears to have contributed significantly to the onset and severity of the depression. In that view, it quickly failed. Yet the philosophy of the twenties prevailed through the depression and was largely restored throughout the thirties. Australia passed through a severe test during which the basic stability of society was preserved with less overt antagonism between conflicting groups than developed in European countries, Britain or the USA. If this was failure, it was also a remarkable achievement. The common view that actions by government that cancel out are merely pointless waste may miss a basic object - perhaps *the* basic object - of the use of public means.

Some long-term consequences of the First World War

Attention is confined here to some long-term implications of war rather than war controls themselves. One outstanding accompaniment of the war was very rapid inflation, comparable to the experience of the 1970s. Until 1912-13, prices (measured here by the implicit price deflator) had been rising very slowly, at a simple annual average rate of 1.4 per cent since 1900-01 (1.3 per cent compound). From 1912-13 to 1919-20, however, inflation escalated to 10.2 per cent simple annual average (8.0 per cent compound). This was an experience common to Western countries, though there were some special scarcity conditions in Australia that prompted local pressures.

Also in common with most Western countries, the aggregate level of *real* gross domestic product (the matter is more definite in terms of real product per head) had actually fallen between 1912-13 and 1919-20. In fact, in the Australian conditions, particularly arising from belated export movements, the real decline in aggregate real product is probably undermeasured at 10.7 per cent. The combination of reduced real goods flow and greatly increased domestic price levels created severe regulatory problems at the beginning of the twenties, particularly in relation to labour markets and manufacturing.

The problems of the war, in this long-term context, might be specified in terms of a manpower drain, the drastic reduction in supplies of imports and the ability to secure income from, but not to move, large stocks of primary products. The manpower drain led to little in the way of wartime labour control. Indeed, the outstanding consequence for the labour market was the escalation of wage rates and, above all, the progressive spread of the basic wage (not necessarily recognised as such) across industry. Though the basic wage was not yet universal by 1918, it was very nearly so; the war was a major influence setting this wage rate floor in the labour market and providing the basis on which, in the inter-war years, skilled workers could build a complex structure of margins. In addition, the wartime price changes made wage-administering authorities and employers more conscious of the need for a closely administered system of cost-of-living adjustments.

So far as imports were concerned, the war meant severe restriction on shipping to Australia, giving local producers almost exclusive access to the domestic market. As a result, a large number of new industries was introduced in electrical goods, machinery, a variety of metal products, chemicals, rubber goods etc. In addition, other non-processing industries were able to expand in the absence of foreign competition. By contrast, the simpler processing industries were checked. The war on the one hand introduced a variety of 'overexpanded' or 'new' complex manufacturing that was exposed to risk of foreign competition, and on the other hand it retarded the growth of the simpler processing industries, implying the potential, subject to foreign competition, for post-war acceleration.

Primary production that had developed to the stage of substantial export by 1914 experienced, perhaps, the greatest disruption both in activity and in market experience. Early wartime measures of internal regulation soon merged in the British Government Purchasing Contracts. Formal organisations, with powers of acquisition, were established for most commodities. There were complex structures of Commonwealth Boards, including growers' representatives, State Boards, London Boards and a network of agents. These operations were funded by administrative arrangements with all the banks to provide for advances to growers, at fixed interest. Funding quotas were allocated to each bank. Most of these arrangements persisted until 1920 when almost the whole control system was dismantled, except for wool. But large stocks had accumulated in wartime as output continued high in most rural products due to good seasons and problems of ship delivery to export markets persisted. Decontrol meant the abandonment of British Government buying and of Australian Government acquisition and the cessation of British price-fixing. Markets were in considerable disarray, with prices of some rural products rising far above all contract prices and others falling below as a 'free' market returned. The conflicts in experience led to corresponding conflicts in producers' attitudes to proposals for free-trade marketing schemes. The major immediate problem areas, in 1920, were in wool, meat and butter, where the existence of huge stocks or greatly expanded output complicated the return to peacetime private market operations. The complications were greatly increased as prices began to move sharply down on world markets from the beginning of the 1920s and as the inter-war trends towards agricultural self-sufficiency began to develop.

Inter-war economics and politics

The Australian growth of aggregate real product in the inter-war years averaged approximately half that of the pre-1914 period, implying a quite drastic retardation of growth rates. Australian public and private policy continued with attempts to push population expansion ahead. Although the growth of population and of workforce slackened relative to before 1914, it was artificially sustained by public action. Australian population grew faster than the population of most Western countries. At the same time, Australian growth of real income per head slackened greatly between 1918 and 1939. Neither foreign (especially British) nor domestic market prospects were propitious. Increasing trade restrictions aggravated export problems. Subsequently the depression led to severe retardation in both overseas and domestic markets.

Nevertheless, Australian determination to sustain population growth through immigration remained. The nature of the age and sex composition of the immigrant population meant that workforce increased faster than total population. It is not paradoxical to suggest that the relative retardation of real domestic product is partly explicable by government attempts to control the rate of growth of population and workforce. Private pressures and public policy were based on the assumption of artificially expanding opportunities for labour absorption. Depression problems apart, the prospects confronting each of the major interest groups encouraged the government measures of tariffs, bounties and subsidies for manufacturers, tariffs and organised marketing with financial supports for farmers, and tariff-supported arbitration for wage earners. This was 'protection all round' - an attempted accommodation of conflicting interest between major private groups competing for a larger share in the existing cake and in the very limited increments of greatly retarded growth rates.

In the conditions of an increasingly heavily administered price structure, the measurement of the changing structure and growth rates is extremely complex. The measured real performance implies that, while the real growth rate of GDP almost halved in the inter-war years compared with before the war, the real growth rate of exports almost doubled. Before 1914 the Australian economy had moved much more *towards* the export of a larger variety of rural products. Substantial export development during and after the war brought the Federal trade power and regulatory processes into greater prominence as the 'new' rural industries of before 1914 shifted their stance in the inter-war years from predominantly serving the local market to large-scale exporting. This last development was a central issue for Australian public regulation.

At the same time, in long-run terms, the real growth of manufacturing value added slackened greatly, to well under half the pre-war rate. As a result of the war and immediate post-war shortages, the more complex manufacturing had lifted by 1919-20 to a little over half the total employment and value added in manufacturing; these manufacturing groups increased their share slightly by the end of the 1930s, implying a slightly faster growth rate than occurred in simpler rural-related processing industries. Given the protective wall established to encourage the latter industries, the interesting feature is the relatively similar growth rate of these processing industries compared to the rest of manufacturing: processing began the inter-war years with substantial dominance of the domestic market whereas the the more complex industries had the opportunity of faster growth through import replacement.

Another important structural change between the wars was the somewhat more rapid growth of skilled professional and service groups. The simple trichotomy of primary, secondary and tertiary obscures the relative increase of very highly trained members of the workforce. For these groups, the conditions of entry to skills and to occupations became a matter of considerable importance.

Table 4.1 gives a little more detail of the change in some major components as average annual growth rates including, for convenience, comparisons with the pre-war years. The value measures are in current prices. It should be reiterated that the widespread development of administered prices obscures the meaning of these comparisons. For what they are worth, they imply, throughout, a drastic

TABLE 4.1 **Pre- and inter-war average annual growth rates (%) (current prices)**

	1900–01 to 1913–14	1919–20 to 1939–40
Gross Wool Proceeds	4.2	− 1.1
Agric. Gross Product	11.2	+ 0.3
Dairy Gross Product	6.6	+ 4.0
Manuf. Gross Value Added	11.2	+ 5.7
Banking and Finance	6.3	+ 5.2
Professional and Domestic Service	5.0	+ 1.8
Distribution Factor Earnings	9.5	+ 2.3
Public Bus. Undertakings	8.0	+ 2.5
Public Services	9.1	+ 4.4
Public Construction	13.4	+ 2.2
Private Construction	1.4	+ 3.3
Exports	5.0	− 1.0
Imports	7.5	+ 0.1
Current Gross Domestic Product	8.9	+ 2.4
Real Gross Domestic Product	5.9	+ 3.0
Wage and Salary Earners	3.3	+ 1.7

decline in the growth rate of every major segment of the economy. Some special areas moved ahead faster, particularly manufacturing, banking and finance and public services; and, less definitely, construction activity and 'alone amongst the primary industries' dairying became relatively more significant in current terms. It may be noted that, in real terms, dairying became much more prominent than the current price measures imply.

Given the long-run decline in Australian export prices from post-war peaks, the current price increases conceal the very considerable growth in the volume of output from the rural sector. This volume increase did not, however, lead to comparable job opportunities in rural areas. Widespread mechanisation and fertiliser use with increased yields in almost every rural product enhanced the labour-saving characteristics of a basically non-labour-intensive farming. Along with increasing job opportunities in city manufacturing and services, the inter-war years brought a major change inducing a marked shift of population to the cities. As officially measured, metropolitan populations rose from just over 40 per cent of the total in 1920 to almost exactly 50 per cent in 1939. Social and economic problems of city communities became much more prominent matters of regulatory attention in almost every area - of public facilities, wage and salary regulation, business activity and operation.

No abbreviated comment on trend characteristics of the inter-war years can omit the deeply disturbed course of economic activity: immediate post-war disturbances followed by the slight recession of the beginning of the 1920s, the severe world-wide depression beginning in

1925-26 in Australia and reaching a trough in 1931-32 and, finally, after a slight recession during 1937-38, the preparation for the Second World War. The major depression led to a severe balance of payments crisis, drastic decline in export prices, and widespread high unemployment. These general problems and the micro-disturbances contained within them created the first demand for macro-economic management, the response to which we will need to discuss as a separate issue.

With the rise to prominence of the Commonwealth, the political success of the various parties at the Federal level acquired much greater significance than before the First World War. In practice, the Federal political record is an extremely clouded one. *Nominally*, 'anti-labour' governments ruled throughout the inter-war period except for a brief Labor episode from the end of 1929 to the beginning of 1932 (and even then without Labor control of the Senate). This might suggest that conservative parties substantially controlled the Federal government for almost the whole period. In reality, however, it was a former Labor Prime Minister who headed a conservative government (including four other ex-Labor Ministers in Cabinet) until 1923. The rise of the Country Party forced the defeat of this post-war government, but not before major legislation on tariffs and war pensions had been determined. Even after the defeat of this mix of ex-Labor and conservative Ministers, one ex-Labor Minister remained in Cabinet.

After the defeat of the Labor Government in 1932, the Labor Treasurer became Prime Minister of a conservative government until 1938, including amongst the Ministry three ex-Labor Ministers. The role of these ex-Labor Ministers has never been properly explored. The experience raises doubts as to the freedom of conservative business interests to act without accommodating directly to some Labor attitudes, and it raises the question whether it was really only in the five years 1924 to 1928 that conservative interests were able to govern without substantial direct constraints by Labor attitudes.

Some similar experiences occurred at the State level and though their power was now declining, State Governments remained the dominant governments in internal affairs. Thus a defecting Labor Premier (with four ex-Ministers) ruled a Nationalist government in New South Wales from 1916 to 1920. Indeed, Labor largely dominated New South Wales politics until 1932 when conservative governments assumed power for the rest of the thirties; in Queensland, conservative (non-Labor) governments attained Treasury benches only from 1929 to 1932, an exceptional Labor 'success' story; in South Australia fortunes were about equally shared between Labor and non-Labor parties; in Victoria Labor was forced into a minor governing role.

It would appear, therefore, that during the inter-war years there was no clear opportunity (except, perhaps, in Victoria) for anti-Labor governments to dominate over long periods or to provide continuing interest representation and there were considerable periods in several States during which Labor policies could be developed in government. Whether this represented merely a confusing influence in the emergence of allocative policy in a continuing pressure towards the accommodation of interest of major social groups or led to greater bureaucratic independence must remain a question - but one of central importance in Australian history.

Rural regulation

Stabilisation of prices and farm incomes were the immediate issues confronting the rural industries after the First World War and it was with these that official regulation was preoccupied throughout virtually all the inter-war years. Nevertheless, at all times, stabilisation was confused by the belief, persisting until 1930, that rural expansion remained a major area for Australian economic growth. In principle, price and income stabilisation problems might have been approached by measures, separately or in combination to provide

(i)   organised marketing, internally and internationally - a 'monopolistic' intervention at the disposal stage;

(ii)   support of farm incomes by measures such as bounties and other fiscal and monetary subventions;

(iii)   product improvement and increased efficiency per unit of farm input;

(iv)   the controlled allocation of resources within the rural sector and between rural and non-rural activities; and

(v)   direct restriction of commodity output by the rural sector.

Given the widely accepted object of a high rate of immigration (for reasons of defence, to enlarge the domestic market and the workforce), the last option did not appeal. Throughout the twenties, net immigration fell only a little below net natural increase, implying that migrants plus children born of migrants accounted for over half of the net population increase of the period. In addition, in the years immediately after the First World War, bureaucratic commitment to rural expansion remained; in the depression after 1930, an underlying objective of the Labor Government was to achieve recovery through rural export expansion.

It was on the first four options that regulatory approaches concentrated. To some extent, the fourth option, the allocation of resources towards non-primary activity tended to discourage the growth rate of rural activity *vis-a-vis* manufacturing and services, at any rate by comparison with pre-war policies. The urban activities of manufacturing and services were perceived as offering, relatively to rural output, greater opportunities for expansion than had been acknowledged before the First World War.

There were special Federal interests in soldier settlement encouraging long-term pressures for expansion of rural activity. More grandiosely, British-Australian policies were developed for 'Empire resettlement' to encourage, under the local oversight of the Development and Migration Commission, expansion of Australian domestic markets and export production by dispersal of Empire populations. Separately, the independent actions of the governments and sectional interests in each Australian State tended to generate conflicting ambitions in rural stabilisation and development. In particular, Western Australia and Queensland sought to develop incentives to rural land occupation and rural production, while New South Wales attempted to achieve an increased market share in rural exports of the 'new' rural industries.

Western Australia most clearly illustrates the development attitudes. From the beginning of the century, Western Australia had been preoccupied with population growth and the encouragement of entry into rural enterprise. Now, in the twenties, much more direct and thoroughgoing public efforts were made to achieve rural expansion and substantial export status. The State Industries Assistance Board established in 1914 played a key role in Western Australia farm development that trebled the area under wheat between 1920 and 1931 (the total Australian area doubled). The Board provided credit for entry into farms, funded improvements and clearing, provided systematic inspection of farms, advised on technology and products, supplied machinery parts, paid sustenance to farmers themselves, subject to approval by inspectors, and met the wages bill of farm labourers. Some 25 per cent of the farms so supported were not wheat farms. But the Board strongly favoured wheat production and, in 1920, this style of intervention applied to farms accounting for a third of all Western Australia wheat produced. This intervention was, however, a declining force in the twenties. By 1925, the Board's role contracted so that it dealt with only 15 per cent of Western Australia wheat, and at the end of the twenties, the Board regulated in this manner a mere 2 per cent.

Queensland adopted a different approach as the only State, throughout the inter-war years, with *compulsory* wheat pooling, a guaranteed high price for wheat and organised marketing under the joint control of producer and government representatives. The pool provided for compulsory marketing through a board and the provision for progressive payments to growers, the initial payment funded through Treasury advances. A more complex scheme of support applied to sugar and other Queensland rural output. But the key objective was to achieve expansion not constraint.

The small Australian share in world markets and a late start in rural exporting made these expansionary approaches by the different States more explicable by comparison with the policies of output restriction adopted elsewhere in the world, particularly in North America during the 1930s. But the different policies of each State confused the pattern of Australian allocative principles and procedures, and exacerbated the exporting problems and the viability of Australian farming as a whole, thereby inducing closer State or eventually Federal government intervention.

In consequence, one key element in Australian rural regulation was the provision for quasi-monopolies in marketing a large variety of products. One of their objects, with State government support, was to confine the market in each State as the preserve of the producers of that State. Such an approach depended on protection from foreign competition, a constraint that is discussed later. This approach was encouraged also by the growing restrictions on international trade, also referred to later. But the development of quasi-monopolistic organisation is so dominant and so dependent on public-private sector relationships as to warrant independent discussion.

Only one substantial rural industry, wool, escaped this design. Almost all wool was exported and the domestic market was minor. Until 1925, the price of wool was supported by the British-Australian Wool Realisation Association (BAWRA) which gradually moved surplus wartime stocks into world markets and disposed of them as joint British and Australian property. This controlled run-down of stocks allowed the wool-producing industry to adapt to peacetime circumstances and, by the mid-twenties, to resume private auctions. Thereafter only one wartime regulatory carry-over remained - the remnants of the system of detailed wool-grading.

The first of the regulatory possibilities ((i) above) achieved a progressively dominant presence in almost all other rural industries. Yet this possibility allowed for a variety of techniques and degrees of public participation in the reduction of private competition. In all cases, the Federal tariff was essential to provide a high degree of domestic protection. But, subject to this, the mode of regulation varied through

(a) statutory authorities, with government and producer representation in control, with power to acquire and with public funding support;

(b) compulsory pooling of output, without a statutory authority, with public funding support to cover progress payments from pools;

(c) voluntary pooling with various modes of public support, including physical pooling facilities and public funding of pool payments; and

(d) the legal registration of grower organisations to provide the minimal conditions for private monopolistic practices and the legal acceptance of such monopolistic practices as might be adopted other than the imposition of overt charges on inter-State trade.

In all cases, the formation of grower organisations was essential. We can only illustrate here the extensive spread of associations of growers, forming a hierarchical and criss-cross pattern. In general, growers' organisations were late to develop and this evolution awaits proper study. The United Pastoralists' Association (1890) was one very early organisation, followed by the Pastoralists' Federal Council of Australia, mainly representing large pastoralists (specialised to wool). From the latter evolved (1920) the Australian Woolgrowers' Association combining large pastoralists and mixed farmers. The Primary Producers' Association formed in 1916 in New South Wales was more representative of mixed and small farms and can be regarded as the ancestor of the Australian Wheat Growers' Federation (1930). The most specialised organisation to emerge was the United Cane Growers' Association (1913), eventually established as the Australian Sugar Producers' Association. Progressively, as differences of interest and particular policy conflicts sharpened, greater specificity of groupings occurred as in the Australian Wool and Meat Producers' Federation (a breakaway from the Australian Woolgrowers' Council in 1939) representing mixed farmers, and the Australian Dairy Farmers' Federation (1942). Interlocking relationships were established at the national level.

Beneath these national bodies, many State and regional organisations were established by the early twenties, particularly stimulated by post-war instability. In most cases, these organisations became affiliates of the larger organisations. Pressure group activities were differentiated at Federal and State levels, designed to propose, influence or oppose legislation by the appropriate government, to provide advice to farmers on the significance of government action, to circulate information on prices, production and trade and to present appropriate agricultural statistics.

An important feature of these bodies was public support through their legislated authority to engage in monopolistic practices. Consumers' interests were rarely recognised by public action. In practice, the ability of these bodies to engage in effective monopolistic practices was by no means uniform. Producers throughout Queensland - not only of sugar but also of fruit, peanuts, poultry products, meat and even wheat - achieved the most comprehensive organisation. In particular, Queensland, until the end of the twenties, alone achieved State-supported compulsory wheat pools, under statutory authority, with State funding support.

Wheat pools that were statutorily organised during the war were abandoned elsewhere by the beginning of the twenties. Thereafter the experience of the voluntary pools was highly variable as between the States. The pooled wheat in Western Australia fell below 50 per cent of the State's output by 1929-30, reached a low of only 16 per cent in 1936-37 and then rose by 1938-39 to 28 per cent. In Victoria and South Australia, a broadly similar decline occurred by the beginning of the 1930s and thereafter the pools became insignificant. In New South Wales the voluntary pools were minor after 1926-27. These voluntary pools were, in substantial degree, government-supported and -financed co-operatives. Co-operative pooling introduced action, however limited, to organise progressive payments (in contrast with the cash price paid by merchants in the private market), to fund these payments until realisation of proceeds and to standardise (or grade by quality) output under public authority.

After wool, wheat marketing was the least regulated of primary products during the inter-war years. The lack of close regulation during the twenties was due partly to conflict of growers' attitudes, partly to confusion of government attitude and particularly policy conflicts between State governments, on the expansion potential of wheat farming. The case of Western Australia has already been illustrated, concentrating on regulation to encourage expansion. Different inducements to expansion were provided in other States, as in New South Wales railway branch line building, freight rate concessions and the adoption of very large-scale Federally financed storage silos.

The extraordinary confusion of attitudes reached its peak in the early 1930s with the Federally inspired call to wheat farmers to produce their way out of depression. A tragicomedy of unrealised promises of high price support, of unlegislated relief bills and of disallowed support legislation induced large-scale expansion in the face of drastically falling export prices. The result was the need for priority attention by government to provide relief to farmers in the thirties. Debt moratoria in 1930, the scaling down of interest commitments and the extension of repayment periods imposed on creditors were part of the consequences of other anti-depression intervention. Provision for relief payments (funded initially by a Commonwealth flour tax during 1933 to 1936) continued until after the Second World War. As wheat export prices rose after the depression, Australian wheat growers succumbed in 1937 to the regulatory device that had spread through many of the other rural products, the adoption of price equalisation. This was the statutory provision for a two-price system, with high domestic prices provided behind a tariff and the dumping of exports on world markets, and the proceeds from the two markets pooled according to overall outcome not according to individual experience of sale at home or abroad.

The conditions for quasi-monopolistic price discrimination were established for sugar in 1901. In was not until the mid-twenties that sugar exporting made export dumping possible. In the meantime, the State support for domestic marketing arrangements of organised producers had secured, for these producers and millers, the possibility of large-scale price differentials as between Queensland and other States. Until 1936 this was achieved for most producers by legislated marketing arrangements and by inter-State agreements of producers and traders, effectively preventing the export of crops, most importantly wheat, from other States to Queensland. This type of quasi-monopolistic agreement between State organisations, reaching agreement to preserve own-State markets to producers, proliferated throughout the States and throughout most commodities, including wheat, meat, dairy produce, fruits, poultry produce etc. with legislative and financial support of government. These agreements, in several cases executed by statutory bodies, had variable success but, at the very least, represented State tolerance and generally active State support and statutory recognition of quasi-monopolistic practices.

These 'monopolistic' practices, despite support by State Governments, would not have been nearly so successful without Federal tariff protection. This protection was also fundamental to the development of price equalisation and the 'two-price system', amplifying government support of quasi-monopoly by producers. This system developed, in the inter-war years, for butter, cheese, sugar, dried fruits, canned fruits, meat and, eventually, wheat. The Paterson Butter Scheme of 1926 illustrates the basic procedures: a high Federal tariff on imports, the provision for a levy on butter produced by factories, the payment to farmers of a bounty on exports, the grading of products under supervision, the averaging of prices on home and foreign markets and the government funding of equalisation payments in advance of realisation. Initially, the levy was voluntary and some butter factories refused to co-operate. In 1934, the levy became a statutory charge. At the same time and until 1936, the Federal Government provided for the licensing of inter-State trade, thereby directly providing, by regulation, inter-State price differentials. On an average, Australian prices exceeded export prices by some

20 to 30 per cent. The enhancement of returns overall to growers was subject to the price elasticity and size of demand in export and Australian markets. A variety of attempts were made to restrict domestic production of any near substitutes (e.g. in the case of butter, restrictions were imposed on margarine in the twenties), thereby reducing the price elasticities of demand. Farmers were further encouraged to expand output, move into export markets and to sustain labour absorption in rural activities. The schemes depended on a large fraction of output being sold on domestic markets where prices could be artificially manipulated, and the main output effects depended on the opportunity to enlarge exports. The schemes had considerable 'success' in encouraging output, despite the instability of world markets and rising trade constraints.

With a substantial role in organising producers' marketing arrangements, the Federal Government became much more prominent in promoting export sales. Wool remained outside this net, though official efforts to promote foreign wool consumption were made in the thirties. For those commodities subject to two-price systems, a variety of boards was established in Britain to assist producers directly in the export disposal of these goods. Throughout the thirties, however, these were primarily for promotional purposes. The Federal Government intervened also in trade regulation as the UK market became progressively less attractive after 1930 and, in the Ottawa Agreement, attempted to encourage diversification of markets. The effects of these activities appear to have been relatively slight prior to 1939.

The third option referred to above was a continuing interest of government in the form of experiment stations, agricultural education and extension services. This was the 'bread-and-butter' approach of the State Departments of Agriculture. In practice, it appears that the resources of these Departments were severely stretched and increasingly thinly spread in the inter-war years. In place of the typical technological advice in production processes, these Departments appear to have become increasingly concerned with quality and grading, recognising the severity of export competition and also the opportunity for this type of intervention through the existence of farmers' organisations, statutory authorities and compulsory and voluntary pools. The existence of these bodies made farmers more directly exposed to bureaucratic influence, a fact that was to become a major source of weakness to them between 1942 and 1950.

In the meantime, however, a new factor intervened, significantly affecting the role of government in influencing the output per unit of farm input; this was the Commonwealth Government establishment in 1921 of an organisation that as the subsequently named Commonwealth Scientific and Industrial Research Organization became the vehicle for Federal scientific and industrial research. By the end of the twenties, this body had begun to influence fertiliser use, pasture development and, in the end most importantly, the control of pasture predators. This influence reached fruition, in quite dramatic terms, after the Second World War.

Manufacturing encouragement

In the Lyne Tariff of 1908, the principle of protection was fully accepted as Federal policy. In addition, this Tariff discriminated in rates as applied to British and other imports - the principle of British preference. It was the Greene Tariff of 1921 that established actual high protection, lifted the average tariff rate to about twice the level of the Lyne Tariff and the British Preferential Rate approximately 50 per cent higher and introduced the Most Favoured Nation rate. Under tariff rates at 1921 levels, the provision for bylaw entry - the admission of dutiable goods free of duty where no local competition was threatened - became a more significant regulatory device to strengthen the allocative influence of the tariff. The new tariff was preoccupied with industries that had developed during the war. But its protective influence was considerably confused by the development of worldwide inflationary movement between 1912 and 1920; the confusion is compounded by the very substantial wage increases in 1920-21, awarded by wage-fixing authorities in Australia. No study of this inflationary episode has been made and we cannot, therefore, be very definite as to whether the Australian manufacturing sector was merely exposed, as 'new' industries, to world competition, or whether, in addition, local prices and costs, especially wage costs, had moved ahead of Australia's main trading countries. Available price statistics suggest the following limited comparisons:

	Wholesale Prices		Retail Prices	
	UK	Aust	UK	Aust
1913	1000	1000	1000	1000
1920	2832	2279	2550	1651
1923	1621	1787	1790	1544

These data are conflicting. Australian prices did not rise nearly as rapidly as Britain's up to 1920 so that the Greene Tariff may have been more protective than appears. But British prices fell much more heavily after 1920, eroding the real protection offered to Australian manufacturers. In this comparison, the retail price movements are probably the more relevant comparison, but it is still a very crude one for this purpose.

The actual additional protection is clouded for another reason. With more highly fabricating industries at stake (higher domestic value added in output), the increase in effective protection of the Greene Tariff may not have been nearly as significant as the increases in the overall rates as compared with the Lyne Tariff may suggest.

These issues warrant more thorough research. But in the light of the virtual absence of world-wide inflationary pressures in the inter-war years, the developments from the date of the Greene Tariff become much more significant than the 1921 increase itself following the establishment of the Tariff Board. The Board became a major body in the regulation of manufacturing, providing a statutory authority for the continuing review of tariff levels, and, in addition, of proposals for other means of manufacturing assistance - controlling bylaw applications, providing for bounties on local production, and recommending alternative modes of assistance with or without tariff variations, including transport rebates, subsidies on production or tax concessions.

The Board provided throughout the twenties an accommodating tribunal for claims for higher protection by individual manufacturers or associations. This established a procedure largely negating general policy considerations and reducing the necessity for manufacturing coalitions. In general, the Board appears to have accepted most claims, without considering closely the case of need or the efficiency of the industry. The Board became, in certain conditions, an important instrument in allowing survival of inefficient firms, the entry of small-scale business and, generally, in restraining increases in scale. On the other hand, where entry costs were high, the Board's approach contributed to the earning of 'excess' profits. By concentrating on nominal tariffs, the Board's approach appears to have given greater encouragement, through the higher implicit effective tariff, to rural-related processing industries (relatively small value-added component), though the deliberate discrimination in tariff levels attempted to accommodate the 'needs' of more complex industry.

The generalised statistical outcome of the Board's hearings have been reported by .G. Hall (1958), adapted as shown in Table 4.2.

The Board's activities need to be seen in the light of Table 4.3 which shows indices of the British preferential and general tariff rates.

The rise in tariffs was accelerated sharply by the Scullin Tariff adjustments of 1929-30, lifting British Preferential and General levels by approximately a third. This increase was more significant than all of the Board's activities of the 1920s and represented a macro-regulatory measure to deal with the balance of payments crisis in the depression. It was adopted at a time when the Board was becoming increasingly concerned about the height of the Australian Tariff. The Scullin Tariff was accompanied and followed by quantitative restrictions on imports during the deepening depression, adding further to domestic protection. Additional tariff restructuring and rate increases were

TABLE 4.2 **Tariff changes by Tariff Board 1924-25 to 1938-39**

	Increase	No Change	Total Not Reduced	Reduction
1924-5	14	13	27	1
6	16	17	33	6
7	40	27	67	8
8	8	5	13	2
9	22	18	40	2
30	31	57	88	8
1	21	41	62	21
2	7	24	31	24
3	9	23	32	58
4	7	13	20	59
5	13	22	35	86
6	6	24	30	46
7	9	27	36	52
8	12	21	33	26
9	19	35	54	31

TABLE 4.3 **Indices of tariff levels 1919-20 = 100**

	British Preferential	General
1914	88	78
1918-19	78	71
1919-20	100	100
21	105	104
22	106	108
23	107	108
24	107	107
25	108	107
26	117	114
27	118	116
28	122	118
29	122	118
30	166	155
31	204	181
32	221	194
33	212	201
34	155	195
35	152	192
36	141	185
37	137	184
38	135	184
39	133	182

Index by A.T. Carmody. Cit. A. Hunter (ed.), *The Economics of Australian Industry*, p. 186.

made by the Government and the Board in 1930-31. By 1929-30, nominal tariff levels were 50 to 60 per cent above the Greene Tariff rates and were reinforced by quotas and import prohibitions in a desperate attempt to cope with depression problems. Subsequent increases in 1930-31 made Australia one of the highest tariff countries in the world.

The devaluation of the exchange rate, forced by the private sector in 1931, gave additional protection. Thereafter, much of the Tariff Board's problem was to restore some semblance of order as recovery developed from 1933. In practice, the general tariff level was very slowly reduced to 1939 but, given the 25 per cent exchange devaluation, the real tariff level of 1939 was significantly above the Scullin Tariff. The British preferential tariff was moved downwards, to stand nominally some 20 per cent below the level of the Scullin Tariff but actually representing a level of tariff rates in real terms in 1939 slightly above the Scullin rates. Note, however, that the peak tariff level (B.P.) was in 1931-32 (see Table 4.3). The 'Scullin Tariff' is a misnomer in that it was created by a large number of successive adjustments, not by a single legislative act.

This relative nominal decline in British preferential rates was largely the product of the so-called Ottawa Agreement of 1932 at which systematic preference to British goods was accorded in exchange for preferential treatment of Australian exports by Britain. Behind the tariff attained in the depression, Australia could well afford to bargain exposure of domestic manufacturing to British (but not other) competitors in exchange for increased British purchases of primary products.

Bounties were also provided on Tariff Board advice. These were applied during the twenties, almost always in conjunction with (occasionally as an alternative to) tariffs, to iron and steel products, cotton, sewing machines, fencing and netting wire, manufactured tobacco, and flax. In the thirties, some additional items were added - small ships, paper, tractor engines and rope and cordage. Of some significance, illustrating a slightly more discriminatory approach, the Board actually recommended against both duty and bounty on engines and chassis for motor vehicles. This was at a time when the Federal Government was initiating action to establish a complete motor vehicle industry in Australia, in opposition to industry opinion. But this is an important matter warranting separate discussion.

During the First World War and in 1938, the Federal Government attempted to establish private industrial enterprises, with manufacturing opposition. These industries were not the only initiatives of government in manufacturing. But each was more than ordinarily important in the whole frame of industrial development. The one (iron and steel) provided the foundation of heavy industry and the other (motor vehicles) was designed as the basis of mass production of consumer goods, each with a proliferation of related industrial activity. The first initiative also pushed the Federal Government towards the Greene Tariff and related action with respect to the iron and steel industry - basically stabilisation measures that dominated inter-war industrial regulation in a manner closely akin to the stabilisation of rural activity. But in industrial regulation there developed a much more significant attempt to encourage manufacturing expansion.

The Tariff Board procedure directly brought manufacturers into the public decision-making process on tariffs, subsidies or by-law concessions. The nature and circumstances of representations by manufacturers need thorough explanation. But it is also the case that bureaucratic objectives had a major role to play in implementing regulation and in promoting domestic manufacturing. Several circumstances may be suggested as underlying this bureaucratic presence: the commitment to large-scale immigration, amongst other things enlarging the domestic market for and labour inputs into manufacturing; defence commitments of the Federal Government (a key to the establishment of the steel industry); public sector commitment to social overhead enterprises requiring large-scale inputs of goods; and a commitment to public sector investment in overhead assets depending on very large purchases over a restricted but industrially vital range of goods. Obviously, there was an interplay between these activities and private sector interests; the essential point is, however, that these public sector tasks made governments major consumers in a way that most other governments in the world were not. An important allocative process was opened through these activities.

The foundation of the steel industry during the First World War and the abortive effort to establish the motor vehicle industry in the late thirties are, in considerable degree, explicable in these terms. Both were immediately government initiatives. Both were seen as calling on intervention by Federal, State and local governments, with an array of measures from tariffs, subsidies, preferential purchasing arrangements by government, provision of concessions in land acquisition, water and power supplies, rural services etc. It was not till after the Second World War that the car industry project was actually undertaken. The BHP (originally conceived as a government undertaking) faced severe financial problems at the beginning of the twenties. Tariff protection apart, regulation begat regulation as governments were drawn further and further into support of the steel industry by the deliberate promotion of related steel-consuming industries to provide for a viable group of steel producing and consuming firms.

In general, with small-scale enterprise and limited local expertise and skills, manufacturing was much more dependent on relatively detailed intervention. But it was intervention to alter the composition of industry by enhancing prospects in the domestic market and not, yet, in the detailed conduct of business. This intervention was the more readily available, not merely from the attempt to sustain population growth and labour absorption in manufacturing but also because State Governments vied with each other to attract manufacturing activity to each State and particularly to each capital city. So developed an intricate pattern of parochial intervention in the supply of land, power, water and rate concessions that provided important support - and helped to fragment industry and limit economies of scale. The small number of States in Australia helped to bring this style of intervention to the fore. Oligopolistic competition by State governments is deeply ingrained in Australian history, reflecting separate developmental and political ambitions of each State.

State Governments were most important in encouraging manufacturing through capital investment. The influence of public capital outlays operated directly by linkage effects and more generally through the provision of urban and especially metropolitan overhead facilities and amenities. They were much more substantial throughout the 1920s and the second half of the thirties than before 1914. Urban-located (wharves, roads, buildings, electricity power stations, urban rail and tram, and water and sewerage in particular) and urban-related (water supply reservoirs) expenditures rose between 1900 and 1929 from approximately 40 per cent of gross public capital formation to almost 80 per cent. With public investment rising, in the late twenties, to approximate £ 90 million per annum (cf. gross product of manufacturing at £ 130 million), this public action represented a massive allocative influence. Direct inputs into manufacturing were supplied by government institutions in the form of power and water supplies, high capacity rail freight facilities and roads. There is some evidence that some of the services based on these facilities were provided to manufacturers at unit charges significantly less than those placed on other consumers, particularly in power and water. The provision of these facilities and services also offered amenities and travel facilities encouraging the agglomeration and intra-city movement of workforce and consumers.

There has been some comment on public investment linkages in encouraging private domestic manufacturing through deliberate preference to local suppliers. Certainly, it was not uncommon for public authorities to profess that preferential treatment was available and provided to local suppliers. It is more difficult to ascertain the dimension of preferential treatment. For particular firms, some specific preferential treatment may have been acutely important. What is less clear is the aggregate implication of government preference. We might compare the share of domestically produced materials, equipment and machinery supplied locally in total goods inputs into public investment activity with the similar components in private investment. Table 4.4 shows the available estimates, none of which can be accorded a high order of accuracy.

TABLE 4.4 **Share of local supplies in total goods inputs into investment %**

	Public Sector	Private Sector
1920–21	56.0	52.3
22	62.7	58.6
23	62.2	58.0
24	63.9	60.5
25	64.6	61.2
26	66.5	63.4
27	64.6	62.0
28	63.7	60.4
29	62.6	61.6
30	63.8	60.7
31	72.1	69.8
32	81.4	81.7
33	79.6	79.6
34	79.1	79.1
35	75.8	75.3
36	75.2	74.6
37	75.2	74.3
38	72.7	71.3
39	75.5	74.9

Derived from N.G. Butlin, *Australian Domestic Product* .... The basis of calculation is described on pp. 142 ff.

Conceivably with the exception of the first half of the twenties there appears to be no substantial difference between the public and private sectors in routing purchases to local suppliers. Even in the first few years, the difference is not marked enough to support any confident judgement. It is possible that there was a similar preference given by the private sector to local suppliers. It is also possible that any such private-to-private preference may have been prompted by government regulatory influence. Reference has already been made in the early development of the iron and steel industry and in metal manufacture, to specific government intervention, partly prompted by BHP Ltd, to assist in the local array of steel-producing and steel-consuming private concerns inducing a sequence of intermediate local transactions between these concerns. One interesting area of investigation in tariff negotiations could be the question of coalitions between firms trading support for tariff protection for preferential private purchases; or bureaucratic/political pressure making tariff protection conditional on this type of collusive business practice.

However, it is not necessary to rely on these possibilities to suggest that a very substantial, if relatively narrow, manufacturing stimulus appears likely to have stemmed from public investment. Australian manufacturing was not sufficiently sophisticated to supply a large fraction of machinery in the inter-war years; increasingly machinery became a major component of total imports (except in the major depression period). There was a significant difference in the composition of public and private investment so far as machinery purchases were concerned. Generally, machinery purchases accounted for some 20 to 30 per cent of private investment, by far the greater part of which was not available from domestic suppliers. By contrast, public investment rarely included a machinery component in any year in excess of 3 per cent. Its impact was much more directly on the manufactured goods that Australian industry was or was becoming most equipped to supply - bricks, timber, quarry products, pipes, cement, steel rails, girders, steel shapes, fencing wire, sheet steel etc. If public preference was a significant factor, it appears likely to have been primarily in steel products beyond the simple stage of rail manufacture and in some special areas of electrical goods of which governments were substantial consumers. But, basically, it appears to have been the nature of public investment and the composition of its inputs that gave its linkages a major role in inducing manufacturing growth in these particular areas, rather than preferential treatment of local suppliers. However, it must be recognised that the steel industry had a peculiar importance for wider manufacturing development and the initial successful establishment was conditional on the assurance of large-scale public purchases behind a high tariff.

It appears that preferential treatment of private firms through the current rather than the capital outlays of government may have been more substantial. Again a relatively narrow but different range of manufacturing was affected - in particular office equipment, paper, books and the miscellany of office supplies. In these there was greater scope for import competition and greater opportunity for government preferential treatment. These practices had been well established before the First World War. The scale of these current expenditures are, of course, obscured and grossly diminished if one thinks in social accounting terms of current government consumption. Investigation of this issue must proceed on the basis of gross purchases.

Public intervention in service markets

Much of the discussion on both rural regulation and tariffs has an immediate relevance to wholesale and retail firms and may be read in this light. Wholesale importing and domestic trade in many primary products were progressively subject to the allocative influences - specifically the regulated pricing - flowing from State marketing schemes, the (at least) permissive support by the States to 'monopolistic' organisations and practices and the legal prescriptions endeavouring to determine the geographical source of inputs of rural products into commercial transactions. Given the permissive attitude by government to the existence of monopolistic practices, little appears to have developed in the way of commercial regulation other than the spread of these marketing schemes (basically producer support systems). Some innovations occurred but with comparatively little significance - for example the requirement to register shops in Victoria and subsequently in New South Wales.

The gradual extension of some zoning and building control regulations made some further invasion into the freedom of market behaviour and the extension of water and sewerage services carried with it increasingly prescriptive requirements to convert households to services and to fund these services. These regulations were generalised most importantly in the New South Wales Local Government Act, 1919 providing for the authority of municipal and shire councils to supervise and regulate building construction within their area, a power reinforced in 1935. These powers were only progressively proclaimed and were not universally applied by the time of the Second World War. They provided for non-uniform standards prescribed for different areas and for zoning of land. These regulations related essentially to new, not existing, dwellings and to extensions. The basic regulatory device was the general requirement to submit building plans for approval and amendment. Some slight tightening of health protection provisions was made, and safety regulations for customers were extended. Building heights became subject to restriction. None of these represented much beyond pre-1914 regulations.

Some extension of building controls was the consequence of the introduction of new services into or new materials used in buildings. So the spread of electricity consumption was followed by the specification of fire precautions and protection from electrocution in homes. In turn, these fed back to technical prescriptions for certain products. Similarly, the more extensive development of sewerage and water supply was accompanied by rules defining conditions of installation and, in the last resort, conditional requirement of installation as alternative public services were phased out. Early development of consumer durables such as washing machines encouraged restrictive rules on location and the prescription of their location in specified laundry areas.

In the field of insurance, the States continued to await regulatory provisions by the Federal Government - to such an extent that in-

surance in New South Wales remained substantially unrestricted except by the general terms of the Companies Act. However, in other
respects, the insurance market changed following Commonwealth entry into income tax so that tax concessions and encouragements to insurance provided by the Commonwealth (in a rudimentary manner
from the First World War) spread to the States until the tax system
was made uniform in 1942. These encouragements took the form
primarily of (a) concessional deductions of superannuation and insurance premiums from taxable income; (b) the freedom from taxation on companies of income from superannuation funds; and (c) the
deduction of specified proportions of public debt interest from taxable income. In fact these offset certain imposed requirements of investment in safe (public) securities. But they represented, in total, a
substantial encouragement to saving through insurance and an improvement in yields on insurance policies.

The provisions were, in one light, an alternative to publicly organised welfare (pensions) extension; from our point of view they gave a
bias towards a particular mode of saving and a particular source and
pattern of investment. They appear to have enhanced the role of insurance companies as financial intermediaries in housing finance,
substituting for now-suspect building societies; and laid the early
ground work for the post-1945 emergence of insurance institutions as
major competitors of the trading banks as financial intermediaries.

Throughout the 1920s, little change in banking regulation occurred, apart from the acquisition of the note issue by the Commonwealth Bank in 1924. The attitudes of the trading banks and of
the Commonwealth Government in the twenties largely ensured that
the Commonwealth Bank should eschew ordinary deposit and advance competition and should confine itself to a predominantly supportive but not intrusive reserve role. In practice, this supportive role
suddenly became a control one as the Commonwealth Bank was
plunged into the crisis of depression.

With the growth of incorporated enterprises and the capital
market, private bank funding was progressively declining in the inter-
war years from its position of dominance before 1914; in addition,
self-financing by business (an unknown quantity) almost certainly
became increasingly significant. The private banks were mostly committed to rural and real estate financing and to commercial and personal overdrafts. They faced a declining role in an industrialising
economy. This diminution of role was not merely a change within the
private sector, if only because the process of industrialisation was a
managed one, subject to extensive government intervention. To this
extent, the gradual change in the position of the banks may be seen as
an important indirect and unintended consequence of government interference in the structure of the economy.

Depression weakened their role further. Some of the changing relationships were formalised in the Commonwealth Bank's acquisition of overseas reserves under the Mobilisation Agreement and the Bank's final assumption in 1931 of the management of the exchange rate. Moreover, the Commonwealth Bank, during the depression, effectively displaced the private banks as lender of last resort to the Commonwealth Government. Though much of the relative shift in power was not formalised and, in fact, denied in evidence before the Royal Commission on Banking in 1936, the basis was already laid for a subsequent drastic reduction in the role of the private banks in Australian business activity and policy making after 1945.

Some regulatory intervention developed in transport as motor vehicle use increased. The rapid pre-1939 growth of the private motor car did not yet yield mass car use and so personal constraints on car and road use remained slight. Primary attention was directed towards regulation of private transport as public carriers, largely to integrate them with major government business undertakings so that they served as feeders to public transport rather than competitors. In metropolitan areas, rate and route regulation of private buses was established from the early twenties with a subsequent trend towards public displacement of private activities and the extensive development of publicly owned and operated urban transit. These transport measures are of special interest in that they represented exceptional adversary acts by government, acts out of the supportive mainstream of allocative and regulatory policy.

Labour market regulation

The high tariff protection in the inter-war years partly encouraged entry of new firms into manufacturing and expansion of existing local manufacturing by reducing foreign competition and raising profitability; it was also a means of meeting demands for money wage increases by trade unions. That the sequence of tariff increases, price increases, wage rate increases and further tariff increases obscured the movements in *real* wages, meant a confused regulatory procedure and provided for progressive intervention. As each conflicting interest made some gain (e.g. in wages), more support was sought by others (more manufacturing tariff intervention or more support for farmers) in spiralling demands for regulatory intervention.

The recognition of these elements of conflict led to the identification of two criteria of wage fixation: the protection of real wage standards, and the capacity of industry to pay. In addition, however, the demands of industry for skilled labour and the change in trade union organisation led to a complex hierarchy of wage rates fixed by arbitration authorities in awards of margins for skill payable above the platform of the basic wage.

By 1913, over 500 separate wage-determining authorities had been established. This array represented a diversity of wage-fixation methods and awards that provided little satisfaction to trade unions, employers or governments. The existing unions were still uncertain as to the choice between, or ability to secure, access to the State tribunals or the Commonwealth Court. By 1913, only seventy-eight unions, with a membership of 352 000, had achieved a representation extending beyond one State. It was not merely wage fixation but union recognition and union preference, particularly the last, that attracted unions to the Federal Court. Moreover, the part-time, inexpert nature of most Boards encouraged union organisation to move towards federated or Australia-wide organisation. By 1920, the number of federated unions had risen to ninety-nine, with a membership of 543 000, or just on 80 per cent of total union membership. This proportion of membership in federal unions remained substantially constant throughout the inter-war years. The Australian Council of Trade Unions was established in 1926. The number of State Boards authorised to fix wages had slightly diminished by 1920 but the ability of trade unions to bargain between State and Federal authorities had greatly increased. This ability was a major bone of contention between governments, employers and unions. To this extent, public constraint was diminished and the opportunity of unions to manipulate the regulatory array was enhanced as private labour organisations adapted to the public institutions they confronted. In the longer run, there was, in fact, a mutual adaptation.

Despite the initial weakening of public influence, the persistent tendency was for labour market control to increase. In certain respects, this was foreshadowed in the Royal Commission on the Basic Wage in 1920, reporting, on a cost-of-living basis, in favour of a very large increase in money wage rates. The attractiveness of the Federal arbitration system to unionists was considerably enhanced. Nevertheless, access to the Federal Court was constrained by the necessity to establish a dispute extending beyond the limits of one State. Accordingly, inter-war wage regulation remained an intricate mixture of State and Federal awards. Though the Federal Court proceeded to develop the Higgins' concept of a basic wage, each State tribunal (except Victoria and Tasmania) had its own concept and measure of a basic or 'living' (minimum adult male) wage throughout almost the whole of the inter-war years. Thus it was not until 1937 that New South Wales adopted Federal rulings for the basic wage.

It was the 1920 Royal Commission that shocked the (various) judges into an appreciation of the conflict between the achievement of a real wage standard and the ability of industry to pay. During 1911 to 1913, the Commonwealth Bureau of Census and Statistics had been developing the necessary information, a price index to measure a constant regimen of consumption, and the State Bureaux had been similarly preoccupied. The evolving price index, and the cost of living, became a major topic of inquiry from 1913 to 1920, and the Royal Commission on the Basic Wage extended its own inquiries into contemporary living standards and costs of living. It is symptomatic of the contemporary regulatory problem that the legal mind grappled unwillingly with the concepts of base-weighted and current weighted price indexes. In the end, it opted for the 'A' Series index, with occasionally changed weights. This approach was forced by union pressure in the inflation between 1912 and 1920. By the beginning of the 1920s, the current equivalent of the 1907 Harvester basic wage standard had been generally attained and the regular adjustment of this standard in accordance with the 'A' Series was adopted in 1923. This continued until 1930. The approach to wage determination was thereby extended beyond the realm of restraining industrial violence and limiting disputes to the routine but piecemeal adjustment of the basic wage in accordance with changes in retail prices.

Initially, the basic wage was applied to adult males; by the mid-twenties, the matter of female relativities was standardised, accepting the female rate as, generally, five-eighths of the male basic rate. But as women workers were accommodated, male workers moved above the basic wage. By 1937, when the New South Wales Industrial Court moved to adopt the Federal basic wage standard, every one of the 'main occupations' listed in the *Labour Report* received minimum wage awards above either the New South Wales or Federal basic wage. All had managed to establish a 'margin' (however minute) for 'skill' above this standard rate. In the meantime, the various authorities had adjusted the basic rate upwards during the twenties, varied it for an across-the-board depression cut of 10 per cent in real terms and restored part of the standard by nominally argued adjustments, particularly so-called prosperity loadings. The basic wage became relevant from early in the 1920s not primarily as a minimum but as a floor on which some margin might be claimed and awarded; in the parlance of the 1970s, it represented 'partial indexation'.

The union pressure for margins dominated the Court bargaining throughout inter-war years. Margins determinations were generally declared separately, occupation by occupation, evaluated one at a time with only limited consistency of each award relative to others. In particular, the Commonwealth Court made no *general* margins awards though some general principles were enunciated in the Engineers' Case of 1920 (the one inter-war occasion when substantial attention was paid to general principles). In practice, margins varied closely with the level of employment. They tended to rise progressively above the basic wage to 1929; in the depression, margins narrowed drastically; and then, after 1934, they were progressively restored.

Formally, the wage-fixing authorities purported to hear arguments justifying claims for skill. There is little evidence that they investigated these claims closely. Certainly, they had no staff that would have made possible a thorough assessment of skill claims. Particularly during the twenties, the authorities adopted practices corresponding, in principle, to the Tariff Board - receiving argument and, in general, acquiescing in a substantial part of claims made. Principles were replaced by rules of thumb and under the pressure of union practices, rules of thumb became mere expedients. This degeneration was expedited as unions were in a position increasingly to appeal to either State or Federal authorities by creating the appropriate 'dispute'. In response, both State and Federal Governments sought to alter the constitutions and modes of operation of their respective wage-fixing bodies, without much effect. During the late twenties, in particular, industrial relations were relatively unstable. The number of disputes was large and the severity and length of strikes tended to increase. It was not until 1929 that strike activity declined heavily, to remain suppressed until the Second World War.

This was a regulatory process with limited restraining effect. Policing of awards depended on unions and employers; enforcement depended on the wage-fixing authorities or on the relative strength of employer or employee groups. Lacking policing or enforcement functions, the authorities were largely compelled to throw intractable disputes back to the market for determination by deregistering recalcitrant unions or by imposing penalties until labour organisations conformed to legal declarations. In either case, this procedure meant, de facto, imposing on unions the task of direct 'negotiation' with employers to report to the authorities the terms of settlement that were then duly enshrined in legal determinations.

Possibly the most important implications of wage fixation were to encourage the growth of large craft unions and to accelerate the growth of union membership, and, in the depression, to sustain unions in existence. Perhaps above all, it achieved a discrimination between particular groups of workers in a detailed classificatory system.

For some skilled groups, the process of bargaining through legal agencies meant that their wages increased very much faster than many professional salaries in the inter-war years. But it cannot be concluded that this was the product of regulation as distinct from bargaining power. Indeed, there was a substantial amount of collective bargaining outside tribunals when unions could thereby secure preferred treatment. So far as union membership is concerned, the biggest growth was before 1920. Indeed the proportion of the employed wage and salary earners who were members of unions changed comparatively little, fluctuating between 45 and 50 per cent, despite the depression. This may indicate a major benefit (a partial monopoly) to unions: their preservation as entities despite severe unemployment in the depression because it was employed *union* members who were legally protected by arbitration awards.

The authorities largely eliminated, by their rules of adjustment, the necessity of unions or employers to argue basic wage cases in predominantly economic terms - cost-of-living adjustments in a situation of extremely slow productivity growth disposed of the main issues and tariff adjustments made handsome contributions towards 'the capacity of industry to pay'. On rare occasions, as in the depression 10 per cent cut in all wages, general economic policy issues came to the fore, and the adjustment of wage rates by 'prosperity' loadings allowed authorities to adumbrate vague principles of economic policy. There was, in fact, little reason but a great deal of specious pleading from both sides.

The Commonwealth Court became increasingly important particularly after 1930 with the State tribunals progressively taking a secondary role. The State authorities nevertheless continued to play an important role in small-scale disputes and in respect of small unions, and in the detailed working conditions of labour. Despite the increase in the workforce and its considerably greater complexity by 1939, very little increase occurred in the inter-war years in the number of awards or variations made. Regulation was slowly becoming a national process, and by the application of common rules in awards, decisions in particular cases came gradually to define generalised conditions of employment across wide ranges of industry.

Government intervention in the labour market was not confined to fixing the price of labour. Direct action to increase the aggregate workforce and its skill composition was considerably more important in the inter-war years than it had been before 1914. Most obviously, the repatriation of ex-servicemen was a massive, managed workforce recovery, effectively completed in 1920. During the twenties and the second half of the thirties, large-scale assisted immigration was resumed (there was a small net loss by migration in the first half of the thirties). This assisted immigration attempted to attract both rural and urban workers. But increasingly, assisted immigration concentrated on attracting more skilled (urban manufacturing) labour as the primary technique to enhance skilled human capital.

Nevertheless, in the twenties, State Governments turned their attention to another mode of increasing human capital by the development of technical education, reinforcing and institutionalising the old apprenticeship procedures of the unions and employers. Until the First World War, the emphasis in education and training had been on primary education, a skeleton provision for an elitist secondary education and an even more elitist tertiary system. In the inter-war years, high school populations remained largely part of the elite. But beside them, a variety of technical schools and technical colleges expanded to permit the training of youth for industrial employment. These became, briefly, important training institutions implying State-subsidised supply of technically trained workers for private business (and, of course, the public sector as well).

Early macro-economic management 1927 to 1932

Public intervention in labour markets, rural and industrial activity, public investment and borrowing and assisted migration appear to have been important contributory factors in the instability of the Australian boom in the twenties and the depth of the ensuing depression. The movement into recession appears to have begun in 1925-26, initially turning around declining export incomes and a slackening in private investment. As general instability became clear by 1928, the need for overt macro-management became pressing.

Beginning in 1925-26, public sector behaviour was, in part, inadvertently counter-cyclical - an increase in public borrowing and investment, the growth of deficit budgeting during the second half of the twenties coupled with progressive increases in tariff protection and the increased subsidisation of some areas of rural activity. These measures were certainly not introduced inadvertently or with as little awareness of possible results as has typically been suggested. Though one should not make too much of the point, they foreshadowed a Keynesian solution. They were certainly confused. But it would be seriously incorrect to perceive them as unconscious or unintended. Thus the Development and Migration Commission's *Report on Unemployment and Business Stability in Australia* (1928) disclosed sharply rising levels of unemployment from the end of 1926. There was no appreciation of the dire prospects ahead. Nevertheless, the Commission firmly asserted the *State* Governments' primary responsibilities to counter unemployment and the necessity for public works by 'Government Departments, public undertakings and municipalities'. The Commission acknowledged that increases in these works in order to cope with unemployment were in fact being undertaken. In the prevailing climate and expectations the Commission regarded these measures as 'expensive palliatives'. At the same time, a key figure, D.B. Copland (1928, p. 35), was strongly urging governments that (government works) 'projects *upon which loans* are to be expended should be in hand with all plans prepared, so that they could be undertaken when a trade depression develops'.

Meanwhile, the Tariff Board had been repeatedly sounding a warning, from as early as 1925-26, against the drift of wages in Australia above the (directly competitive) British wages. This warning had been generalised by 1927-28 to cover all relative costs in Australia and Britain. Simultaneously, growing trade union pressure on the arbitration systems had led to increasing public sector dissatisfaction with the propensity of the unions to manipulate the State and Federal arbitration systems to their advantage. This was most highly dramatised in the attempt by S.M. Bruce to abandon the Federal Court - an attempt leading to his political defeat.

It appears that already throughout 1927-29, conscious, if incoherent and inappropriate, measures of macro-management were being attempted before the election of the Scullin Government in 1929. The route adopted had some elements of consistency - public works expenditure, deficit financing, export subsidies and foreign borrowing proceeded along with progressive and quite rapid increases in import restraint through tariff increases. But the extent to which the economy was closed off from imports and to which exports rose failed by far to match the growth of external imbalance; restraint on money wage increases was not easily achieved. Once the decline in export incomes worsened in 1929 and 1930, the domestic efforts at macro-management had become a source of weakness. It is, incorrectly, at this point that most discussions of anti-depression action begin.

The actions taken during and after 1929 focused on the Commonwealth, not the States, but were increasingly the product of private pressures. Severe external instability required Commonwealth action to close the economy, given rapidly declining export earnings and very high overseas interest commitments. The newly elected Federal Labor Government introduced a radically increased and broadened tariff schedule in November 1929 (the Scullin Tariff), together with quantitative import restrictions. This Tariff largely disregarded the Tariff Board and hence limited the opportunity for any group to protest. The 1929 action was followed by further tightening of restrictions in December 1929 and June 1930 (in 1931 a primage duty was introduced). The number of items subject to duty increased by these three steps from 259 to 418 and the movement of items in the various customs duty rates shifted the whole emphasis of the tariff structure to concentrate nominal duty rates in the range 55 to 75 per cent. Coupled with severe quantitative restrictions in the first half of 1930, the major drain on foreign resources due to goods imports was stopped.

In a move closely related to the constraint on imports, the Commonwealth Treasurer was pressing for formal Reserve Bank powers in November 1929. A Bill to provide this was abandoned though the Commonwealth Bank secured an important emergency power to control all available gold in Australia, thereby acquiring power over the Australian gold and bullion holdings of the trading banks as well as the gold of traders. This strengthened the Commonwealth Government's power to ration gold disposal in London and to conserve gold to give priority to the public sector's London commitments. This power increased the tensions between the Commonwealth and private banks, though the latter were increasingly drawn into the placement of substantial deposits with the former during the depression. Initially, the official policy was to preserve exchange parity with sterling but in the early months of 1930 the Australian rate was allowed to move into a substantial 8 per cent discount.

Australian economists in June 1930 were arguing for the abandonment of cost-of-living adjustments of wage rates. In fact, retail prices affecting the indexes used by the arbitration systems had been falling during 1929. Throughout 1930, money wage rates were falling as adjustments to declining cost of living were made. By the end of the year, awards under the Commonwealth Court, for example, had been progressively lowered by approximately 10 per cent due to these adjustments. At the end of the year, the Commonwealth Court, in a railways case, considered the desirability of a *further* wage reduction to achieve a *real* and not merely a money wage reduction. Accordingly, in January 1931, the 10 per cent real wage reduction was made and was applied subsequently to other industry awards. The Court urged the State bodies to follow suit, all but New South Wales conforming.

It should be appreciated that British money wage rates had been virtually unchanged throughout 1920 to 1930. During that period, Australian money wage rates had increased by some 20 to 25 per cent. The Australian reductions in the depression crisis period went far towards bringing money wage relativities back into line. With approximately a 50 per cent increase in tariff rates and a money wage rate reduction approximating 20 per cent, two major macro- measures had been adopted by January 1931.

Macro-measures were preoccupied with the sharing of the 'sacrifice' in the depression. By 1930, export producers and the unemployed were acknowledged as the two immediately suffering groups. By 1931, it was recognised that wage earners in employment in the private sector had now largely joined the sufferers. The finger was pointed at the public sector, to beneficiaries of the public sector (pensions) and to recipients of government bond interest.

In June 1931, the Premiers' Plan was adopted. Simultaneously with this Plan, interest rates and the gold reserve ratio were reduced, relaxing the legal constraints on bank advances but also and more importantly freeing gold for shipment to London to meet government obligations. The adoption of the Premiers' Plan followed an additional major change forced by the private sector, the exchange devaluation initiated by the Bank of NSW in January 1931. The Plan briefly preceded, by three months, a British devaluation of 20 per cent, a devaluation that Australia followed so that the Australian exchange devaluation *vis-a-vis* other countries was more severe than that implied by the Bank of NSW initiative. At this point (in December), the Commonwealth Bank assumed responsibility for managing the exchange rate.

It is remarkable in this context that there has been so much serious debate of the Premiers' Plan as a recovery factor, given all the surrounding action. Equally it is extraordinary that little attention has been given to the long-term efforts in restraining public outlays on infrastructure throughout the thirties. The Plan provided for a target reduction of all government expenditures of not less than 20 per cent (including wages and salaries and pensions) below the 1929-30 levels, debt conversion to reduce interest payments, increased taxation on consumers, a reduction in bank interest rates, and the provision for private mortgage relief. Apart from the last, the Plan was an attempt to enforce 'sacrifice' on the public sector, i.e. expenditure cuts and balanced budgets, and formally acknowledged (in a way that subsequent post-war policies did not) the equity issues of general economic management. As a minor provision, it provided for restricted outlays on relief works to assist the unemployed.

The Plan was never fully achieved; as a recovery scheme, it was intended to be read in the context of other major measures adopted and to be treated as a whole. Its significance lay perhaps essentially in directing the attention of all governments to the emergency of severe depression. That it could be taken seriously, within the limits of the Plan's measures, as a major contribution to recovery is scarcely now credible. Indeed, it is illustrative of the limited expectations of the Plan that eight months later, in February 1932, the New South Wales Government announced default on foreign loans, an announcement leading to High Court restraint, the legal attachment of the New South Wales Treasury, and, in May, the sacking of the Premier.

The New South Wales action reflected particular Labor Party approaches and an antipathy to British capital. Its revolt was accompanied by an important concession by the Federal Government, the issue of a Relief Works Loan in April 1932 and, in the month immediately following, the initiation of a large-scale relief works program and the beginnings of a more definite recovery approach. Closely related with these was the introduction of relief proposals for small-scale farmers who were in as much distress as the unemployed.

Relief for unemployed workers and for farmers remained an acutely important policy problem throughout the thirties, particularly as recovery was slow and incomplete. The fear of mass unemployment remained after this episode as a deeply ingrained fear that was to underlie a great deal of government policy and intervention for most of the succeeding forty years. Its imprint on public-private sector relationships emerged most clearly after 1945 when the adoption of

Keynesian management procedures led to the application of stop-go policies in macro- regulation. One of the outstanding implications was to superimpose on all post-1945 allocative regulation the short-term constraints of maintaining full employment and the preservation of aggregate external and domestic balance. The essential consequence was the diversion of attention away from long-term allocative regulation and the preoccupation with short-run and aggregative policies. Economic allocative strategy became submerged by aggregative, full employment, criteria and the reliance on generalised macro-controls. Many of these controls were constraining in contrast with pre-1939 experience. And public policy became much more centralised.

5

All the Restrictive Practices Known to Man 1945 to 1975

Introduction

The tendencies to centralisation of allocative influence were greatly strengthened and accelerated during and after the Second World War. Centralisation and the introduction of constraining measures, qualifying the underlying supportive relations between the public sector and private interests, were, perhaps, the two outstanding characteristics of allocative and regulatory intervention after 1945. Centralisation in Federal authority, combined with the application of nation-wide influences, carried ambivalent implications. There was a strong tendency for private organisations to change to match national administrative and legislative bodies so that a corresponding concentration of private interest occurred. So long as a commitment to full employment policies remained, Federal authority appeared as the most effective instrument for designing and executing national policy. This perception reached its heights in the national integrating efforts of the Whitlam Government. On the other hand, centralisation exposed public intervention to evolution of public policy at a single political and bureaucratic level and to efforts to reverse the trends towards so-called 'big government'.

Centralisation was accompanied by the evolution of more general rules and influences with greater speed of operation and by the spread of influence to almost every area of private decision-making. It encouraged the primacy of Federal bureaucracy, particularly in Federal financial, monetary, economic and social policy, with States and local authorities progressively downgraded to subsidiary government agencies - until the mineral boom. The role of the Federal bureaucracy accentuated opportunities for autonomous action by government and focussed private pressures at the Federal level.

In part, this evolution was a designed change, initiated by Labor Governments during the Second World War and deriving from wage-earner preoccupation with full employment needs and pressures for reform in social welfare, supported by bureaucratic interest in these areas. The resulting wartime change in fiscal provisions and subsequent monetary control altered drastically the relative roles of the different levels of government.

But neither changes in relations between levels of government nor adjustment of national private interest groups explain the evolution adequately. Closely associated with the tendencies to centralisation and constraint was the influence of the nature of economic and social development. The main thrust of this development, particularly through changes in foreign trade, international investment flows, the entry of foreign enterprise and technology, and the post-war disturbances in European populations, was to bring many issues formerly less important or dealt with at sub-Federal level within the constitutional ambit of the Federal Government. To that extent, the centralisation was unintended. Increasingly, moreover, allocative and regulatory influences related to foreign interests that replaced domestic Australian interests. The opportunities for bureaucratic autonomy and centralised intervention were both enhanced - until the mineral boom - in so far as public intervention bore more directly on non-Australian private interests rather than domestic interest groups, particularly in manufacturing and immigration.

Over all these changes lay the effects of the commitment to full employment and macro-economic policies. These commitments introduced, substantially for the first time in Australia, strong elements of constraint on private decision-making for aggregate economic purposes rather than for purposes of particular markets. It is appropriate, therefore, to look in this chapter at macro-economic circumstances and policies before investigating the changing network of public intervention in these markets.

The Second World War

The duration and intensity of the war established a dominance of Federal authority with far-reaching and long-term consequences. The war concentrated constitutional authority in the Commonwealth. It allowed the Federal Government to exercise directive and allocative powers not normally available to it. The scope and nature of these consequences were radically altered by the election of a Labor Government in 1941.

From the long-run management view, perhaps the fundamental change was the Uniform Tax Agreement of 1942, transferring income tax powers to the Commonwealth, including both personal and company taxation. This change needs to be appreciated in the light of prior developments - the 1927 Financial Agreement providing some oversight of State borrowing and capital projects by the Commonwealth; the experience of macro-management from 1929 to 1932, with the consciousness of Federal management potential; the introduction of the Grants Commission, allowing the Commonwealth to manage the evening-up of State financial relativities; and the operations of the Premiers' Conferences influencing budget allocations. The Uniform Tax Agreement was introduced in circumstances particularly advantageous to the process of centralisation in the Commonwealth because of the subsequent three war years and because of the extension for almost five years after the war of Federal defence powers under National Security Regulations. By the end of the Labor Administration in 1949, the financial primacy of the Commonwealth was largely confirmed. This was expressed not merely in terms of Commonwealth control of tax rates and concessional provisions but also by the Federal constraint on all public borrowing and the change to funding of much of State capital outlays through ordinary revenues raised by the Commonwealth.

The pattern of primary product acquisition, corresponding to the experience of the First World War but carried to a wider range of rural output, was largely established in the first two years of war. The system of statutory marketing boards was extended into the peacetime economy after 1945. Rural marketing regulation that had been partially developed before the war became more tightly structured.

The period of most intense war effort, throughout 1942 and into 1943, provided the occasion not merely for the exercise of close directive control to achieve a maximum war effort and maximum reduction of civilian activity but also for the application of Labor social objectives within these limits of wartime aims. This experience was to be important in the post-war economy, particularly in terms of direct import controls and in control of capital expenditures. Moreover, in the war circumstances, both conservative Coalition and Labor Administrations brought business, trade union and academic groups into the planning and administration of wartime controls, introducing into the Commonwealth public service an exceptional array of expertise for public sector operations.

The rapid creation of full employment, the attraction of many new entrants, particularly women, into the workforce and the opportunity for high earnings created potentially intense inflationary risks, in the context of tight constraints on civilian production. Severe taxation measures were required to constrain these risks, coupled with provisions for deferred pay and for exhortations to support war loans. Experience important for post-war administration of a full employment economy was being gained, and the mechanisms for combining fiscal, monetary and trade measures in dealing with domestic balance were being established.

This experience was the more advantageous as partial reconversion towards peacelike production occurred during and after 1943. Then, although this reconversion concentrated on primary production, renewed opportunities developed for a substantial range of manufactured output.

The reconversion was a limited one. Nevertheless, it provided the wartime Labor Administration with the experience of guiding and directing private factories towards output more akin to civilian needs (even though the output was absorbed in defence requirements). This allowed the wartime government to adjust the economy towards actual peacetime production. Accordingly, at the end of the war, the Government was the more adapted to the restoration of private decision-making, aware that it had, in taxation and monetary controls and in trade and capital issues controls, the essential general powers and existing control procedures to manage a reasonably orderly transition to a peacetime economy. Perhaps the crucial problems that the public sector faced were the risks of inflation and the physical dilapidation of all plant and equipment, including the physical assets of the major public business undertakings, and, in the longer run, the fears of post-war recession and the importance of planning for the maintenance of full employment.

Summary comments on economy and politics

The years immediately after the war were a period of severe shortages due to wartime reductions of civilian output, slow reconversion to peacetime production, drastic deterioration of plant and equipment, physical shortages of key imports and constraint on supply of domestic key materials and equipment. Juxtaposed against these conditions, pent-up consumer demand and accumulated financial assets due to wartime earnings and high employment created strong inflationary pressures. At the same time, economic policy was based on the assumption that post-war inflation was likely to yield serious post-war recession.

The Korean War accompanied by a wool export boom freed the economy from many of these problems. Prevailing government attitudes changed also with the election, in 1949, of a conservative Federal Government. Massive earnings of foreign, especially dollar exchange, led to similarly massive import purchases. Though much of this foreign importing yielded consumption goods, it also provided much needed supplies of plant and equipment for the restoration of domestic production, especially for manufacturing. At the same time, foreign capital was attracted in increasing volume into the Australian economy, with American capital vying for the first time with British for dominance in new additions to direct foreign investment in the private sector. Public overseas borrowing dropped to minimal levels and, for the first time in Australian history, the private sector was able to attract large-scale capital inflow without public sector competition.

For the two decades after the Korean War, the Australian economy operated with near full employment, slight recessions occurring with troughs at 1952, 1956, 1959, 1961, 1966 and 1971. This full employment was associated with a large-scale inflow of migrants so that population growth rose until the early sixties to annual levels well above inter-war years. Thanks to the accession of skills during the war and the skills contained in the workforce acquired by migration, this human capital was now able to contribute to much more complex activities. Greatly enhancing these local human skills, American capital inflow into manufacturing, in particular, was accompanied by the inflow of technology and managerial skills. These were basic factors in leading not merely to rapid sustained growth in aggregate real output but also to (for Australia) relatively high rates of growth of output per head. At an average annual 2.5 per cent (2.3 per cent per annum average compound) growth rate, this per capita 'improvement' was about twice the inter-war performance and approximated the achievements of the heyday of growth in the period 1860 to 1890.

Part of the explanation of increased per capita performance was that Australia experienced for the first time the conventional Western structural change, a shift to manufacturing, in circumstances in which manufacturing output per unit of labour input was high and rising relatively to rural activity. At the same time, at least during the sixties, very substantial improvements in technology in the rural sector led to recovery in per capita output and a substantial decline in the share of the workforce as inputs in rural activity. The major technical changes were the introduction by government of myxomatosis to destroy rabbits, the main pasture pests, opening the opportunity for large-scale pasture improvement with sown grasses and fertilisers, including aerial applications.

Australian manufacturing had acquired most of the advantages of being backward. Mass consumption of consumer durables had not developed extensively before the war and until 1950 these goods were in very short supply. Motor vehicles, refrigerators, radios, washing machines, vacuum cleaners, electrical, rubber, plastic and chemical goods and petroleum refining invited the interest of foreign manufacturers and it was into these, in particular, that American, British and subsequently European and Japanese capital flowed. Scale of establishments rose, and, with takeovers by foreign firms, scale of enterprises also increased substantially. Australian manufacturing became structured in highly concentrated forms - one of the most concentrated of any western country - even though it was often also fragmented in terms of establishments.

By the early sixties, doubts about the long-term viability of this development were arising. The question of the appropriateness of large-scale foreign control was increasingly raised. The composition of manufacturing, containing a substantial fraction of high-cost inefficient firms and products, appeared even more generally dubious. Similarly, the development of rural activity appeared to have been achieved with a highly wasteful use of capital inputs and the preservation of a significant number of rural producers whose incomes were now relatively low, earning very low rates of return on capital (e.g. dairying, fruits). Moreover, with these doubts in mind, the wisdom of sustained high immigration was challenged and with it the fundamental tenet of Australian faith, development to provide jobs for an expanding population.

Though rural prospects recovered in the sixties, the failure of manufacturing to move from an import-replacing stance to very substantial exporting (some export activity did develop) was an important factor encouraging the redirection of capital and labour into different channels. This redirection led to massive redevelopment of the major cities and their geographical extension. Property development was one of the activities of the sixties transforming city centres, aiding large-scale shifts in city populations and encouraging the development of new housing. Both a dwelling construction boom and a boom in inner-city office space followed. The city property boom was the product of a number of major factors, including the very long time lag in providing new inner-city structures (little development since the 1920s), the concentration of population in the cities, the greatly increased standards expected by city dwellers because of long-sustained prosperity and the growth of financial intermediaries servicing property development.

Closely associated with this city boom (in Western Australia, intimately so) was the development of the mineral boom. This was already foreshadowed but inadequately perceived at the beginning of the sixties. Iron, bauxite, copper and coal formed the basis of this mineral boom, moving a great deal of the impetus in economic development to the 'outlying' States of Queensland and Western Australia. Mineral exports rose rapidly as foreign capital moved into direct exploitation of Australian mineral resources. By 1970, these exports, sold on varying bases by term contract and direct sale to Japan, the USA and Western Europe, had become important contributors to Australian export earnings. Oil and gas discoveries provided a major import-replacement and freed Australia, for a time, from close dependence on much imported petroleum.

After the Korean war, creeping inflation had developed particularly from wage pressures. After 1965, Australian consumers were insulated from overseas oil prices, with artificially low oil and gas prices set internally. But the mineral and property booms both appear to have been important in accelerating wage pressures and by the early 1970s, reinforced by rising prices for energy, inflation began to gather force. Export prices offered for Australian rural products increasingly reflected world prices and added to Australian money incomes. Import prices similarly reflected world price movements and added further inflationary pressures to Australian costs. Lack of monetary and financial constraint by Conservative Governments particularly from 1970 to 1972 and by the Labor Government during 1972 to 1975 significantly accentuated inflationary pressures.

By 1975, Australia was firmly affected by high rates of inflation and unemployment. Domestic prices were rising faster than in many Western countries and for the first time in over forty years a serious problem of unemployment (concentrated on the new entrants to the workforce and on married women) had developed. World recession led to slackening mineral export sales and to the introduction of new uncertainties in mineral development. Belated fiscal and monetary constraint was attempted in 1975 by the Labor Government. It was left to a new conservative government to introduce a series of changing and conflicting policies in an effort to reduce inflation at the cost of increasing unemployment, after the dismissal of the Whitlam Government. Nevertheless, throughout these final years, wage rates continued to rise, limiting the opportunities for employment and for the control of inflation.

In the light of the post-war dominance of the Federal Government and the progressive testing and extension of interpretation of the Constitution, it is with Federal political experience that one must be chiefly concerned. It may be suggested that, with Liberal-Country Party Government from 1949 (subject to the short interval of the Whitlam Labor Governments, lacking control of the Federal Senate), there was a sea-change in the Australian political and government scene. This was the first long-sustained period in which non-Labor parties were in government at the Federal level and able to apply Liberal political philosophy with little constraint other than a commitment to full employment.

State experience was much more confused. Victoria actually flirted briefly with short-lived Labor Governments. But apart from New South Wales, the basic experience of State politics was to favour non-Labor governments. A strong withdrawal from conventional electoral support for Labor combined with internal party disputes significantly weakened the influence of Labor parties throughout Australia. Though fortunes fluctuated, the Federal Government was placed in a stronger position to deal with the States.

This change may have encouraged another alteration in the governing structure through the concentration of the bureaucracy in

Canberra and the greatly increased professional strength of that bureaucracy. It is an important issue to consider whether Federal political (and financial) dominance combined with a powerful bureaucracy working geographically apart from the mainstream of Australian economic and social experience may have introduced a much stronger element of public sector independence in Australian governing processes. Moreover, this bureaucratic change was also accompanied by a dominance of economic and more general social science professions at the Federal level confronting predominantly technical professions in the State bureaucracies - a confrontation that created major problems of communication and understanding in a Federal system.

Macro-management and allocative implications

In discussing macro-management, we are primarily concerned with its allocative rather than its aggregative consequence. Post-1949 allocative measures in general cannot be sensibly discussed except in a context of macro-management, partly because of the strong allocative content of macro-measures, partly because macro-management altered quite drastically the operation and the time horizons in other specifically allocative policies. This change can be perceived as a major cost of full employment. Because of Keynesian influence, and the commitment to full employment, macro-management was a pervading, conscious and persistent object of Federal government policy, overriding many specific micro-considerations and affecting the application of long-term allocative principles. The policy-forming influence of economists was concentrated in the Federal government, lacking the capability to intervene in many micro-areas but powerful in fiscal and monetary controls and in the control of exchange rates and trade. This Federal power was greatly enhanced by the 1942 Uniform Tax Agreement, adding much greater strength to budgetary controls through which allocative influences operated as a crucial part of macro-management. The years from 1949 to the mid-sixties were, in general, ones of rapid economic expansion, productivity increase and rising real income per head with recessions occurring as minor fluctuations around very high levels of employment and comparatively slow price rises (apart from the Korean War episode). Stable full-employment policies and macro-management implied a high degree of centralisation of allocative influence in almost every area, because of the intermittent but frequent subjection of subsidiary micro-policy to macro-needs, as determined at the Federal level.

Initially, after the war and into the fifties, Federal preoccupation was with the preservation of price constraint in full employment. During this early period, despite the strength of the Australian balance of payments, the commitment to support sterling limited Australian reconversion to peace. Subsequently, after the Korean war, the Australian foreign balance became increasingly a policy claimant. Throughout the attempts at macro-management, budgetary measures emerged as a means not merely of private sector management but also of Federal constraint on the public sector. For most of the period, the emphasis was on the use of fiscal policy for control of (constraint on and stimulus of) the private sector. But increasingly into the sixties, the conscious Federal control of the public sector as a whole came to the surface. It was not until 1972 and 1976 that, in two different senses, the basic political philosophies in the management of both the public and private sectors became explicitly central issues of policy. Until then, variations and readjustments of public sector activity were designed primarily as a means of direct or indirect manipulation of private sector behaviour on a short-term basis, very largely to influence allocative decision-making in securing domestic and foreign balance at high levels of employment. It was initially the Labor Government's reformist ambitions after 1972 that led to strong Federal interventionist pressures on the public sector itself, though there had developed earlier strong pressures in one direction related to pricing policies of public business undertakings. Partly arising from these Labor activities, the development of inflation and of unemployment induced, after 1975, a reverse intervention to constrain the public sector presence in the economy by reducing the absorption of labour, demands for capital inputs, the supply of underpriced services and the scale of financial transfers. This reversal of attitude did not greatly affect, however, the degree to which the public sector intervened in private decision-making.

There were, of course, major issues of allocative policy distinct from macro-objectives. But many policy areas that had had essentially allocative purposes before 1939 were profoundly constrained to the requirements of macro-management. The most obvious of these were the use of import restrictions (including the tariff) to 1962 and the partial adaptation of labour market regulation to the needs of general economic management. On the other hand, it should be reiterated that many of the macro-management measures had - and were explicitly intended to have - allocative influence though essentially in short-run perspective. And, ironically, some major macro-measures led to much closer, more specific and more arbitrary intervention in private decision-making - a behaviour pattern that some might regard as the essence of 'big government'. During economic fluctuations, each recession brought action to check an unstable boom and each was followed by measures to restore employment and output. It is not implied that macro-management was appropriate, efficient or equitable.

Indeed, a good deal of the subsequent criticism of Keynesian management policies obscures the fact that actual policy measures were often inconsistent, too harsh or inadequate, too early or too late. These difficulties were partly the product of economic and political realities, but they appear also increasingly to have stemmed from the limitations of theoretical prescriptions. One of the current problems, gradually emerging, was the fact that, although wage rate increases were checked in periods of restraint, they moved sharply ahead as recovery was promoted. Another problem was the inadequate attention, in macro-management, to questions of restructuring the economy to achieve more productivity gains.

There is no space here to recount the multiplicity of measures, still less the proposals for macro-management in successive boom and recession situations. It is, perhaps, useful to outline a little of the variety of approaches and the increasing problems of management. The Korean boom and accompanying inflation followed the limitations of supply of key resources (energy, transport, steel) and restrictions on imports due to sterling area weaknesses, and occurred shortly after the freeing of constraints on wage adjustments. The export boom enormously increased pastoralists' income. Control measures actually adopted focused on a very modest levy on wool sales to fund a reserve price system and the prepayment of income tax by pastoralists as measures to constrain liquidity; encouragement was offered to increase imports to support domestic expansion, an increase in imports that the Federal Government actively participated in by securing an IBRD loan to fund the import of tractors, earth-moving equipment and railway and electricity plant and equipment.

While it was, perhaps, essentially American action to unload wool stocks and cancel war textile contracts that defused inflationary pressures, the import boom led to a sharp check on growth and to a rise in unemployment. In addition, this was the first time in Australian history in which the budget was used for anticyclical purposes: stringent controls on capital issues, Loan Council constraint on borrowings, a rise in the bond rate and a 'horror' budget, with increased income tax, profits tax and sales tax, reduced outlays on public works to achieve a budget surplus. At the same time, Reserve Bank measures were adopted to increase special reserve deposits in order to restrict liquidity.

One of the major delayed effects of the Korean War boom and inflation was the abandonment, in 1952-53, of the cost-of-living adjustment procedures in wage fixation. Hindsight may suggest the lack of wisdom in this action: union power in a situation of full employment was probably too strong to make any effective wage control possible but it could be interesting to explore whether the old practice of (in effect) partial indexation could have slowed down the rate of increase of

wage rates. The substitution of common rule application of determinations in respect of claims by key unions for margins and loadings
adjustments appears to have accelerated the subsequent rate of increase of wage rates in recovery episodes. More closely related to the
Korean boom and the associated import surplus that developed was
the adoption in 1952 of stringent quantitative import restrictions that
allowed direct bureaucratic intervention in determining the types and
quantities of goods to be imported subject only partially to price and
competitive conditions. In addition, the post-war immigration scheme
was checked on the grounds of the short-run capital demands of the
immigration program.

Subsequent stop-go measures acquired some greater subtlety, partly reflecting the more secure political position of the Liberal-Country
Party Government. These measures were, to some extent, aided by the
separation of the Reserve Bank from the Commonwealth Bank and
the increasing use of monetary as compared with fiscal controls. Until
this central banking separation occurred, inevitable conflict occurred
between Commonwealth and private trading bank interests, with the
latter resisting constraints imposed by the former when these constraints led to the invasion by the Commonwealth Trading Bank of the
advance business of the private banks.

This was not, however, until the fifties were past. This institutional
change followed the gradual development of informal advice, consultation between private banks and the Commonwealth Bank, and
the development of Commonwealth directives, paving the way
towards a more flexible interest rate policy and the beginnings of
deliberate open-market operations by the Commonwealth Trading
Bank. Increasingly, attention was turned first to monetary and second
to fiscal policy as modes of government intervention in preserving the
stability of rapid private expansion; progressively less attention was
accorded to public contribution in that private development. As
macro-controls became broader during the fifties, there remained in
the background, however, the determination to intervene directly and
specifically in the preservation of external balance through variably
applied quantitative import restrictions. These restrictions, despite the
aggregative   objective,   were   often   specifically   applied   with
discriminatory, allocative intent. The use of quantitative import controls, in fact, reflected the limitations of the conservative Coalition
Government: the unwillingness of the Country Party and of farm interests to countenance exchange rate flexibility placed a major restriction on stabilisation policy.

Macro-measures inevitably crop up in discussing allocative and
regulatory actions with respect to the major markets of the economy,
as indicated later in this chapter. However one major area of *aggregate development* policy in which government participated directly

was in the support of large-scale immigration throughout the fifties. But even this was subject to the short-term checks and spurts of stop-go policies. These policies were applied variously to restrain or stimulate consumption, capital outlays, imports and liquidity *and the related private decisions* depending on the current conception of the sources of short-run inflationary pressures or of the retardation of private activity.

This method of approach to stabilisation was perhaps inevitable given the constraint imposed by the objective of domestic full employment. It was also feasible so long as there was sustained private economic development and improved productivity. By the end of the fifties, the prospects of this private development revolving around manufacturing and rural development were increasingly clouded. But while growth continued, public stop-go policies took priority over older, pre-war, emphasis on public intervention in the growth and structure of the private sector. Particularly in the area of capital formation, government tended to withdraw relatively from its long established role in providing the social overhead facilities of the economy. This had major implications for the underlying transport provision of the economy and, in the long-run, for the efficiency of private operations. As a counterpart of this withdrawal, government participated actively in some development and allocative decision-making in the private sector, of which the encouragement of mass consumption of motor vehicles was one and the support for home ownership another. The long-term consequence was to induce a new range of interventionist measures, in transport, in energy, in financial and in environmental policy. The contention that regulation begets regulation might on this occasion be corrected to the proposition that non-regulation leads to (lagged) greater regulation later. In the Australian case, however, there were major externalities of private action with which governments were eventually forced to deal, in circumstances where inflationary pressures made belated intervention even more unpalatable. But this was only one area of the allocative measures of government after 1949 and we need to look at these more directly.

Services regulation

A great many of the management approaches to private services in the immediate post-war years were restrictive - a novel and, in the main, passing phenomenon in Australian economic history.

The details of *immediate* post-war constraints are not directly relevant to this outline, except for two major points. First, these post-war controls were widespread and detailed and encouraged a strong and widespread political backlash leading to powerful pressures for the 'freeing' of the market. This applies alike to such circumstances as long-continued rationing of electricity or petrol and to the more general but more central attempts to control the banking system. Secondly, some post-war restraints led to long-term issues in difficult regulatory tasks as in the attempts to control the medical profession, to nationalise the banks or to innovate in airline development. The peacetime restructuring and expansion of the economy, immigration and population growth, increasingly concentrated in the capital cities, were a complex product of private behaviour and public policy. But in all these changing economic and social circumstances was a basic element: the growing centralisation in the Commonwealth and, directly or indirectly, the much greater centralisation of allocative policy. This centralisation had, however, an ambiguous implication: in certain circumstances, it strengthened and speeded the process of regulation; in other cases, the administration of regulation and the development of new policies were constrained by the Federal control of the purse limiting interventionist ambitions in the States. In the post-war years, the Federal Government became so important in the regulation of basic services that it is appropriate to recount the development of regulation as a process evolving around the Commonwealth.

To underscore the point, fiscal and monetary policies and measures of the Federal Government impinged on almost every area of business, often with (apparently) unintentional or at most only half-intended effects. Income tax changes, concessional allowances in tax deductions, company taxation and related allowed deductions, sales taxes, import duties and excise duties spread a vast net of substantial and variable influence on the behaviour of domestic trade and service activity, making them increasingly dependent on public regulatory policy and making the Federal Government increasingly the target of interested pressure groups in search of government benefit or the avoidance of government constraint. At the same time, pressures on State Governments to find new sources of revenue led to the spread of a variety of new taxes - such as on entertainment - that impinged most importantly on the delivery and consumption of services.

Policy measures of governments operated through private business decision-making, most importantly in the behaviour of financial intermediaries. One needs to identify the changing specific regulation of banking and other financial institutions. But to confine attention merely to specific monetary regulation would lead to the conclusion that there was, after 1949, a decline in the controls affecting the monetary and banking system. There is, however, a different point of view: macro-regulation of the Federal Government depended primarily on fiscal policy at the beginning of the fifties with fiscal policy made up of a variety of aggregative and specific restraints on or encouragement to selected business sectors. These fiscal measures flowed back, directly or indirectly, onto the banking and financial system, inducing changed behaviour through diverse channels, nonetheless substantial because of their diversity.

Monetary measures formed part of macro-regulation during the fifties. However, they came to be gradually more prominent during the sixties until they were leading instruments of macro-regulation in the early years of the seventies. This does not imply that they were particularly successful; it conveys, however, that generalised monetary measures, centralised in the Federal Government, became far more important in the operations of the Australian economy than they had been twenty years before. To this extent, a greater centralisation of regulatory approach occurred in the banking and fiscal sector in a manner broadly conforming to other centralising processes.

This change in emphasis needs to be borne in mind in considering the direct approach to the regulation of monetary institutions. During the twenty years after the Second World War, the monetary role of the banks declined progressively and heavily. On the one hand, the mass consumption of consumer durables depended on and stimulated the growth of hire purchase, an area outside the conventional advance policy of the private banks. On the other hand, the rapid development of manufacturing was accompanied by direct foreign investment, new capital issues and self-financing. These represented activity to which the private banks did not easily accommodate.

The first major peacetime measure providing for regulation of the trading banks was in the 1945 legislation that, in general, codified wartime controls, placing the responsibility for foreign exchange transactions, capital transactions and the authorisation of current international transactions on the Commonwealth Bank; reducing the role of the private sector in the management of the Commonwealth Bank; providing for the special accounts of the private banks with the Commonwealth Bank to be continued in order to control bank lending; and, in addition, instructing the Commonwealth Bank to develop its trading and specialised activities - especially the newly-formed Industrial Finance Department - in active competition with the private banks. The legislation was challenged, only on limited grounds, but successfully. The Government's response was to attempt nationalisation of the private banks; this, too, was challenged successfully and the Government defeated in 1949.

The new Liberal Administration which came into power in 1949 took until 1951 to make any changes; then it restored the board of management of the Commonwealth Bank. Under pressure from the private banks, the Liberal Government took further steps in 1953, this time to restrict the competition of the trading sections of the Commonwealth Bank and to reduce the tightness of control exercised through the Special Account procedure.

The private banks were still not satisfied, nor was their influence exhausted, but it was not until the end of the 1950s that they could effect any further change. In the meantime, the Commonwealth Trading Bank continued to expand its business and to introduce many innovations to Australian banking which the private banks were eventually to adopt themselves. It is probably true to say that the competition of the Commonwealth Trading Bank was almost as important in shaping Australian banking as the more formal instruments of regulation.

Central banking in Australia was faced with formidable problems after 1945 and during the 1950s. The controls created and refined under the 1945 and 1953 legislation were not fully adequate in this context. Macro-economic management relied heavily on fiscal policy. However, central banking also suffered from two specific handicaps - a rigidity in interest rates, weakening as the decade advanced, and a growth of other financial institutions operating outside the orbit of central bank controls and of direct Federal constitutional authority.

The growth of non-bank financial institutions resulted from a combination of circumstances (not least of which was the tight control exercised over banks) and with some private bank encouragement represented an escape from control exercised by the Commonwealth Bank and a break from the conservatism of the private banks.

Conventionally, these growing areas had been legislated for in the States. Thus, hire purchase business had grown some twenty-five-fold from 1939. At the mid-fifties the control of this business had been limited to State legislation that concentrated on a small range of formal and legal issues of personal entitlements, far removed from the massive post-war significance that the business acquired: hire purchase contracts were regulated to provide that title remain with suppliers but to allow buyers to take possession of goods; regulations allowed buyers to terminate hiring at any time subject to repossession on non-payment of due rates. Some consumer protection devices were established but the only substantial constraint on the growth of business was in a relatively heavy stamp duty on hiring contracts. The funding of these contracts attracted large specialised service companies that were largely free of direct public restraint.

The private banks, meanwhile, had remained restive under the banking controls and had not ceased to campaign for their further reduction. There followed a major restructuring of the Commonwealth Bank in 1960 under the legislation passed in 1959. The trading activities of the Bank were diverted to a new institution, the Commonwealth Banking Corporation operating under its own management. There was to be no more competition between the central bank and the private banks. The central banking functions of the Commonwealth Bank were to be continued in the Reserve Bank of

Australia and the Special Account procedure replaced by a system of Statutory Reserve Deposits with limitations on their functioning which had not been applied to the special accounts. The new arrangements, including the loss of its trading departments, and the growth of non-bank financial institutions were to make the Reserve Bank turn more and more to market-oriented measures of control, specifically the use of interest rates, and this itself was to lead to further financial diversification.

In the meantime, the recession of 1960-61 drew attention to other aspects of financial control. Private insurance companies, as one kind of major institutional investor, lay within the constitutional ambit of the Federal Government, but the Commonwealth - apart from tax concessions to companies and policy holders and apart, also, from a requirement that companies lodge small deposits with the Federal Treasurer - had made little move with respect to insurance. Even the 1945 Life Insurance Act made little change, achieving no more than a uniform mode of handling business and the establishment of an Insurance Commissioner with powers of supervision over companies' viability (or conduct). However, the insurance companies' holdings of government securities had been steadily replaced for two decades or more by real estate assets and industrial financing. Some other institutions also found Commonwealth Government securities progressively less attractive than they had been. This, indeed, was a concomitant of rising interest rates, which had begun to move up about the middle of the nineteen-fifties and gathered strength at the turn of the decade; it had the effect of reducing the liquidity of holdings of government securities on which a capital loss would be sustained on disposal.

Early in the sixties, therefore, the Commonwealth Government moved to exercise its taxation powers to oblige life insurance companies and other bodies to hold certain proportions of their investments in Commonwealth Government securities. In effect, it created a captive market; it limited the extent of the increases subsequently required in interest rates to attract funds to governmental purposes and introduced some new distortion into the allocation of resources.

Throughout the sixties the monetary authorities strove for the establishment of control through the manipulation of interest rates and sought the development of a short-term money market to encourage trading in Commonwealth Government securities to facilitate changes in market rates. Thus, towards the end of the sixties, the central bank was able to enter into a formal arrangement with a small group of dealers to extend to them lender-of-last-resort facilities (on the English model) ensuring their viability and the existence of a formal and continuing market.

These steps represented a new emphasis in monetary control and they implied the establishment of a wider regulation and a more comprehensive monetary control than concentration of regulation on banks' liquidity had given. It was an evolution in which the tight control of banking having encouraged the development of non-bank financial institutions and the growth of those institutions, together with the weakening of banking controls, led the monetary authorities to seek measures to extend their influence. This they did without legislation and, indeed, with the co-operation of the private sector which saw in the more market-oriented approach greater individual freedom even if the area of control was widened.

The extension of control was not, however, without its cost. The market-oriented measures were less specific in their effects than direct controls and, more importantly, much more slow-acting and, indeed, uneven in the speed of effect on individual institutions and kinds of activity. The gain in comprehensiveness was at the cost of a lack of specificity and speed in operation and sometimes in effective strength, as became clearer in the seventies.

The problems of the seventies, and constitutional developments (in the form of a new legal interpretation of the Federal corporation power), induced a return to direct controls that was stillborn; in 1974, the Labor administration introduced and passed in the Federal Parliament the Financial Corporations Act but the succeeding Liberal administration refrained from implementing the part of the Act conferring direct controls on the monetary authorities.

In general, it may be suggested that in the field of financial services greater and more centralised regulation was achieved, then partly lost because of private sector changes and constitutional limitations. Then during the sixties it was partly private sector developments and partly the greater concentration of Federal policy on monetary as compared to budgetary policy that brought these services back towards centralised regulatory influence.

Little Federal action was initiated in respect of Stock Exchanges and their services. The mining boom brought growing pressures for some increased oversight but it was not until this share market boom in minerals was over that any significant regulatory development occurred. Similarly, with respect to company legislation generally, the alarms and excursions of the sixties left a substantially hands-off position, reflecting the range of private interests opposing government intervention.

Just as in financial services, so in medical and health services controls emerged from Federal Labor Government initiatives. Ostensibly, the Labor Government failure to introduce its full scheme of health provision turned or was made to turn on a particular regulatory device, the use of special prescription forms. In fact, the opposition was a concerted confrontation by the medical profession to resist inroads into the system of largely 'unfettered' private medical business based on publicly funded university training and publicly supported hospitals. The Federal Coalition Government success in establishing the form of Labor's proposals turned on co-operation of doctors with a more sympathetic Government and the concentration on insurance principles with limited regard for assistance to low-income groups. Federally subsidised insurance schemes combined with income tax concessions in a progressive tax structure provided powerful support to the private medical profession and encouraged strong inflationary pressures through consumption of medical services and price escalation by a quasi-monopoly profession. These matters are more fully discussed in Chapter 8.

Implicit in the treatment of the medical profession until 1972 was the prevalent Federal Government support for or acceptance of 'monopolistic' organisation and monopolistic practices. In the area of services, this became increasingly important as the scale of retailing and wholesaling enterprises expanded, as takeovers and concentration of business occurred. Price leadership, tied producer-seller relationships, retail price maintenance and the development of larger and more powerful trade associations illustrate the outcome of this institutional development during the fifties and sixties. The support for registered associations offered by both Federal and State Governments was extended to a wider range of professional services in which specialised businesses developed rapidly as part of the sophisticated economic growth after 1950. All the restrictive practices known to man were exploited in the Australian economy with the legal support of the public sector.

These developments brought opposition particularly from consumer and academic groups, but there was another factor increasingly disturbing the Australian scene, the entry or attempted entry of foreign business accustomed to different competitive circumstances or seeking the relaxation of existing restrictive practices to facilitate entry. In practical terms, although there were some minor and ineffective State attempts to cope with monopolistic structure and practices, they carried little administrative significance partly because State Governments themselves, however pro-Labor, were preoccupied with growth and the attraction of business to the States. The Commonwealth had (see Chapter 8) sought unsuccessfully, through a referendum conducted by the Labor Government, to enlarge its constitutional powers to deal with monopoly; it had to be content with the short-term National Security Regulations until 1949 when the new Liberal Government demolished most of the antimonopoly provisions.

The first step towards a reappraisal of monopoly regulation came in 1965 with the repeal of the *Australian Industries Preservation Act*

1906 (the equivalent of the Sherman Anti-Trust Act) and with the substitution of the Trade Practices Act - legislation passed after five years of prolonged and uncertain political and public debate.

The Act provided for a Commissioner and a Register of Trade Agreements with a Tribunal to review complaints of monopolistic practices. Only one form of behaviour, collusive tendering and bidding, was prohibited; all other practices were subject to examination by the Commissioner and, on his exclusive complaint, by the Tribunal sitting if it chose *in camera*. The Act provided for the registration of agreements, not practices, with no constraint on business structure, including mergers. In all, the Act was severely watered down by business pressures and represented a very weak and largely nominal provision for constraint of monopolistic practices. On an average, between 1969 and 1973, approximately fifty agreements were investigated annually by the Commissioner out of some 14 100 agreements registered in 1973 - though it would appear that many of the 'investigations' were actually carry-overs from preceding years and the real number of separate cases was much less than this very small number. The secret operations of the Act and the Tribunal largely defeated any purpose they may have had. Moreover the Act operated in circumstances of considerable constitutional uncertainty until the High Court ruled the Act, apart from its clauses on resale price maintenance, invalid in 1971 (in the Concrete Pipes Case) but, at the same time, pointed to methods whereby the legislation could be remedied. The new legislation so produced in 1971 was restricted to corporations only. By this legislation, monopolistic practices of individuals and unincorporated business carried out within the limits of one State were unrestrained. At the same time, the provision against resale price maintenance was introduced in 1971, though the teeth to this provision may have been established more by trade union threats to blacklist suppliers than from legislative and administrative intent. It awaited the passage of the 1974 Trade Practices Act under the Whitlam Government to attempt a more organised attack on monopolistic practices.

Symptomatic of the prevalent attitude to these practices from 1950 to 1974, public sector business undertakings were themselves deeply committed to and regarded themselves as dependent on 'monopolistic' practices, using the coercive power of government to regulate competition. At the same time they were subject to regulation to provide for discriminatory pricing and service delivery. The most artificial but also perhaps the most effective of these, leading to mutual public and private sector regulation, was in the emergence of the two-airline policy whereby Federal Ministers directed a change from competitive behaviour by TAA through the sharing of government business by TAA and Ansett (formerly ANA) to the controlled scheduling of flights by both, the requirement of similar passenger and freight charges, control of aircraft purchases and public subsidies of purchases. Closely related to this evolution, Federal Ministerial commitment to Qantas led to close regulation of all aspects of international carriers with respect to flights to and from Australia, attempting to preserve the Qantas market share and sustain its 'profitability'.

Airline controls became increasingly relevant to private sector operations as air freight carriage and airline passenger travel escalated. But side by side with these controls were the more traditional public sector regulations of land transport in response to the rapid growth of private motorised transport (for further discussion, see Chapter 10).

Immediate post-war regulation of railway services was predominantly a matter of State determination (see Chapter 10). Initially, the State authorities were preoccupied with the declaration of classes of users rather than discriminatory treatment opening railway services to personal or political manipulation. Non-Labor administrations tended subsequently to reinforce preferential charging, particularly for rural users. For our present purposes, however, regulation of transport is concerned primarily with regulation of private transport. We are not concerned here with organised public transport services. Before 1940, primary attention was directed towards taxing and licensing private transport services to serve as railway feeders. With the substantial cessation of railway expansion after 1940, interest was directed to 'co-ordination' of transport services.

In practice, regulation was divided between private passenger services and freight transport. The chief regulation of passenger services related to licensing of operators and approval of fares. In the case of freight, the matter was more complicated. Licensing systems provided entry rights where transport services did not compete with public transport; this competition was prevented. In addition, in some States (New South Wales and Queensland primarily) systems of road haulage taxes were adopted to limit long-distance road haulage, a procedure spreading throughout the States. In fact, section 92 of the Constitution led to loopholes and restricted public intervention because of the legal restraint on imposts on inter-State trade. The consequence was to encourage registration of hauliers in low-tax States. It is of some interest that not only were these regulations restrictive of competition but in the States in which revenue surpluses were earned these surpluses were generally paid to competing public transport services, exaggerating the anti-competitive consequences of private transport regulation.

Regulation of much of land transport services was clearly related to metropolitan development and land and service use. Implicitly, regulation of taxi services has already been referred to. With growing personal car use and increased congestion, entry controls and parking regulations increasingly restrained vehicle entry into city areas. These restrictions had limited relevance in the fifties but became increasingly significant thereafter.

Metropolitan concentration and the varied pressures on land led to much greater concern for land use zoning - though incompletely applied - and the application of location constraints on service operation, including residential services. More importantly, increasingly close supervision of the provision of building services, house occupation, densities of housing, plans and specifications developed with increasing population pressures on urban land. On the other hand, some relaxations of constraint occurred, partly due to pressures on land and services, partly due to changes in materials, architectural design and engineering with the extension of building heights.

Finally, with the changing nature of urban living and of urban economic activity, concern over environmental quality and of services related to the environment became more prominent from the early fifties. Initially directed towards air pollution, more restrictive regulations were imposed on the service operators yielding or disposing of pollution. Typically constraints took the form of direct physically specified restrictions; rarely did control take the form of taxation or market-like signals to induce a lower level of output or consumption or changed technology to reduce penalties. Until 1972, however, little action was taken beyond limited controls related to air particulates together with some largely ineffective efforts to police the operations of private waste disposal services. It remained for the Whitlam Government to make its particular influence felt after 1972 and for State governments in the same period to respond to pressures of environmentalists within the limits of State constitutional authority.

Labour market regulation 1945 to 1965

Some States continued to make basic wage awards through all or most of the second world war. But the suspension of the 'needs' award and the 'loadings' in the basic wage by the Commonwealth Court in 1940 had extensive implications because of the adoption of Federal basic wage awards by Victoria and New South Wales by 1937. This suspension continued until the end of 1946 when an 'interim' award was made. In the six-year interval, major changes in wage structure and in workforce composition had occurred: widespread entry of women into the workforce, particularly in manufacturing; the adumbration of a Federal basic wage for women; the dilution of the workforce; adaptation of margins standards; and the cost-of-living adjustment of the 'needs' standard in the basic wage. The suspension of the 'needs' adjustment combined with high wartime and post-war taxation had significantly reduced the real wage 'floor' represented by the basic wage.

Reconsideration of the 'needs' award in 1946 was taken up as a resumption of the suspended hearings of 1940 as a result of an application by the Federal Attorney-General during what was a Standard Hours Case in 1946. The 1946 award, particularly as an 'interim' award, was the product of direct (Labor) government intervention. The six-year suspension reflected government determination to hold wage increases in a highly inflationary situation. The deliberate relaxation of constraint on the lower levels of wage rates represented a significant reduction of relative margins for skill, margins that had already been shrinking because of the non-adjustment of margins for price increases.

Tardiness in the relaxation of wage constraint and the narrowing of margins may have been part of the issues in the frequency and severity of labour disputes in the second half of the forties. It was, perhaps, unfortunate that the effects of this relaxation, once begun, were working through the wage structure at the outbreak of the Korean War. Then intense inflationary pressure, from external sources, accelerated the increase in price-adjusted wages and encouraged the spread of over-award agreements. A major task confronting the new Liberal Administration was to recover control of labour prices.

Radical changes in regulatory principles were initiated in 1953-54, reversing the basic approaches of the Federal Labor Government. In September 1953, the Federal Court announced the abandonment of quarterly cost-of-living adjustments - the indexation of the 'needs' component of the basic wage. In November 1954, the Court substituted new principles on which all determinations were proposed subsequently to be based. The foundations of these principles remained obscure but in essencé they provided for

(a) a large-scale increase in margins in the metal trades;

(b) the recognition that these margins would need successive reconsideration to ascertain a 'true' value;

(c) the provision for a flow-on to other employees; and

(d) the advice to other tribunals already adopting Federal awards and others that regarded the Federal Court as 'of persuasive authority' to adopt these Federal proposals and the provision for proportionate adjustments throughout industry.

These rulings provided for the rapid flow-on of a particular Court decision to a large fraction of Australian workers. For those not directly affected, the flow-on depended on claims in other jurisdictions and was not necessarily complete or consistent. Nevertheless, this 1954 award was critical in the Australia-wide process of wage bargaining and wage determination for the subsequent thirteen years. It initiated a highly (if not completely) centralised system in which a trial claim for margins adjustment was to a large extent automatically applied proportionately across the board. It introduced explicitly the concept of 'comparative wage justice' so that relative margins were preserved. It provided the foundations for wage leadership by the metal trades as a powerful skilled union. It invited the successive reappraisal of margins as National Wage Cases. And it implied the opportunity for the assessment of altered relativities between occupations on the basis of 'true values'. From this obscure reference came subsequently the even more obscure search for the assessment of 'work value' - to a large extent affecting highly skilled and particularly professional groups seeking to upgrade their rewards for skill.

Major determinations followed this 1954 decision, setting a basic wage and margins adjustments in 1959, 1963, 1965, 1966 and 1967. In 1967, the division into basic wage and margins was abandoned and the concept of a 'total wage' was adopted. In addition to these five major margins cases, there were also Basic Wage Inquiries held by the Commonwealth Court in 1956, 1956-57, 1958, 1959, 1960, 1961, 1964 and 1966. In only two years between 1954 and 1967 was the Court not engaged in major general investigations and determinations.

In the 1959 Metal Trades Case, the Court introduced a new procedure of a *proportionate* increase in the margin for metal trade workers, with flow-on provisions. Accordingly from this point, djustment of wages across industry was made faster by the apparent simplicity of the rule of thumb of across-the-board proportional adjustments. In practice, declared percentage changes in margins for the major occupations accentuated also the wage push towards inflation. This procedure continued until 1967.

The invitation in the 1954 Metal Trades Award to attempt to determine the 'true value' of margins also led other tribunals both at the Federal level (especially the Public Service Arbitrator) and State tribunals to engage in Work Value Inquiries. The Federal Court itself became deeply immersed in a Metal Trades Work Value Case in 1966. These investigations led the tribunals into a highly detailed examination of work performed, the characteristics of occupations and occupational gradings and the nature of skills on a scale and to a degree that they had not formerly undertaken. Work value cases were undertaken partly to establish margins not previously determined. More frequently, they were a response to pressures from groups anxious to improve their relative wage and salary status. The declaration of the 1954 Metal Trades Award provided for percentage adjustments to existing margins in other trades, provisionally regardless of the existing relevance of those margins. The Court and its associated tribunals initially adopted the practical wisdom of varying relativities on rule-of-thumb basis where 'comparative wage justice' was regarded as seen not to be done by single proportionate adjustments. But the recognition of comparative wage justice provided different unions with the grounds for frequent appeal to catch up on Court awards to particular groups. This initiated a spiral of claims for comparative justice, which in a condition of full employment was not easy to restrain. It was in the extreme cases of these claims that full-scale 'work value cases' were undertaken.

The relevance of Commonwealth awards in these major basic wage and related margins cases may be seen from the fact that, by 1963, they applied immediately or by automatic flow-on to 42 per cent of male wage and salary earners. But, in addition, New South Wales and Victorian awards accounted for an additional 26 per cent of male workers. Since these tribunals followed the basic Federal declarations, sometimes with some delay, the Federal decisions were dominant with respect to 68 per cent of all male workers. In practice, the other States followed relatively closely. During the fifties, in effect, the whole system of wage regulation had become highly centralised in the Federal Court, with other tribunals to a large extent *de facto* derivative agencies. Before the second world war, a central feature of labour market regulation was that it had achieved a high degree of rigidity in wage rates. The experience of the fifties and sixties provided a technique for the rapid upward adjustment of rates.

The contrast between pre-war and post-war speed and scope of intervention and of the centralisation of regulation is well illustrated in the determination of standard hours. The determinations on the 44-hour week occupied most of the 1920s and 1930s and in some cases extended into the war. First granted as a general rule by the New South Wales legislature in 1920, the reduction in hours was withdrawn in 1921. In 1920, also, the Commonwealth Court granted a 44-hours' week to two industry groups but reintroduced a 48-hour week in 1921. Legislative action in Queensland provided for a 44-hour week in 1924 and similar legislation followed in New South Wales in 1926. The Commonwealth Court adopted the 44-hour week in 1927 in an engineering case and permitted individual applications to be brought under the ruling, subject to investigation of the nature of the industry, foreign competition and the financial status of the relevant enterprises. The depression was partly responsible for the delay in extending the provision for reduced hours under Commonwealth jurisdiction. Apart from New South Wales and Queensland, no legislation was passed so that employees in these other States not subject to

Federal awards faced a long-drawn-out process of individual application and disposal, extending over fifteen years from 1926 to 1941.

By contrast, the conversion from 44 to 40 hours, as applied subsequently to all workers under all jurisdictions, was confined effectively to six months, 1 July 1947 to 1 January 1948. Here the Commonwealth Court took the lead, and, as evidence unfolded, the New South Wales and Queensland Parliaments again legislated for universal application; the Western Australian Court of Arbitration adopted the Commonwealth ruling, a decision followed by the other States. The abrupt introduction led to considerable opposition from employers and two cases were brought, in 1952-53 and 1961, seeking extension of standard hours in conditions of recession. Both applications were rejected by the the Federal Court and no further action was taken.

In certain respects, this instance exaggerates the speed and completeness of centralisation of wage regulation. New South Wales was the first to fall most completely in line with Federal decision. Victoria maintained cost-of-living adjustments to the basic wage until 1956 and Queensland until 1961. Queensland also maintained more definite regional differences in wage rates. But these along with some independence in Western Australia and Tasmania were relatively minor deviations from centralisation.

Full employment in a regulated market was an occasion for a considerable number of changes in relativity and in the award of substantial fringe benefits. Female wage relativities were raised from the latter part of the war until, in 1969, the principle of equal pay was accorded. Paid annual leave was provided Federally for all relevant workers in 1963, having first been adumbrated in 1936; the Federal ruling was followed by the States almost immediately. In 1964, long-service leave was provided by the Commonwealth Arbitration Commission for a very wide range of workers, reaching its full extension in 1966. This determination followed earlier initiative by State tribunals (e.g. New South Wales in 1951) but in most States the award of this benefit was not completed until after the 1966 decision of the Commonwealth Commission.

Perhaps not surprisingly, the period 1950 to 1965 was one of the least disturbed by industrial disputes in the twentieth century. Regulation was increasingly expedited and determinations applied widely throughout Australia by flow-on provisions. Determinations were basically favourable to employees; in sustained boom conditions, high awards did not lead to unemployment other than in slight recessions. In regulatory terms, this comparative peace was shattered soon after the Commonwealth Commission resolved to abandon basic wage and margins decisions to initiate a 'total wage' concept and to adopt systems of National Wage Inquiries in 1967. This decision placed wage determination centrally in macro-regulation, with wage adjustments being determined explicitly with primary attention to general economic conditions and much less to the particular characteristics of specific industries. In the management approach of the Federal Government, the older equity considerations declined and the role of wage rates as a price to clear the market acquired increasing prominence. One effort was made specifically to restrain wage demands: the introduction of wage indexation that harkened back to the system adopted in the 1920s and abandoned in 1953.

Briefly, this lowered concern with equity was reversed under the Whitlam Government, when Federal intervention in National Wage Cases became a means of supporting larger wage demands, leading to a significant redistribution of income. These increases enhanced inflationary pressures, reduced the ability of the market to clear labour supplies and introduced new threats to the arbitration system. The final contribution of the Whitlam Government in this area was to use wage indexation in an effort to preserve the income redistribution that had been achieved. This was a return, in principle, to the system abandoned in 1953, through it was now applied to all wage incomes. The incoming Fraser Government limited the application of indexation in attempt to restrain wage inflation.

Rural regulation to 1972

The outbreak of the Second World War quickly brought the introduction of wartime powers of acquisition of virtually every rural commodity by the Federal Government and the establishment of statutory boards to carry out the process of acquisition, price control and disposal of output. A multiplicity of regulatory authorities was accordingly established, in the main strongly representative of growers' interests. Without following through the details of wartime regulation, several points are worth noting.

1. The pre-war establishment of growers' associations simplified the identification of grower representatives. While permitting this representation, the easy identification also exposed the different industry groups to political and bureaucratic influence. Acting as sources of information and advice and offering channels of communication in wartime emergency, they speeded the application of wartime controls. This was particularly important in the light of wartime and immediate post-war output and price policies.

2. This exposure became immediately relevant to rural output and manpower measures. The first reaction was concern at the prospect of wartime stock accumulations as in 1914-1918. Hence output restriction was imposed in the first half of the war. Growers were licensed,

output possibilities determined and manpower withdrawn from rural activities. Under American influence, Australia was required to convert to a wartime rural supplier and output policies were reversed in 1943, with manpower reallocations and priority diversion of inputs of machinery and fertiliser to farming. Though this reversal was largely negated in the short run due to drought, it gave farming a head start in the conversion to peace.
3. Drought conditions nevertheless led to the immediate post-war concern with farm incomes and the stabilisation of farm activity. This was particularly pressing in the light of the relief needs for food in Europe.
4. The exposure of grower representatives to central regulation was also peculiarly important in that as members of statutory boards they were required, for substantially a decade, to administer the reversal of the pre-war two-price system: partly to restrain domestic inflation, partly for purposes of protecting consumers, domestic prices were generally held below world prices. In post-war conditions, this reversal of regulation required a greater emphasis on subsidies and bounties on production and was exposed to increasing stress as world inflation developed ahead of price movements in Australia.

The immediate regulatory provisions after the war were designed, then, to provide for the stabilisation of farm prices and incomes and the equalisation of prices across the two general markets, domestic and international. But since domestic prices were held below world prices, the problem of subsidising domestic as distinct from foreign sales became a somewhat more complicated regulatory problem. This was in part resolved by the determination of guaranteed prices to growers based on costs of production and the subsidising of prices to cover the margin between domestic prices and production costs. In the circumstances of high world demand, no proposals for output constraint were considered; on the contrary official measures were designed to encourage output expansion. What was not foreseen in the fifties was the scale of expansion and increase in farm productivity that subsequently occurred; nor was the speed of the reversal of relationship between domestic and export prices anticipated.

Given the dimension of output, a very severe income constraint was imposed on wheat growers until the fifties. Guaranteed prices by regulatory bodies led to relatively little subsidy payments to any industry thanks to high world prices. The control of the direction of sales flow, except in the case of the dairy industry, transferred very large sums from growers to consumers until after the Korean War. Publicly controlled bulk storage and pooling of output had largely withdrawn from farmers' control the ability to shift sales to preferred markets.

This problem was accentuated during the Korean War. But it was as quickly reversed with rapid price declines for farm products in the early fifties. Then, and continuing into the mid-sixties, the guaranteed price provisions, pooling and controlled marketing restored the pre-war arrangement of domestic prices sustained artificially above world prices. But an additional element was added. The early post-war guaranteed price schemes proposed the setting of prices at 'cost of production'. As world prices (and more particularly, equalised prices) fell below the cost of production of the least efficient high-cost producer, the question of subsidising farmers became a significant problem of regulation.

During the fifties and first half of the sixties, no attempt to constrain production was made. The boards that had existed under National Security powers were converted to civilian statutory authorities. Enabling legislation was provided by Federal and State authorities to permit producers to take regulatory initiative in the establishment and running of marketing boards and to protect them and the relevant governments against legal challenge. Import restraints were provided and State quotas established to protect boards and growers from overseas or inter-state competition. The quasi-monopoly structure of the rural industries, developing before the war, was now much more firmly established. Regulatory prescription varied from commodity to commodity, with its degree of detail indicated by the legislation for a Federal poll-tax on hens to strengthen organised egg marketing.

The extent of the changing income constraint on and change in protection provided to rural industries may be indicated approximately in Table 5.1. Table 5.1 shows the approximate calculation for the years 1948-49, 1955-56 and 1964-65, indicative of a strong movement towards the pre-war restoration of 'protection all round' in the farm sector.

TABLE 5.1 **Measure of protection for agricultural products, 1948–49, 1955–56 and 1962–63 (world prices = 100)**

	1948–49	1955–56	1962–63
Butter	89	114	139
Cheese	87	105	111
Wheat	73	93	102
Sugar	78	104	126
Eggs	85	108	119
Dried fruits	97	108	113
Barley	77	97	100
Rice	94	104	109

Source: Williams, ed. (1967, p. 309).

The administered guaranteed prices, paid on aggregate production and based on marginal costs, operated to support inefficient farming and to provide 'surplus' profits to above-marginal farmers. It encouraged expansion of small-scale farming that would not otherwise have been viable while providing large-scale benefits to large, more efficient farming. The preservation of high-cost farming implied an allocation of resources towards the rural sector that would not otherwise have occurred and created a major social problem of restructuring that was becoming recognised by the first half of the sixties.

Advantages to large-scale farming and encouragement to allocate resources in rural activities were not, however, confined to marketing and guaranteed prices. Statutory boards were able to take a much more prominent role than before the war in the promotion of sales and negotiation of overseas disposal. Thus the entire overseas marketing of beef, mutton and lamb came to be regulated by the Australian Meat Board which acted as a principal in negotiations determining guaranteed prices in the UK market and in setting shipping charges. By the early sixties the Board came to control directly the disposal of 45 per cent of beef and 33 per cent of mutton exported and operated a licensing system to control the kinds of meat exported and their destinations and, by organising slaughtering inspections, attempted to regulate export quality.

In the case of wheat, a trading monopoly was assured by complementary State and Federal legislation so that the entire export disposal of wheat and flour was subject to the Australian Wheat Board. Under the Board's authority, the storage and rail transport of wheat was handled by grain elevator boards acting as the Board's agents, government funding of advances to growers was assured by the Commonwealth and later the Reserve Bank and the Board administered progress payments to growers as wheat was progressively sold.

In domestic marketing, statutory controls became much tighter. Thus in the marketing of fresh milk, control was operated by milk marketing boards under State legislation. The Boards, with defined regional monopolies, were authorised to purchase milk and sell at prices fixed for both producers and consumers and thereby also controlled distributors' gross margins. The Boards were empowered to fix prices, determine vendors' areas, license suppliers, distributors and vendors and enforce minimum health and quality standards.

The organisational structure became increasingly a State-supported and -funded 'monopoly' system. Underlying this were other major measures to assist farm expansion and to induce resource allocation towards farming. The most continuous system of intervention, apart from the long-established freight concessions on railway carriage, was through Federal tax intervention and the provision of special subsidies.

It is typically claimed that, until 1947, farmers were provided with investment incentives through depreciation provisions only to the extent, standard throughout business, of tax deductible allowances based on the expected lives of assets. Formally, this is correct. However, it obscures the fact that under tax provisions up to 1947 farmers could claim depreciation allowances *plus* replacement outlays. In part, at least, there was a double depreciation provision. In 1947, however, farmers were allowed to write off by tax claims full outlays related to land improvement and land clearing, including dam construction. This concession was followed in 1952 with the provision that depreciation allowances on other capital outlays were raised from those based on life expectancies of assets (generally at 2.5 per cent p.a.) to as much as 20 per cent p.a. At the same time, farmers continued to claim replacement outlays as fully tax deductible.

The incentive to purchase capital equipment and to invest in new capital assets was substantially enhanced by these measures. The benefits of such a measure were gained most importantly by those able to fund these outlays, a benefit attracting not only large-scale farmers but others who looked to farming as a subsidiary investment outlet - the so-called 'Pitt Street' farmers.

These incentives coincided with another public sector input into farming, the introduction of myxomatosis virus to destroy rabbits as pests consuming both pastures and grains. Myxomatosis was the product of happenstance and research by the CSIRO, subsequently supported by ANU. The destruction of rabbits by virus disease and subsequently by poisons represented a major act of 'biological warfare' by the public sector. It opened the way to pasture improvement and to the expansion of grain production. As such, it represented the fruition of public sector research and development, dramatically enhancing the production possibilities of the rural sector.

Closely related to myxomatosis was the public sector research into trace elements and the related significance of fertilisers in Australian farming. Experimental studies of plant introduction, combined with fertilisers, trace elements and the elimination of rural pests, opened the way for large-scale expansion of rural activities - a way that had been largely blocked since the early thirties by rabbits as rural pests. In the early fifties, these public inputs transformed the growth potential.

The ultimate aid to expansion, given the absence of restraint on production, was the introduction of subsidies to fertiliser application. This became a major provision in the early sixties, based on rule-of-thumb criteria. The emphasis was to favour large-scale rural enterprise and those farmers who were sufficiently liquid or creditworthy to support property acquisition, increase in farm size and new capital outlays. Increasingly, intervention to 1965 led to declining viability of small-scale farming. The basic approach at the beginning of the century, closer settlement, was in process of reversal. So, too, was the willingness of government to continue subsidising guaranteed prices without production limits. This changing attitude was coupled with the growing consciousness that restructuring was necessary.

These changes of allocative approach emerged haltingly and with some considerable inconsistencies. It is important, nevertheless, to register that declining public sector support for unconstrained private production decisions and increased public concern for direct intervention to restructure rural activity emerged in the course of the ten years 1962 to 1972 and particularly after 1965.

This change was signalled in 1962 when the Federal Government set a ceiling on dairying industry bounties equal to the payments made, on an average, over the preceding five years. The cost-of-production criterion for price guarantees was abandoned. But the important decision to alter rural regulation was made in 1968 with the Wheat Industry Stabilisation Plan, affecting a large part of the rural sector. The cost-of-production basis of guaranteed prices was abandoned and guaranteed prices were linked instead to world price movements. Wheat quotas were set to limit price guarantees to a given proportion of average deliveries of the preceding five years, a recognition that preceding guarantees and subsidies had encouraged the generation of unmanageable surplus. It is possible also that British movements towards the EEC may have prompted attempts to cut back output.

These approaches implied a substantial decline in incomes for marginal producers. In 1968, the Federal Government initiated a limited program of restructuring. It established a fund ($25m) to apply to 1968 to 1971, to assist large farmers to buy out small ones, amalgamating holdings into larger units in the dairy industry. The scheme provided credit to purchasers and also allowed for the subsidised exit of small farmers by compensating purchasers for unwanted improvements included in a regulated sale price. This method of restructuring was applied to non-dairy farmers in 1971. A variant was added to grant a small loan to sellers to assist in re-establishment out of the industry. The schemes required detailed inspection and evaluation of farms to be sold and the assessment of net worth of departing farmers. In practice by 1972 only a small number of farmers were induced to transfer out. In the longer run, greater success was achieved with the restructuring of dairying.

The regulation of industrialisation

For a variety of reasons, the Federal Government played by far the leading public sector role in the regulation of post-1945 industrialisation in Australia. State Governments continued to offer, on non-market terms, facilities in the form of access to land, overhead capital of roads and transport services and the supply of inputs in the form of energy and waste disposal. However, these facilities and services were primarily relevant to location of manufacturing and particular specific types of activity such as vehicle and accessory manufacturing, petroleum refining (in which the Commonwealth, in any event, had important regulatory control) and in extra-metropolitan decentralisation measures (again, chiefly the supply of land and overhead facilities). While, before 1939, the vast proportion of manufacturing enterprise was local Australian enterprise with a significant British presence, and while the factory enterprises were largely Statewide in terms of establishment ownership, the States had a significantly more exclusive authority. After 1945, the States were more concerned to compete for the location of particular establishment segments of nation-wide concerns and indeed, for fragments of foreign multinational enterprises. Moreover, the nature of industrial development after 1945 pushed the States further and further into some old and some new forms of constraint as distinct from encouragement, and in this they were joined by local authorities. Metropolitan concentration of factory activity imposed greater pressures for land-use controls and factory extensions on existing industrial land. The zoning controls became much more prominent as a constraining element. In addition, factory inspection systems for purposes of safety conditions and employees' welfare acquired greater restraining significance, particularly with trade union power underpinned by sustained high employment. Finally, the particular technological developments of industrialisation, combined with its area concentration, led to increasingly powerful pressures to restrain particular modes of industrial technology - initially air pollution through particulates, subsequently other air polluting emissions, the disposal of dangerous solid wastes and, eventually, the disposal of massive liquid waste flows. Many of these constraints emerged from the impact of private technology on the public sector itself rather than the pressures of environmental or conservation interests. Thus the most impelling pressures for effective inspection and the ordering of systematic liquid waste disposal under public sector approval appear to have arisen from loss and damage to public sector property and workforce rather than from complaints over the loss of environmental amenity.

These tendencies to increasing *constraint* in some areas of factory decision-making evolved, however, partly as a product of the growth of manufacturing.

The post-war regulation of manufacturing became much more Federally centralised than it had been before 1939. In this respect, the trend of regulation followed the pattern of both labour market and rural regulation. In the long run, the financial power of the Commonwealth was an important contributory factor, with Federal powers enhanced by the Uniform Tax Agreement 1942, the influence of the Loan Council and Premiers' Conference and the adoption of Federal funding of much of State capital works from current Federal revenues. From these powers flowed such consequences as exclusive Federal company taxation and its variation, Federal investment allowances, Federal payroll tax and indirect taxes imposed on manufactured products by the Federal Government.

The war itself provided an additional major factor, placing Federal authorities astride the decision-making process in factory activity. The retention of National Security powers for the first five years after the war, in circumstances of inflationary pressures, extensive shortages of key materials and the degeneration of physical plant and equipment in factories, placed major authority in the hands of the Federal Government. This authority was exercised, within the confines of the general objective of emphasising private decision-making in conversion to peace, above all through some price controls, general capital issue controls, controls (often indirect) over bank advances, exchange controls and the regulation of imports.

It is relevant to the process of centralisation that, in the early post-war years, this Federal regulation applied at least as much to State and local works activities as to private manufacturing decision-making. Initial Federal action attempted to transfer *existing* factory establishments to private enterprise decision-making. But priority was, perforce, given to the restoration of radically degraded social overhead facilities (that were largely provided by State and local authorities) in order to restore the basis of the private manufacturing system. Thus extreme energy and transport shortages had to be overcome before effective private conversion operations could proceed. The allocative decisions of State and local authorities were accordingly closely controlled to provide a central direction. This centralisation was enhanced initially by the necessity to import much of the basic plant and equipment not only for public sector restoration but also for private recovery and growth. The subsequent dependence on much imported equipment for large-scale factory development preserved this Federal authority beyond the short run of National Security powers. Immediate post-war problems of the British economy, the weakness of the sterling area and Australian commitment to protect the sterling area (however wavering that constraint was) added strength to Federal authority in the rationing of imported equipment.

It is part of Australian political mythology that the election of the conservative Federal Government in 1949 restored free enterprise and reintroduced a climate favourable to a free market system. It is possible that this claim may have some justification for the two years 1950 and 1951, during the Korean War. In the high boom conditions created essentially by American war procurement purchases of Australian wool, intense inflationary conditions developed; with massive dollar earnings, the general restriction on importing was removed and similar massive private importing occurred. During 1951, with the cessation of American procurement orders, inflationary pressures dissipated, severe balance of payments disequilibrium developed and substantial local unemployment appeared. The belated result was the reimposition of Federal direct controls and the close (if variable) budgeting of all imports throughout the fifties; for some important imports direct restrictions persisted beyond 1960.

The extensive industrialisation whose peacetime basis was laid during the fifties was, therefore, established in conditions of direct Federal control and oversight of the entire range of imports and the allocation of import quotas that were key to this industrialisation. Import restrictions had been imposed in 1939. Thus for substantially two decades (except for 1950 and 1951), the high protective tariff of Australia ceased to be the essential instrument of protection. Indeed, in so far as tariffs were still relevant considerations in import competition, their significance was in many cases also eroded by inflation, particularly after 1949. Import licensing and quota restrictions became the key regulatory instruments for macro- and micro-economic policy directly determining the conditions of domestic competition with foreign imports but also regulating the flow of foreign inputs into local manufacturing. From this point, direct import restrictions, combined with the tariff, also became key negotiating instruments arranging the terms of direct foreign investment in and the acquisition of foreign technology and managerial skills by Australian manufacturing.

We are not concerned here to attempt to 'explain' industrialisation, but merely to try to define the interrelations between public and private action in the process. In practice, the very large increase in direct foreign investment (with accompanying technology) automatically brought many new enterprises within the Federal constitutional ambit without conscious public initiative. Industrial development became intimately linked to the Commonwealth trade power as foreign newcomers, not yet geographically located, sought to move behind the Australian quota and tariff barrier and to produce locally rather than supply by trade. Trade, budgetary, monetary, exchange and immigration powers - all centred in Federal authority - were the main conditions for controlling foreign entry. It is not intended to imply in what follows that the whole process of manufacturing development in the fifties, in particular, was the result of Federal policy and intervention. There were strong incentives for foreign interests to move into the Australian economy by direct new investment or by the takeover of existing firms. Nevertheless, the mode and circumstances of this entry and the takeover process was significantly influenced and the structural outcome significantly altered by Federal intervention. One of the most important structural implications was the preservation - perhaps, though the data are inadequate, the increase - of restrictive market structure and restrictive practices and the very high degree of business concentration in Australian manufacturing.

Quota and tariff measures were not the only major points of government intervention. Massive injections of human capital were supplied by sustained, large-scale immigration programs with public support, supplying skilled and semi-skilled labour and enlarging the local market. Exchange controls provided a means of oversight of capital transfers and the repatriation of profits. Domestically, the terms of company taxation and the provision of investment allowances were important factors affecting allocative decisions through Federal action. So, too, were the adaptations of domestic indirect taxes. In addition, the provision of bounties on specified ranges of manufacturing activity provided added allocative effect. As manufacturing expanded, Federal export promotion programs moved to support private initiative.

Finally, but by no means least, direct Federal (and State) intervention in the initiatives to establish particular important manufacturing projects did more than merely signal Australia as a genial host of foreign capital: it provided the security of public commitment to projects and the assurance of benefits and concessions to private interests. However, initiation of direct foreign manufacturing enterprises tended to be followed by Australian government administrative pressures to increase the Australian 'content' (the local value-added component) ostensibly to enhance the domestic advantages of foreign activity. This led to increasingly close oversight and performance testing by the public sector and the use of market-sharing devices, importing concessions, the threats of arranged 'competition' (perhaps, more accurately, publicly controlled market sharing). This was most notably the case with motor vehicle manufacture, attempts to introduce which went back since the pre-war years. The attraction of General Motors into full-scale Australian manufacturing was accompanied by land and service facilities, quota priorities on imported inputs and tariff concessions on imported inputs including by-law entry. Similar concessions were offered to other car manufacturers and a local oligopolistic situation established with 'local' foreign manufacturers and importers. The existence of substantial imports was an important condition for sustained pressure to increase local manufacturing content.

Except for two areas, the public sector exercised no prohibitions on the activities into which direct foreign capital might flow either by direct new investment or by takeover until the mineral boom. The mineral boom brought confused and changing efforts to establish formulas limiting foreign interest in mineral projects. But until this boom was fully developed only two non-manufacturing areas were prohibited for foreign investors: television and radio broadcasting and banking. For manufacturing in general, there was open house to foreign capital, to the limits of total ownership and control. This implies also that there was an unfettered process of takeovers of local firms and, indeed, in the fifties and sixties extensive takeovers occurred.

The ability to direct entry through trade controls and concessions, to structure market shares, to induce growth and Australian content, combined with the permissive attitude to takeovers, enhanced the tendencies to oligopoly and high market concentration that is a basic feature of Australian manufacturing. Closely related to this, the public sector support to domestic restrictive practices in providing the legal foundations for trade associations gave positive encouragement to widespread monopolistic practices throughout Australian industry. By the early 1960s, several hundred overlapping trade associations existed, registered under public sector support, providing for a variety of restrictive practices of price fixing, tied purchase and sale arrangements, collusive tendering and the like. By the mid-sixties serious doubts were beginning to surface about the wisdom, whether on grounds of efficiency or equity, of these restrictive practices and oligopolistic structures. In the meantime, foreign enterprise was firmly ensconsed in Australian manufacturing - so much so that almost a third of all company profits after tax were payable overseas.

Some of these processes of intervention required only general directives or simple variations of rules where changes occurred in policy or administration. This was true of provisions such as company taxation, investment allowances and indirect taxation. These were, however, also most exposed to the variations of macro-management and opened industrial development to the short-term 'needs' of stop-go policies. Others, however, led to detailed bureaucratic intervention, whether in assisting in the promotion or expansion of industries or in the structuring of markets. In this respect, the programs of immigration and of trade controls were perhaps the most far-reaching and intricate.

Large-scale immigration programs adopted after the war appeared to resume the pre-war course of expansion. The devotion to high immigration targets persisted into the early sixties until this basic tenet of Australian faith came seriously under question. Initially acquiring displaced persons, the migration program may properly be looked at in the longer run as an interventionist approach to the acquisition of human capital above all to service the labour input requirements of industrialisation. Particularly in the fifties, when the Australian additions to the workforce by natural increase were abnormally low, these public endeavours were more than an alternative to the local genera-

tion of human capital for factory purposes. Indeed, as the public sector supported this migrant inflow, it embarked on large-scale support
for higher education with a massive increase in student retention in
(generalised) secondary education and in tertiary education, limiting
the flow of the Australian-born into sub-professional skilled employment.

The use of trade measures was, however, much more extensive and
opened up a large array of political and bureaucratic modes of intervention not merely in the promotion of manufacturing but also in
the protection of existing industry and the structuring of markets.
This was particularly the case throughout the fifties with the generalised application of import licensing and quota restrictions. But even
after tariffs were restored in the sixties as the dominant protective instrument, the commitment to furthering the Australian content of
manufacturing sustained a great deal of detailed political and
bureaucratic attention to manufacturing.

The general application of quota restrictions from 1952 to 1960
placed the Federal Government in the position to provide
discriminatory encouragement to particular industries, to induce a
discriminatory allocation of imported inputs and to provide
discriminatory protection against import competition. That it had indeed in a major way pursued non-market objectives emerged most obviously once the role of the Tariff Board was restored in 1960. The
more independent appraisal of the Board made possible a careful
assessment of protection needs and the extent of encouragement that
had been given to high-cost industries in the fifties. An investigation
and assessment of the Board's appraisal would be an important
research task. It would also be important to explore the extent to
which the use of quotas for macro-management purposes conflicted
with the allocative policy of government and of the market.

The introduction of quotas led to action directly affecting the
relative profitability of different industry areas. Administration
depended on planning total import levels over varying time horizons
(a Cabinet decision), the systems of preference in quota allocations to
be provided (Cabinet, separate Ministers and officials), the methods
of administration and the prescription of rules for importers
(Ministerial and official) including progressive adjustment of allocations between different applicants and users, the establishment of a
network of day-to-day licensing and the provisions for dealing with
hardship cases and anomalies (officials). The scale of public sector intervention is displayed in the fact that, on an average, some 300 staff
members of the Department of Trade were required to assess and
decide on some 150 000 cases and authorise the issue of some 500 000
licences annually, while the Department of Customs and Excise actually issued licences and Reserve Bank officials authorised the alloca-

tion of foreign exchange. It should be recognised that these decisions would have been made by private traders under a tariff system. It is also relevant that a high proportion of importers were also final consumers of the licensed imports so that quota administration directly regulated, in many cases, domestic industrial activity and not merely the business of wholesale importers. So extensive was this direct intervention that only 2 per cent of all imports (actually passengers' luggage and imports from Australian Territories) were exempt.

Initially post-war quota control had been part of the Australian commitment to the sterling area so that import budgeting and the control of the source of imports were directly influenced by advice from the British Government on the changing state of 'hard' currencies. Throughout the whole period, the US dollar was the primary target for constraint but after the Korean War and the upsurge of Australian dollar earnings, policy in allocating quotas between different currency areas became essentially a matter of Australian decision-making. This became most importantly the case as US direct investment rose rapidly in Australian manufacturing. Then, it became an important instrument of public sector intervention that quota and tariff concessions on imported inputs were made to chosen foreign investors - essentially implying relaxation of quota restrictions on US supplies of plant and equipment and hence more severe constraint on other importers of US goods.

There is no space here to attempt to describe the details of the varieties of quota systems. The import budgets varied considerably in severity because of macro-management considerations. Import licensing and quotas were used as a key method of coping with both internal and external balance. The system that was adopted under conservative administration in 1952 was regarded as a temporary measure. Controls tightened throughout 1953 and then were progressively relaxed to early 1955. Thereafter a renewed period of tighter control was applied to 1959, this time on the assumption that the system might be an enduring feature of public sector regulation. Relaxation after 1959 brought, in fact, a strong business revolt against the system (and widespread academic criticism) leading to its abandonment as a general system in 1960. Quota restrictions continued to apply to a limited range of imported goods until 1962 when these too were freed. Thereafter quotas were applied intermittently to specific goods as special protective devices (e.g. textiles). Essentially from 1962, the tariff was restored as the mode of protection and the Tariff Board resumed its former role. But now the Board functioned in an environment of public and private interest that was very different from its pre-1940 experience.

When the tariff was once more revealed, it acquired an immediate significance that was essentially an unintended and long-term echo of

1929 to 1931. Subject to the relatively minor adjustments of the tariff during the thirties, the *formal* structure of the tariff was that established for emergency anti-depression purposes by Scullin in 1929. But the relevance of this structure was, in 1960, radically altered. This was due to three sets of circumstances:

(a)   The range and complexity of Australian manufacturing had expanded radically.

(b)   The sources of foreign competition with this manufacturing had shifted away from Britain and the Dominions and, in the main, also from those countries that had been accorded Most Favoured Nation treatment.

(c)   The Tariff Board, in its pre-war adjustments (reductions), had not paid significant attention to the General Tariff since this was largely, at that stage, of strictly formal relevance. The General Tariff level was accordingly the extremely high level of the 1929 Scullin tariff and it was this tier of the tariff that was now particularly relevant in 1960.

The Tariff Board resumed its conventional procedures of case-by-case consideration of applications for increased protection referred to it by the Minister, who had first been convinced by interested manufacturers that a case for reference existed. The Board did not undertake the studies of general investigation that it was empowered to attempt; it was rare that references for reduced tariff rates were made.

Accordingly, the Tariff Board had a much greater interventionist role than would otherwise have been the case. The failure to respond to the task of catching up with the realities of trade and industry had, however, other implications. The case-by-case review of special pleading applicants led to further creeping protection. Perhaps more importantly (the matter needs much closer investigation) the ad hoc tariff adjustments created wide inconsistencies in the treatment of different commodities. Since it was those that faced cost-price squeeze that appealed for higher protection, the process of review appeared to maximise the encouragement to least efficient output, and intentionally or unintentionally, low-cost firms were accorded the opportunity for higher profits.

This highly differentiated and piecemeal protection came increasingly under fire and the first step purporting to achieve a more systematic and more centralised intervention in industrial structure through tariff measures was made in 1968. Then the Tariff Board proposed and began to undertake a 'general review' declaring broad levels of effective protection to be allowed and adumbrating a policy of limited protection at less than 50 per cent. In fact, the Board's first attempts at measurement of effective protection showed that effective protection in the industries investigated (machinery and metals manufacture) was between 50 and 80 per cent.

The approach to protection as a general policy had become increasingly confused in the late sixties, with conservative governments reluctant to move but enfiladed by manufacturers' pressure and consumer and academic criticism (and Tariff Board reluctance to continue ad hoc protectionist procedures). In 1971 the Board undertook for the first time an effective large-scale review covering a combination of industries that had not been exposed to Board assessment for many years under the old appellant systems, to consider these industries in terms of interrelated commodities, to base evaluation on effective and not merely nominal rates of protection and to narrow the range of protection provided. These changes in approach led to heated public dispute between the Federal Government, manufacturers and the Board, a dispute that was a major factor in the demise of the Board and the substitution of the Industries Assistance Commission in 1972. In practice, this represented success for manufacturing enterprises, the Commission acting in the traditional case-by-case mode of the Board. Efforts by the Whitlam Government to expose Australian manufacturing to greater competition, including across-the-board tariff reduction, were a passing phenomenon in a society in which business was determined to use public means to preserve the status quo and to avoid the task of distributing the private costs of rationalisation. Moreover, governments accustomed to supporting the growth of manufacturing appeared to lack the initiative to act to achieve a selective restructuring. Efforts in this direction implied a denial of national ambitions that had persisted for at least half a century. The strength of a supportive role of government (subject to the conflicts of macro-economic policy) had become an obstacle to rational action.

Part Three
Social Policy

6

The Poor and the Needy 1901 to 1914

In the twenty years before 1914 major shifts in the balance between private and public decisions in fields of behaviour formerly subject almost exclusively to private choices within and beyond the market laid the foundations of Australia's welfare state. The labour market was constrained in a variety of ways. Most importantly, State-backed industrial tribunals brought widening sectors of employment under minimum-wage rules that, more and more, became associated with the consumption needs of a small family. Employers were required to compensate those injured at work and the families of those killed. The place of government in what had previously been regarded as the domain of private charity for those not in the workforce was changed and enlarged. Taxpayers were compelled through government budgets to contribute to cash transfers paid as pensions for the aged poor and invalids, as allowances to some widows and deserted wives with dependent children and as maternity benefits for women. The range as well as the volume of education services and of institutional health care services that governments subsidised or provided at a nominal direct charge, or at no charge, was increased.

This altered the patterns and the distribution of consumption and determined the minimum supply of those services. Moreover, by 1914 conferences of all political parties had discussed, and sometimes incorporated in their platforms, public action to provide pensions for widows and orphans, cash benefits for the unemployed, the sick and injured, and wider access to better hospital facilities. Australia's social laboratory was in process of establishing, through intervention in the labour markets, through cash transfers and through public services, floors to incomes and consumption of those in and outside the workforce. These developments were decades in advance of many other Western countries.

These developments implied a fundamental change in the role of government with respect to the individual. It had its origins in the hardening consciousness of class and the changing character of

Australian capitalism that emerged in the 1890s. Awareness of class was already highlighted in the great strikes at the beginning of the decade, the 'conflicts between Capital and Labour'. It was sharpened as depression brought reduced employment, income and wealth, reversing drastically the prospects of security and prosperity apparent over the preceding three decades and decimating trade union organisations built up before 1890. Expectations that had faithfully served a generation were shattered.

Universal male suffrage for the lower houses of colonial parliaments had already given some influence to low-income voters. Payment of members of parliament, the abolition of plural voting, and nascent political Labor parties based on trade unions enhanced that position. Unrepresentative upper houses remained the bastions of conservatism. A feature of the new Commonwealth parliament was therefore very significant: both houses were elected on a universal adult suffrage. In those evolutionary days of the party system in Australian politics, Labor members derived their power and their immediate legislative interests from their ability, as the only cohesive group, to exploit the bargaining weaknesses of the shifting coalitions that formed governments.

Though inspired by considerations of class and trade union interests, the development of this broad welfare program met with remarkably little opposition. To some extent this was because the changes were not always achieved by legislation. Some were due to bureaucratic, judicial or ministerial action - action not undone by subsequent legislation. The attitudes of many people who, from self-interest, might be expected to have resisted public intervention were tempered for several reasons. Organisational and political weakness of manufacturing employers led to bargains struck with trade unions. Backward-looking liberal lawyers and middle-class 'radicals' introduced important mediating influences. Other conservatives saw or came to realise that there were benefits to be gained from greater social stability. Ultimately, it is this seemingly widespread coincidence of private interests in the desirability of shifting certain responsibilities into the arena of collective choice that needs to be explored.

Social Security

For most of the first half of the twentieth century public social security benefits (veterans' benefits apart) were designed with the express purpose of advantaging limited dependent groups outside the workforce - the aged, the young and the disabled. That preoccupation could be sustained only because Australians thought they had solved the question of protecting the worker who was employed, and his family, and until the 1930s regarded unemployment as a temporary and (for most) infrequent hazard. Government intervention in the labour market influenced the level of employment and sought to influence the distribution of incomes between labour and capital, between workers in different industries and between workers with different skills. The series of experiments in the regulation of industrial relations from around the turn of the century was so fundamental to the welfare package that it is necessary to start with an account of how the floor to wages was established.

A floor to wages

The origins of the 'basic wage' that became an almost sacred feature of Australian life lay, institutionally, in the conjuncture of two issues that attracted increasing attention in the late 1890s. One related to the conciliation and arbitration of industrial disputes. The other grew from a concern about conditions in a few 'sweated' industries in which outwork, piecework, and/or the employment of women or Chinese were associated with very low wages and earnings.

In 1890 the idea of industrial arbitration was anathema to most trade unionists: direct confrontation and the strength of union organisation had proved effective. By contrast some employers, though by no means all, saw in it the only possibility of restraining the intransigence of labour. After the crushing defeat of the unions in the maritime strike in 1890 and in those of the following four years, interests were reversed as the strength of trade unions dwindled. Employers saw no need for state intervention: they could win any dispute. Organised labour turned more and more to politics and to arbitration, particularly compulsory arbitration whose finding was binding on both parties. Stable industrial relations served the interests of white-collar consumers and employers. Moreover, both these groups could see other potential advantages to themselves, especially when arguments were couched in terms of restoring the old, conservative parities. Experiments with various forms of arbitration and conciliation during the 1890s influenced the inclusion in the Commonwealth Constitution of power to legislate for arbitration and conciliation in respect of inter-State disputes. Compulsory arbitration was introduced in New South Wales in 1900 and in Western Australia by Acts of 1900 and 1902 and by the Commonwealth Act of 1904.

Arbitration bodies were designed to settle disputes between specified employers and organisations representative of employees and, by use of the common rule in the New South Wales and Commonwealth jurisdictions, to extend the terms of settlement to other parties similarly situated. Their wage determinations were equally specific to named occupational tasks and categories. The initial legislation contained no provision for them to establish, as they later did, a minimum wage across all industries. In practice, that function developed from the way the Victorian Government, in 1896, dealt with six 'sweated' trades. Wages Boards were created to fix minimum wages or rates for the trade over which each had jurisdiction. Enforcing the awards was a function of government factory inspectors. Public regulation of wages by this means, which was later adopted in South Australia, was extended to other trades and industries in and after 1900. Employers' interests were diverse, yet by and large they were persuaded to support, or at least not to oppose resolutely, the introduction of Wages Boards not only for sweated trades but also for the others. 'Unscrupulous' competition was a threat to importer and local manufacturer alike. Some employers, mistakenly as it turned out, saw the Boards as a restraint on the re-emergent strength of unionism. Others offered firm, though temporary, support as a means of securing working-class support for protectionism before and immediately after Federation.

The labour movement pursued other ways to influence wage rates. Through deputations and political representatives, trade unions urged governments and local authorities to set minimum wages for public employees, to use day labour rather than private contractors on public works and to include minimum wage provisions in public contracts. This pressure had limited success. In 1894 the New South Wales Government insisted that public works contractors pay no less than the current wage; in 1900 the Melbourne City Council put a minimum wage clause in its contracts and the New South Wales and Victorian Governments respectively made that requirement of suppliers of steel rails and of candles and clothing; and in 1902 the Commonwealth Public Service Act set a minimum for adult males employed under its provisions. Even where concessions were won they related, like the awards of industrial tribunals, only to specific groups and types of employees. Yet there was a broader purpose behind the demands: to re-establish the pre-depression market influence that governments had exerted on general, as well as on specific, wage levels. The altered pattern of economic activity doomed that hope from the very start. Nevertheless, it was in this elliptical fashion that the development of concepts of a 'living wage', below which *no* unskilled worker should be paid, began to overlap with the setting of minimum wages for specific occupational groups.

Although 'a minimum wage for all classes of workers' was incorporated as a plank in the platform of parliamentary Labor in New South Wales in 1898, employers were among those whose advocacy had been heard even earlier. Liberals like Deakin, Peacock and Sir Samuel Griffith, disturbed by the fall in wages for unskilled labour, raised the issue in 1893 and 1894. It was taken up, though with its humanitarian character distorted, by some Victorian employers who proposed that a single minimum wage should replace Wages Board determinations in 'sweated' industries and by some protectionists who saw it as a trade-off for labour's continued parliamentary support for tariff protection.

Important employers gave the notion of a minimum wage their backing early in the new century. Labour's anxiety to lift wage levels by non-market means was raised to new heights between 1903 and 1905 when Victorian Wages Boards and the New South Wales Court were weakened by legislative change and judicial attack. It was at this point that the political consideration of securing workers' support for at least some semblance of a protective Australian tariff induced manufacturers to accept, however reluctantly and temporarily, (potentially) wider public intervention in the labour market. The Excise Tariff Act of 1906 set a duty on the domestic production of agricultural machinery equal to the new import duty but provided that the excise would be waived if the manufacturer paid fair and reasonable wages. All but the most sophisticated and far-seeing manufacturer might be excused for believing that their support for this would not involve them in difficulty. Discussion of minimum wages had been conducted in terms that, over the preceding decade, had become less and less precise: the 'union rate', the 'current rate' and the wage paid by a 'reputable' employer. Specific minima had been set on these and similar criteria. But what could be made of a 'living' wage or of 'fair and reasonable'?

What employers overlooked was judicial autonomy. G. C. Heydon, President of the New South Wales Arbitration Court from 1905, indicated that he would be guided in his judgements not only by current market rates and prosperity within an industry but also by a duty to provide all workers with 'some small degree of comfort'. Mr Justice Higgins of the Federal Court went further when ruling on H. V. McKay's application for a declaration that wages paid at his harvester factory were 'fair and reasonable' in terms of the 1906 Excise Tariff Act. Higgins interpreted 'fair and reasonable' by bringing together the concepts of a minimum wage and of a living wage. The rule he set then and invoked subsequently was that every unskilled adult male worker's wage should be 'appropriate to the normal needs of the average employee regarded as a human being living in a civilised community ... sufficient to ensure the workman food, shelter, clothing, frugal comfort, provision for evil days, etc.'[1] This was the first time these criteria alone were used to determine a minimum wage, and Higgins set a monetary sum that he thought would satisfy them. Equity, not clearing the market, was the fundamental principle.

---

[1] *Commonwealth Arbitration Reports, 2*, pp. 3 and 4.

Ten or fifteen years passed before the concept of Higgins' minimum standard was generally accepted. Nevertheless, in 1912 Labor governments in New South Wales, Western Australia and South Australia legislated for judicial determination of 'living' or basic wages. In other States, tribunals adopted the practice in the 1920s. Ten or fifteen years passed too, before the real value of the Harvester wage was generally attained as the base rate, even though the Federal Court was concerned enough with its maintenance as early as 1911-12 to seek the Commonwealth Statistician's help in measuring price movements. By that time however the notion of a general minimum, determined by elements of an independent judiciary supported by the power of the state, had become too firmly entrenched to be dislodged by the use of available political power.

The unemployed

Even during the long boom before 1890, unemployment resulting from sickness or intermittent lack of work was a familiar experience for Australian workers, especially the unskilled. The circumstances of the boom itself created a generally sustained demand for labour and governments were easily persuaded to advance their public works programs in recessions as unemployment relief. In the 1890s, however, financial stringency restricted this outlet. Long-term continuing unemployment became a reality, trade union membership fell heavily and a new and potentially demanding set of interests was built up.

Despite those interests, there was little change in the ways the unemployed could get help to maintain minimum levels of consumption. A few of the richer craft unions, like the engineers, provided unemployment benefit; some skilled workers could use savings; many depended on family and even distant relatives. The unemployed were largely beyond the ambit of organised charity. Their wives and children sometimes received outdoor relief - gifts of food, clothing or fuel, occasionally rent money - from benevolent societies. Some private charities provided a meal, bread or a night's lodging to itinerants looking for work. Destitution, rather than unemployment, was typically the qualification for charitable assistance. While meetings, demonstrations and deputations mounted by the unemployed concentrated on persuading governments to create jobs for them, it was widely acknowledged that governments had a broader responsibility. Thus, Labour Bureaus were established to bring vacancies to the notice of job seekers. That in New South Wales had the added function of distributing rations to those in 'absolute want', and was officially classed as a charitable society. Labour colonies and labour farms were set up. Their original purpose of providing training to suit the destitute urban unemployed for rural occupations was rapidly downgraded and they became short-term stopover points where food and shelter could be got in exchange for nominal work. City dwellers were given railway tickets to go gold-fossicking or rabbiting. Rationed, unproductive relief work was provided at 'wages' that were indeed charitable relief.

These measures were typical of the variety of actions forced on governments by a general unwillingness to countenance widespread starvation and, implicitly, by apprehension that social tensions might become unmanageable. None of them made any basic alteration either to the relative roles of public and private action or to the prospects of those facing future unemployment. It was not until late in the first decade of the new century (with low unemployment) that, stimulated primarily by debates that led to the British unemployment insurance legislation in 1911, serious consideration was given to national insurance that would provide a floor to an unemployed worker's purchasing ability. Attitudes soon polarised and hardened. Conservatives favoured and Labor rejected a system that explicitly sought from wage earners a major proportion of the funds needed to support the unemployed. The perceptions of self-interest that these attitudes embodied were already of long standing and remained powerful elements determining social security provisions for another generation.

Protecting those not in the workforce

For the greater part of the nineteenth century the private sector played, overall, the dominant role in Australian welfare services and assistance. The basic premises were that care of the needy was essentially a family concern; that those who could should help themselves lest assistance sap their independent spirits and create a class of dependent poor; and that where assistance was justified it should be given in kind rather than in cash. It was built upon the charity and philanthropy of a Christian middle class - what Beatrice Webb called 'a class consciousness of sin' - that carried with it a deep fear of being cheated. Charity was to help the *deserving* poor and directed to benefit primarily the aged or infirm, the young and, such was the nature of the religious ethic, those for whom there was a chance of moral rehabilitation. The origins of these attitudes clearly lay in British values, reinforced perhaps by the very high living standards and prosperity sustained in Australia for thirty or forty years before the depression.

Private, non-profit, charities and religious groups provided a range of welfare institutions and services. Indoor relief, consisting at least of a bed for a night and at most of subsistence throughout the remainder of life, was available in institutions catering for the aged and infirm (often in association with hospitals, with which they had much in common). Other institutions provided that assistance to 'special' groups: orphans, inebriates and 'fallen' women, destitute women and children, old colonists or distressed actors, for the deaf, dumb and blind, and for released prisoners. Outdoor relief took the form of occasional meals, food, clothing, fuel or vouchers drawn on co-operating storekeepers. This became an increasingly pressing function in the 1890s. The charities were subsidised with public funds including, in some cases, statutory transfers of revenues from various categories of fines etc. Of 218 charitable societies and institutions reporting to the Victorian Statistician in 1904 only twelve were entirely independent of the public purse, and across Australia in the second half of the 1890s the institutions providing indoor relief received public aid equivalent to between a quarter and a third of their total expenditure.

Two dependent groups helped in these ways were eligible also for government assistance. For the care of the aged and infirm most governments established grim asylums. Destitute or neglected children were cared for in orphanages or, increasingly in the last decade of the century, boarded out with foster parents or indeed with their own mothers. Governments also made meagre provision for the support of Aboriginals, satisfying objectives of social control rather than of charity.

In the twenty years before 1914 the relative roles of public and private activity were altered substantially. Governments were induced to pay maternity benefits to all mothers, cash pensions to the aged poor and invalids and cash allowances to some deserted wives and widows.

One strand in the reassessment of attitudes and values that resulted in the Victorian and New South Wales old-age pension legislation in 1900 was the erosion of the belief that cash grants would create a dependent class devoid of thrift. Accompanying that was a strengthening rhetoric that society owed a right to those whose lives had been spent labouring to the common (Australian) good. It was an extension of the Australian nationalism that Gollan (1955, p. 146) saw: 'an equalitarian social doctrine, a belief in equality of opportunity, and a conviction that in Australia man had a right to the good life'. The preambles to the legislation made no bones about it. The Victorian Act referred to 'the duty of the State to make provision for its aged and helpless poor', and the New South Wales Act stated that 'it is equitable that deserving persons who during the prime of life have helped to bear the public burdens of the Colony by the payment of taxes, and by opening up its resources by their labour and skill, should receive from the Colony pensions in their an old age'. The right to old age free at least of desperate poverty was reinforced by a growing appreciation that putting people in institutions was not the only or best way of relieving want. This stemmed in part from conditions in asylums, with healthy and dying often jumbled indiscriminately together, man and wife often separated. From the late 1890s

Queensland applicants for assistance were offered an 'indigence allowance' as an alternative to institutional accommodation.

The age structure of the population exacerbated the problems of charity and fanned the self-interest of those who in later years might become claimants. Australia's immigrant base, and especially the influx during the 1850s, had created exceptional age groupings. But in the 1890s, the echo of this immigration was the growing percentage of old people, many of them without private support. In 1881 only 25 per thousand of the population was aged 65 or more; in 1891, 29; and in 1901, 40. Practical charity and practical politics were sensitive, however, not so much to the proportion of the population that was aged as to the absolute increase in their numbers. Over the decade of the 1890s net additions to those over 65 years amounted to almost 60 000 - two thirds of the number existing in 1891. Even more tellingly, perhaps, the number of aged women increased a third more rapidly than that of old men, and this group was the object of greater social and charitable concern.

That an increasing proportion of this rapidly growing group would become applicants for charity was assured by the conditions of the 1890s. Unemployment was disproportionately high among the aged and late in the decade, when recovery was far from complete, labour legislation began to threaten the jobs of those whose physical productivity was relatively low. In Victoria, licences exempting employers from paying award wages were sometimes issued in respect of specified workers who were old or feeble and factory inspectors often turned a blind eye to unlicensed below-award payments to others. Some third of all persons aged 65 and more in Victoria earned their own living in 1904, indicating how dependent on work they had been before pensions became available in 1901. Nor was lack of work the only new source of poverty among the aged. The collapse of financial institutions, especially of building societies, wiped out the savings of many. Friendly societies were thrown into disarray and their ability to pay continuing sick benefits to aged members as they had occasionally done was severely curtailed. Moreover, many of the aged poor lacked the full network of family affiliations that existed in the lands of their origin, particularly the one in five old men who had never married.

The increasing visibility of the aged poor aroused concern in a variety of quarters. That concern became formalised by the establishment of parliamentary inquiries, in the evidence presented to them and in their findings and recommendations. In 1900 the Victorian and New South Wales pension legislation was passed. In 1908 Queensland joined those two States and in the following year the Commonwealth instituted an Australia-wide system.

There was remarkably little overt opposition to those Acts. Inside parliaments, opponents were possibly quieted by knowledge of electoral pressures outside. Wage-earner support for an automatic right to a non-discretionary pension paid from public funds is readily understandable. It provided simultaneously for a protection potentially available to all in the future, a reduction in 'unfair' wage competition and therefore a strengthening of effective regulation of minimum wages, and a redistribution of income to the very poorest to which, so it was widely thought, the working class did not greatly contribute. Social reformers like J. C. Neild, a New South Wales insurance agent, Member of the Legislative Assembly and later Senator, who prepared his own influential report on pensions and charitable relief overseas, and the Rev. F. R. Boyce and others, took equally comprehensible positions. The alliance formed early in the 1890s between middle-class reformers and labour leaders was indeed central to the rapid spread of support for age pensions. A good deal more research is needed, however, to explain why others either supported or did not oppose this sharp break with the past. Was there a common benefit for which middle-income groups generally were prepared to pay? Did employers welcome a scheme that lifted from them a moral obligation to retain on their payrolls at least some of their aged workers? Were there other reasons why employers accepted that the support of indigent old people should be the responsibility of taxpayers? Were voluntary subscribers to private charitable organisations so perturbed by the prospect of supporting more and more aged poor that they were prepared to insist that others be coerced to assist, even though they might lose the special cachet assured by their own voluntary contributions?

There was, however, nothing like the same broad agreement on how pensions (and other social security benefits of the period) should be funded, on who should provide income transfers to the very poor.

One view was that benefits should be paid for by that part of the community from which most recipients would come. Proposals for funding old-age pensions, if they were in fact to be met from the public treasury, therefore included taxes on wages, tea, kerosene, totalisator transactions, sports and billiards as well as fines for drunkenness. All would have fallen exclusively, or most heavily, on wage earners. Forms of compulsory insurance were also suggested, some covering the whole population, all requiring annual contributions from those insured and making no call at all on public funds. It was an easy step from this to the proposition that not only should potential beneficiaries contribute largely to current benefit payments but that contributors alone should benefit. These became tenets of conservative political faith. From the passage of the Commonwealth Old Age Pension Act until the 1940s, conservative parties looked to national insurance, funded primarily by the direct and indirect contributions of those insured, to provide any new social security benefit.

Labour's rhetoric, on the other hand, insisted that old-age pensions (and, later, other social security benefits) should be met from the public purse without taxation of wage earners. The persistence of this rhetoric until the early 1940s suggests the existence of a widespread illusion that 'public funds' were provided by taxation of the rich and that pensions and other benefits represented a redistribution to the very poor from the rich.

In fact, no special taxes were levied to meet the social security expenditures approved before 1914. Implicitly they were all funded from increased customs and excise revenues. While much more work on the incidence of the different revenue sources is needed it seems indisputable that wage earners, skilled and unskilled, contributed the major part of the funds from which the reformist, progressive policies these years were financed.

The legislation introducing old-age pensions drew heavily (as did much of the Australian social-laboratory legislation) on the corresponding New Zealand measure, first introduced in 1896 and eventually passed in 1898. In both New South Wales and Victoria pensions became payable to all persons aged 65 or more (excluding Aboriginals, Asiatics and aliens) who were poor, who had lived in the State for twenty-five years (twenty years in Victoria) and were without moral or criminal taint. The maximum pension was 10s a week (reduced in Victoria in 1901 to 8s and raised to 10s again in 1907) except that in New South Wales a married couple received a joint maximum pension of only 15s. Both States allowed for a sliding scale of pension depending on the degree of poverty. New South Wales followed the New Zealand example of defining the poor in terms of their means: no pension was payable if an applicant had an annual non-property income exceeding £ 52 or possessed property with a net value of £ 390 or more; the maximum pension was payable only if other income was not greater than £ 26.

The Victorian pension was regarded by the Premier as a charity, not as a right, and by the Tasmanian Statistician, in evidence to the Commonwealth Royal Commission (q. 5146), as 'a pauper's dole'. In 1901 it was designed to bring a pensioner's income to 8s a week provided the net value of property owned was less than £ 160; if, on the other hand, the value of all goods owned was less than £ 25, a pensioner was able to augment a full pension by up to 2s a week earned by personal exertion. (In 1907 Justice Higgins set 42s a week as the living wage for a man, wife and two or three children.) The Victorian Pensions Commissioner might moreover refuse the pension or grant it at a reduced rate if the applicant appeared physically capable of earning his living. Victoria alone provided that relatives might be ordered to care for a pension applicant. The restrictive nature of the Victorian scheme is evidenced by the fact that the proportion of pensioners in the relevant age group in both 1904 and 1908 was 17 per cent in Victoria, but 32 per cent in New Zealand and close to 40 per cent in New South Wales

The New South Wales Act also entitled invalids aged 60 to 64 to pensions providing other pension conditions were met. In 1907 a conservative ministry extended that right. Non-contributory pensions were granted to persons over the age of 16 years who were incapacitated for any work by invalidity or accident and who were not in charitable institutions or in receipt of an old-age pension. The maximum annual pension of £ 26 was adjusted in accordance with a means test and the extent of support provided by relatives. The number of pensions granted in the first half year of the Act's operation was equivalent to nearly one tenth of the number of old-age pensioners in the State, and after two years to over a quarter. This Act was the first truly innovative piece of social policy to reach the Australian statute books this century and the number taking advantage of it indicates the extent of the problem. When incorporated in the later Commonwealth pension scheme it complemented Workmen's Compensation Acts, passed in most States by 1914, that placed on employers the responsibility of compensating those injured at work.

The Commonwealth pension scheme, operative on 1 July 1909, closely followed the New South Wales precedent with slight variations in means test, in provision for married couples, in tests of character and in residence conditions. A major amendment of the Act in 1912 allowed the value of an applicant's home to be disregarded in the means test. This represented a significant easing of access conditions, for the property limits originally established in 1901 allowed a New South Wales pensioner to own an ample house (valued at up to £ 390) and a Victorian a modest one (£ 160). The most innovative section of the Commonwealth Act was that pensions were to be payable to women on attaining the age of 60 rather than 65. The 1908 Act also incorporated provisions, operative from December 1910, for invalidity pensions of up to £ 26 a year.

The real significance of Deakin's legislation is that it was the first *national* expression of social welfare policy involving non-contributory benefits paid from public funds. It extended pension rights to the aged poor irrespective of their State of residence - including those in South Australia and Tasmania, whose Premiers had said that pensions would not be introduced in those States - as well as those whose migration between States had been a disqualification under existing State pension schemes.

The other Commonwealth initiative was the 1912 Maternity Allowances Act, introduced by Fisher's Labor Government. The allowance was payable to any woman, married or unmarried and regardless of her means and character, on the birth of her child. This was the second, and the last, Australian 'first' in social policy during this period: no other country offered this benefit on either a non-contributory or a universal basis, let alone both. The allowance was generous, equivalent to a fortnight's pay at 1907 Harvester rates. Its fundamental justification was that it assisted the needy to secure adequate pre- and post-natal nutritional and medical care (a doctor's obstetrics charge was three guineas, a trained nurse acting as midwife charged over £ 2).

In addition to the cash benefits it paid to aged and invalid pensioners in the first decade, the New South Wales government paid an indirect cash benefit to some widows and deserted wives. It took the form of the boarding-out allowance paid to foster parents of destitute and 'neglected' children. Since 1896 it had been within the power of the State Children's Relief Board to select as 'foster parent' the mother of such a child. Through the exercise of administrative discretion, the number of mothers deemed worthy of caring for their destitute children rose rapidly after 1900. In that year just over a quarter of the children financially supported by the Board lived at home; by 1914, more than a half. The number of widows and deserted wives who were assisted in this manner probably doubled, or more, over the same period and in 1911 (before their number had materially increased as a result of eased access conditions afforded by the Labor Government) was equivalent to a tenth of all widows in New South Wales under the age of 55. Moreover, by 1912 the allowances paid to this group of 'foster parents' had been lifted to the maximum normally payable in respect of each child - 5s a week - instead of the minimum, as had been the rule in the first half of the decade.

State governments continued to subsidise private charity in much the same ways as they had in the 1890s. Two important changes appear to have taken place, however. In the first place, the revenues of private charitable institutions and societies (excluding hospitals) formed a smaller part of total resources devoted to charitable purposes, although in real terms the revenues themselves rose. Private charity institutions providing indoor relief - the need for which might (or might not) have been reduced by the introduction of old-age pensions and the increased availability of hospital beds (see below, p. 169) - suffered the most. In the second place, the extent of government subsidy to institutions and societies not providing general hospital services declined: in Victoria, from 42 per cent of their revenue (including subsidy) in 1903 to 27 per cent in 1913, and in New South Wales from 21 to 7 per cent between 1901 and 1913. These changes took place in the context of greater use, per head of the population, of the various forms of institutional relief. They suggest that increased provision of public and semi-public (hospital) welfare services were associated with a relative diminution in private charitable effort. Further study is needed to determine the extent to which it was the product of the relative diversion of public funding from the private to the public and semi-public services, of a relative reduction in private support of charities, or of a change in the nature of demand for indoor welfare services.

Education

In discussing education in this volume, we are concerned primarily with its welfare and redistributive implications. Nevertheless we cannot avoid reference to public and private roles affecting the growth of human capital.

Nineteenth-century background

In the last third of the nineteenth century the role of governments in education was transformed in all the Australian colonies. That transformation had three major components. First, to eliminate illiteracy, attendance at school or an approved alternative was made compulsory for all children within prescribed ages, generally by 1900 between 6 and 13 years. Second, governments themselves established and staffed secular (i.e. non-denominational) schools open to all who chose to enrol. Third, governments withdrew their subsidies to private, notably denominational, schools. The basic Acts were passed during the 1870s, the New South Wales Act of 1880 being the last. Subsequent Acts were needed in some colonies to complete the pattern, the final one being that in 1895 abolishing general subsidies to Western Australian private schools.

In Victoria and Queensland, government education services were always provided free of direct charge. Even in New South Wales and Tasmania, where fees were still charged in 1900, however, the service was heavily subsidised. In New South Wales, primary school fees covered only 12 per cent of running costs. Moreover, though the payment required was low in relation to wages (3d per child per week, or 7s - just over a day's unskilled wages - to cover the minimum period of compulsory attendance for a year), the very poor could be exempted from fees (14 per cent of New South Wales gross enrolments were exempt in 1900). Further, the greater portion of non-government primary schooling was, by the end of the century, privately subsidised. The compulsory and secular components of the legislation stimulated greatly increased provision of school facilities by orders associated with the Roman Catholic Church. By 1900 they accounted for 12 per cent of all primary school enrolments. The fees charged were nominal; church collections and other income were used to transfer income

among Catholic families in accordance with student dependants; and
there was a transfer from other church activities, including the services
of teaching orders, to families with children.

Rural Australians were particularly benefited by government
school systems. Outside the main cities and towns, the population was
spread sparsely over a very large area. Had the supply of educational
facilities been left to market forces alone there is little likelihood that
they would have been provided as very small-scale institutions for
many country children. But in 1884, for example, nearly three New
South Wales government schools in ten were attended by fewer than
twenty pupils, enough to warrant merely one teacher and scarcely
enough to attract private enterprise except at a relatively high price to
consumers. By 1910, 44 per cent of its schools were in this category.
Governments dominated by rural interests could more readily pro-
claim the public good of rural literacy.

The new approach to elementary schooling in the last thirty years
of the century changed consumption patterns considerably. Most of
those who would formerly have paid for the service were now subsidised and those who would otherwise have foregone schooling were provided with a direct service. The very rich continued to engage private
tutors or enrol their children in exclusive fee-charging schools; a
number, perhaps 6 or 7 per cent, continued to make use of private
non-Catholic schools, with modest ambitions and charges. By the end
of the nineteenth century, government primary school education was
distinguished from many other welfare services in that, in order to ensure its accessibility to the children of the poorest citizen, access was
made free, or nearly free, to all children. The overall redistribution
seems to have favoured the middle- and lower-income groups.

Formal post-primary education, on the other hand, was provided
mainly by private, fee-charging, non-Catholic schools and availed of
by a small minority of children. A few of these schools received
statutory endowments from governments. Universities, whose new
graduates numbered only 300 a year, were financed by private philanthropy, students' fees and, to the extent of about a third of their expenditures, by government grants and endowments.

Developments, 1901 to 1914

In the first decade or so of the century there were significant
developments in the provision of educational services. They were concerned, most notably, with the extension of public education into the
secondary and technical fields. The spurs to this were various: a
keener appreciation of the economic importance of schooling,
stimulated undoubtedly by concern in Britain about Germany's
technological successes; changing concepts of primary school objec-

tives and curricula and of teacher training; a need to increase the supply of primary public school teachers to keep pace with student numbers (whose age group formed an increasing proportion of the population - another substantial echo effect of the pattern of past immigration); a desire to give more substance to the democratic goals attributed to the public systems; and, in some States at least, an embarrassment of students beyond the age of compulsory schooling who continued coming to classes.

In 1901 secondary education was almost entirely a matter for private schools. Although there had been eight government high schools in New South Wales in 1884, by 1901 only four remained. None existed in other States, though Queensland quite liberally subsidised ten private grammar schools and the private Perth High School was subsidised by the Western Australian Government. Provision for other students willing and able to go beyond the primary school curricula was made in New South Wales at Superior Public Schools which, in addition to the first five ordinary primary classes, offered two subsequent classes; and, in Victoria, through the offer of special additional subjects at ordinary primary schools for which fees were charged.

A reorganisation of the public education sector, begun hesitantly from about 1906-07 and culminating in sweeping changes in the four years 1910 to 1913, established a public system of secondary schooling for the intellectual elite. The impetus for this seems to have come from bureaucrats rather than from politicians or private groups interested in the 'products' of schooling. One of its results and, in part, one of its stimulants, was the creation of human capital capable of serving the growing needs of service industries. In New South Wales in 1913 there were 15 public high schools, in Victoria 22, in South Australia 24, in Queensland 6, in Tasmania 2 and in Western Australia 1. Most States provided super-primary departments in primary schools or central schools at post-primary level from which transfer to high school was possible. All were based on entry and progression by merit. New South Wales went furthest, perhaps, in creating in 1911 an integrated system of schooling in which post-primary students were streamed according to ability into different vocation-oriented tracks according to their ability to surmount a succession of examination hurdles.

Wider availability of public secondary schooling had implications for financial conditions of access. By the turn of the century public primary education was free, i.e. without fees, except in New South Wales and Tasmania. New South Wales abolished fees in 1906; in Tasmania from 1901 they were paid into the Treasury instead of remaining the perquisites of teachers and were abolished in 1907. Fees charged to high school students in New South Wales were much more substantial than primary school fees had been, meeting a third of the recurrent costs of high schools in 1907. They were abolished with the introduction of the new system in 1911. Victoria and South Australia alone maintained fees at public secondary schools after 1913. But all States, fee-charging or not, made substantial provision of scholarships, bursaries and exhibitions: 130 in Victoria; 368 in Queensland in 1913; over 1200 in New South Wales for students of public and registered private high schools, technical and agricultural schools. Through these public access conditions New South Wales, under the Bursary Endowment Act of 1912, acted to limit the freedom of private school curricula. The influence of public school curricula on those of private schools was first felt when the system of certification of students by examination spread, as it was bound to do, to private schools. Moreover, as part of the reorganisation, the Government altered the composition of the University of Sydney's governing body to accommodate, for the first time, representatives of the State (comprising a third of the University Senate); raised its endowment of the university and tied subsequent increases to growth in the number of 17- to 20-year-olds in the State; and fixed the number of publicly funded scholarships to the University at one to every 500 17- to 20-year-olds.

All these changes had their main impact on the middle class and more particularly on groups like skilled tradesmen - those whose appreciation of the values of education was most highly developed and whose income and home backgrounds permitted and encouraged continued education for their children. Yet, striking though the developments in schooling were, they were really portents of the future. Working them out, putting flesh on the skeleton, was the basic task of the systems over the following thirty years.

By the first decade of this century there was, in addition to primary and secondary schools and the universities, a variety of other educational establishments, many of considerable age. Alone among them, business colleges specialising in typing, shorthand and office methods were conducted by private enterprise. The rest, including those specially related to mining and agriculture, were funded by governments by 1901. At that time some were directly controlled by a government department, others by local councils. Although students were charged for their instruction, their fees met only a quarter of current expenditure in 1912 and that proportion had been falling since 1900. Technical education was very limited, designed to train small numbers of skilled tradesmen: from bootmaker through commercial artist, fitter and turner and metallurgist to wool classer. Those subsidised were, consequently, drawn primarily from working-class backgrounds. For them, technical training was attractive, offering advancement to the higher income and status that skill conferred.

In this area, two changes were under way early in the twentieth century. One was the closer integration of technical with other schools. New South Wales had brought technical education firmly under the responsibility of the Minister of Public Instruction in the nineteenth century. Queensland did so in 1905 and Victoria in 1910. Western Australia's continuation classes, Victoria's junior technical schools and New South Wales technical schools, all introduced after 1901, provided a link between the general and the technical educational settings. This integration made it easier to award scholarships at the technical institutions. These developments owed something to both public and private concern over the shortage of skilled labour - the need to enhance human capital in specific ways - and the pressures of private industry to limit its financial commitments to the development of that (mobile) human capital. Even by 1912 average weekly attendance at technical school classes throughout Australia was only three times as large as that at high schools and expenditure per head of the Australian population 1s 2d compared with the 13s 10d spent on primary education. Manufacturing employers may have thought this too little but they had a more fundamental influence on general technical education that was a potent factor in the second change that took place. This change found fullest expression in New South Wales, where technical colleges were increasingly restricted to the tuition of apprentices and of people studying subjects very closely allied to the needs of the jobs they held. The services made available to develop skills more generally were deliberately restricted so that the system could serve the needs of employers more immediately and directly. Moreover, New South Wales educators held, it was not the function of technical colleges to produce fully trained artisans. Rather, they should provide theoretical instruction to supplement on-the-job training. These tensions have continued to plague Australian technical education to this day.

Health

Like education, health services raise questions of public and private choice with respect to redistribution and welfare on the one hand and to human capital on the other. Health care services in the decade before Federation were basically provided through the market. When they needed attention, those who could afford it were treated at home. Perhaps one in five of the population in the 1890s was a member of a friendly society providing the services of associated doctors and pharmacists. The costs of these services were negotiated between society and supplier and were met from the insurance fund established by members' contributions. Those who could afford neither private medical costs nor society contribution were treated at home by family or friends advised, perhaps, by the pharmacist; or they sought admission to a hospital.

Hospitals existed essentially to provide services to the very poor. Most were established by religious and charitable organisations or by groups of philanthropic subscribers (whose subscriptions, or gifts, formed a significant source of revenue); medical services were provided on an honorary basis. Most were charities, subsidised by governments to the extent of 45 to 50 per cent of their total running expenses. Admission was generally free; in many hospitals it was dependent on a recommendation from a subscriber and in New South Wales the Government Medical Officer assumed that role on behalf of the government.

Except in South Australia and West Australia, where special conditions existed, few ordinary hospitals were operated as government services. On the other hand, most hospitals for the insane were financed and managed by governments. Unlike the few (licensed and regulated but unsubsidised) private asylums for the insane, they recouped only a small proportion of their expenditure from patients' families or estates. Inmates were predominantly poor; possibly the richer insane, unless positively dangerous, were cared for at home - or perhaps, as popular novelists insisted, were stripped of their wealth before committal.

The role of hospitals was changing even in the 1890s. By the 1930s, instead of being regarded primarily as places in which the less fortunate died, they had become central points in the health care of the whole community. What began this transformation was aseptic surgery and then aseptic hospital treatment generally. This gradually enabled hospitals to offer treatment that was often more successful than that given at home or in a doctor's surgery. A number of important consequences were apparent by 1914.

In the 1890s, there were a few profit-making hospitals seeking trade. Privately owned (often by medical practitioners or qualified nurses), not subsidised from public funds, they accepted only fee-paying patients and catered to the well-to-do. Since 1890, such establishments in Victoria had been obliged to be registered by the Board of Health after inspection and to be conducted subject to regulations made under the Public Health Act. The first year's operation of the parallel New South Wales Private Hospitals Act, 1908, revealed that the number of such hospitals in the State had mushroomed to 454 by 1910. Only 139 'public' (i.e. charitable) hospitals, receiving money from government and obliged to treat the poor without charge, existed at that time. The difference was that private hospitals were very small and the majority licensed for lying-in only.

The increasing willingness of people to be treated in hospital meant growing pressures on hospital accommodation. Between 1901 and 1913 the number of in-patients treated at New South Wales public hospitals, for example, rose from 24 per thousand inhabitants to 36. Over the same period the number of hospital beds rose from 2.46 per thousand inhabitants to 3.05, the rate of increase in country areas being three times as great as that in the metropolis.

Revised attitudes to hospitalisation encourage specialisation. Hospitals were established during this period dealing exclusively or mainly with, for example, babies, consumptives, women requiring lying-in or gynaecological services, children, those suffering infectious diseases and, in New South Wales, those requiring dental treatment. There were interesting distinctions. In Sydney, the Benevolent Society opened the Royal Hospital for Women at Paddington in 1902 so that its Asylum would not have to house its lying-in clients with aged, infirm and destitute women. While the poor used the Women's Hospital, or more frequently no hospital, the rich and middle-income groups had access to fully satisfactory services at home or in private hospitals.

The New South Wales Government had, by 1914, established its own hospital for consumptives, accepted full responsibility for a formerly privately endowed general hospital in the country, opened its own hospital for babies and two convalescent hospitals and had started to construct a large metropolitan general hospital. It was also making much greater use of its asylums for the aged and infirm as geriatric hospitals. Victoria, least exposed to Labor Party influence and least involved of all State governments in providing and subsidising hospital services, opened government sanatoria for consumptives in 1905 and 1910-11. On the other hand, in South Australia and Western Australia there was a notable increase in the percentage, as well as the number, of general 'public' hospitals that were not operated by the state.

The gradually changing role of hospitals was already creating tensions between different interests that were to become more pressing in the future. Should any patient able to pay for treatment be admitted to a 'public' hospital, a hospital subsidised by government? Private hospitals could meet those demands through the market. Doctors felt their general practice business threatened if 'public' hospital treatment were not restricted to indigents. In the absence of such a restriction, how were hospital administrations to meet the new demands and yet maintain the quantity and quality of services available to the poor? Charging those who could afford to pay was a partial solution. Again, faced with loss of income, medical practitioners argued that they should not provide free services in hospitals to patients who could pay the hospital charges. Further, unless hospitals set their fees at levels that effectively excluded the mass of wage earners they could not fully cover their costs. Hospitals did in fact admit patients from a widening range of income groups. The other issues were not resolved. The inevitable consequence was mounting pressures for government subsidies.

What happened in New South Wales in response to this before 1914 had long-run implications. Government needed better advice on the justification of hospitals' requests for aid and on rationalisation of services. Hence the Board of Health was built into a powerful regulatory body. Many of the powers exercised or sought by the Board were essentially extensions, in relation to public hospitals, of the regulation imposed by the 1908 Private Hospitals Act. The emergence of a professional bureaucracy specialised in health care brought with it a new set of vested interests - just as the slowly increasing professionalisation of school-teaching and the use of professional educators as administrators did in education services. The Labor Government, in power from 1910 until 1916 with a policy of reforming health care services and widening access to them, greatly encouraged this development. Its forceful Health Minister, indeed, raised far-ranging policy issues including even the nationalisation of hospitals that, for the first but by no means the last time, aroused the antagonisms of the vested professional interests of medical practitioners, pharmacists and friendly societies.

Between 1901 and 1913, the expenditure of public hospitals more than doubled in current prices, a substantial increase even in real terms, and their revenues absorbed an increased share of total revenues devoted to charitable purposes. With the exception of Victoria, State governments continued to provide a half or more of hospitals' receipts. Their role as subsidisers was to change little in the inter-war years; but regulation of hospitals was to become progressively more comprehensive. To the extent that those who were able to pay for treatment made more use of hospitals, the thrust of the subsidised expansion of those facilities before 1914 was to give them some advantage they had not previously had.

7

The Heroes and the Hungry
1919 to 1939

The comprehensive social policies developed by political parties before the First World War found scant practical expression in the next thirty years. The social security measures put into effect between 1900 and 1914 were introduced by a generation that had lived in Australia when it was, from 1860 to 1890, one of the world's richest countries - possibly the richest per head of population - and had shared the shock of the reversal of its condition in the 1890s. They were introduced as the riches seemed to be reappearing and were framed to accord sympathy and support for those who, to a numerical extent unimagined in the 1880s, were grossly disadvantaged. Australia's prominence, both as a social pioneer and as a rapidly developing economy, receded after 1914. The country was to face a period of very slow growth and another of severely retarded living standards which, in themselves, constituted a major impediment to the implementation of new measures, as well as a source of poverty.

The loss of momentum can be attributed partly to political perceptions of group interests. Urban conservatives, particularly at the Commonwealth level, became what Greenwood (1955, p. 289) called 'the not wholly legitimate heirs of the nationalist tradition' with which the propensity to social experimentation had been closely linked. But they were nationalists of an industrial capitalism, devoted to economic expansion and constrained by the illiberalism of their coalition allies, the new Country Party. The philosophy of the labour movement became less cohesive, and Labor parties' policies less incisive, as the events of 1916 in Australia and of 1917 in Russia sharpened divisions among reformists and between reformists and radicals. Moreover, when Labor ministries took office in the States before the 1930s they too looked to economic expansion as the source of social benefit. The labour movement and Labor parties were concerned primarily with the real wages of those in the workforce rather than with redistributing income to those who were poorer. Moreover the ability of political parties, conservative and reformist, to give effect to the policies envisaged in 1913 was constrained by rhetorics from which they could not readily escape and which they could not bring to realisation. Liberal sections of the conservative Commonwealth governments in power for most of the inter-war period aimed to provide income support to workers without appreciable cost to others by means of national insurance. Vested business interests prevented effective legislation. The rhetoric of the labour movement was that income support schemes should be financed through direct taxation of people richer than the workers themselves. State Labor governments discovered that this was impractical, both fiscally and politically. The burden of most changes they did make to their welfare systems was in fact shared by the groups from whom the recipients of the advantage were expected to be drawn.

Nevertheless, although these years are often described as being barren of social security innovations, two very significant additions were made. In the first place, the horrors of Flanders and pride in a nation's baptism by fire came to compete with liberal philosophy and divert attention to a new demand: the needs of, and the compensation owed to, the war-wounded and war-bereft. Various veterans' benefits curbed the potential of this new source of extreme need - and may have curbed too the continuation of earlier welfare promises. Throughout the 1920s, the effects of the war were to channel policy attention away from the poor, the needy and the economically disadvantaged to the expatiation of the losses and risks experienced by servicemen, regardless of their economic background. In the second place, responsibility for relieving poverty due to unemployment was transferred to State governments (not the Federal) when deep depression in the 1930s proved private action inadequate to the task. Providing a massive unemployment dole scheme, makeshift and inadequate though the benefits may have been, altered many long-held interests and attitudes. Besides these two mammoth income support operations other innovations were minor indeed: a system of unemployment insurance started in Queensland; child endowment for Commonwealth employees, and in New South Wales; widows' pensions in New South Wales and, in 1938, Victoria. At the same time, health and education services supplied or subsidised by governments continued to be adapted to make 'more welfare' available to users.

The burden of providing health, education and welfare shifted dramatically between the wars. Before 1914 taxation of personal and corporate incomes was an insignificant element in governments' current revenues. After 1920 it became the most important single source from which State governments raised additional funds. Its contribution to their receipts (after excluding gross revenues from public business undertakings included in their budgets but effectively hypothecated to meeting working expenses and interest charges) doubled between 1914 and 1930, to 30 per cent of the total. In that decade less than 20 per cent of the workforce paid income tax and, in the major States, that group included no unskilled workers and relatively few skilled tradesmen even at its lower margin. In that decade, also, State governments funded 80 per cent of the country's education services and between a third and a half of the hospital services. The first change, therefore, was that their increased expenditures on those services were financed from revenue sources to which the contribution of middle- and high-income earners was of growing importance. On the other hand, the Federal Government, responsible for providing 90 per cent of social security cash benefits by the end of the 1920s, steadily retreated from direct taxation throughout the interwar years. Customs and excise duties, profits from Post Office operations and, in the 1930s, sales tax funded all additional Federal expenditures. Ultimately these taxes were borne largely by wage earners (and exporters) rather than by the relatively few high-income earners who paid Federal income tax, and the burden of Federal pension payments fell on much the same groups in the 1920s as it had before 1914. In 1930, however, State governments were obliged to provide social security benefits to the unemployed amounting to between a third and two thirds of the cost of Federal pensions. These were funded by income taxation vastly extended to include up to 60 to 70 per cent of the workforce. Low-income earners were unable, subsequently, to escape that net. More progressive in its incidence than indirect taxes, the new pattern of income taxation presaged a tax-benefit structure, however, that was to make distinctions between a national insurance scheme and tax-supported benefits increasingly irrelevant.

Social security

There were a number of welfare-related consequences of the 1914-1918 war and its immediate aftermath. One was that rising prices, experienced from the pre-war boom, exacerbated by drought and bad harvest in 1915 and by war-caused shortages, and lasting until the peak of post-war inflation in 1920, depressed real per capita consumption and accentuated workers' demands that wages be adjusted in the light of cost-of-living criteria. The findings of the Federal and New South Wales Royal Commissions into the basic wage, and the evidence presented to them, served both to reinforce the welfare mythology of Higgins' living wage and to make it a reality. Another consequence was the leading role among Australian charities acquired by the Australian Red Cross and the altogether more respected and respectable status accorded to the Salvation Army as well as to the YMCA as a result of their contact with Australian troops. A third, and by far the most important in this context, was the Commonwealth Government's acceptance of formal, wide-ranging responsibility for the post-war welfare of servicemen and their dependants.

Veterans' benefits

Unlike the grace-and-favour pensions granted to some Boer War veterans by State governments, Commonwealth pensions to ex-servicemen were granted as a matter of right due to those who suffered for their country. (In this, their justification had much in common with the argument that old-age pensions were a right due to those whose working lives had helped develop their country.) Initially, politicians and the electorate expected that public means would be confined to those pensions, for which Federal legislative sanction was first secured in 1914. Private interests associated with patriotic funds raised by voluntary subscription (originally to provide additional comforts for the armed forces) expected, when the first wounded soldiers arrived home from Gallipoli in mid-1915, that their funds would take care of the men after demobilisation. Until August 1917, voluntary subscriptions channelled through government-sponsored 'War Service Committees' supported the actual work of rehabilitating invalided ex-soldiers and caring for their dependants. Moreover, an Australian Soldiers' Repatriation Fund to supply ex-soldiers settling on the land with seed, stock, implements and training was opened for subscription by citizens. When some measure of order was imparted to this chaos by the passage of the Commonwealth Repatriation Act in 1917 the magnitude of the undertaking had become more apparent: the Government undertook to provide care and attention to those suffering wounds or war-induced illnesses and to reinstate in civil life those capable of being reinstated. The repatriation and rehabilitation package that was finally prepared was, consequently, a very comprehensive blend of services and cash benefits covering both veterans and dependants. Compensation as the basis of benefit introduced a new note in the provision of publicly funded income support: no longer was need alone the criterion.

All veterans were eligible for assistance to re-establish them in civilian life and employment. They could claim not merely sustenance allowances from the time of discharge until they found suitable employment, including any period of training at vocational school or university, but also the costs of that tuition and cash grants, gifts in kind and loans to help them set up in business. The best known of these schemes is that to settle them on farms. They were as much, if not more, a form of assistance to private businesses as they were welfare assistance to individuals. Statutory preference for veterans in public sector employment (except in Queensland) and effective preference in much of the private sector widened the re-establishment assistance. Veterans could also secure low-interest loans through the War Service Homes Commission to enable them to acquire houses. Although expenditure on sustenance, training and re-establishment continued into the 1930s, they were relatively short-lived aspects of the rehabilitation package.

Cash payments to persons and free medical and hospital attention became the central, enduring features of veterans' benefits. Pensions were paid to veterans whose employment potential was reduced by war service and to widows and dependants (including dependant mothers, fathers and siblings) of those killed or incapacitated. Ex-servicemens' children, including those born after the war, were eligible also for scholarships from public and quasi-public funds, and from 1921 children of deceased or totally incapacitated men received maintenance allowances while being educated, in addition to any other pension payment due to them as dependants. Ill or wounded veterans were entitled to free hospital and medical treatment in respect of war-caused conditions. Access to both groups of benefits was made easier as a result of the continuing pressures exerted by the veterans' association. At their inter-war peak, in 1930-31, war pensions were paid to over 75 000 ex-servicemen and to over 208 000 of their dependants and those of deceased servicemen. They represented cash transfers equivalent to two thirds of the amount paid to old-age pensioners. All these payments were met by annual appropriations by the Federal Parliament and could quite reasonably be assumed to be funded from the income taxes first imposed to meet the expenses of war. What were their redistributive implications?

Until 1936, when the service pension was introduced to assist ex-servicemen who were unemployable but not eligible for war pensions, the main benefits available under the repatriation scheme were not means-tested. (In the depression dependants other than widows, wives, children and widowed mothers were granted pensions only if they were without adequate means of support.) Before that date, however, pensions were related to the degree of disability suffered. Just under a tenth of disability pensions in 1925 (slightly more in 1938) were paid at the rate indicating the veteran's total and permanent incapacity to work. These pensioners can be identified unmistakably as a group most of whom would have been in desperate need in the absence of pensions. Short of detailed investigation of Repatriation Commission records, it is not possible to say more about the welfare implications of pensions for other recipients than that, in terms of the distribution of their income and wealth, those pensioners were probably similar to the rest of the population. It seems probable that any redistribution was a matter of chance and did not form any coherent pattern.

Other social security benefits in the 1920s

The uncertainties affecting an individual's future command of resources sufficient even for minimum acceptable levels of consumption were no less after the war than when political programs to minimise them were formulated before it. Age, invalidity, widowhood, orphanhood, sickness and unemployment could mean the end of a market-generated income for varying periods. Expenses of hospital and medical treatment, even the needs of a large family, could mean the difference between sustenance and extreme poverty. The market offered means to cover some of these risks.

Various insurance arrangements, including endowment and whole-of-life policies, superannuation and workers' compensation insurance, provided an income source to some in the event of widowhood, orphanhood, invalidity and age. Ordinary life insurance was more widely used in the inter-war years than earlier: the number of policies rose from one for each 7.8 inhabitants in 1920 to one for 5.8 in 1939. The average value of a policy, though rising, was hardly sufficient to provide a lasting adequate income for a survivor, even though the typical policy holder earned more than an average wage. Industrial insurance, designed especially for working-class participation with weekly premium payments collected door-to-door, grew even more quickly, but the average sum insured was much lower. Superannuation schemes for government employees were established, or re-established, after 1916 primarily as a consequence of employee pressure. By 1929 more than four in ten government employees, or 6 per cent of the civilian workforce, were able to look forward to retirement pensions, and provisions for their dependants in the event of death, funded by their own and their employers' contributions. Some larger private employers, particularly in finance, similarly subsidised their employees' provision for old age, but their number was small and they probably covered no more than 1 per cent of private employees by 1940. The risks of loss of income during sickness and of incurring large medical and hospital expenses were met, though inadequately and not by all people, partly by workers' compensation, partly through membership of friendly societies or hospital funds. Typically, it was the skilled tradesman and lower- to middle-echelon white-collar worker who belonged to these organisations. The upward trend in savings bank deposits per head of the population, except during the depression, indicates the use made of another market avenue for those who were able to build a private reserve.

The bulk of wage earners, low-income earners in particular, could make little effective use of these market mechanisms to reduce risk. And it was only the very poorest of the aged and invalids, widows and orphans, who could draw public pensions or allowances. Clearly, the sectional interests of these groups meant that any attempt to provide a non-market or subsidised means of dealing with the income and consumption uncertainties facing them would have had electoral as well as humanitarian appeal. No government in the inter-war years chose to take up that challenge in a substantial or lasting way.

Conservative ideologies, so far as they saw any greater public role in social security, were wedded to compulsory national insurance for specified groups of income earners. Conservative Federal governments in power in all but three years between the wars therefore appointed a series of Royal Commissions to report on the problem and unsuccessfully introduced a National Insurance Bill in the 1920s. A decade later, official inquiry preceded the passage of the 1938 National Health and Pensions Insurance Act incorporating most features suggested earlier. Insurance was to be compulsory for all employees earning less than about twice the basic wage. Premium payments were to be shared equally between employees, employers and Commonwealth government funds. Benefits included entitlement to age, widow and orphan pensions and to sickness and disablement payments, and cover against the cost of general practitioner services, medicines and appliances (but not for an insured's dependants).

No matter how far it may have pleased ideologues and Federal income tax payers who could see social good being done at very little cost to themselves, both the general concept of national insurance and the particular provisions of this Act aroused opposition in many quarters. Potential beneficiaries heedful of Labor claims objected to being called on to meet any of the cost, and would have objected even more strongly had they realised that the employers' and Commonwealth government's share would have been largely met from beneficiaries' own pockets in any case. Those who were excluded because they were self-employed even though, like farmers, their cash incomes might be very low, opposed the scheme because it left them disadvantaged. To friendly societies and insurance companies, national insurance operated through government auspices posed a direct threat that might eliminate a substantial part of their business. Other professional interests joined the opposition: the medical profession and pharmacists; State public servants whose careers were threatened by a successful national insurance scheme; and State politicians who resented the Commonwealth's centralising intrusion into areas formerly outside its reach. Consequently, a good many conservative politicians were all too happy to postpone operation of the Act because of the worsening of the international situation in 1939 and, in fact, the Act became a dead letter.

Labor's rhetoric was that the rich should finance amelioration of the condition of the poor and even of the average wage earner. It looked to income tax, land tax and death duties on wealth to accomplish this. In State parliaments, as contrasted with the Federal, electors favoured Labor during the 1920s. In the five years from 1924 to 1928 there were, at any time, Labor governments in four of the six States and for the greater part of the period in five of them. From two of those governments came three pieces of social security legislation. Only one of them, providing for the New South Wales widow's pension, drew on the 'rich'. The other measures placed the burden of supporting reformist expenditures on wage earners themselves.

The Queensland Labor Party, already halfway along its first fourteen years of continuous office, introduced its unemployment insurance scheme in March 1923. It was restricted to but compulsory for those who worked under State awards and by 1925 there were about 150 000 contributors. There was no question of the scheme being noncontributory. The premium for the insurance was 9d a week (doubled in 1928) to which workers, employers and an endowment from general government funds each contributed a third. A detailed study of Queensland Industrial Court cases might determine whether or not employers' contributions became, in effect, deductions from their wages bills and show how export producers fared. The purpose of the scheme was to cover seasonal unemployment (to which workers in Queensland's large sugar and pastoral industries were particularly exposed) and intermittent work such as that on wharves (which was related, of course, to the seasonal export patterns of primary industry) as well as other unemployment. If indeed this legislation owed as much to the non-Labor opposition as it did to Labor policy as Kewley (1969, p. 65) suggests, then the conservatives may have thought their efforts worth the while. In 1921-22 the Government distributed £ 177 000 from general government funds as outdoor relief, predominantly to the unemployed; in 1924-25, when sustenance benefits from the insurance fund totalled £ 188 000, government expenditure was restricted to £ 21 000 in outdoor relief, £ 83 000 in endowment of the fund and its (unknown but smaller) contributions as an employer.

In 1925 the New South Wales Labor Government legislated for the payment of pensions to widows with dependant children less than 14 years old. This formalised and extended provisions previously made under legislation protecting destitute and neglected children. Payment was subject to the applicant satisfying a means test. The Act was amended in 1929 by a non-Labor government to extend payments to destitute widows over the age of 50, without dependant children, and to pay the pension if a dependant child below the age of 16 suffered from a mental or physical disability or possessed special scholastic ability. By 1933 one fifth of all New South Wales widows under 60 years could satisfy these conditions. The maximum pension rate for the widow was the same as that for an age pensioner, plus half that for each dependant. Victoria's Labor-supported government had similar legislation passed in 1938. It scarcely became operative before Commonwealth widows' pensions were introduced in 1942, a subject discussed in the next chapter. No source of funds was earmarked for these pensions. They were paid from increments to general revenues to which income tax was the most important single contributor.

The most controversial of the three measures of interest here was Labor's introduction of child endowment in New South Wales. It represented an attempt to adjust wage earners' incomes to the size of their dependant families, a concern that was inevitable after the marriage of the concepts of a living wage and of a basic wage by Higgins in 1906. Relating a general basic wage to the needs of a family of 'about five' (as Higgins did) clearly created inequities between families. The idea of separating basic wage and family living income gained considerable currency. Between 1919 and 1925 Bills to set the basic wage at a level sufficient to sustain a married couple and to tax employers to form a fund from which to pay allowances to workers' children were defeated in New South Wales, South Australia and Queensland. The basis of the opposition was the direct role that employers were to take in financing the scheme. In the event, child endowment was introduced by the Federal Government in 1920 in respect of its own public servants and by New South Wales in 1926. In both cases it was an alternative to an increase in the real basic wage.

In 1919 a Commonwealth Royal Commission was appointed to determine the actual cost of a basic standard of living for a family of five. The figure the Commission set as a basic wage appropriate to that standard caused consternation: it was more than 40 per cent higher than the current level. Three days after the *Report* was signed, Prime Minister Hughes asked the Chairman a series of pointed questions. The answers were no less pointed: 'From the produced wealth of the country, its children have less than enough in order that the unmarried childless may have more than enough'; but this could be remedied if the basic wage were calculated on the needs of a man and wife and an allowance be paid to children from a fund created by a tax on employers (*Report*, p. 90). The Commonwealth scheme was ostensibly based on this. It set a basic wage rate for its employees above the current rate but well below the previous five-person basic wage adjusted to current prices, and no longer distinguishing, as formerly, between unmarried and married men; an endowment of 5s a week was paid for dependant children providing the officer's annual salary and allowance combined did not exceed £ 400. When fully amalgamated into the public service wage structure, endowment paid to officers with dependant children was directly financed by other officers and, in effect, the basic wage was for the first time split and distributed according to the family needs of employees (*Labour Report*, 1927, pp. 94-5).

The New South Wales legislation had a similar background. In 1926 the Industrial Commission (led by Justice Piddington who was chairman of the Federal Royal Commission on the Basic Wage) determined that the current price equivalent of the New South Wales basic wage should be 25 per cent higher than the existing rate. Concluding that such a steep rise was not economically possible and that it could not, with justice, determine a standard of living and 'associate it with a rigid domestic unit consisting of any specified number of children', it did not change the current living wage and recommended a 'motherhood endowment' as an adjunct to the wage. With the Family Endowment Act of 1927 Labor offered weekly allowances for dependant children on a sliding scale such that no endowment was paid to a family when its weekly income (not solely the wage earner's income) exceeded the current living wage plus 5s for each dependant child. At the same time the Industrial Arbitration Act was amended to define

TABLE 7.1 **Old-age pensions and the State tribunal's living wage in Sydney**

	Maximum age pension as percentage of living wage	Maximum permissible pensioner income[a] as percentage of living wage
1911	21	42
1914	21	42
1915	19	38
1916	23	41
1917	23	41
1918	21	38
1919	16	29
1920	18	30
1921	18	29
1922	19	32
1923	21	38
1924	21	36
1925	24	39
1926	24	39
1927	24	38
1928	24	38
1929	24	38
1930	24	39
1931	21	36
1932	21	39
1933	26	45
1934	26	44
1935	26	45
1936	27	45
1937	26	42
1938	25	40
1939	24	40

[a] i.e. maximum pension plus permissible earning at that rate.

the living wage as that appropriate to a man and wife. In December 1929 the basic wage was declared, by a non-Labor Government, to be a sum sufficient for the needs of a family with a dependant child and endowment of the first dependant child in a family ceased. Endowment allowances were financed by a 3 per cent payroll tax on employers. Many employers and employees believed the burden rested there. Perhaps labour leaders believed it too. In fact, the probable ability of employers (except in export industries) to pass on a good deal of the tax to consumers, the shifting definition of the basic wage and the associated lags between movements in wage rates and in prices ensured that endowment was pre-eminently a transfer of real income between different low-income families.

Concern about the effects of rising prices during and after the war was reflected in changes in the maximum rates of age and invalid pensions payable by the Commonwealth though, oddly in view of the strength of the veterans' lobby, not in the rates applying to war pensions. In 1916, 1920, 1923 and 1925 additions of 2s 6d a week were authorised. The income permitted to pensioners in addition to pension at full rate was increased in 1923 from 10s a week to 12s 6d and the value of permissible property from £ 310 to £ 400. The adjustments were no more than belated recognitions that pensioners had become worse off in the interval. Their position is clearly shown by the relation of their pension rate and maximum permissible income to the Sydney basic wage.

Depression

The onset of severe depression and unemployment in 1929-30 marks a watershed in the history of social security in Australia. On the one hand, demands on public and private benevolence multiplied so enormously that priorities were necessarily altered and private interests broadly assigned to government the responsibility of relieving the distress of, and the dangers to the status quo created by, the unemployed. On the other hand, vast extensions of the direct tax mechanism ensured that virtually all income earners, including lower paid workers in employment, helped sustain the unemployed and their dependants.

Through most of the 1920s unemployment rates for Australia had ranged from 4 to 6 per cent, involving loss of earnings by 100 000 to 150 000 people a year. This was tolerated (though not necessarily accepted) partly it seems because many people thought much of it was casual and seasonal in character or due to workers' illness or old age, partly because it was hoped that charitable organisations' efforts did indeed mean, as the Royal Commission (1927, p.15, italics added) said, that 'there need be few persons in genuine distress who would actually go without *some* sustenance during *periods* of unemployment'.

It was not until unemployment became unusually high, in 1928-29, that special provision was made. The enormity of the problems thereafter, with over half a million persons - over 20 per cent of the workforce - out of work in the worst year, are too well known to bear repetition.

The usual form of government relief, public works, was not at first available because no government would raise loans at the going rate of interest to fund them, and in the short run current expenditures were insufficiently flexible. As the number out of work kept rising, the first priority had to be sustenance relief: cash, food or food vouchers from State government sources or meals from the lengthening queues at hastily extended soup kitchens run by private charities. Slowly, workable administrative devices were found to distribute food relief in roughly equitable ways. At best, it was minimal relief. In New South Wales in 1933, after a number of improvements and with the addition of 'permissible earnings' from casual work, it allowed a married couple with a child (the family unit for which the living wage was calculated) food vouchers worth exactly half the current living wage. For the many who could not find casual work, the basic dole had to suffice: a fifth of the living wage. (By contrast, unemployment benefits for a married man were a quarter of average weekly *earnings* in 1972 and close to 40 per cent in 1977.) Local variations quickly developed into matters of settled policy. In Victoria, South Australia and Tasmania, receipt of sustenance carried with it an obligation to work, unpaid, if and as directed; single girls and women on sustenance in Western Australia were required to work a day a week at a sewing centre.

Sustenance was quickly supplemented and then outweighed by public relief works. They were funded first from State taxation revenue and later from loans and Commonwealth grants as well. Between normal public works that would have been undertaken in any event and those designed solely as alternatives to food relief there is a large grey area of works whose funding cannot be allocated unequivocally to either purpose. In general, though, employment on relief works was basically part-time and rationed, with hours of work and scales of pay eventually in accordance with the recipient's position on the food relief scale. In New South Wales and Western Australia, specially proclaimed relief works were exempted from the minimum wage and certain other provisions laid down in industrial awards.

The administration of these relief schemes was gradually systematised and improved. The system of labour exchanges was extended beyond the capital cities - though just how effectively the New South Wales country police sergeant, for example, operated as a labour exchange is not readily known. By 1937, administering unemployment relief was so firmly incorporated in the establishment that the New South Wales Government was explicitly building on it a new Social Aid Service offering medical benefits and welfare services as well as food relief and job search services. Yet, although it was equitable in concept, the administration of sustenance relief and relief work was too often humiliating in the extreme to recipients. The depression and the relief systems it spawned was a trauma that scarred the consciousness of Australians, white-collar as well as blue-collar, for two generations.

Even though relief was given on what may necessarily have been a grudging scale, it soon became immensely costly. In 1931-32 State governments spent £ 8.6m on sustenance relief alone, a sum 40 per cent as large as all other government-funded cash benefits together (and most cash benefits before 1930 were funded by the Commonwealth). In addition another £ 4m from consolidated revenues was spent in that year to provide relief works, and £ 4.6m in the preceding. In subsequent years, expenditure from loan funds for this latter purpose increased, reaching nearly £ 7m in New South Wales alone in 1934-35. The impact that this relief spending had on taxation practice was never lost.

Most State governments retained the income tax provisions, including tax rates, that were in force at the end of the 1920s. These raised revenue from those earning, generally speaking, more than £ 250 a year. With declining personal and company money incomes, collections fell by an average of a third between 1929-30 and 1931-32, and by a half in New South Wales They were quite insufficient to meet the additional expenditure requirements. Governments therefore imposed new taxes on incomes for the specific purpose of providing unemployment relief. South Australia alone refrained from this course, increasing the rates at which ordinary income tax was charged as its alternative. The new special taxes tapped a class of income earners previously immune. In Victoria in 1930 an income as low as £ 1 a week was sufficient to attract unemployment relief tax; in New South Wales and in Western Australia the exemption level was 30s a week. Rates, moreover; were basically proportional. To collect these taxes, governments instituted various pay-as-you-earn arrangements, with employers deducting tax due from wage payments. This meant that the low-income earner's liability to tax payments depended not on annual income but on earnings each week, irrespective of the number of weeks worked during the year. Tax rate structures were later modified and became more progressive, but exemption limits as low as £ 105 and £ 156 per annum - less than the living wage - were retained as late as 1939. Though renamed towards the end of the 1930s or amalgamated with ordinary income taxes, these taxes were still in force in 1942 when the Commonwealth Government took over all income taxation. The result was to bring about a lasting extension of the direct tax impost to those receiving the basic living wage and even less.

Special taxes provided about half of State government revenues from taxation of earnings through the greater part of the 1930s. Their chief significance may lie in the long-term political effects of the habituation of low-income earners to tax liability rather than in the amounts of tax raised from that group. They nevertheless present an unavoidable challenge: much more work than has been done is required to assess the way they changed the incidence of taxation.

At the same time as these direct taxes on earnings were being imposed, the Federal Government in July 1930 introduced a sales tax levied, at the point of wholesale distribution, on manufactured goods. The initial rate was 2 per cent ad valorem, raised in 1931-32 to 6 per cent and then reduced to 5 per cent from October 1933 and to 4 per cent in September 1936. Until the war years, the sales tax lacked the multiple rates that can give it an element of progressive incidence on income groups (goods can be classified as more or less necessary, more or less luxury) and enable it to be used as a tool of social and economic control. (Those elements became much more pronounced after the war, as part of macro-economic regulation.) Many goods of common consumption were exempt from the tax, but it is unlikely that it fell lightly on wage earners and the unemployed. Each year, from 1933 to 1940, it brought in revehue equivalent to three quarters or more of that yielded by the Commonwealth personal and company income tax and between 12 and 17 per cent of its total tax collections. The incidence of a tax as important as this requires investigation; indeed a thorough study of the history of Australian taxation is long overdue.

The depression increased the willingness and the eligibility of the population to apply for public benefits that were not directly unemployment benefits. The fall in earnings as a result of unemployment or part-time employment increased the number of people with more than one dependant child who qualified for New South Wales child endowment by virtue of their receiving wages near or below the living wage. The number of claims granted (including short-term endowments) was half as high again in 1930-31 as it had been in the previous year; and expenditure nearly doubled between 1930-31 and 1932-33 as claimants' earnings fell further below the means test and thus entitled them to more of the 5s per child per week maximum allowance. A similar, though slighter, movement took place in the number of New South Wales widow pensioners. The diminished ability of some old people to provide themselves with adequate support, even with the help of their relatives, may have eroded some of the social and cultural barriers that formerly discouraged them from applying for pensions. (One should not make too much of this: the proportion of the census-date age-eligible population in receipt of age pensions rose only slightly, from 32.1 per cent to 33.4 per cent, between 1921 and 1933.)

Almost inevitably, the generosity of some existing benefits was reduced and conditions of access tightened. The most significant exception to this were war pensions to incapacitated soldiers; pensions for their dependants, however, were cut. Provisions for child endowment in New South Wales also remained unchanged. The maximum rate of age pension was reduced in 1931 and in the following year further reduced for those pensioners (only 37 per cent of the total) whose non-pension income was more than 2s 6d a week. (The full pension was 17s 6d a week.) The 1932 legislation also tightened provisions relating to pensioners' property qualifications (and made their estates the property of the state so that it might be reimbursed for its charity!) and obliged near relatives earning £ 6 a week or more to contribute to pension applicants' support, the grant of a pension and the determination of the amount being conditioned by that obligation. Maternity allowances were reduced from £ 5 to £ 4 in 1931 and means-tested. New South Wales widow pensioners and their children received lower allowances and had to meet a tighter means test. (Among other things, a widow's means-tested income was deemed to include 25 per cent of the earnings of her unmarried children not living with her.) Most of these changes were amended or repealed within three or four years of their enactment, so that their long-term effect was slight.

Despite these economy measures, the position of pensioners relative to others in the community, employed as well as unemployed, was actually improved for part of the 1930s. Reductions in pension rates lagged behind the fall in prices and subsequent increases ran ahead of adjustments to the living wage. Measured as percentages of the 'six capital cities' basic wage, the maximum rate of age pension and the maximum permissible pensioner income rose from about 22 to 28 per cent and from 36 to 46 per cent, respectively, between 1929-30 and 1936-37 (see Table 7.1 for measurements relative to the State living wage in Sydney). In New South Wales, the maximum rate of a widow's pension was unchanged from December 1929 till February 1933, despite the fall in prices, and it was not until June 1939 that the 1929 relationship between maximum pension and living wage was re-established. In the interval, at least the most needy widows had received additional purchasing power that offset the changed conditions of access to the pension, and most were better off than they had been (relative to others) in the 1920s. Similarly, the real value of pensions to incapacitated soldiers increased rapidly until early 1934 and in 1939 was still above its 1929 level.

Education

In the twenty years to 1938-39 governments' spending on education rose from 4.3 per cent of their total expenditures to 6.2 per cent, or from 0.9 per cent of GNP to 1.4 per cent. This far outstripped the growth of public school enrolments, which were only 20 per cent higher at the end of the 1930s than in 1920. The increase resulted from a correspondence of bureaucratic initiatives inspired by educational philosophy and organisational problems, greater industrial requirements for a more highly educated workforce, and a wider private realisation that formal education provided a springboard for social mobility. The importance of developing human capital was being recognised more explicitly.

The proportion of children staying at school for secondary studies is one very important phenomenon where those three interests came together quite clearly. It rose quickly in the 1920s, fell temporarily during the depression and then rose again. The impact of this trend was borne disproportionately by the public school systems. Between 1921 and 1933 the school participation rate of 15-year-olds, for example, rose by nearly a third, from 20.4 to 26.8 per cent, and total enrolments of that age increased by 60 per cent. Of the 12 000-odd additional enrolments, government schools accommodated nearly 80 per cent. Broadly, the same is true of the enrolment of 16-year-olds and of older students. This put pressures on the supply of public sector services. (In New South Wales fees for secondary schooling were reimposed in 1923 'to help meet interest payments on loans used for its expanded school building programme' - they were hastily abandoned a year later.) The student-staff ratio in secondary schools edged up in the 1920s: in New South Wales, for example, from 17.4 to 19.7 between 1921 and 1929. As depression economy measures began to bite, it rose as high as 22.2 in 1932 and settled to range around 21. (Offsetting this, of course, were the higher qualifications of new staff: university medallists often figured among teacher intakes in the 1930s!)

Increased retention of students beyond the age of compulsory schooling was partly a response to, partly a cause of, continued diversification of public secondary education towards technical and homemaking skills. South Australia's first junior technical school, for example, was opened in 1924 and in the following year central schools, with curricula heavily biased to technical and domestic science subjects, were educationally separated from the primary schools with which they were associated. Facilities in day continuation and technical schools elsewhere were increased and improved. These courses provided for the fastest growing sector of school enrolments in the 1920s, high schools' academic courses for the second fastest: the number of students at New South Wales technical day continuation schools increased by 160 per cent between 1921 and 1929, the number at high schools by 90 per cent. That relationship was reversed after the abnormal peak in total secondary enrolments was reached in the early

1930s. Through the rest of the 1930s high school enrolments continued to rise in most States, though slowly, while technical and domestic science enrolments either fell or increased very slowly. Those patterns suggest that students at technical schools tended, to a greater extent than those at high schools, to come from poorer families to whom the cost of continued schooling was an important matter.

There is no reason, of course, to assume that rapidly increasing enrolments in technical schools necessarily represented an equivalent growth of demand for technical education. To some extent it reflected an administratively contrived grouping of those who could not gain entrance to high schools. It is worth noting, however, that the proportion of students leaving New South Wales technical schools in 1928 and going into the trades and unskilled jobs was twice as large as that of high school leavers.

Enrolments at post-school technical training institutions do not share that ambiguity; students made a deliberate choice. In the 1920s enrolments did not increase nearly as quickly as those in technical and high schools. The big boost came in the second half of the 1930s. How far this resulted from technical colleges and even trade schools attracting students by catering to their recreational interests and how far from an increased demand for strictly trade and technical education by people trying to make good depression-caused, or depression-revealed, deficiencies in their training is not immediately obvious. To know the answers might suggest where the benefits of this still well-subsidised branch of education were being directed.

Other important educational developments included special schools for retarded and exceptionally bright children. Educating children in remote areas had always been one of the major challenges for government school systems. It also proved to be one of their more impressive accomplishments. Travelling schools, part-time schools and subsidisation of parents of very small groups of pupils who engaged private teachers were among the innovations of public education bureaucrats. In 1916 the New South Wales Education Department commenced its correspondence school which, operating from Sydney, utilised the mails and the assistance of mothers to take the classroom to the most isolated homestead. By 1938, 20 000 children throughout Australia received their schooling in this manner. For those only slightly less isolated, the one-teacher school remained a haven of primary school instruction, and special attention was devoted to preparing teachers for the special demands that these schools placed on them. Free or subsidised travel and government-provided hostel accommodation in larger provincial towns went some way to provide access to secondary schooling to students from small rural settlements.

We can identify, however tentatively and roughly, some of the major groups that were advantaged by governments' additional expenditure on schools over these years. Increased expenditure on high schools tended to give more benefits to middle-income earners, though a good number of children from low-income families (as well as some from high-income families) were also subsidised in their use of these services. Country children and their parents were thought to be better off because of the special services extended to them and children from lower-income families may have been the main recipients of the subsidies extended through the provision of technical and domestic science courses in schools. There is, however, another group that began, during this period, to reap slightly disproportionate advantages from government school systems: the teachers themselves. Although conditions varied from State to State, in the second half of the 1920s the number of government schoolteachers over Australia as a whole was increased more rapidly than the number of students; from the depth of the depression through to 1936, the number of teachers was virtually stationary while the number of students declined; and from 1937 until 1942-43 the number of teachers was again increased even though the number of students continued to decline. In this way an avenue was kept open for that large element of the population to whom teaching represented a classic mechanism of social mobility.

Health

Health care services, like education services, became effectively available to and were consumed by a greater proportion of the population. Readily available statistics of hospital care during this period are not good; they should, and can, be improved. In New South Wales, Victoria and South Australia the number of public hospital beds per 1000 persons increased by 10 per cent in the 1920s and 40 per cent in the 1930s; the number of in-patients treated per 1000 persons in these three States and Queensland grew by nearly 40 per cent in the 1920s and by over 50 per cent in the 1930s. The consumption of medical services seems to have increased as well. There is no direct evidence of this but the fact that friendly societies' payments on account of members' medical bills rose considerably faster, between 1914 and 1939, than members' contributions and the societies' other payments is suggestive. These societies reached the peak of the popularity in the twenty years or so before 1930, when their cover extended to perhaps a quarter of the population.

There were important developments and extensions in public and private provisions for child and infant welfare, in the form of baby health centres, pre- and post-natal health education services, day care centres, infant care facilities and medical and dental inspections of school children. Campaigns against major outbreaks of specific infectious diseases as well as long-term programs to eradicate them were organised and financed by governments. These activities were important, but despite some impressive accomplishments neither singly nor jointly did public and private endeavour form a coherent approach to what we now call the problem of public health.

The main thrust of the health care industry lay in the increased provision and use of hospital accommodation, largely financed by governments. Three elements stand out. There was, first, increased centralised oversight and regulation of public hospitals, in the manner foreshadowed in New South Wales before 1914. Most public hospitals, it must be remembered, were voluntary organisations. Only the governance, management, personnel and building specifications of some were determined by statute. Creation of the Victorian Hospitals and Charities Board in 1923, of the New South Wales Hospitals Commission in 1929 and perhaps the grouping of Queensland hospitals into districts in 1923, increased government control of hospitals' policies by making more effective the sanction of withholding a subsidy. Second, largely in consequence, there was an increased emphasis on patients meeting more of the cost of hospital services, illustrated for New South Wales and Victoria in Table 7.2. Third, there was a relative diminution in the importance of public hospitals wholly maintained by government. In South Australia in 1920, for example, there were ten government public hospitals and nineteen non-government, in 1940 twelve and forty-four respectively; and the largest of the New South Wales public hospitals passed from government to 'voluntary' control in the mid-1930s.

TABLE 7.2 **Public hospitals: sources of receipts by percentage shares, selected years**

	N.S.W.				Victoria	
	Patients	Systematic contributions[a]	State aid	Other	Patients	State aid	Other
1920–21	14	—	48	38	16	27	57
1924–25	13	—	44	43	15	32	53
1925–26	13	—	46	41	14	32	54
1927–28	16	—	44	40	15	31	54
1930–31	.24	7	40	29	18	40	42
1931–32	23	8	43	26	19	38	43
1935–36	27	15	43	20	20	40	40
1936–37	24	17	47	23	18	38	44
1938–39	26	16	46	22	20	39	41

[a] Donations made to hospitals, on pre-agreed bases, by hospital-insurance-like funds. May include some payments directly on account of patients.

Sources: N.S.W.: *Statistical Register;* Hospital Commission, *Reports.*
    Vic.: Victorian Year Book.

Making consumers pay more symbolised a major alteration in the role of public hospitals. A compromise was effected between the widened demand for hospital treatment expressed by all social classes and the divergent interests of different groups of medical practitioners. It was not the only compromise open. It continued to make the best medical attention available to the very poor, who were not charged and were treated by honorary medical officers. At the same time, by allowing practitioners (for the first time) to treat other patients, in hospital, on a normal private fee basis, the need for heavy private investment in facilities was eliminated. Fee-charging medical practitioners not only became dependant on hospital facilities largely built and serviced at public expense, but also became key figures in determining hospitals' access policies and practice. Increasingly, public hospital patients were drawn from middle-income groups.

Since early in the twentieth century, at the latest, patients had been expected to contribute, in accordance with their ability to pay, towards their treatment and maintenance in public hospitals. The 1929 New South Wales Public Hospitals Act defined that liability and made the charge legally recoverable. At that time, too, building on earlier proposals, both New South Wales and Victoria encouraged public, subsidised, hospitals to open special wards for private and intermediate patients and thus become 'community hospitals'. The effect of these policies is evident in Table 7.2. It is apparent, too, in the fact that in 1933-34 and the rest of the 1930s only about 25 per cent of in-patients in New South Wales public hospitals were treated without charge. The number of beds in New South Wales private hospitals, however, having reached a peak in 1929, was almost identical in 1930 and 1940, falling between those dates from over a third of the State's general hospital beds to a quarter. To an extent at least, they were being replaced by private and intermediate beds in public hospitals. But the majority of patients were still public ward patients. Many came from the bottom half of income earners, and hospital bills could be catastrophic. To bring realism to the policy of 'consumer pays more', various forms of insurance and insurance-like funds were encouraged. Some exchanged regular donations to a hospital for a member's entitlement to a specified period of free hospitalisation (though not medical care); others provided members with a partial refund of hospital expenses. The New South Wales Hospitals Commission helped initiate some of these schemes; it certainly threatened sanctions against hospitals that did not adopt them. The risk-spreading characteristic of these funds was of undoubted value. At the same time, reference to Table 7.2 shows the extent to which they provided, in New South Wales, mediating mechanisms in a process by which a substantial part of the funding of public hospitals was transferred from private charity to government and from government to user.

All this while, a large and varied collection of general and special hospitals, sanatoria and mental hospitals, offering treatment quite without charge to users, was operated and wholly maintained by the Commonwealth Repatriation Commission for the benefit of ex-servicemen. The Commission's *Reports* are remarkably uninformative about the arrangements it had with medical practitioners at its institutions and about costs incurred in the treatment of different groups of patients. Perhaps this is one reason why the existence and operation of the Repatriation Hospitals seem to have had no impact on the operation and policies of public hospitals subsidised by State governments - apart only from the exchange of clinical findings and the obvious fact that patients would otherwise have been the responsibility of public hospitals. It is probable that archival records could open a worthwhile study of this closed facet of hospital services.

8

Welfare for All 1940-1975

The hesitant recovery of the economy in the later years of the 1930s was succeeded by full wartime employment. There were forebodings, however, about the likely unemployment in the immediate peacetime years. They turned out to be unfounded. After 1945 there was more than a quarter of a century during which the unemployment rate did not exceed 3 per cent of the civilian workforce and was below 2 per cent except in brief recessions. At the same time Australia experienced a rate of growth of real income per head that had not even been approximated since the decades before 1890. Only in the late 1960s, with the onset of stagflation, did confidence in high employment falter. Within this context the place, nature and impact of government social welfare policies altered dramatically.

From the 1940s, welfare policy was increasingly centralised in the Federal sphere. Backed by Federal control of income taxes, by specific purpose conditional grants to States, and subsequently by constitutional amendment, this transfer began during the war. First, the manpower demands of a 'total' war forced Federal attention to education, health and unemployment. Second, politicians and bureaucrats were aware of the need to balance war-directed sacrifices with prospects of a better post-war world. They were equally aware of the profound popular cynicism about the 'world fit for heroes' that had been promised a previous generation. From 1941, moreover, Australia was led by Labor Governments responsive to trade union pressures and to widespread criticism of the social wastes in the depression of the 1930s. They were committed to social change and quite deliberately used wartime measures to prepare for post-war reconstruction. They planned a comprehensive system of social security and welfare broadly similar to and in close association with Beveridge's 'cradle to the grave' approach. Full employment was the central goal, for this was seen as the basic element of social security and perhaps, in the long horizons of peace, the condition necessary to the survival of capitalist democracies. With full employment were to be associated relief for

192

those who might nevertheless be unemployed, greater security for the aged and for widows, improved and more accessible health care, and better housing for the urban poor.

These pressures and initiatives made social welfare policies leading electoral issues, at State and Federal level, in the next thirty years and it was in this period that specific welfare beneficiaries or potential beneficiaries, other than war veterans, first organised as special pressure groups. But there were major conflicts in post-war political and social ideologies that conditioned policy on social welfare. Labor's electoral defeat followed partly from antagonism of particular interest groups to bank nationalisation and 'nationalised medicine'. Reformist government was replaced by conservative coalition government. Subsequent policies (1949 to 1966) favoured middle- and upper-income groups. After 1966, conservative governments were gradually forced again to consider the problems of the traditional needy groups and of those newly recognised (even as, simultaneously, they extended welfare provisions to the well-to-do). The Whitlam Labor Governments (1972 to 1975) went forward in splendid ambition to reform without reducing the welfare of any group in the community. Conservative reaction, expressed through the Fraser Governments, has since been to rein in on all welfare programs.

Despite the deep ideological differences in approach, despite changes in the benefits and services and despite the long period of conservative government after 1949, welfare provisions were vastly extended. To age and invalid pensions there were added in the 1940s child endowment, widows' pensions, unemployment and sickness benefits and assistance of varying forms in meeting hospital, pharmaceutical and medical expenses. Subsequent measures extended government help to students at secondary and tertiary institutions, in private schools and public, both as direct cash transfers and indirectly as grants to educational institutions. Low-income groups were supported through the provision of low-rental housing and legal aid, through support to newly arrived migrants and single-parent families and through the services of social workers and rehabilitation centres to those whose need was for counselling and retraining as much as for financial assistance. Successive governments built on existing welfare activities so that a class of benefits or of welfare recipients, once created, was assured of continued existence. Acceptance of precedent was rudely broken by the Fraser Government.

New relationships between public and private roles in welfare were another change marking the post-war period. The tendency in the pre-1914 and inter-war periods was for public benefits and public and semi-public services to supplant those previously provided by organised private endeavour. During and immediately after the war, this tendency appeared to be confirmed. Since 1949 there has been, instead, a quite conscious public use of the market.

Though probably stronger under non-Labor administration, this has become a continuing feature of Australian welfare. Medical and hospital benefits developed as subsidies to those who insured against risks; income tax concessions encouraged this insurance. The activities and incomes of general practitioner and specialist doctors, of private hospitals and nursing homes and, indirectly, of dentists and optometrists were publicly underwritten. So too were the private health insurance funds. Income tax concessions gave a powerful stimulus to private life insurance and superannuation, for a time limiting potential claimants for public age benefits. Private builders, building societies and private school educators have all been supported by forms of welfare benefit. Tax concessions and benefit supports to individuals, such as those for education expenses or those given as Home Savings Grants, necessarily bolster (and distort) the relevant private market activity. Other measures have been designed to support private non-market operations: subsidies to charitable organisations such as the Red Cross Blood Transfusion Service; tax concessions for gifts to charities (a device of long standing); and certain provisions to encourage accommodation for the aged. Public commitment to the use of the market in the delivery of welfare might be perceived as a relatively efficient system. Whether it is socially efficient - still less equitable - is another matter.

The share of all governments' outlays devoted to welfare (excluding housing and grants for private capital purposes) rose from an average of a quarter in the second half of the 1930s to a third during the 1960s and a half in the 1970s. The way in which this expenditure was financed forms a further important change.

Between 1945 and 1970, for the first time in Australian history, direct taxes on personal and company incomes provided revenue enough to meet the total welfare spending of all governments. Further, Commonwealth income tax reimbursements to the States under the Uniform Tax Agreement, and the general grants that later took their place, sufficed to meet total State welfare payments, and income tax revenues retained by the Commonwealth failed to cover its welfare spending only in 1963. After 1970, States' welfare expenditures exceeded income tax revenues transferred to them by the Commonwealth. The increasing importance of Commonwealth deficit financing in the 1970s greatly complicates questions about funding. Nevertheless, although there are dangers enough in associating any specific expenditures with specific sources of revenue, the whole of the post-war period to 1975 can be very broadly characterised as one in which governments' welfare expenditures were financed by income tax receipts.

The importance of the changed system of funding is that the indirect taxes that financed much welfare expenditure before 1940 were generally regressive in their incidence, whereas Australian taxes on incomes were generally regarded as more progressive. Income taxes, that is, appeared as a more equitable source of welfare funding. (The total tax structure has, of course, a different incidence, as Bentley et al. (1974) and Warren (1979) show, bearing regressively on the lower-income families, almost proportionally on the majority and progressively only on the top 20 per cent. As important as this pattern is for the distribution of 'economic wellbeing' and for redistributive policies as a whole, the role of taxation as a redistributive mechanism is beyond the narrower scope that can be encompassed here. An historical study could be most rewarding.)

In so far as direct taxes and welfare expenditure can be related, it is useful to look at changes in the 'progressiveness' of those taxes after 1945. The extension of State income taxes to formerly untaxed, low-income groups in the 1930s was followed by the Commonwealth's interest in taxation to help finance the war and to control inflationary pressures, by uniform rates imposed throughout Australia as part of the Uniform Taxation Agreement and then by nation-wide resort to taxpayers of the lowest income groups in the name of Social Security Contributions. It has already been suggested that widely accessible welfare budgets became politically feasible in Australia only when income tax was imposed, after 1942, on almost all incomes: all contributed and hence all could receive. But after the war, the additional contributions of wage earners became more significant.

'Progressive' tax rates, rarely changed, meant that rising levels of money income carried wage earners into higher and higher tax brackets. Groups that were in fact at the lower end of current money income distributions became subject to tax rates originally designed for higher income recipients. Moreover, because there was an upper cut-off point in the progressiveness of tax rates, groups at the higher end of the income distribution scale were not comparably affected. For these reasons and others (including the greater number of multiple-income families, tax avoidance and evasion), the incidence of personal income tax on household units (the income unit most relevant to welfare questions) has almost certainly become less progressive than it was in the inter-war period or in 1955. Certainly, its incidence in 1966-67 and 1975-76, the only years for which estimates have been made, was at best one of muted progression. If households are arranged in ascending order of income (defined to include social security cash benefits) then the tax in 1966-67 fell very lightly on the bottom 10 per cent of households and took between 7.78 and 11.07 per cent of the incomes of the next six tenths of households (Bentley et al. 1974). For the remaining 30 per cent of households the tax impact rose from 11.92 to 17.03 per cent of incomes. On the assumptions used by the estimators, taxes on company income, on the other hand, were regressive over the bottom 40 per cent of households and progressive only over the top 20 per cent. It is possible, given rising real incomes and changed savings and investment behaviour, that a greater proportion of people in lower income groups were affected by company income tax in 1966-67 than earlier. Because taxes on company income were a significant proportion of direct taxes a thorough study of their incidence would be desirable.

As lower income groups were increasingly drawn in as tax contributors, there was a pervasive trend for the middle- and upper-income groups to reap more substantial benefits from welfare policies. At times, indeed, the welfare 'needs' of the better off seemed to overshadow those of the poor. Proposals to abolish the means test for age pensions, and steps already taken in that direction, are addressed to the middle- and upper-income households. The main avenues through which these groups have secured a significant new access to public redistributive policies have not, however, been those of social security. They have, rather, been parts of the new post-war welfare package whose benefits are not necessarily caught in the measures of household income used in Australian studies. The continued occupation of low-rental, welfare housing by families whose incomes had risen beyond the qualifying limit represented a welfare cost to the community and, to the extent that people qualified by income were unable to be accommodated and forced to pay higher rentals, a direct redistribution from poorer to wealthier. Medical and hospital benefits provided by government conditionally upon the recipient's membership of an insurance fund clearly advantaged middle-income earners in a way they had not been advantaged previously: the incidence of health care costs became increasingly regressive over much of the post-war period. Both the income tax concessional allowances for schooling expenses and the conditions of scholastic merit on which secondary and tertiary education scholarships and living allowances were awarded clearly favoured the better-off taxpayers and their children. Given the social and economic backgrounds of undergraduates, the abolition of university fees redistributed benefits towards that same group. Indeed the whole sequence of wider access to schools that led to increased qualifications being required of employees in turn inducing children to stay at school longer meant, in essence, that the majority of children of working-class families delayed their entry to the workforce for longer (and at a cost to their families) without generally gaining advantage from it, relative to other children, in their subsequent workforce experience. There is no need to multiply examples.

Taken in conjunction, the ungenerosity of Australian welfare benefits, particularly the traditional benefits that were directed to relief of poverty (relative both to other countries and to average Australian earnings), the pattern of taxation established since the

1940s, and the middle-class capture of substantial welfare benefits suggest a massive shift in welfare objectives and practice since 1949, emphasising the absence of a definitely equitable concern in Australian welfare approaches.

Social security

After the special preoccupations of the inter-war years there was, in the 1940s, a burst of welfare initiatives reminiscent of the concerns of the first decade of Federation. It reflected a new perspective on the condition of the people and established social security provisions that provided a basic framework for the next thirty years. The legislative program was enacted by the Commonwealth Parliament, its originators the reformist Labor Governments supported by trade union interests and advised by a new brand of bureaucrats. Yet it built on a concern with social security and social stability evidenced in the 1938 National Health and Pensions Insurance Act introduced by a conservative government, by the appointment of the National Insurance Commission in the same year, and by proposals for unemployment insurance in 1939. The war reinforced conservatives' perception of the importance of ameliorative social policies, a perception influenced after 1942 by substantially universal income taxation. The pattern of social security that was established had an essentially bipartisan support.

The nine reports of the Joint Parliamentary Committee on Social Security provide an indication of this broad agreement between political parties. Working under the Menzies Government and the succeeding Curtin administration, it recommended a wide range of Commonwealth initiatives in social security benefits and services. Though equally representative of government and opposition in all but its last report, only one of its recommendations was not unanimous. The only difference in political outlooks that is evident in the reports concerned the means of financing social security benefits: an insurance scheme in the only report eprsented to the Menzies Government, income taxation in subsequent reports. The difference is not nearly as profound as may appear at first sight, because universal income tax had made almost all families contributors. It nevertheless had important implications for redistribution, especially at that time.

The introduction of cradle-to-the-grave social security

It was not so much these concerns with social conditions as some economic consequences of war itself that produced the first of the new welfare provisions. War organisation of the economy carried with it certain imperatives. High among them was the control of inflation and its consequences. An immediate fall-out was the introduction of child endowment. In 1941 the Menzies Government legislated to pay an allowance of 5s a week to mothers for all children under the age of 16 other than the first. Like the earlier child endowment schemes in the Commonwealth Public Service and in New South Wales, for which Lang had been vilified by employers, this was an alternative to a basic wage increase. It was to be financed primarily by a newly introduced payroll tax, just as the New South Wales endowment had been, and partly by the abolition of income tax concessions for children other than the first. It differed from previous schemes, however, in being universally available, without regard to family earnings. The principle of universal access had appeared.

Means-tested pensions for widows, among whom were included de facto widows, deserted wives and divorcees, were taken as a Commonwealth responsibility by the Labor Government in 1942, extending income support previously restricted to those in New South Wales and Victoria. Automatic cost-of-living adjustments to age and invalid pensions were reintroduced and the rates increased. In 1943 came cash allowances to wives and children of invalid pensioners and a benefit towards the funeral expenses of age and invalid pensioners. Most significantly in the long run, the blueprint of the scheme for unemployment and sickness benefits (from New Zealand again) was passed in 1944 and became operative in 1945. Means tested for income only, they differed markedly from unemployment relief during the depression. Benefits were in cash, not kind; they were available to people not previously employed as well as to others; they were paid no matter what the cause of unemployment - excepting only direct participation in a strike; and they were available to all who met the statutory qualifying requirements, leaving less obvious scope for the administrative discretion so objectionable in the 1930s.

Within those three wartime years, then, all the social security recommendations made by the Joint Parliamentary Committee as part of its 'Plan against Poverty' were carried into effect. Along with old-age and invalid pensions, maternity allowances and veterans' pensions they provide still the major social security cash benefits.

Proliferation of benefits

After 1945 State governments introduced, or continued to provide, benefits for people in need who slipped through the interstices of the Commonwealth welfare net, especially to widows, deserted wives and their children. New Commonwealth measures after the defeat of Labor in 1949 resulted from identifying special areas of need among those already in receipt of benefits and from identifying groups similar to those already protected. In 1950, for example, the Menzies

Government extended child endowment to the first (or only) child. Presaging future tendencies, it made endowment a wholly universal benefit. Increases in endowment rates to large families, in 1964 and 1967, were aimed at diminishing poverty among large families, but inclusion of student children aged 16 to 21 in 1964 favoured the well-to-do. Similarly, in 1956 pensionable widows were awarded higher pensions if they had more than one dependant child under 16; and in 1963 this was widened by making a payment in respect of first (or only) children and a separate mother's allowance in addition to the pension. Widows and single age and invalid pensioners, who paid rent and were wholly dependant on pensions, were given discretionary supplementary assistance from 1958. From 1967, persons in sheltered workshops were paid at slightly above the rate of invalid pensions as, in 1968, were handicapped children in religious or charitable homes. The Whitlam Government inaugurated a supporting mother's allowance in 1973 to provide assistance to unmarried mothers, de facto wives who had been deserted and others, with dependent children, who did not qualify for a widow's pension. In the same year special benefits were given to orphans and in 1974 allowances were paid to handicapped children living with their parents.

Benefit levels

Despite the array of benefits, the record of Australian governments in social security is marked by a lack of generosity that bordered, at least until the late 1960s, on meanness. Of eleven OECD countries for which evidence is available, only Japan had a lower ratio of public expenditure on income maintenance to 'trend' national income in both 1962 and 1972, and the Australian and New Zealand ratios were the only two to fall between these two years. The real value of a weighted basket of Australian benefits increased by only 13 per cent between 1949 and 1969, while real income per head increased some 80 per cent (Hancock, 1971, Table 7).

In absolute terms, the position of beneficiaries was greatly improved. Rates for age, invalid and widows' pensions (which since the late 1950s have absorbed more than half the Commonwealth's social security expenditure) were adjusted frequently. Since the early 1950s they increased more rapidly than the cost of living. By 1968-69, for example, the real value of a single person's age pension was 40 per cent higher than it had been twenty years earlier; a married couple's joint pension 25 per cent higher and that of a widow, with dependent children over 75 per cent higher. Most of these advances had been achieved in the period of relative price stability in the first half of the 1960s.

An alternative perspective comes from comparison with non-pensioner earnings. Since the war average earnings have outstripped the rise in consumer price indices. A single person's age pension (later a standard pension) was equivalent in 1948-49 to 24.2 per cent of Australian pre-tax average earnings per male unit. During the Korean War boom it fell sharply, then oscillated within a narrow range around an average of 21.5 per cent from 1950 until 1967, after which it troughed at less than 19 per cent. That fall motivated the 1972 Labor government's objective of raising it to the equivalent of 25 per cent of average male earnings. Yet increased affluence among the rest of the community is not necessarily evidence of the development of secondary poverty among pensioners. Age pensioners, in particular, received a variety of supplementary assistance: the pensioner medical scheme and funeral benefits, concessions from public enterprises in reduced telephone rentals, fares, radio and television licences and reduced local government rates. Eligibility for these fringe benefits was governed, from 1955, by a means test more stringent than that applied to applicants for the pension itself, thus easing the circumstances of poorer pensioners.

Not all benefit recipients were as fortunate. The rate of endowment for children other than the first doubled between 1941 and 1948, a much more rapid rise than that in the cost of living. The basic rate then remained unchanged until 1976, when the whole system of endowment was replaced by the family allowance scheme and the withdrawal of tax concessions for dependent children. Nevertheless, despite the additional protection afforded large families in 1964 and 1967, the real value of endowment benefits to a family with six children, Hancock found (1971, Table 7), was no greater in 1969 than in 1949. (Other benefits have, however, been made available to particularly disadvantaged people with dependent children.) The maternity allowance, similarly, was not changed between 1943 and its abolition in 1978. Irregular adjustments after 1949 helped to protect the relative real value of unemployment and sickness benefits, but the tendency was for them to be eroded. An unemployed man with dependent wife and one child was 'best' off in 1952 with benefit at a third of average earnings per male unit; subsequently he was worst off in 1968, when it was equivalent to less than a quarter. Mounting pressures towards a 'liberalisation' of conservative government policies towards the end of the 1960s, and the Whitlam Government's efforts to improve the lot of welfare beneficiaries generally, led to a substantial rise in the relative value of unemployment and sickness benefits between 1969 and 1975. In the June quarter of 1975 the unemployed man with dependent wife and one child received nearly 43 per cent of average earnings per male unit, and despite both rising unemployment and continued inflation that relationship was maintained until at least June 1978.

Widened access

As the relative value of benefits fell they were made more readily available. Universal access to child endowment, maternity allowances and unemployment benefits has already been noted and widened or universal access to other welfare services and benefits is highlighted elsewhere. The trend is best evidenced by liberalisation of the means test. A national insurance scheme projected in the 1938 Act would have eliminated means-tested pensions for those covered by the scheme. That concept was abandoned during the war. By the late 1940s, nevertheless, the principle of universal age pensions had been accepted, at least in terms of political rhetoric, by Labor and non-Labor parties alike. Over the next quarter of a century political pressures were exerted, through the bureaucracy and informal private networks to give effect to this rhetoric and thus overcome the relative loss of advantage that inflation's erosion of the value of middle-class private market savings had created. Many adjustments were made to the means test in line with changes in general economic conditions. More fundamental relaxations occurred in 1954 when income from property was excluded from the test; in 1961 when the merged means test treating income and property as interdependent became operative; in 1969 when the tapered means test stretched to almost double the old limits of income-property at which pension eligibility ceased; and in 1972 when people whose means did not exceed three times the maximum rate of pension were still eligible for some pension payment. The age-eligible population in receipt of pensions, full or partial, rose from 37.5 per cent in 1947 (slightly higher than the 32 per cent recorded between 1911 and 1933) to 67.8 per cent in 1973 (see Table 8.1.) From there it was not such a large step for the Whitlam Government to eliminate means tests for those aged 75 and over in 1973 and for those aged 70 to 74 in 1975. Pensions, however, became taxable, though a partial offset was given in the form of a special rebate on account of age. Similar changes were made to the means tests for invalids and widows, though tests were retained for all applicants, with similar effects on participation rates.

Increased rates and wider access are competitive. It was certainly budgetary constraints that, in immediate terms, bedevilled and delayed all promises from the 1940s on to abolish the means test for

TABLE 8.1 **Percentage of age-eligible persons in receipt of age pensions**

1947	37.5	1967	53.2	1972	62.0
1954	42.1	1968	54.6	1973	67.8
1957	45.7	1969	55.5	1974	72.9
1961	51.0	1970	60.2	1975	76.1
1966	52.9	1971	61.2	1976	75.4

age pensions within some specified period. More testingly, commitment to a new program is a result of competition, also, with other potential new programs. In part, tension arose from conflicts between the political and social implications of efforts to extend eligibility or assist the poor further. Contained in the process of choice were issues of political and bureaucratic objectives and the types and importance of private interests affected. Opposing a universal age pension in 1950 Chifley was more 'concerned about the people on the lowest rung of the economic ladder, who suffer great hardship under present living conditions'; and Cairns, at a Labor Party conference in 1967, said 'There are 600,000 people at the lower end of the pension scale living in poverty. There must be a proper sense of proportion. I don't want to see this party become a middle class party too quickly ... ' (quoted by Kewley 1969, pp. 292 and 406). Despite such protestations, the tension in that case skewed political actions, for a considerable time, to favour a little for many at the expense of further bettering the position of the poorest pensioners. The effect of gradual inflation on the value of the savings and property income of middle-income groups had created pressures to obtain additional retirement income. In turn, though, resolving the tension in that manner tightened the screw further and created new tension that was released only by the simultaneous provision of greater access and increased real rates of pension. The belief that the distribution of costs could be ignored appeared in the Whitlam Government's view of the economy as a 'magic pudding'. By contrast but not surprisingly, with increasing funds required after 1974 for unemployment benefits government subsequently moved in an opposite direction, endeavouring to restrict access by imposing longer waiting periods and stricter 'work tests'.

Redistributive implications

The income status of some recipients of some benefits can be gauged fairly accurately. In June 1975 just under a half the people receiving widows' pensions, invalid pensions and supporting mothers' benefits had no assessed income apart from the benefit (Department of Social Security, 1974-75, Tables 5, 21 and 26). It is possible that some of these beneficiaries may have received income from property, not included in the assessable income used for means testing, but it is improbable that this would change the calculation by more than a few percentage points. This means that, at a time when Australian average earnings were over $8000 a year, those pensioners were dependent on public support ranging from $1872 to $2444. Only 17 per cent of all beneficiaries in these groups received an assessed income (which excludes income from property) in excess of $1040, in addition to their pensions.

It is more difficult to generalise about the poverty status of age pensioners because of the greater extent of home ownership among them (probably increased since 1908) and the likelihood that income from property is greater and more widely spread than in some other pensioner groups. It is significant, however, that the proportion of age pensioners entitled to maximum pensions who also owned their homes increased from 58 per cent of all age pensioners in 1971 to 63 per cent in 1978 and that the proportion of all pensioners entitled to full pensions declined from 79 per cent to 69 per cent over the same period. Similarly, while nearly 92 per cent of all age pensioners were eligible, under a means test stricter than that used for the pension itself, to enrol in the Pensioner Medical Scheme in 1959, twenty years later the proportion had shrunk to 79 per cent. The means available to that 70 per cent or 80 per cent of pensioners were nevertheless very limited. The redistributive thrust of child endowment, handicapped children and sheltered workshop allowances as well as of veterans' pensions is unclear though it is likely that distribution of recipients' family incomes pretty well matched that of the population as a whole.

At a more general level, however, two sets of findings are extremely important. First, the Australian Bureau of Statistics survey of income distribution in 1973-74 (Tables 19 and 23) indicates that a half of all government social security cash benefits (defined to include government educational scholarships and rehabilitation payments as well as age, widows', veterans' and invalid pensions and unemployment, sickness and special benefits and tuberculosis allowances) went to households, including single person households, whose total annual income inclusive of the benefits was less than $3000. In that year average earnings were over $6000 and the median income, including benefits, of all income units was over $5200. But nearly a third of income maintenance payments, defined in this broad way, went to households whose total income exceeded average earnings and 40 per cent went to households whose total income was above the median. Second, Podder and Kakwani (1975, Table 5) in the only study of its kind show that in 1966-67 the net effect of the government taxing original incomes and then supplementing them with cash benefits changed the share of lowest quintile of families from 2.9 per cent of original personal incomes to 7 per cent of personal disposable incomes. The share of the second lowest quintile increased from 13.7 to 14.2 per cent and that of the highest quintile was reduced from 41 per cent to 37.2. The net position of the other 40 per cent of families, relative to all others, was scarcely changed.

Voluntary organisations

The continued existence of poverty despite the extension of welfare since 1940 was evidenced in the *Reports* of the Henderson Commission on Poverty. At a time when social welfare is absorbing close to 50 per cent of all public authority expenditures, discussion is turning to other ways of meeting and financing needs: negative taxes, national superannuation, 'demo-grants' and so on. These proposals have long-term significance. In the meantime private charity is still being called upon to supplement public provisions. This supplementation is far from the primary role voluntary organisations played in 1900. Over the past two or three decades, a new relationship has emerged between government and charitable associations: while government provides cash benefits it has withdrawn almost completely from the direct provision of welfare services that was characterised by its orphanages and asylums at the beginning of the century and the private sector is called upon more to deliver welfare services associated with income support. We know virtually nothing about charity dispensed through families or through voluntary organisations. To ask the extent of help given to unemployed people by near relatives; to ask how many orphaned children are cared for by families; to ask how many aged parents live with their children: these questions indicate merely some of the dimensions of our ignorance. It seems, though we cannot really be sure, that voluntary organisations tend to be even more concerned now than formerly with the systematised provision of services (meals on wheels, aged persons' homes) that are directly subsidised by government.

It is no easy task to assemble adequate statistics portraying the activities of these organisations. However, official statisticians no longer try, which is unforgivable. There are indications, however, that even before unemployment in the 1970s increased the calls on their help, voluntary societies' assistance to individuals in cash and kind, while proportionately much less now than in (say) the 1920s, was widespread and probably increasing. Between 1950 and 1970, for example, total charitable expenditure of the Society of Saint Vincent de Paul rose nearly sevenfold (average weekly earnings during the same period rose nearly fourfold). Nearly half of that 1950 expenditure took the form of relief in cash or kind; about 60 per cent of it in 1970. Similarly, the 'family welfare' expenditure of Brisbane Legacy increased from $49 000 in 1965 to $76 000 in 1970, the largest category of expenditures being those for 'weekly sustenance'. While the number of cases considered annually by Brisbane Legacy rose from about 600 in 1952 to 1000 in the late 1960s the persons relieved by the Society of Saint Vincent de Paul jumped from 33 000 in 1950 to 316 000 in 1970. But statistics of this sort are no better than straws. Despite the formal association of charitable organisations into the Australian Council of Social Service nearly twenty years ago very little is known of them. Research is needed on their functions and activities.

Education

Growth of education services

The post-war growth of Australian secondary industry into technically more demanding fields; the technical transformation of primary industries requiring complex machinery and biological and chemical knowledge; and the changing character of service industries, especially public administration and community and business services with informational and interpretative functions - all demanded a more highly skilled workforce. The need to develop and improve the stock of human capital transformed education provisions between 1945 and 1965. Participation rates rose greatly. Both as response and cause came a wider variety of educational facilities; greater emphasis was placed on post-school technical and other vocational education; schooling became more flexible, more student-oriented; access to education was democratised; prevailing educational philosophies were metamorphosed.

The restructuring of educational facilities and opportunities coincided with an enormous expansion of the population in those age groups most likely to seek formal education. With demographic factors reinforcing economic requirements, the resources devoted to education increased dramatically. Total expenditure on education rose from about 1.75 per cent of GDP in 1950-51 to 4.1 per cent in 1967-68 and to 6.2 per cent in 1975-76. The pattern of public sector spending changed significantly. In the inter-war years governments' education outlays were almost wholly devoted to services provided in kind by State governments. After 1945, funding of education became more centralised in the Federal Government which financed 5 per cent of all government outlays on education in 1950-51, 20 per cent in 1969-70 and over 40 per cent by 1975. In the process, financial assistance to students and to private schools meant that cash transfers became much more significant.

The pressures on education services in the twenty years after 1945 were intense. The number of children aged between 5 and 14, for most of whom schooling was compulsory, increased by 40 per cent between 1947 and 1954 and by 30 per cent between 1954 and 1961. They were 15 per cent of the entire population in 1947 and nearly 20 per cent in 1961. After the absolute decline in numbers in the age group between 1933 and 1947, and after the diversion of resources out of education during the war, public and private schools were unprepared for the new demands made on them. Overcrowded classrooms, abbreviated teacher training programs and a rapid change in the sex ratio among teachers became apparent in the 1950s.

A more lasting and influential pressure for change came from the increased demand for education services by those for whom it was not compulsory. Between 1955 and 1965, as war, post-war and immigrant babies grew older, the number of 15- to 19-year-olds jumped by 80 per cent and their share of the total population rose from 6.6 to 9.1 per cent. This alone would have swollen senior high school enrolments. Yet by far the greater pressure came from sharply increased participation rates.

In 1954 only 15 per cent of those aged 15 to 19 years were at school. New South Wales evidence suggests that the proportion had been rising steadily since the late 1940s. After 1954 retention rates soared, rising sharply and continuously until the early 1970s. Over the next twenty years, increasing retention rates accounted for three quarters of the additional enrolment of 15- to 19-year-olds. Even the increased retention of 15-year-olds that resulted from raising the statutory school leaving age to 15 between 1960 and 1965 is swamped by other forces. The detailed figures in Table 8.2 speak eloquently of the revolution in the attitudes of students and their parents. They do not indicate, however, the revolution that occurred in the attitudes of education administrators. From the mid-1950s moves were started to make secondary school studies more appropriate to the nature and aspirations of the increasing proportion of students already choosing more schooling, and to abandon the concept of elite, competitive entry to high schools. It was not until New South Wales secondary schooling was reorganised in 1962, for example, that entry to high school automatically followed completion of the standard primary school years. (Although the examination-based Qualifying Certificate was

TABLE 8.2 **Australian school participation rates, by age, 1933 to 1977**

Age last birthday	1933 %	1954 %	1961 %	1966 %	1971 %	1974 %	1977 %
15	26.8	42.6	60.9	73.4	81.5	81.6	86.0
16	14.7	19.3	30.5	43.1	53.7	53.8	58.6
17	7.4	9.4*	12.1	17.9	28.8	29.7	32.0
18	3.5	n.a.	4.7**	5.3**	7.6	6.7	6.8
19	1.7	n.a.	n.a.	n.a	1.3	1.2	1.4
Total 15–19	10.8	14.8	22.7	27.8	34.9	35.5	37.6
Total population aged 15–19 ('000)	613	592	809	1,055	1,122	1,205	1,275

*   17 and over as % of 17-year olds.
** 18 and over as % of 18-year olds.
Sources: 1933 Census; ABS Schools, Demography and Estimated Age Distribution.

not awarded after 1938, competitive conditions were maintained in practice by the criteria used by departmental committees that determined who was permitted entry.) The interaction between participation rates and the content and organisation of schooling continued (and still continues) to be one of the elements in a most complex sociological process.

As a result of population growth, changing age structure and choices by students and their parents, schools' clientele nearly trebled between 1947 and 1977 - from 1.2 million students to nearly 3 million. The real cost of providing school services rose even more dramatically, approaching a fivefold increase. Coping with the increased school population, its changing geographical distribution and the effects of new educational philosophies on the design of new schools considerably increased capital expenditure on buildings. The major source of the escalation of costs, however, was labour. Between the early 1950s and the mid-1970s, the total number of State government employees nearly doubled. The proportion who were public school teachers rose from 9 per cent to 17 per cent. The gross staff-student ratio was significantly reduced after the mid-1950s. The Australian average had been about 1:22 in government schools at the end of the 1930s; it rose to 1:28 in the late 1940s and to 1:30 in the mid-1950s. It fell rapidly through the 1960s to 1:21 in 1973 and to 1:17 in 1977. Moreover, major changes in qualifications required of new teachers and, more recently, in the structuring of promotion positions exerted additional pressures on salaries. It is probable that teachers' salaries, standardised for qualifications, the proportion of men etc., increased faster than the average rate of wage and salary inflation: teachers can create demands for their services by supporting better educational services to students. It is interesting to speculate how much slower the escalation of costs might have been in the absence of the pressures they exerted on politicians and parents (voters) as well organised professionals.

As costs of public school services increased, the proportion of State governments' expenditure from Consolidated Revenue Funds that was devoted to education rose from 14 per cent to 25 per cent between 1950 and 1965. State finances were strained, as these demands competed with other demands including hospital services and public transport. Governments nevertheless persisted in providing services to all who sought them, whether or not they were of compulsory schooling age, though without guarantee of quality of their provisions.

The finances of private schools were strained even further. Roman Catholic primary schools suffered most severely. While the socially elite private schools kept waiting lists despite increased fees and were able to raise funds through appeals to the community, systemic schools had to replace the low-cost labour of teaching orders with lay

staff. Catholic primary schools in the Melbourne Archdiocese are an
example: before 1950 almost all their staff were members of orders, 60
per cent were in 1960 and only just over a third were in 1970. At the
same time, their employment policies were influenced by staffing provisions in government schools. The public sector was threatening to
crowd them out. The emergence of the strongly Catholic-backed
Democratic Labor Party from the split in the Australian Labor Party
in the mid-1950s provided an effective way of expressing these special
interests.

Support for private schools

It was within this context that the Commonwealth began to make
finance available to public and private schools and to school children,
and State governments began to make grants to private schools from
their own general revenues. This brought to an end a period of some
ninety years during which the financial isolation of private schools
from public funds was jealously enforced.

The success of Menzies' 1963 promise to fund the construction and
equipment of science laboratories in non-government and State
government high schools indicated the electoral value of the new
policies. From 1963 Queensland paid per capita allowances to private
schools and in 1967 gave further assistance in the form of general purpose grants. From 1965 Victoria provided an interest subsidy on loans
for new private school buildings and direct per capita grants in 1967.
Non-government schools in New South Wales had access to the
Government Stores (and the advantages of bulk buying) from 1954
and received interest subsidies on building loans and from 1965
private school secondary students received a means-tested allowance
and the textbook allowance that was made available to all secondary
pupils from 1966. Direct per capita grants were paid to private
primary schools from 1968. The Commonwealth Government
capitalised on this by funding library buildings, beginning in the
1968-69 financial year.

In 1969 the Commonwealth Parliament passed the States Grants
(Independent Schools) Act offering per capita payments to all non-
government schools as contributions towards meeting their recurrent
expenditure. In 1972 the per capita rates were increased, States invited
to make matching payments in the future and special capital grants
made available for both State and private schools. The 1969 Act was
the first to authorise payments benefiting private schools alone. This
step was by then no longer revolutionary. It confirmed the trend to use
public means to support private schools and pupils that cut across the
traditional focus of government attention on government schools. The
discriminatory treatment is illustrated by the fact that government
schools, which enrolled some three quarters of the secondary school

population, were allocated 63 per cent of Federal funds voted for science laboratories over the period 1964 to 1971. It was this, among other things, that stimulated activist supporters of government schooling to seek a judicial ruling on the constitutionality of Federal assistance to denominational schools. (In 1981, judgement was finally given against the case they mounted.)

The basis of Commonwealth support was changed by the Whitlam Governments, which determined to assist both public and private schools in a way that discriminated on a basis of the relative needs of *individual* schools - on the understanding that State governments maintained their own expenditure. Even so, only 72 per cent of grants recommended by the Interim Schools Commission for 1974-75, that were allocable to sectors, were for government schools (then enrolling 82 per cent of pupils). The Commission acquired a considerable influence on the content and organisation of schooling. This was an extension, albeit a very major one, of the influence that had been exercised through the bodies responsible for approving building projects under the science laboratories and library schemes. After 1975 the Fraser Governments diminished the Commission's apparent influence in these directions and reintroduced the greater bias to discriminatory support of non-government schools, including the richer non-government schools, that had characterised the late 1960s.

This innovative and expanding government support of private schools, at both State and Commonwealth levels, failed to sustain the enrolments of those schools. In 1958 non-government schools enrolled 24 per cent of Australian school children; in 1975, 21 per cent. It appears that private schools concentrated their efforts on primary schools, leaving governments to cope directly with a larger share of the more costly, and more rapidly expanding, secondary school services. Private schools' share of secondary enrolments fell from a third in 1961 to just under a quarter in 1975, of primary school enrolments from 22 per cent to under 20 per cent. How different the institutional pattern of services supplied might have been had there been no public assistance - or much more - is a question that future research may pursue.

Cash benefits to students

As important as these direct payments to schools may have been, Commonwealth secondary scholarships were publicised as more clearly redistributive. First awarded in 1965, they were designed 'to encourage able students to complete the last two years of schooling'. But scholarships were awarded competitively and without means tests, providing allowances for living and fees. Similar scholarships were awarded for technical studies following the third year of secondary schooling. In its last year of office, the McMahon Government determined that, from 1973, more scholarships would be awarded and that part of the benefit would be subject to a means test. This scheme was terminated by the Whitlam Government at the end of 1974 and was replaced by a wholly means-tested scheme with grants for living expenses only.

These scholarship schemes had three main effects. First, they reinforced the development of a centralising, overseer role for the Commonwealth in education. Second, they altered the pattern of the States' education benefits to individuals. As they developed during the first half of the 1960s (as part of the process of the democratisation of secondary schooling) State scholarship provisions tended to fall into one of two groups. Either, as in Victoria, there were a great number of awards each worth comparatively little but made without reference, generally, to parental income and therefore having little impact on the distribution of 'economic wellbeing'; or, as in New South Wales, they were less liberal in number, more liberal in value, means tested, and therefore enhanced the possibility of upward social mobility for a few members of the low-income group. The Victorian Government, for example, awarded over 20 000 new scholarships tenable at government or private secondary schools in 1969. (Only 2500 were awarded in 1958.) To State school pupils the scholarship was worth $78, spread over four years; private school pupils received an additional $50 a year to assist with their fees. The annual award of new New South Wales secondary school bursaries in the same year totalled only 3900. At a time when the annual value of average weekly earnings per employed male unit was $3700, the awards were means-tested to parental incomes of $3999 and $2000 for senior and junior bursars respectively.

The Commonwealth initially offered 10 000 new awards annually; the basic benefit for most of the period was $250 but students at private schools could receive up to $400. In 1973 the number of new scholars was raised to 25 000, all of whom received $150 benefit with those who met a means test receiving up to an additional $250. Throughout most of the period Commonwealth awards were thus substantial, and went mainly to the middle class which had also derived most benefits from the concessional income tax deductions for education expenses introduced in 1952. The effect of wholly means-testing the scholarships in 1975 was dramatic. Awards held in 1974, not means tested, exceeded 48 000; there were only 12 000 means-tested recipients by 1976. State awards, on the other hand, had either been worth very little or were reserved, essentially, for the poor. It is most unlikely that either the Commonwealth or the State systems individually could have developed or maintained its observed characteristics in the absence of the other.

Third, the means-tested elements of Commonwealth, and to a smaller extent of State, scholarship schemes did indeed provide support to members of low-income groups. That support may have proved decisive in determining many individuals' ability to undertake or to persevere with school studies.

Tertiary education

The rapid growth of primary and secondary school services appears almost puny compared with tertiary education. There were six times as many university students in 1977 as there had been in 1946, while the number of school students 'merely' trebled. Moreover, in 1977 there were almost as many students at colleges of advanced education (a type of educational institution represented only by a few teachers' training colleges and other vocational or technological institutes in 1947) as there were at universities. Where there had been six universities (not counting the Canberra and New England University Colleges as separate entities) in 1946, in 1977 there were nineteen and, in addition, seventy-four colleges of advanced education; and where their teaching and research staffs numbered 1837 in 1946, thirty years later there were twelve times as many. That spectacular growth was intimately associated with the increased participation rates of children in senior secondary schooling and with Commonwealth intervention in the financing of post-school education.

In fact, Commonwealth intervention in education began during the 1939-45 war, when manpower planning became a matter of prime importance in supplying both the armed services and local industry with appropriate skills. Various industrial occupations were exempted in varying degrees from military service. At the same time certain forms of training were needed. Thus the Commonwealth set up a technical training scheme, using the facilities of State technical schools and colleges, through which passed about 120 000 trainees up to June 1947. The entire costs of this training, including all necessary additions to premises and the salaries of teaching staff, were met from Commonwealth revenues. Federal governments had only a tiny pre-war presence in education. This training scheme was, then, a huge leap into uncharted country. In addition, however, in the interests of manpower planning, undergraduates in medical, dental, engineering and some other faculties were granted reserve occupation status and, from the beginning of 1943, the newly formed Universities Commission offered means-tested financial aid to students in approved undergraduate study. In this process, Labor developed a firm commitment to intervene more widely in education, especially tertiary education, when the war was finished. Its political opponents accepted that same commitment - though undoubtedly with different social objectives - after they won power in 1949.

The Commonwealth's entry into the field of educational cash transfers to individuals during the war was consolidated and vastly extended over the following thirty years. The original scheme of financial assistance for undergraduates was continued until 1950, drawing legitimacy from the 1946 constitutional alteration, though it was dwarfed by the massive support given to returned servicemen to acquire retraining at universities. It was replaced in 1951 by a more general offer of scholarships, awarded solely on merit, that provided tuition fees for all holders and living allowances at the maximum rate to those whose families met an income test then equivalent (as it happened) to roughly four fifths of average male unit earnings. In 1966 this scheme was extended to students at colleges of advanced education. By 1973 Federal scholarships paid tuition fees for more than a quarter of all first degree students at universities and colleges of advanced education; 43 per cent of full-time students were in receipt of scholarships. In addition, a scheme of postgraduate scholarships was inaugurated in 1959 which in 1973 provided benefits for one in six higher degree students. These scholarships virtually displaced State provisions. In New South Wales, for example, only 115 university bursaries were funded in 1954, falling to 97 in 1971; Commonwealth scholars in New South Wales in those years numbered 3393 and 12 370. State governments, however, offered numerous scholarships and allowances to trainees for the teaching and other branches of their services, bonding them to accept employment, and in 1973 assisted one in ten bachelor degree or diploma course students at universities. In so far as States have waived or relaxed the bond, the allowances became more attractive to many students.

Federal means-tested living allowances provided, on a superficial interpretation, an element of redistribution. They helped support a rapidly growing number of tertiary students (Table 8.3) and by 1977 were awarded to two of every five full-time first degree undergraduates at universities and colleges of advanced education. Even more impressive was the increase in the number of students eligible to claim the maximum allowance payable (Table 8.3, rows 3 and 4).

Students qualified for allowances either because their parents satisfied certain income tests or because they were independent of parents and their own incomes were below specified limits. The redistributive implications were not necessarily the same. Dependent students could claim the maximum allowance in 1966 if the adjusted parental income was below a figure that was the annual equivalent of two thirds of Australian average weekly earnings; in 1973 and 1977 the limit had risen to above 80 per cent. In 1973 only a fifth of all families with dependent children had incomes below that cut-off point. The eligible income group is under-represented on Australian campuses; yet row 3 of Table 8.3 suggests either a marked increase in that representation or a shift to full-time studies by part-time students

TABLE 8.3 **Proportion of full-time university and C.A.E. students receiving Commonwealth living allowance**

		1966* %	1973 %	1977 %
1.	Receiving living allowance	15.9	23.7	40.9
2.	Receiving allowance at less than maximum rate	10.1**	12.2	15.3***
3.	Receiving maximum allowance, dependent on parents	4.5**	7.5	12.8***
4.	Receiving maximum allowance, independent status	1.3****	4.1	12.8***
	Number receiving living allowance	8368	24686	70414

*   Universities only.
**   Students receiving slightly less than maximum benefits are included here as at maximum.
***   Estimated on the assumption that the characteristics of students in receipt of living allowances at universities and colleges of advanced education matched those of all tertiary students in receipt of allowances. This might lead to an overestimate of dependent students receiving the maximum allowance and an underestimate of those with independent status.
****   May include some students on less than maximum benefits.

Sources: Commonwealth Scholarships Board, *Annual Reports; Report on the operation of the Student Assistance Act, 1977;* ABS, *University Statistics, Colleges of Advanced Education.*

from poorer families. At the other end of the scale, a student was ineligible for an allowance only if parental income was between 50 per cent higher than the national average (1966) and about 80 per cent higher (1973). Most students in row 2 of Table 8.3 received allowances appropriate to incomes closer to the bottoms than to the tops of these ranges.

Students who claimed independent status formed the fasted growing group (Table 8.3, row 4). Independence could be established in 1966 by being not less than 25 years old, by being married (or, later, having a lasting de facto relationship) if under the age of 25, or by having been self-supporting for the previous five years (subsequently changed to three years, to two of the preceding five years, and eventually to the two preceding years). Of this group the proportion married and under 25 years of age rose between 1968 and 1973 from 35 per cent to 44 per cent. Between 1973 and 1976 those qualifying as self-supporting jumped from 26 per cent of the total to 44 per cent. There is no way in which the true income status of the group can be determined, though the children of middle- and upper-income families may have exploited the system more readily. The 1976 decision of the Fraser Government to require 'independent' students to have spent two years full-time in the workforce was a belated recognition of some of the moral hazards.

To stress those characteristics of some independent students is, in one sense, merely to direct attention back to the fact that the majority of tertiary students who received Commonwealth assistance, of whatever form, were from the more affluent classes. This was so even after the changes introduced by the Whitlam Government. The abolition of tertiary education fees in 1974 was, de facto, a newly established grant to students whose fees had not been met by scholarships. It should not, nevertheless, completely divert attention from the fact that while the occupational and income background of undergraduates remains overwhelmingly middle and upper class, means-tested Commonwealth living allowances *have* made it easier for some students from lower socio-economic groups to gain entry to tertiary education. (How many more students from low-income backgrounds there may have been had there been stricter conditions determining scholarship awards, and higher benefits, is a worthwhile speculation.)

Commonwealth scholarships undoubtedly increased the effective demand for tertiary education. That stimulus was supplemented, however, by the lure of qualifications that would lead to high incomes and status positions, by rising living standards and by a casual job market that - for most of the post-war period at least - made it easier for families to maintain students of workforce age and for students to maintain themselves.

No such qualification attaches to government stimulation of the supply of tertiary education services. With the Commonwealth forcing the pace, government funding of tertiary institutions increased immensely. Without that support universities would not have been able to meet the demands that were in fact (and in consequence) placed on them and colleges of advanced education would probably not have existed. In the process of providing services on those expanded scales, universities, and later colleges of advanced education, became essentially quasi-government organisations.

The post-war Commonwealth Reconstruction Training Scheme (CRTS) involved the central government in much more than paying living allowances and tuition fees to ex-servicemen wanting a university education. In addition, there were so many CRTS students - 38 per cent of university enrolments in 1948 - that it was necessary for the Commonwealth to pay the States and the universities for the capital costs of erecting necessary buildings and plant and to subsidise universities for the extra running expenses of teaching CRTS students. In the years up to 1950 total government grants (including those from the Commonwealth) provided from about a half to two thirds of university receipts, fees from students (including CRTS) from a third to a quarter. CRTS funding wound down quickly and, under pressure from the universities, the form of Federal assistance changed.

From 1951-52 the Federal Government supplemented its home-grown role in respect of the Australian National University by making grants to the States to meet parts of universities' recurrent expenditures, grants partly conditional on the levels of States' own support and of fees received from students. This proved to be entirely inadequate. The Murray Committee recommended much higher levels of Commonwealth assistance in 1957. The Government associated the continuation of that increased funding with the creation of the Australian Universities Commission, in 1959, to recommend triennial grants for both recurrent and capital purposes. Under the Commission's guidance the Commonwealth made possible the great expansion of facilities that followed. By the mid-1960s the funding pattern had stabilised, with roughly 45 per cent of universities' revenue coming from the Commonwealth, 35 per cent from State governments, and 10 per cent each from students' fees and other sources. In 1973, with the agreement of the States, the Commonwealth assumed full financial responsibility for universities. At the same time it decided to abolish tertiary tuition fees that had, in any case, been met largely by Commonwealth or State scholarships or by internal concessions within the universities themselves. This rendered all the more potent and important the additional function which the Commission's power over the purse strings had already enabled it to exercise: that of co-ordinating 'balanced' development of universities in the national interest. Not only had there been a degree of rationalisation of specialised teaching and research facilities and avoidance of some unnecessary duplication of facilities, there had also been a degree of educational judgement exercised between competing projects and positive encouragement of new approaches in some major areas of tertiary training.

A similar sequence developed in areas of tertiary study not undertaken at universities: the Martin Committee in 1964, Commonwealth capital and recurrent funds for colleges of advanced education through specific purpose grants to the States from 1965-66 and the creation of the Commonwealth Advisory Committee on Advanced Education (later, the Australian Commission on Advanced Education). Developed from existing State-funded technological or specialised education institutions or newly formed, colleges of advanced education were always funded primarily by Government. Until the Whitlam Government's initiatives, student fees provided a relatively small share of total receipts, Commonwealth grants about 40 per cent. At about the same time the Commonwealth commenced making capital grants to the States for teachers' colleges and for facilities for training pre-school teachers. From 1974 these institutions, too, have been wholly dependent on Commonwealth funding.

The infusion of Commonwealth funds into education changed the priorities in public spending. Those funds were directed to purposes accepted by the Commonwealth and, when made available as specific purpose grants to State governments, frequently carried a requirement that they be matched from State treasuries. In the 1950s and 1960s, Commonwealth initiatives may seem to have led to a disproportionate diversion of funds into tertiary education that limited States' abilities to improve primary and secondary services. The continued neglect of technical and further education may appear as partly attributable both to that emphasis on higher education and to the thrust of effort into schools introduced·by the Whitlam Government. The greater percentage increases in public expenditures on tertiary education shown in Table 8.4a, and the low percentage increases in expenditures on primary and secondary schooling, seem to confirm that view. Yet, to the extent that we can put to one side absolute levels of expenditure per student in the base period, Table 8.4b suggests tertiary education was the least well-favoured sector of education in the 1960s. By the sixties, enrolments pressured more fiercely on facilities for the upper than for the lower age groups, whatever the political rhetoric of the day.

Despite the apparently favourable position it occupies in Table 8.4, technical and further education remained the Cinderella of the household. The high percentage increases shown·in the 1960s arise in important measure from the exceedingly low levels of expenditure that

TABLE 8.4 **Percentage increases in public expenditures on education, by purpose**

	a	Expenditures		
	Primary and secondary	Technical and further	Tertiary*	Total expenditure**
1963/64–66/67	38	81	56	45
1966/67–69/70	45	62	59	50
1969/70–72/73	67	48	74	68
1972/73–74/75	83	94	90	86
	b	Expenditure per student		
1963/64–66/67	26	63	13	
1966/67–69/70	35	58	14	
1969/70–72/73	62	27	40	
1972/73–74/75	79	24	52	

*   Includes colleges of advanced education and teachers' colleges.
** Includes general administration and research, transportation of students and other education programs.
Source: Calculated from R.B. Scotton and Helen Ferber, *Public Expenditures and Social Policy in Australia,* Vol. 1. *The Whitlam Years,* Tables A3–2.4 and A3–2.2.

existed in 1963-64 - lower, per student, than that on primary and secondary schools. They also reflect, especially in the mid-1960s, the introduction of Commonwealth technical scholarships and grants for technical training facilities. Before the end of the 1960s the Commonwealth's share of total government expenditures on technical education (including special purpose grants to States) had fallen back to a fifth and State governments could not sustain the slight momentum that had been generated. Despite industry's long recognised and highly publicised need for skilled workers, it was only in the mid-1970s that acceptance of the report of the Labor-appointed Committee on Technical and Further Education at last presaged a real diversion of funds into this branch of education.

Health

Labor's health schemes 1942 to 1949

Since the early 1940s the most contentious of all welfare issues has been access to health care services.

Labor's legislation between 1944 and 1949 was designed to bring comprehensive health care within the reach of all Australians by extending equal assistance to all. This was a distinct break with past practices of State governments as well as with traditional concern that it was the poor and needy who required public assistance and protection. As the influential Joint Parliamentary Committee on Social Security reported (*Sixth Interim Report*, para. 123), 'The best medical service, including specialist service, is now available to the rich who can pay for it, and to the poor to whom it is provided free. Upon the large middle income group, prolonged illness or major surgery frequently imposes very considerable hardship ... such conditions are unjustified and inequitable.' In its *Seventh Interim Report* (para. 8) it noted 'the very high proportion of the cost of sickness represented by hospital expenses, and [that] this, at present, falls particularly heavily on the middle income group'. The 'poor' were indeed poor, benefiting from means-tested free public hospital care and treatment by honoraries and from general practitioners' philanthropy; the 'middle income' group included the bulk of Australian wage earners to whom Labor's welfare schemes were directed. Among the beneficiaries, however, were to be included the 'rich'.

The 1944 and 1947 Pharmaceutical Benefits Acts proposed to meet the cost of specified pharmaceuticals prescribed by doctors. The 1945 Tuberculosis Act financially assisted States to maintain and extend their services and provided generous cash allowances to TB sufferers to stay in sanatoria until cured. (The benefits became payable in 1948.) By agreements made between the Commonwealth and the

States under the 1945 Hospitals Benefits Act the Commonwealth undertook to pay the latter 6s a day for each occupied bed in public hospitals on condition that public wards were free and admission not means tested and that charges to other in-patients be reduced by 6s a day. A similar subsidy was offered to private hospitals. The National Health Service Acts of 1948 and 1949 authorised the Commonwealth to establish or arrange the establishment of medical and hospital facilities or by agreement to take over State facilities. It authorised the establishment of a medical benefits scheme, government paying half the fees charged by all doctors who, by participating, accepted a scale of maximum fees, and patients paying the other half directly to the practitioner. Few of these Acts became operative.

The chief stumbling block was the organised opposition of the medical profession based on its fear of nationalised medicine and on its belief that it, not government, was the proper judge of health care services and policies. The profession mounted a successful High Court challenge to the 1944 Pharmaceutical Act that threatened the constitutional validity of all Commonwealth welfare benefits other than age, invalid and repatriation pensions. A referendum in 1946 transferred certain specified social welfare powers to the Commonwealth and showed wide public support for Federal policies. Nevertheless, subsequent Labor legislation, including the medical benefits scheme, foundered on the profession's refusal to co-operate. Effective health legislation with which the doctors would co-operate was not introduced until the first three years of the Menzies administrations.

Liberal administration, 1949 to 1972

The changes that the Menzies-Page scheme introduced were much more than a confirmation of the influence of the organised medical profession - the profession which had originated the proposals and on whose co-operation their success depended. Even though they fulfilled some of the essential welfare objectives sought by Curtin and Chifley, they reflected the very different philosophy that motivated the conservative government. Labor's programs were to be financed by direct, progressive taxation of incomes, the benefits available to all on the basis of health 'needs'. Redistributive implications were obscured by the confusion between 'needs' and 'effective consumption' of health services. The Menzies-Page scheme identified specific 'needy' groups - veterans, age, invalid and widow pensioners - for full public support. For the rest, public policy sought to encourage private choice through subsidised insurance - a publicly guided use of the market. Those who chose to be their own insurers were left free to do so (in practice they received less direct and often unintended public benefits).

There were four strands in this system of assistance. The first, providing free life-saving drugs, was introduced in 1950 and was basically the same as that proposed by Labor during the 1940s (and then rejected by the medical profession). The Pensioner Medical Service was the second. From 1951, medical services provided by participating general practitioners to Commonwealth pensioners (other than veterans entitled to free medical services) and their dependants were made without charge to the patients (ironically under Labor's National Health Service Act). A wider range of free medicines, also, was made available to pensioners than to the rest of the community. Medical practitioners and pharmacists were paid from government budgets, the former on a concessional fee-for-service basis negotiated with the Australian Medical Association, the latter at rates agreed with the Pharmaceutical Guild. Both schemes retained patients' freedom of choice of doctor. Neither was possible without the active co-operation of the professions.

Conditions of access to both schemes were subsequently modified. From 1959 non-pensioners were required to meet a flat-sum part of the cost of benefit prescriptions. Co-payment has been retained since then. A special means test for entry to the pensioner medical service was introduced in 1955 to exclude those who became eligible for pensions solely because of liberalisation of the pension means test. On the other hand, free public ward treatment of pensioners was introduced in the 1960s and a special pensioner nursing home benefit in 1973. Being funded mainly from income tax, these benefits represented a redistribution to means-tested pensioners and perhaps from richer to poorer consumers of pharmaceutical products. However, pensioners did not rank high among Commonwealth governments' priorities. Between 1950 and 1975, health payments on account of pensioners and other specifically identified low-income groups (see below, p. 220) did not reach even a third of all expenditures on hospital, medical and pharmaceutical benefits.

The other two strands of the Menzies-Page scheme provided assistance for the mass of the population. Their essence lay in encouraging private health insurance and, with that, the retention of a substantial element of market activity, subject to public subsidy.

The new hospitals benefits arrangements, implemented in 1952, retained the Commonwealth payment to States that had been initiated in 1945 (and increased to 8s a day in 1948) but required the States - Queensland alone standing out - to reimpose charges averaging about 18s a day for beds in public wards. The Commonwealth undertook to pay another 4s a day to hospital patients who were insured in a voluntary fund that gave a benefit of at least 6s a day. That is, an insured person was fully covered at least against public ward charges (more expensive insurance could be taken for wider cover). In the following twenty years, treatment in nursing, convalescent and rest homes was included. Despite rising hospital charges, the ordinary Commonwealth benefit was never varied and the additional benefit increased only in 1958. However, special Commonwealth benefits and subsidies were made available to specially disadvantaged groups unable to meet funds' contribution rates or their rules: the chronically ill during the Menzies administration; families earning less than the basic wage, those on unemployment and sickness benefits and recently arrived migrants from 1969.

The medical benefits scheme introduced in 1953 operated in a very similar manner. Benefits were paid, in respect of charges for a variety of medical services, to patients who were privately insured. Special subsidies, again, were provided for those insured persons whom funds' rules made ineligible for full fund benefits. Subsequent alterations met the expanding range of medical services that technological change produced or were prompted by the rising costs of medical care. However, the proportion of charges met by the Commonwealth benefit consistently declined until the mid-1960s. It substantially exceeded the level attained in the first year of operation only in and from 1971 following the Gorton Government's decision to limit to $5 a patient's direct contribution to the newly introduced 'common fee' of any single service. The basic format remained unchanged until 1975.

More research is needed on the age and income structure of insured persons before confident statements about redistributive effects can be made. It seems, however, that the separate elements of this scheme had different redistributive characteristics. The Commonwealth benefit itself probably took from the richest and gave to the poorest. Those who were insured and were among the 16 per cent of families that, in 1966-67, made up the lower income groups (paying 3.2 per cent of taxes on incomes), undoubtedly gained. It is uncertain whether this occurred as a result of their incomes, their age or their health status. The effects of the universally shared rise in real incomes and of generally higher standards of education makes the link between poverty and illness less certain now than it was at the beginning of the century. Nevertheless, unpublished official estimates (ABS, Australian Health Survey 1977-78) indicate that people from household units with annual incomes of under $4000 visited doctors more frequently than those from higher income groups, as did those who were retired or unable to work. As there are many pensioner households among the low-income group, the more significant relationship may be between age and illness, many aged also being poor, than between income per se and illness. On the other hand, the 4 per cent of households that paid direct taxes at the top rates in 1966-67, and provided over a quarter of the total collected, undoubtedly paid more in taxes than they received in benefits.

Other aspects of health insurance tended to make the overall incidence of health costs among insured persons regressive. Insurance premiums were regressive and were deductible from income taxed at rising marginal rates. That part of insured persons' health costs borne directly by patients - not met by insurance and Commonwealth benefits - increased up to 1975. This also attracted tax concessions thereby further advantaging the well-to-do.

Government subsidisation of private health care expenditure as a social welfare measure posed many serious questions encouraging active public discussion from the mid-1960s and influencing the Labor Government's program from 1972. One issue was equity, another access. The proportion of the population insured was estimated at 39 per cent in 1954, 73 per cent a decade later and 78 per cent by 1972. Some uninsured were pensioners covered by other schemes. The remainder were predominantly drawn from three groups: young single males, recent migrants from Mediterranean countries, and low-income families. The claims of the last two groups, at least, had electoral substance. Moreover, it was clear that low-income groups took out the cheapest insurance. This meant either that they directly met a higher proportion of their health costs than others or that they helped swell hospitals' and doctors' bad debts (or were assisted by cross-subsidisation by differential charging) or that they received inadequate health care.

Another question dealt with the economic efficiency with which the health insurance funds were managed. In 1961-62 administrative expenses and reserve accumulation took about 19 per cent of members' contributions (equivalent to 23 per cent of the fund benefits paid to them) and ten years later management expenses alone, of all funds, were still over 11 per cent of contributions. These were higher than the administration costs of other insurance systems: perhaps economies of scale could be won by a monopoly.

Medibank

The essential aims of Labor's Medibank scheme, for which legislative approval was finally obtained in June 1975, were three: to make access universal to basic medical and hospital care; to fund that access more equitably; and to do so more efficiently. Medical benefits equivalent to at least 85 per cent of fees scheduled in the Act (more if it were required to keep patients' direct payment for any single service to $5) were provided to all Australians in respect of all medical services previously covered by government benefits. Accommodation and treatment in public wards, when it included treatment by hospital doctors, was available without charge; for those who preferred other than public wards or other than hospital doctors, there was a reduced accommodation charge. In return, State governments received Commonwealth grants equal to half those hospitals' net operating costs (i.e. their total operating costs less receipts from fees); private hospitals received a uniform per diem allowance for each patient and deducted it from their charges.

Medibank was to have been funded by a proportional levy on taxable incomes supplemented by grants from general revenue. In fact, this part of the proposal was abandoned because of opposition in the Senate and the whole of the scheme's cost during its fifteen-month existence was met from general revenue - or formed part of the deficit. Regressive concessional income tax deductions granted for contributions made to health funds ceased. There was substantial redistribution from the richer to the poorer. Pressures by the medical and hospital insurance funds kept them alive and, though their benefits were not accompanied by any additional government benefits, their provision of cover for the 'gap' between benefits and health costs and for forms of health service not included in the government scheme, ensured them a considerable continuing custom. Administrative costs consequently remained a higher proportion of total health expenditures than they might otherwise have been.

This structure was quickly and confusingly dismantled by the Fraser Governments after 1975.

Hospitals

Throughout the period since the war, the Commonwealth continued to provide repatriation hospital services without charge to patients and to support its territorial public hospitals, and State governments to subsidise public hospitals within their boundaries. But the new role the Commonwealth assumed in 1945 and subsequent changes in its assistance policies altered the whole pattern of public hospital revenues. As Table 8.5 shows, Labor's first hospitals scheme sharply reduced the share provided by patients' fees. That gap, and the one left by the virtual disappearance of receipts from private charity, was filled by governments' greatly expanded support from personal income taxes. During the first twenty years of the Menzies-Page scheme, governments which in the 1930s had contributed less than half of public hospitals' receipts, provided from two thirds to three quarters. Though patient fees in that period were a higher proportion of revenue than they had been from 1946 to 1950, they were nevertheless probably less important than they had been in the 1930s. From Australian patients, on average, in the 1960s and early 1970s came a share that was close to that which came from public ward patients alone in Victoria before the war. However Queensland maintained free public ward accommodation without means tests and Tasmanian public hospitals had very few beds not in public wards. The more useful long-term comparison is in the single-State statistics: Victorian patients, public and private, provided a slightly higher proportion of

TABLE 8.5 **Sources of public hospitals' maintenance revenue — percentages**

	Commonwealth government*	State government	Patients**	Other
Victoria				
1934-35	—	36.2	26.2***	37.6
1939-40	—	45.4	27.3***	27.3
1942-43	—	40.0	37.7	22.3
1949-50	19.5	49.8	17.7	13.0
1963-64	19.3	50.3	25.3	4.5
1964-65	18.4	49.0	28.2	4.4
1965-66	15.9	50.1	30.0	4.0
1966-67	15.3	48.6	32.6	3.5
1967-68	16.3	47.2	33.1	3.4
N.S.W.				
1934-35	—	45.0	40.7	14.4
1939-40	—	44.5	45.0	10.5
1942-43	—	43.1	47.5	9.4
1949-50	18.2	64.4	14.6	2.7
1963-64	16.4	50.3	32.1	1.2
1964-65	16.0	50.8	31.9	1.3
1965-66	15.8	53.4	29.5	1.3
1966-67	16.2	48.9	33.4	1.5
1967-68	16.4	50.1	32.2	1.3
Australia				
1963-64	17.7	55.5	26.8	1.8
1964-65	17.2	55.0	27.8	1.8
1965-66	16.2	56.5	27.8	1.7
1966-67	16.2	54.0	29.7	1.7
1967-68	17.0	52.8	28.4	1.8
1967-68	19.5	52.8	25.8	1.8
1968-69	19.1	54.2	24.9	1.8
1969-70	19.7	56.1	22.4	1.7
1970-71	18.6	59.5	20.4	1.5
1971-72	18.7	54.8	25.2	1.3

*   Includes hospital benefits paid to patients.
**   Exclusive of Commonwealth benefits but inclusive of hospital insurance fund benefits and systematic contributions.
***   Intermediate and private patients' payments represented only by the small profit made from the operation of those wards.
Sources: 1934-35 to 1949-50: The Charities Board of Victoria, *Annual Reports;* Hospitals Commission of N.S.W., *Annual Reports,* calculated only for those medical, surgical and obstetric hospitals that, in 1949-50, were under the Commonwealth Benefits Scheme. Commonwealth assistance estimated in respect of N.S.W. and of public wards in Victoria.
          1963-64 to 1967-68: Australia. Senate Select Committee on Medical and Hospital Costs (June 1970), *Report,* Table 39.
          1967-68 to 1971-72: Australia. Hospitals and Health Services Commission, *Hospitals in Australia* (1974), Table 3.1.

receipts than public ward patients had in the 1930s, patients in New South Wales a considerably smaller proportion.

Since the war, State governments have quite categorically accepted the role of funding public hospital deficits, and with it an intensified interest in hospitals' pricing policies. The achieved shares of revenue displayed in Table 8.5 reveal only some of the tensions to which their policies about pricing were subjected. Average costs per occupied bed in Victoria almost doubled between 1950 and 1955, increased by nearly 60 per cent in the following decade and by another 50 per cent between 1967-68 and 1971-72. These movements were typical of those that influenced hospital deficits throughout Australia. States had to choose that blend of increased subsidy and increased fees that best met their political needs.

Their choices, which varied between States, further changed redistributive trends. By and large, it seems that fees were raised more rapidly than costs in the 1950s, slightly less rapidly in the 1960s; and that, except in New South Wales in the 1950s, public ward fees rose more rapidly than intermediate ward and they more rapidly than private ward. This made hospitalisation relatively cheaper for those who used private wards (and who benefited disproportionately from the regressive character of insurance rates and tax concessions). It also meant that those users were more heavily subsidised from State public funds, for not since the early 1940s had Victorian private ward fees, for example, exceeded average bed-day costs. At the same time, some States specifically earmarked some receipts such as the surpluses on lotteries or taxes on poker machines and totalisator turnovers, to partly fund hospital deficits. The importance of regressive taxes diminished as hospital deficits grew and especially after the Commonwealth undertaking, under the Medibank scheme, to meet half the States' commitments.

This continuing, and increasing, Commonwealth presence in hospitals' funding gave it a much greater influence in the determination of their fees. Partly at its behest, private and intermediate ward fees were raised more, proportionately, than public ward fees in the 1970s in an attempt both to meet escalating costs and, after 1975, to shift more of them to consumers. A different set of options has been widely canvassed more recently, including the reimposition of means-tested entry to public wards. This would be in keeping with policy since 1975: that those who can should pay and that government's main assistance should be reserved for those who cannot pay. It would be at the expense of those lower and lower-middle income groups, unable to meet the test, for whom hospital insurance at higher rates would become a disproportionately heavy burden.

Cost containment, however, has become the major objective of the Fraser Government, ironically tending to give the Commonwealth an initiating and supervisory role in hospital rationalisation. This concept was first developed by Labor in the 1940s and explored again by the Hospitals and Health Services Commission in 1974; State instrumentalities had attempted to promote rationalisation with varying success, by increased centralisation and tighter control. Until the 1970s the only direct role the Commonwealth played in determining the expansion of facilities was restricted to its grants to States for the specific purpose of maintaining and constructing tuberculosis hospitals (first made in 1949-50 following the 1948 legislation) and for constructing mental hospitals (1955 and 1964 legislation).

Yet during this period the number of hospital and nursing home beds increased greatly and the way in which they were provided was almost completely attributable to Commonwealth policies. The number of hospital beds rose from 7.72 per thousand persons in 1956 to 8.23 in 1962; and the number of beds in hospitals and nursing homes from 8.36 in 1963 to 10.09 in 1972. That expansion was undertaken primarily by private enterprise responding to public inducement. The number of beds in private institutions trebled between 1956 and 1972, lifting the provision from 1.83 private beds per thousand persons to 4.08. Beds in public institutions increased, however, by less than half, and the number per thousand rose from 5.89 only to 6.01. Statistics compiled on a different basis indicate a much slower growth of capacity since 1972 despite the continued surge in the number of private hospital and nursing home beds.

This whole pattern of changing allocation since the 1950s was a direct response to the rapid development and middle-class appreciation of private hospital funds themselves, which the Commonwealth effectively underwrote, to the payment of the Commonwealth's own benefits to private hospitals or to patients in them, to the extension of benefits to patients in nursing homes and to the subsidisation of the construction of nursing homes for aged persons and, since 1975, of the operation of others. This policy was appropriate for patients in nursing homes requiring different care from that available or appropriate in a public hospital. To the extent, however, that private hospitals and nursing homes cater predominantly for wealthier patients, that encouragement was far from the sense of concern expressed earlier in the century. Moreover, there is a real possibility that too many resources have been attracted to nursing homes.

Other health policies

The same encouragement to private decision-making to provide welfare services is evident in other Commonwealth policies. These included making specific purpose grants to States so they could encourage voluntary groups to organise emergency housekeeper services and home care services (including paramedical) mainly for age pensioners (1951 and 1956) and be reimbursed part of their assistance to the Red Cross Blood Transfusion Service (providing they first met 90 per cent of Red Cross costs); direct subsidies paid to voluntary organisations such as those providing family planning services; and, from 1954, direct subsidies to voluntary organisations to provide accommodation for the aged (on conditions that encouraged them to seek their clientele from among the well-to-do aged).

Equally, despite the Chifley Government's aim of improving and rationalising the delivery of medical services with a salaried staff and the Whitlam Government's effort to establish community health centres, also using salaried staff, almost every government intervention in this area eventually reinforced the private provision of medical services on a fee-for-service basis. The whole structure of the medical benefits scheme guaranteed this. If the scheme did not actively encourage a greater supply of medical practitioners it certainly did nothing to impede it. Where there was one doctor to every 856 Australians in 1961 there was a steady rise in the ratio so that there was one to every 644 in 1976 (though they were unevenly distributed). The pattern of medical services was certainly responsive to income rewards offered by the structure of insurance and government benefits, and the multiplication of specialists and specialities went beyond what might otherwise have been expected. Governments were prevented, by the strength of the Australian Medical Association, from grasping the potential given them by their place in the benefits system effectively to control practitioners' incomes and incentive to create 'unnecessary' demand for their services.

Although in health, as in education, government outlays after 1945 were increasingly focused on transfer payments, new services were provided. Prominent among them are those relating to environmental health and problems associated with drug dependence, welfare counselling services, rehabilitation training services for various categories of invalids and later for widow pensioners and Commonwealth pathology services. Some State governments have themselves undertaken to provide emergency housekeeper services to assist families at times of crisis. At the same time many of the welfare service programs that existed in the inter-war period have been vastly expanded, whether in the form of baby health centres, kindergarten and pre-school services, or massive campaigns against communicable diseases such as the mass compulsory chest X-ray program and vaccination against poliomyelitis.

There can be little doubt that government interventions in the market for health care services will continue to generate controversy and conflict for many years to come. The vested interests and vested expectations created in the past thirty years will not readily acquiesce in welfare objectives that cut across the incredibly varied and multi-directional redistributional outcomes that have been established.

Housing

Social security cash benefits and government provision or subsidisation of education and health services have always been the prominent elements in public welfare. Even in 1900 expenditure for these purposes weighed heavily in budgetary considerations - much more so today - and schools and hospitals stand as enduring concrete reminders of government's presence. Intervention in the market for housing services, by contrast, remained inconspicuous until the 1940s - almost something of an afterthought - even though in fact the Queensland Government had first acted in this way as early as 1909 and all governments did so from 1920. Housing policies, however, made small direct demands on the public purse until after 1945 and the forms that intervention generally took cloaked it with many of the trappings of private enterprise and so it did not stand out. Intervention has been of two kinds: that which facilitated home ownership; and that aimed at providing low-cost rental housing of acceptable standard to low-income earners.

Government home ownership programs before 1940 were founded on the proposition that private lenders - individuals, building societies, insurance offices and banks - charged interest rates, required purchasers' deposits, and imposed repayment periods all of which were beyond the means of many who earned moderate and low incomes. The most general form of intervention was the creation of a government or semi-government lending agency drawing on public funds. That this action was directly related to the gap in the finance market left by the collapse of building societies in the 1890s, their very slow recovery in the early decades of this century and the continued suspicion with which savers viewed their operations until the late 1930s is a possibility that would repay investigation.

In 1910, the Queensland Government's Workers' Dwellings Board offered loans of up to £ 300 at 5 per cent repayable over twenty years. The few building societies lobbied vigorously against the enabling legislation: parliamentarians quoted their interest rates at between 6 and 8 per cent and their repayment period was eleven years. From 1912, South Australia and Western Australia and, from 1919, Tasmania also channelled public funds into home purchase advances through State banks or special statutory authorities. The New South Wales Housing Board entered the lending market in 1919, the year in which the Commonwealth established the War Service Homes scheme to finance home purchases by veterans and their dependants. All of these agencies had from their inception, or later acquired, the power to erect or supervise the construction of dwellings for borrowers. Although supervision may have lifted standards of workmanship in construction and even of house design the agencies, working through private building contractors, could reduce construction costs only when they built groups of houses. The New South Wales Housing Board and the Agricultural Bank of Tasmania, the only authorities within this group to follow that course before the 1930s, respectively built only 376 and 150 group houses.

Victoria from 1910 (with important changes in 1920) and New South Wales from 1913 eased access to housing finance in a way that did not use public funds. State Savings Banks, substantially independent of the Minister to whom their governing bodies were ultimately responsible, were given the power to invest their own funds in home purchase advances. Government funds were made available to the New South Wales bank only from 1934 until 1937, to enable it to raise its limit on a loan from 75 to 85 per cent of valuation. By 1928 both banks had power to construct houses and in a long program, begun in 1926, the Victorian bank had by 1940 built 238 houses at Fisherman's Bend. Finally the 1927 Commonwealth Housing Act created a mechanism whereby funds in the Commonwealth Savings Bank, together with such loan funds as the Commonwealth Treasurer might grant the bank, could be advanced to prescribed State and municipal instrumentalities for lending to home purchasers. The New South Wales Government Savings Bank and the lending authorities in South Australia and Western Australia entered into agreements with the bank but little advantage could be taken of its resources before monetary stringencies curtailed its operations in 1929.

The conditions on which these agencies provided loans varied widely. The maximum that could be borrowed in terms of the original legislation was £ 300 in Queensland (1909), £ 500 in South Australia and £ 550 in Western Australia (1912) and £ 1000 in Victoria (1920). The initial equity that purchasers were required to contribute ranged from nothing to a third of the valuation. Maximum term of the loans was as much as forty-five years and as little as twenty. Interest rates in July 1921 extended from 5 per cent to 7 per cent. These terms were all more favourable than borrowers could obtain from other lenders. Moreover, with the very significant exceptions of the War Service Homes scheme and the New South Wales Government Savings Bank scheme, from 1920 eligibility for these loans was determined by an income test. Although this excluded the well-to-do it was, nevertheless, such groups as skilled artisans and clerical workers rather than poorer people who were most advantaged. These groups were eligible for loans under all limited schemes except the Queensland Workers' Homes (1919): in October 1920, when the New South Wales basic wage was 85s a week or about £ 220 a year, the maximum permissible taxable income under the Queensland scheme was £ 260, the permissible gross income under the South and Western Australian provisions was £ 300, and for applicants to the New South Wales Housing Board and the Victorian State Savings Bank £ 400. In addition, they more readily than other workers could accumulate the deposit of up to £ 200 that all but the Agricultural Bank of Tasmania and the New South Wales Housing Board required. The lending scheme most closely attuned to the needs of the poor was that operated by the New South Wales Housing of the Unemployed Trust from 1934. Paradoxical though providing 'unemployed or necessitous persons' with access to housing finance may appear, the Trust had built and sold 833 houses by 1943 and had financed the purchase of building materials used by another 1946 borrowers to construct or extend houses with their own labour.

That workers' loans schemes promoted home ownership cannot be doubted. Between 1909 and 1943 some 63 000 borrowers benefited by their existence, 45 000 of them building new houses as a result. Over the same time, the unrestricted advances from the War Service Homes administration and the New South Wales Government Savings Bank provided home ownership for over 21 000 and 41 000 families respectively.

The third form of intervention facilitated home ownership by moderate and low-income earners more by implication than by restricting the borrowing clientele. In order to reduce purchasers' initial equities, in the late 1930s the governments of New South Wales, Victoria and South Australia either guaranteed repayment by building societies of money borrowed from banks, insurance offices etc. and used to make advances above 80 per cent of security valuation, or indemnified the societies against losses made on that part of their loans.

These various home ownership programs had their origins in concern about high house rents, inadequate housing conditions in inner-city areas and constraints of private financiers. The first two were precisely the concerns that one might expect to have led to slum reclamation and government housing projects offering low-cost rental accommodation, yet in practice this was not a typical response before the late 1930s. The New South Wales Housing Board was set up in 1912 and by 1918 had constructed a 'model' suburb of 315 houses at Dacey Garden Suburb (Daceyville) about 8 kilometres from Sydney GPO. These houses were for rental only. In 1919, however, the legislation was amended so that the Board's subsequent constructions, at Daceyville and elsewhere, were for sale only, not for rental. It was thought that in this way the Board would make a greater contribution to overcoming the housing shortage. The Sydney Municipal Council was given power to erect workers' housing for rental in 1912 and by

1927 controlled four blocks of flats with 165 dwellings. Victorian municipalities limited themselves to houses for sale. Similarly, although the Western Australian Workers' Homes Act of 1912 and the Queensland Workers' Homes Act of 1919 initially gave the authorities power to construct for rental purposes, in the first case it was never used and in the second it was withdrawn by amending legislation before the authority began operations.

Significant planning for government provision of rental accommodation commenced only after the slow-down in building construction during the depression and the renewed reformist concern with insanitary and crowded living conditions in slums diverted policy makers' attention to it. As a demonstration project, the New South Wales Housing Improvement Board built a small estate of 56 flats in Erskineville in Sydney using it to accommodate persons moved from condemned dwellings nearby. In 1936 the South Australian Housing Trust was set up with powers to build, sell or lease houses. It limited itself to rental operation and by 1943 was providing low-cost accommodation to about 1900 families. In Victoria a Housing Investigation and Slum Abolition Board created in 1936 recommended the appointment of an investigatory Commission which in turn recommended legislation, passed in 1938, that gave it the necessary powers to clear slums and build low-rental housing specifically for low-income earners.

The scale, and for short periods the character, of public housing policies was transformed after the 1939-45 war. In 1945, after fifteen years of depression and war when few houses were built, when long-term deficiencies remained and when maintenance work was restricted, there was a housing shortage officially estimated at more than 300 000 dwellings. Slum conditions had deteriorated further. In the following thirty years, but more particularly in the years to the mid-1960s, State housing authorities undertook large-scale building activity and, from the early 1960s, slum clearance programs, that contributed substantially to the amelioration of both problems. The funding, if not wholly the initiative, for these efforts was primarily of Commonwealth origin.

Housing Agreements between the Commonwealth and all States except South Australia were made under enabling legislation passed in 1945. The Commonwealth made funds available as special loans which the States were to use for the construction of low-cost housing for rental. The terms of these loans represented a considerable subsidy compared with normal commercial 'economic' rents. Moreover, rental rebate arrangements were written into the Agreements so that, essentially, basic wage earners or families with lower incomes would pay no more than 20 per cent of their income in rent. The losses from this were to be shared between the Commonwealth and the State.

Four major changes were made to the basic Agreement over the following twenty-eight years, three of them changing its original emphasis considerably. The thrust of the Labor Government's arrangement was the provision of rental housing to which low-income earners would have access. The sale of houses constructed under the Agreement was not prohibited but the Commonwealth's objective was secured by a clause requiring the State to pay the full proceeds of the sale to the Commonwealth immediately. A buyer, consequently, needed to raise finance for the purchase through a third source which, in the circumstances of the first half dozen years after the war, was a difficult process.

The Menzies Government's first amendment of the scheme, made during the currency of the initial ten-year term, permitted States to sell their houses on credit terms. As in other welfare areas, the Federal Government now moved to stimulate - by active public intervention - a greater use of the market and less attention to equity. Within four years sales totalled more than three quarters of an average year's construction under the Agreement. In the new Agreement signed in 1956 considerable new emphasis was given to the promotion of home ownership at the expense of the provision of rental housing. Though funds continued to be provided at about the same levels as in the immediate past, at a greater concession in interest rates to compensate for the withdrawal of the Commonwealth's sharing of rental losses, 20 per cent (later 30 per cent) of the total was to be made available to terminating building societies for re-lending to private home builders or buyers. The remainder of the funds was available for construction for rental or for sale as each State individually determined. The decision of the New South Wales Government to allocate only a fifth of its 'own' share to construction for renting was indicative of future trends.

Subsequent renegotiations of the Agreement in 1961 and 1966 produced few changes, but a completely new approach was taken in 1971. States were to depend on normal Loan Council allocations for the bulk of their funds for housing construction paying interest at the going rate; they were to receive a small ($1.25m) annual grant towards the cost of reduced rents for needy families occupying housing authority dwellings, and a special annual grant of slightly more than twice that amount to be used for low-income housing and assistance to specialised lenders like building societies. The requirement that 30 per cent of States' borrowing be lent to building societies or State lending authorities was retained. A new Agreement, to last until 1977-78, was negotiated by the Whitlam Government in 1973. It reverted, in part, to the spirit of the 1945 agreement, offering special loan funds to the States on condition that while no more than 30 per cent (nor less than 20 per cent) of the total was to be made available to private home builders or buyers through building societies etc, no less than 85 per cent of the remaining funds was devoted to housing for low-income earners and no more than 30 per cent of an authority's family dwellings could be sold - and then only to means-tested buyers.

Some State authorities continued to construct houses with State finance. Housing authorities in South Australia, Queensland and Western Australia were primarily responsible for the fact that the number of dwellings provided on State initiative between 1945 and 1973 was almost a half that produced with Commonwealth funds. In addition, they developed their own supplementary programs of building, for example, for State employees. Both Queensland and South Australia indeed had created special, though limited, schemes for housing the aged before the Commonwealth legislated in 1954 to subsidise voluntary organisations building such accommodation.

The Commonwealth, too,had other housing programs, some integrated with the Commonwealth State Housing Agreements. It continued to facilitate home purchases by veterans and since 1964 (with the exception only of the Whitlam years) made cash payments under the Home Savings Grants scheme to young people who saved for the purpose of buying their first home - a notorious instance of a public subsidy to those already well-off. In 1965, it created the Housing Loans Insurance Corporation to encourage institutional lenders to advance higher proportions of their valuations and the provisions of the 1959 Banking Act specified housing loans as one of the few avenues in which the funds of private savings banks could be invested. Its assistance with housing for the aged was extended to nursing home accommodation and from the late 1960s it made special provisions to help house needy Aborigines.

The impact of these various schemes was substantial. Between 1947 and 1971 the stock of dwellings in Australia doubled, from about 1 920 000 to 4 010 000. Over a third of the additional dwellings were built for government authorities or for buyers whose purchase loans were financed from Commonwealth funds. Over 365 000 dwellings were built under Commonwealth State Housing Agreement arrangements or on State governments'·initiative. In the thirty years after 1945 the War Service Homes scheme made it easy for over 313 000 families to own their own homes, some of them newly constructed; funds made available to building societies and other lenders under those Agreements were lent to over 130 000 home purchasers. Some 350 000 families benefited from the Home Savings Grant scheme and about the same number had their loans insured with the Homes Loans Insurance Corporation.

In 1971 governments were landlords of 5.8 per cent of all Australian dwellings and of 7.5 per cent of all flats. They had, however, sold half the dwellings they had constructed to tenants who were clearly not poor. A significant proportion of these tenants by the early 1970s were well above the accepted poverty line while an equally significant proportion of poor families rented private housing. State housing authorities, that is, had moved far from any original concern with welfare delivery. In this transformation they encapsulated much of the adaptation of Australian social policy since 1945.

Part Four

Public Enterprises

9

Statutory Profits

Australian public enterprises covered large areas of transport and communications, water and sewerage, electricity and gas, and banking and finance together with a miscellany of competing 'socialist' enterprises (see Chapter 2). Given their significance in the Australian economy in 1901 and today, their organisation and performance are important matters. Virtually no attempt has been made previously to study their history so that, more than any other part of this book, the following chapters explore new territory.

In the circumstances, this section is selective in terms both of performance and structural history and of enterprises covered. Four types of public undertakings are discussed, including the largest: in Chapter 9, water and sewerage and electricity; in Chapter 10, railways, urban transit and air transport; and in Chapter 11 postal and telecommunications. Further research on these and other public businesses is needed. Although the issues raised vary according to the type of enterprise considered, we have focused throughout on monopoly characteristics and the related organisational structure, as well as on the degree of enterprise autonomy.

Criteria on which to measure performance are extremely difficult to define and apply. In particular, simple concepts of business surpluses are of dubious value for a number of reasons. Chiefly, the specification of performance of competing or alternative private enterprises is by no means clear cut. This is because the public enterprises considered are mostly monopolies or quasi-monopolies, so that the modes of pricing and the coercive influences introduced, along with opportunities to fall back on general budget support, affect the interpretation of performance. Also, when public enterprise is considered as an alternative to regulated private monopoly, questions arise as to the extent to which the varieties of private influence brought to bear on public monopolies would also have borne on their private enterprise alternatives. Finally, in the absence of measures of the external benefits and costs of public undertakings (subjects long overdue for investigation), neither internal nor social rates of return can be freely deployed to assess outcomes.

So far as is feasible with available data, we have tried to explore recorded enterprise surpluses, to give some indication of externalities, to examine pricing policy and investment criteria, to identify the process of cross-subsidisation (preferential treatment of particular consumers) and to examine the extent to which public undertakings have been able to sustain or increase their 'monopoly' power. Interestingly enough, we have found ourselves as much concerned with the displacement of public enterprise by private as with the opposite crowding-out process. There are other issues that might be investigated and other enterprises that might be included. The following chapters are preliminary investigations which we hope may encourage further study.

Consequences of public ownership

The major Australian public enterprises (see Chapter 2), with the chief exceptions of TAA and the Commonwealth Bank, have been natural or artificial monopolies constrained, as are all monopolies, by the threat of competition from substitutes. The evidence of the lack of large unregulated natural monopolies elsewhere leads to the conclusion that if these enterprises had not been publicly owned they would almost certainly have been subject to government regulation. Because they were owned by the public sector, however, a potential form of conflict between some private interests - private owners of regulated 'public utilities' - and the public sector has been largely avoided in Australia. A different set of conflicts developed, between the managements and workers of the public enterprises, and their political masters. How were public enterprises to be controlled by the minister, government or parliament and for what ends? Towards an answer to this kind of question, Australia has contributed innovation and experimentation with the statutory corporation, given greater or lesser degrees of autonomy and responsibility. A notable example was the Victorian Railways in the 1890s (see Chapter 10). Relationships between the enterprise and public (political and bureaucratic) interests are different when the enterprise is publicly owned from when it is private. And the public-public relationship has developed during the last eight decades. In particular, the long-term trend has been towards more autonomy for enterprises and, for those capable of it, greater reliance on retained earnings as a source of investment funds.

Public ownership has not only been a form of regulation of natural monopoly. It has also been a means both of creating or sustaining a monopoly, and of introducing more competition within private monopolised or cartelised industries. This last - government as competitive supplier - is illustrated by some of the history of the 'petty socialist' enterprises founded in the 1910s and 1920s as well as by the Commonwealth Bank and TAA (Chapter 10), at least in their earlier years.

It is therefore not always easy to attribute to the public form of ownership what we find remarkable in the behaviour of public enterprises and in the relations between the enterprises, the rest of the public sector and private interests. Some features do stand out, however, as being peculiar to public enterprise or more pronounced than in private enterprise. First, the ability to run an enterprise or economic activity for indefinite periods at a loss is largely confined to the public sector. Some activities were begun as enterprises which were expected, or so it was claimed, to cover costs eventually. When they failed spectacularly, like some of the irrigation projects (Davidson 1969), they were then declared to be projects of national importance, to be operated without close regard to commercial accounting and hence with general budget support. Other activities, like broadcasting, or symphony orchestras and opera companies, were never seriously labelled as enterprises, although the option was open for attempts to have them cover costs from receipts. Public enterprises and organisations making losses generally do not vanish as quickly or surely as do failed private enterprises.

Next, the pricing policies of public enterprises differ from those of private. The public sector has the ability to tax, that is, cheaply to compel the transfer of money. This power can be used as an alternative to or as a variety of public enterprise pricing of, for example, water and sewerage services. More importantly, the public enterprises appear to have engaged in a greater degree of price discrimination or cross-subsidisation than private business. They have been used or have acted to provide discriminatory benefits to advantage particular groups. Private firms do use price discrimination, but it is more likely to be designed to increase the profit of the owners than to help one set of favoured customers over another.[1]

More generally, public enterprises are run with much less attention to maximum overall profit. Though the matter must be more heavily qualified after 1950, governments have not exploited the monopoly power of enterprises as a source of indirect 'tax' revenue to anything like the fullest extent. Market or monopoly power has been dissipated on unprofitable extensions of business, on the pursuit of technical rather than economic objectives, on featherbedding or on preferential

---

[1] See Richard A. Posner, 'Taxation by Regulation', *Bell Journal of Economics and Management Science*, 2, 1, 1971, pp. 22-50.

treatment to particular interest groups. Public enterprises offer attractive prospects for the distribution of political favours especially since their cost can be disguised.

The public enterprises include big businesses that have had or are still having considerable influence on Australian economic and social life. They merit more attention than they have received from economists and historians. Perforce, some of what follows is business economics. Always in mind, however, are questions relating to the relative autonomy of the public sector in Australia, to changing attitudes to the use of monopoly power, to the pressure that customers or suppliers have exerted through political mechanisms upon the conduct of enterprises, and to the effects that the public enterprises have had on private activity. It is not that completely different considerations are involved in the assessment of public enterprises, but that some aspects of conduct, structure or performance are much more prominent in public than in private enterprise.

Profitability

Profitability remains a useful if crude way of summing up the performance of an enterprise, although it suffers from a number of defects as an indicator of net economic benefit. Unfortunately there are serious data problems involved in calculating the rate of return to capital of public enterprises, relating to the meaning and measurement of capital. Much of what we say about profitability relies on the accounting conventions of the individual enterprises.

One rough indicator of profitability is the ratio of surplus to product generated by the public enterprises (Table 9.1). The figures in Table 9.1 which are very preliminary and involve some guesswork, are to be taken as indicative of trends more than of levels. They suggest buoyancy in surplus to 1910, as the economy recovered from the depression of the 1890s and severe drought. This was a period of rapid, if variable, growth in railway investment, and of constraints on

TABLE 9.1 **Share of surplus in gross product generated by public enterprises, 1902 to 1975 (%)**

1902	33	1939	31
1905	36	1950	6
1910	38	1955	15
1915	27	1960	27
1920	26	1965	35
1925	26	1970	37
1930	26	1975	21
1935	38		

the Post Office. It was a period also in which State governments were subject to a peculiar degree to market constraints - limited income tax gave little opportunity for subsidising enterprises, and commitment to overseas lenders emphasised the importance of meeting interest obligations, particularly after the stresses of the 1890s. On the other hand, State governments confronted comparatively weak private interest groups.

The decline in the surplus ratio by 1915 was due to special circumstances of drought during the war and problems associated with transport and storage of rural products together with large concessions given by the PMG to rural customers. During the 1920s, relaxed standards for major public investments helped to keep the ratio down (in fact, surpluses are likely to be overstated). Here rural interest groups had achieved industrial organisation and political prominence at a time when the States were able to use, on a much greater scale than ever before, the weapon of income tax - in this lay the source of coerced revenue that permitted enterprises to fall back on 'general budgets' to the advantage of now well-organised private interests. Depression seriously eroded public enterprise profitability at first; however, deferral of expenditures and some recovery of demand more than reversed the change.

The immediate post-1945 years show a very sharp decline from wartime peaks, the result of a price-cost squeeze and of Labor policies. The rise during the 1960s is striking. It derives from an increasing move towards self-finance of capital works, implying the greater use of monopoly power. Amongst other things, this reflected pressures on public undertakings from Federal authorities (relying on centralised fiscal power), and the responses of some major enterprises themselves to funding problems.

The profit records of the largest enterprises, railways and the Post Office, are looked at in some detail in Chapters 10 and 11. The railways displayed, within the kind of fluctuations indicated by Table 9.1, a long-term tendency to a declining rate of profit. At the start of our period, the railways were almost covering all their costs, including interest. At the end, they could earn only 70 cents for every dollar of working expenses. By and large, the Post Office has paid its way, with the important provisos that during 1945 to 1960, it was not charged interest on its capital borrowings, and that various of its major branches made losses at different times.

What are we to make of these records? In Chapter 10 we argue that railway accounting does not capture the full economic benefits afforded by rail. (This problem is not unique to railways - all public enterprises generated externalities that they could not capture.) In particular, railways enhanced the value of the land they served, and these 'external benefits' did not appear in rail accounts. Also, railways were forced to build and run unprofitable lines, and offer various freight and fare concessions. Therefore, the profit or loss of rail services does not reflect accurately either the economic value of their operations, or the quality of internal management and workers. There are additional considerations. Railways were the most exposed, amongst the leading public enterprises, to the erosion of an initial monopoly position because of competition from the private sector. Persistence with railway operation in these circumstances accentuated the risk of low enterprise yields. Moreover, as railways encountered competition, they were also subject to increasing pressures for discriminatory benefits to be provided to a variety of private groups.

As already mentioned, the combined postal, telephone and telegraph accounts conceal patterns of profit and loss between and within branches. These services have been run so as to provide increasing subsidies to rural Australians. Until the 1920s, the large losses were made in rural mail delivery. Profits made elsewhere in postal services covered these losses, and those on telephones and telegraph. In the thirties, rural telephone losses began to mount as the service was improved and the financial criteria for rural services were relaxed, reflecting, we suggest, the force of rural pressures and the availability of budgetary resources (especially income tax) to subsidise enterprise performance. Because of technological and other factors, the overall profitability of the postal services tended to decline, whereas that of telephones increased, aided by important changes since 1945 in the method of financing this capital-intensive service. From a simple economic point of view, the profitable branches or sections were using their monopoly or market power, thereby causing one kind of economic inefficiency, while the losing branches were using up too many economic resources, thereby causing another kind of inefficiency.

A separate but related issue arises when the profit records of the water and sewerage authorities are considered. These authorities have generally been charged with the task of covering costs from revenue. They have mostly succeeded in this. If they made too much revenue then rates and charges were reduced or new expenditures found to soak up the surplus; if too little, then rates and charges were raised. Due to the nature of the revenue received, being more a tax than a price, a comparison of the rate of return to capital in urban hydraulic services with that in ordinary businesses is a dangerous one to make. The water authorities can, in the extreme, increase their revenues by changing the rates charged on properties, rather than by changing the excess water rate. To some extent, the authorities have a 'captive market': an increase in rates may not lead to a reduction in the amount of water consumed. Therefore, the authorities may have been able to make capital investments that were not economically worthwhile, and yet maintain the appearance of a respectable profit record. In particular, there is only a fairly faint shadow of a 'market' test to be seen in the authorities' accounts when expansion of services is undertaken. A similar comment can be applied to capital investments in roads in Australia. The nature of the revenue - mostly licenses, fees and excises - makes the 'rate of return' a dubious tool with which to approach the question of when there has been too much or too little or the wrong kind of road building.[2] Many of the problems in assessing public business decision-making arise, therefore, from the system of public charging, not merely from any intrinsic characteristic of public enterprise.

Our final comment on profitability relates to electricity, which, as Chapter 2 shows, was a hungry user of investment funds after 1945. Investment in power generation has come in large lumps, and a single unprofitable project can make a noticeable difference to the overall rate of return of the power industry. Also, the power industry is vulnerable in the sense that fixed charges - interest and depreciation - make up such a large proportion of cost. Hirst (1963, p. 124) reports that these two items contributed 40 per cent of cost for the industry as a whole, hydro and thermal, in 1960-61, and McColl (1976, pp. 40 and 44) reports a similar figure for thermal in 1972-73, and nearly 90 per cent for the Snowy hydro. Some of the power investment errors are the kind of errors a private enterprise business might have made; others, however, seem to have been intrinsic to public decision-making. Despite these errors, and because of the rapid rate of growth in demand for electricity, the rate of return in the electric power industry after 1945 has been halfway decent. McColl (1972) puts the rate of return on capital at about half that in manufacturing. Such calculations are difficult for before World War II, due to fragmentation of the industry, and the shift to public ownership.

Natural and artificial monopoly in water and sewerage and electricity

The major public enterprises all have some characteristics of both natural and artificial monopoly. But the mix varies greatly in each case and there were important historical developments, in both the public and the private sectors, altering the bases of public 'monopoly'. It is convenient to begin in this chapter with the more recently established public enterprises in water and sewerage and electricity.

A persistent element of natural monopoly in these two enterprise groups arises from indivisibilities at the network level that make it less

---

[2] See Bureau of Roads, *Roads in Australia*; Neutze (1978).

costly to have a single supplier of reticulated water, or sewerage, or electricity within each 'local' region, rather than many suppliers: there is a plentitude of possibilities for natural monopolies in local retailing. In time other elements emerged that led to the establishment of large, integrated networks at the wholesale level. These were economies of scale in headworks and mains in the case of water and sewerage, and in generating facilities in electricity; in both cases, other economies were available in the process of distribution, at both wholesale and retail levels. Local retailers remain in electricity but have vanished in urban water and sewerage.

Public enterprise in these areas emerged relatively late in Australian development, even though public action in some form extends back in the case of water supply at least to the 1840s. The substantial public intervention in water and sewerage was made during the 1880s and 1890s though even then sewerage was a matter of a great many dispersed undertakings. In this case, there were a number of alternative services that consumers might use - pan delivery systems and septic tanks, in particular. So far as electricity is concerned, it was not until the First World War that long-distance transmission was feasible as a result of technological change. Hence, here also, small-scale enterprise was possible, although at relatively high cost, competing with available alternatives of candles, kerosene lamps and gas for lighting, and gas and solid fuel for heating and cooking.

An important process in the twentieth century for water and sewerage and electricity (unlike railways and telecommunications) was the building up of monopoly structure and the displacement of smaller public and private enterprises. This 'monopolisation' was not altogether one-sided. The competition for the consumer dollar ranges over a large area and there are many minor commodities whose competition nibbled at the edge of growing public monopoly. In many respects, large-scale public monopoly in electricity and sewerage emerged at the earliest in the interwar years and was firmly established only after the Second World War. In country towns, small public monopolies had been established for water and sewerage in the nineteenth century but there remained small enterprises throughout (except where merged with the metropolitan giants).

More than in any other area, large-scale water and sewerage monopoly depended on artificial intervention and led to the establishment of what we might call 'captive customers'. Some captive characteristics came to relate to electricity consumers but for different reasons and with significantly fewer restraining bonds. The development of water and sewerage systems derives partly from 'environmentalists' concerned with public health in the nineteenth century, though lack of medical understanding and a low public or private valuation of amenity delayed and limited action. Once the basis of service delivery was established, however, public organisations were provided with a variety of non-market weapons with which to bind customers to them: to impose property rating or set basic charges based on property values, wholly or partly disregarding volume of consumption; to require connections; to regulate the consumption of alternative services; and to introduce discriminatory or preferential charging systems that could be revised when connections were made. A basic consequence followed: public enterprises could raise charges without decline in consumption. Less directly, the adoption of charging systems not related to volume used distorted consumers' decisions and encouraged a dependence on public supplies.

In the case of electricity, large-scale monopoly evolved through the displacement of both small public and private institutions. Some much more attenuated artificial means were adopted to attract and hold customers through combined base and unit charging systems. In this case, the attachment of consumers was achieved more strongly by the costs of installations in buildings and the financial implications to consumers of providing parallel competing services (e.g. electricity and gas). In encouraging these installations for electricity, public bodies were able, through access to general budgetary support, to offer larger incentives or persist with incentive systems for longer periods than private enterprise might have done. Once appropriate installations in buildings were made, prices could be adjusted without much alteration in consumption. These policies appear to have had their place in the activities of distributors. Nevertheless, as became clear with the energy crisis and the development of natural gas supplies, the commitment of customers to electricity essentially was market-determined, unlike the more obviously unavoidable commitment of water and sewerage users.

Water, Sewerage and Drainage

Organisation

Various forms of organisation have been adopted partly in recognition of the 'monopoly' characteristics of these public enterprises. The supply of these 'essential services' was and is carried out by a large number of local authorities, statutory boards or commissions, State or Federal government departments. The boundaries of the areas under the control of a local or statutory body differ according to the function involved, and have been added to progressively. Most of these bodies today, in the cities at least, are engaged in the construction and maintenance of headworks, the management of catchment areas and disposal plants, and in reticulation. In addition, the Melbourne and

Metropolitan Board of Works has responsibility for town planning (since 1948), foreshore protection and inner-city highways (both since 1956). The degree of autonomy of the bodies has varied over time and between cities. In South Australia, the authorities are State departments. In Queensland, water and sewerage for cities and towns has long been left to local government, with the Brisbane City Council since 1928 including amongst its functions sewerage and, until recently, water for Brisbane and surrounding districts. When established in 1888 (legislation had been passed in 1880), the Sydney Metropolitan Water and Sewerage Board took over the city water supplies and sewerage works constructed by the State, the city and councils in the County of Cumberland. It had quite limited powers over its bylaws, catchment areas and finances. Although the Sydney Board had a majority of indirectly elected local members it was, until 1924, restrained by an annual parliamentary expenditure vote and required to pay all revenues into consolidated revenue; the Minister of Public Works had to approve all works costing more than $200, and his department carried out the construction. The reconstructed Sydney Board was freed of these restrictions, empowered to raise its own loans. In 1972, the Board was again reconstituted, this time to remove indirect local government representation, all members being appointed (although some from a panel put forward by local councils). The Melbourne Board was given extensive powers in its initial Act (1890) to make certain bylaws, expand its water supply area with consent of the councils involved, and to borrow up to $10 million. Its powers were extended by subsequent legislation. Until 1959, the Melbourne Board was subject only to Parliament, not a Minister. In that year, the Minister for Local Government was given veto powers over any works exceeding $20 000; in 1968, in reaction to criticisms of water restrictions, the Minister's supervisory powers were extended. Water supply in country towns in New South Wales is mostly left to local government; in Victoria, the State Rivers and Water Supply Commission (1905), directly or indirectly through local water authorities, is responsible.

Supply of 'needs'

The water supply system requires two levels of works, headworks and reticulation. Headworks include: storage dams to handle variations in demand from year to year and between seasons; intermediate and local storage to meet diurnal fluctuations in demand; and mains. The problems of water supply have varied from city to city, depending on rainfall conditions and the proximity of suitable catchment and storage areas. Storage capacity has increased in large, discrete amounts whereas annual consumption has tended to increase relatively steadily. Thus in the Sydney Board district, average water consumption per head per day (including all uses) rose relatively slowly in the first quarter century from 180-odd litres to 200; more quickly in the next to 330 litres; and then moderately in the third to reach about 470 litres.

The working rule of the Sydney Board was to store sufficient to meet a repeat of the longest recorded drought plus one year. This rule did not prevent severe water restrictions during the long drought from the late 1930s to the early war years. The Board had been forced to delay completion of the Nepean storage during the Depression, and had not been able to commence the Woronora dam, completed in 1942, as early as it wished. During the water shortages in the 1930s, the Board as a responsible statutory body was exposed to public criticism that it did not relish (and which, to a large extent, it had not earned). Its next major dam, the Warragamba, completed in 1960, increased the Sydney water storage capacity by more than a factor of three. Water from the first stage of the Shoalhaven Scheme was pumped in 1976. In Melbourne, the Board has had a less conservative policy (and more secure water supply) and for most of the period maintained in storage a volume less than annual consumption. The completion of the Cardinia Reservoir in 1973 doubled the system's storage capacity, but further water was desired. After a political battle over irrigation and city water, the Melbourne Board has begun to develop the Upper Thomson, against a cheaper source, the Big River (Neutze 1977, p. 39). Adelaide and Perth have both fully tapped their more convenient catchments. Only Brisbane and Hobart, of the State capitals, continue to enjoy cheap supplies.

The whole basis of decisions about the headworks has been an engineering notion of 'needs' rather than the economists' concept of 'demand' (that is, quantities that would be consumed at various prices). A series of expert inquiries into the water requirements of the major cities have, almost without exception, used projections of past trends in population and per capita consumption to arrive at estimates of needs, and hence of investment programs. Only in the last few years has the Australian Water Resources Council sponsored an investigation into the likely effects of higher water charges on urban water use. Of course, costly metering equipment is required whenever excess charges are to be levied, and considerable portions of our cities, especially the older suburbs, remain unmetered.

Most sewage disposal since 1900 has been into water bodies. Where the ocean (as in Sydney) or a large river (as in Brisbane) are handy, sewage has been discharged largely untreated until pollution of the beaches and rivers became a major political issue in the 1960s and 1970s. Extensive sewage treatment has been carried out before discharge in Adelaide, Perth and Canberra. In Melbourne from the

1890s sewage was piped to the Werribee farm for treatment and use, and the treated water discharged into Port Phillip Bay. The new southeastern scheme will have its outlet 56 kilometres away in Bass Strait.

In this century, most urban residences have been connected with reticulated water soon after construction (with exceptions in Sydney in the period of material shortages after World War II); the same cannot be said with regard to sewerage services. The Melbourne Metropolitan Board of Works was set up in the 1890s to solve problems of pollution of the Yarra by upstream cities - marvellous Melbourne had not been sewered as extensively as had Sydney in the 1880s. By 1901, 75 per cent of the Sydney population with water connections also had sewer connections; the figure for Melbourne was less than 40 per cent (quickly raised to 88 per cent by 1911, however). Less than half Perth's population enjoyed sewer services until the 1930s; Brisbane did not achieve half until the 1960s. During rapid suburban growth in the 1950s, the authorities did not keep pace with sewerage demand, and despite efforts in the 1960s (especially in Sydney and Brisbane), the early 1970s found 20 per cent of the population of these four cities still using septic tanks or removable pan services. To some extent, these alternatives, particularly septic tanks, represented private and government responses to the very high cost of sewerage installations in some areas.

Granted that there were, in places, preferred alternatives, why did authorities with such wide powers as the water and sewerage boards allow such long delays to occur between water connection and sewering? The explanation lies partly in the fact that sewering a city is more costly than watering it, and in the fact that the demand for sewer services was more price-elastic (because households had more acceptable alternatives for the sewer than for town water).

The boards have used various criteria to judge the desirability of extending water and sewerage services. In Sydney, until 1892, a return of 6 per cent on a project's capital was required by the Board. From then until the 1930s, the Sydney Board required guarantee bonds or deposits from individuals and councils, ranging from 4 to 8 per cent; after 1919 councils could levy special rates to meet deficiencies under the bonds. The criteria were progressively relaxed until in 1937 the State guaranteed the first 2.5 per cent return, leaving councils responsible for the remainder. However, the State also required a reference to the Minister of Local Government of proposals involving large deficiencies.

Rating system

Water and sewerage authorities have generally been charged with the task of covering costs from revenue. They have mostly succeded in this. If they made too much revenue, rates and charges were reduced (as for example in 1909, when the Sydney Water Board complained that it was not allowed to make provisions for a renewals fund) or new expenditures found to soak up the surplus; if too little, then generally rates and charges were raised. Due to the nature of the revenue received, a comparison of the rate of return to capital in urban hydraulic services with that in ordinary businesses is a dangerous one to make. Sewerage charges have almost always been based on property rating until the past ten to fifteen years, during which industrial effluent released into sewers became much more important. In the case of Sydney, a standard property rate applied from 1904; until then, differential rating on assessed property values varied from region to region. In the case of water supply, the introduction of meters was Board policy effectively from the beginning. But by 1902, only a little over 10 per cent of the more than 100 000 improved properties were metered. This position changed progressively so that some 60 per cent were metered in 1960 and over three quarters by 1975. Although metering opened the possibility of charging by volume of water consumed, the pressure of large numbers of unmetered properties compelled an alternative approach. This was made through imposition on properties of a rate intended to allow an estimated basic consumption. However, the Board recognised the large usage for domestic gardens and, for those properties 'with gardens', it added a 'garden rate' according to size, as a proxy for additional water consumption above basic allowances. (At various times the Board also prohibited some water uses.) Subsequently property valuation systems were made more sophisticated to provide a rating substitute for garden allowances. Thus the Board has, for a considerable period, operated with four distinct systems side by side - property-rated sewerage, volumetric waste discharges, property rating for basic water consumption and excess water charges where metered.

The financial return from service extensions depended chiefly on the costs of extension and the aggregate ratable value of the properties serviced. Apart from extracting guarantees, the Board could react to proposals for unprofitable extensions by delaying work until assessable values rose sufficiently as population density increased. An alternative was for the property owners to finance the reticulation works themselves, and in the 1960s the practice grew of developers offering to do that. Previously, developers had been required to construct local roads. By the end of the 1960s, developer contributions to reticulation were enforced in most cities, and extra added for headworks. A consequence was that established suburbs were sewered after new subdivisions. (In the late 1940s, the Sydney Board's policy to sewer new housing developments brought angry responses from established but unsewered suburbs.)

Local levies to meet commitments under guarantees represented a divergence from the principle of uniform rating adopted by the Sydney Board in 1904. Before that year, sewerage rates had depended on whether or not pumping was required (i.e. on an obvious cost differential). It was also expected that the new southern suburbs' sewerage scheme would be self-supporting, with a separate rate to be struck; in the event, legal considerations dictated that the Board do what it preferred to do, that is, charge a uniform rate throughout the metropolitan area. The argument used by the Board, namely, that the benefits of the works were enjoyed in common, does not justify a uniform rate unless it is assumed that these common benefits (e.g. fire protection from water supply and improved public health) dominate the benefits. Unsewered areas did not pay for the advantages they secured from the fact that the city was more pleasant because of sewerage.

Drainage presented a different aspect of the question. The expenditures required were very far from uniform and the benefits fairly local: for example, the Board noted in 1904 that the cost of drainage of the Marrickville Valley exceeded the aggregate ratable value of the properties before drainage. Nevertheless, the Board departed radically from the principle that each area should bear its own costs. Firstly, once sewerage was installed, the separate drainage rates (which lasted until 1951) were subsumed into the sewerage rate. Secondly, for the areas with drainage but no sewerage, a uniform drainage rate was charged from 1951 after the Board had secured the necessary legislation, in order to obviate the need to keep 'numerous small accounts' and to free the Board of 'the consequences of a high rate in any individual area where substantial work might be required' (1951 *Report*). One speculates whether the Board would have been as keen on uniform rates if, in the early 1950s, it had been able to tap surpluses (of revenue over working expenses) to finance capital works, or had been able to use surpluses from one part of the enterprise (say, water) to subsidise losses in another part (say, drainage). What would these consequences be? Presumably that some drainage rates, if set to cover costs, would be so high that the area concerned would strongly object to the carrying out of the drainage work. A relatively small rise in drainage rates elsewhere, in consequence of uniformity, might allow the Board to engage in more drainage works than otherwise. The form of cross-subsidisation favoured by the Board, therefore, is a regional one, where the variations in the gap between price and cost arise on the side of cost.

The managements of the water, sewerage and drainage enterprises have generally covered costs in the metropolitan areas. Avoiding deficits, unfortunately, does not ensure complete economic success. Because revenues have been derived in large part from rates, even after 'excess water' charges have applied, and not from charges per unit consumed, there has been an important element of underpricing which arises as follows. A water rate is set at say $200 for a particular property. Water charges are then at the rate of, say, 10 cents a kilolitre with an 'allowance' of 2000 kilolitres (that is, 1 kilolitre per 10 cents of water rates charged).[3] For rate payers consuming less than their 'allowances' or with unmetered properties there is no financial incentive to reduce consumption. It costs the community more than zero to secure extra water, and yet those consumers are encouraged to treat water as if it were free. If the costs to the community of extra water were 10 cents, then those consumers paying 'excess' charges would be responding to an appropriate marginal price when deciding whether to consume more water or less. It is likely, however, that the cost has been more than the rates charged for 'excess' water, the authorities having set those charges at something like the average cost of water production and reticulation, not the marginal cost. Average costs have been rising (apart from general inflation) because communities have been forced to tap more distant or inconvenient water sources to serve extra demand.

Besides leading to over-consumption, the water rating system raises issues of equity. The *average* 'price' of water consumed varies between users according to the extent by which consumption falls short of or exceeds the allowance. In particular, the household and business sectors tend to use less than their allowances, and the manufacturing sector more. Manufacturing, then, pays a lower average water 'price'. It can be said, therefore, that water users in manufacturing are subsidised by other users.

Cross-subsidisation may help explain why the water rating system has not been changed to force most users into excess rating. Also important are the attitudes of the water authorities towards their dual responsibilities to meet demand and cover costs. The method of rating is satisfactory to the water authorities because it goes a long way towards ensuring that each year's costs are met by revenue, whereas relying more heavily on excess charges would bring the risk of revenue shortfalls either in very rainy years, or years so dry that water restrictions are needed. (The Melbourne Board has had a Rates Equalisation Fund to help avoid too frequent a change in rates.) Besides, pricing at marginal cost would tend to produce surpluses and a surplus was a sign for rates to be reduced, at least until more recent times when the boards were empowered to finance works from revenue.

---

[3] This is a simplification. The 'price' for water use beyond the allowance has often been set below the 'price' used to convert the water rates into the allowance (e.g. 8 cents rather than 10). Also the 'price' might decline to say 7 cents or 6 cents for users of large volumes of water. Perth has recently begun much more complete water pricing.

Both the inequity and the incentive to over-consumption were moderated in Sydney in 1975 by the passage of a sliding scale of rates (in conjunction with the change from annual assessed value to unimproved capital value for residential properties).

Similar considerations of equity and efficiency arise from the changing methods used by the hydraulic authorities to fund capital works. For a long time, the Boards in Sydney and Melbourne relied upon loan funds (supplemented by grants and advances from State governments), for which they had to compete against other public claimants. After the Second World War, the centralisation of public works funding, operating partly through the Loan Council, restricted enterprise projects. In the mid-1950s, the Sydney Board was reporting that its requests to the Loan Council were being only half met; meantime, public complaints were common about the lack of progress in meeting the sewerage backlog that had built up particularly during and after the war. One response of the Boards was to accept and, later, demand private developer contributions to reticulation and headwork costs as new suburban expansion occurred. Another was to resort to revenue financing of works. This implied the greater use of monopoly power to increase rates and charges in order to enlarge surpluses. This latter process went so far in Sydney that in 1969, one third of capital expenditure was financed by provisions from revenue. When it began a policy of 'self-finance' of capital outlays (for drainage and river improvements) in 1956, the Melbourne Board stated that it wished to avoid imposing on rate payers the crushing burden of interest that would have followed upon the use of loans. It is difficult not to believe that most customers would prefer loan financing to a system that forces today's customers to pay for works that will benefit customers in the future, particularly given that those current customers are still paying for assets established using loan funding during preceding decades. Nevertheless, in making this adaptation, the water and sewerage authorities were acting in a manner more akin to private enterprise.

Electricity supply

The electricity supply industry has evolved from being a mixture of privately, publicly and jointly owned enterprises, to being almost completely publicly owned. Generation, transmission and distribution initially were on a small local scale with a substantial private presence, typically by private franchises given by urban authorities. Since the First World War, long-distance transmission has provided opportunities for large economies of scale. By 1930, defective statistics suggest that close to two thirds of all power generated originated publicly.

Today one or a few authorities in each State run very large plants mostly located near their source of fuel, if coal fired, or at their source of water power, if hydro-electric. This implied a very considerable increase in scale and concentration. The systems within and between several States are now interconnected, requiring transmission over great distances. Distribution is now almost entirely in public hands, although not fully centralised within each State. In part, a high growth output has been due to the relatively low rate of electricity price increase, and in larger part to the shift in demand by households (appliances, heating, cooling), industry (including large users) and commerce. The earlier sources of demand - lighting and electric traction - have become far less important. In the process of growth, the peak load problem of the industry has worsened, with consequences for pricing policies and investment strategies.

Supplementing the State enterprises, the Snowy Mountains Scheme, begun in 1949, introduced a Federal government presence in the generating process, based on an agreement between three States (New South Wales, Victoria and South Australia) and the Federal Government. This project, subject to heavy criticism, provided an important influence encouraging the development of the southeast Australian electricity grid.

Demand

Apart from generation of electricity for consumption within a plant or works, the first important uses of electricity in Australia were for the lighting of buildings, and for street lighting in the late 1880s. By the turn of the century plants had also been established for electric street tram traction in Sydney, Melbourne and Brisbane, and later other cities. Electric traction may have been the fastest growing component of demand into the 1920s, with the electrification of trams and suburban trains in Melbourne and Sydney. Other sources of demand, however, soon became as important. By 1920-21, half the horse-power in New South Wales factories was electric, and electric-powered factories provided more horse-power per worker than did other factories. The advantages of electric power were chiefly in the decentralisation made possible within the factory. Rather than power distributed by physical (and often noisy and unsafe) means like belts, shafts and gears, each machine could have its own motor.

The most impressive users of electric power, besides the electric trams and railways, were large industrial concerns. In Tasmania, one of the chief purposes of developing the State's hydro-electric power resources has been to attract industry. The Electrolytic Zinc Ltd plant at Risdon (established 1917), was in the 1930s still drawing more than half the power of the Hydro-Electric Commission's only station, Waddamana 'A'. Aluminum production was attracted to Bell Bay,

Tasmania, in 1955 by cheap power. Tasmanian electric power has been considerably cheaper than that of the mainland States; this attraction was added to by charging lower prices to industrial consumers than to domestic or commercial consumers (a practice fairly common in all States, at least in the 1960s and 1970s) and by especially low rates for the very large users. With the advent of the mineral boom and its processing potential, State government action to provide very large increases in electricity supply for metal refineries became a leading policy concern in several States.

Within the home, in the 1920s electric toasters and irons (which could operate without the need for the kitchen stove to be lit), became quite common. The larger uses within the home, aside from lighting, were for heating and cooling (especially stoves and electric refrigerators and later, space heating and air conditioning), and were diffused more slowly. Indeed the mass consumption of large domestic appliances was a post-1945 phenomenon in Australia. The electricity supply industry, during the 1950s, encouraged the 'all electric' house by a special low tariff (similarly, the gas supply industry encouraged the use of gas) with the consequence already mentioned - the building up of a peak demand period associated with home cooking, heating and cooling. According to the 1947 census, almost all metropolitan residences, over 90 per cent of other urban residences, and almost half of rural residences had electric power connections though these were predominantly for cooking and to a less extent for small water-heating appliances. By 1971, encouraged by subsidies, the rural connection rate was close to 100 per cent.

Organisation

Because the first important uses of electricity were for public purposes - lighting of public buildings, street lighting and, later, electric traction - it is not surprising that there was appreciable public authority involvement in supply from the 1880s and 1890s. Electricity generation was by municipalities (Melbourne City Council, 1896) or by private companies under franchise to the councils or by joint public and private bodies. The capital costs were not so large as to be beyond private companies, especially when assured of a local monopoly and indeed, though adequate statistics are not available, it appears that private or joint (private-public) institutions predominated.

When widespread reticulation began, the capital costs imposed more serious constraints on entry or on private mergers in a pre-1914 economy in which the domestic supply of investible funds was very restricted and the capital market ill formed. There were advantages to consumers and to large enterprises to be had from co-ordination, involving the choice of frequencies and voltage, and the potential savings of capital costs per unit of output through the interconnections of systems with different demand patterns (especially peaks). These advantages were sought, as has been common, more by public means than by private co-operation. Their achievement did not, however, require everywhere the wholesale public ownership of generating or distribution facilities, although by the early 1930s public enterprise accounted for perhaps two thirds of the total output generated. A variety of ownership patterns continued, with a trend toward public ownership, faster in some places (Tasmania, Victoria) than in others (Adelaide's electric power was provided by private companies until 1946). By the 1950s, perhaps more than 90 per cent was publicly generated. An almost total displacement of private activity had by then occurred.

In both Tasmania and Victoria, public ownership occurred more fully and rapidly because of State government desires to exploit natural resources in a manner and on a scale that precluded private ownership because of capital costs and managerial experience. The Tasmanian Hydro-Electric Department was set up in 1914 to take over from a private company that attempted unsuccessfully to develop the Great Lake region. The Department supplied power to private distribution companies until 1930, when the newly formed Hydro-Electric Commission took over generation, transmission and distribution.

Eggleston speculates whether private enterprise in Victoria would have succeeded in developing the Gippsland brown coal fields; in the event, it was not given the opportunity (Eggleston 1932, p. 161). The Victorian government was concerned to decrease the reliance on New South Wales black coal, the supply of which had been seriously interrupted by industrial disputes, and when severe technical problems were encountered by the State Electricity Commission of Victoria (set up 1919), the project was pushed ahead. Distribution in the metropolitan area was still by the Melbourne City Council and the Melbourne Supply Company, a private company, and the success of the SECV depended on securing the right to supply these retailers. It did so after a struggle with the Melbourne City Council in the late 1920s. Retailing of electricity is still carried out by municipal and local councils.

The first major power station in New South Wales, Ultimo, was built for the railways to run their ancillary electric tram services. To this extent, the Department of Railways followed its common practice of (public) vertical integration. It was also able to sell off 'surplus' power and therefore gain advantages of scale. By 1907, the Railway Department generated half the electric power in New South Wales. The trend to public ownership was strengthened by a change in the Local Government Act that empowered municipalities to generate and supply electricity, and although some (e.g. Balmain, 1906) franchised private companies for those purposes, the tendency was for municipal generation. The Sydney City Council took over private firms in 1904 and later, and became an important supplier of electricity. The railways opened a second station at White Bay, and began to sell power in competition with the Sydney City Council. This competition was resolved in 1919 in favour of the Council as wholesaler. When the Council opened its Bunnerong Station in 1929, the railways had no excess power to sell largely because the electrification of metropolitan railway transit absorbed available output. An effort at co-ordination of the industry was made in 1938 with the appointment of an Electricity Advisory Committee, and again with the formation of the Electricity Authority of New South Wales in 1946. This latter body brought about the amalgamation of local distributors into electricity county councils. Immediate post-war power shortages, which were extreme, exerted a powerful pressure towards co-ordinated provisions. The Electricity Commission of NSW, created in 1950, acquired the power stations being operated within an interconnected grid by four large electricity organisations, and has expanded that system to include most of the State. Retailing is still done by the electricity county councils under regulation by the Authority; there are four councils supplying electricity in Sydney.

The lines of division and control in the mid-1960s were horizontal in New South Wales   and vertical in Queensland. The Queensland industry was largely unco-ordinated until the advent in 1938 of the State Electricity Commission of Queensland. About seventy local undertakings generated and distributed electricity in the late 1930s. These the SECQ had, by 1945, integrated into five regional boards controlling generation and distribution along the eastern seaboard. By further consolidation, the system by the 1970s comprised three main grids, southern, central and northern, the first two having been interconnected. The regional boards are the electricity retailers, along with Dalby and Brisbane Councils (the latter buying its power from the Southern Electric Authority).

As already mentioned the Federal government entered electric power generation in 1949 with the Snowy Mountains Scheme, a project of grand proportions, which diverts waters of the Snowy River into the Murray River, and waters of the Eucumbene (a Snowy tributary) into the Tumut (a tributary of the Murrumbidgee). The work began in 1950 and was completed in the mid-1970s, and was the largest engineering project in Australian history. The water is used to drive six main power stations and for irrigation. The power, after an allotment to the Australian Capital Territory, is fed into the Victorian and New South Wales systems in the ratio 40:60 to cater to peak electricity demands in those States. The capital costs of the project are to be recovered from consumers of the electricity generated.

Investment errors

Because the construction of electricity generating plants absorbed such huge sums of money, it was important that decisions on them be economically sound. Electricity investment decisions have come in for a considerable amount of criticism from economists. McFarlane, an advocate of more (if better) economic planning, says that 'the record of some State electricity commissions in investment planning and policy has *not* been impressive in the past and a rather long catalogue of errors could be constructed' (McFarlane 1968, p. 96). He hastens to point out that only part of the blame falls on the commissions' internal decisions, and that part falls on the system of Loan Council finance. In his examples of errors, two Victorian projects, the Kiewa hydro scheme and the Morwell project, figure prominently. Only in discussing the first does McFarlane cite Loan Council difficulties - the new Federal government in 1949, bent on carrying out the Labor plans for the Snowy, refused loan funds. This does not seem to be a particularly convincing argument given the change of Federal government in that year and the opportunities to alter the allocation of capital funds.

The most recent assessment of a series of electrical investment decisions was made by McColl (1976). He applied differential cost-benefit analyses to four decisions. They included the Victorian decision to make the state independent of imports of New South Wales black coal, following the strikes of 1949 (the Morwell project which McFarlane also examined). McColl concludes that the project was not economical except at a low discount rate (5 percent), and only then if Morwell is 'forgiven' the cost of the very uneconomical briquetting enterprise. Next, McColl examined whether New South Wales could have saved costs by using nuclear power, and concludes it could not have. Third, he calculates that in Tasmania thermal generation of electricity became more economical than hydro in the late 1960s. Last, he supports the work of Davidson (1969) and others that the Snowy scheme was uneconomic because of the insignificant returns from irrigation, again except at low discount rates. Of the four comparisons, only in the second - nuclear versus coal power in New South Wales - was the actual decision justified economically. Technical efficiency did not guarantee economic efficiency.

Were the errors of the kind that private business also commits? Two of them, Morwell and the Snowy, were decisions taken at a time when shortage of electric power was seen to be a major obstacle to economic development after the war. Moreover, black coal was in uncertain supply because of Communist influence in unions. Further, in the late 1940s, coal-fired power generation was replaced by oil-fuelled stations after the hydro projects were committed. In fact, there is a common feature to all the actual decisions taken. The three State governments chose to use the fuel which was found in abundance in their own State. The Commonwealth, on its part, pressed ahead with the only energy source it could reasonably command, which was water 'owned' by a number of States. It did so at the expense of cheap hydro power at Kiewa (according to McFarlane) and cheaper thermal power. A higher degree of self-sufficiency was obtained in power, but at a cost to electricity customers and others. No doubt private business displays some similar preferences, for example, for 'in-house' production over buying in, or for plowing back profits rather than finding new fields for investment. And the security obtained by higher degrees of self-sufficiency was valuable. Nevertheless, it seems likely that political factors overrode economic ones in the preferences shown by these four governments. There was, also, an important bureaucratic consideration: the Snowy Mountains Scheme had been fully articulated in the 1930s by Scandinavian consulting engineers and was high on the priorities of the post-war Labor Government's bank of works projects proposed as defence against postwar unemployment. To that extent, it was 'taken off the shelf' when interruptions to black coal supplies reached crisis proportions.

Hindsight reveals that thermal power generation became much more efficient in the last few decades, that the Joint Coal Board did a remarkable job in reorganising New South Wales black coal supplies, and that fuel oil became very cheap in the 1950s and 1960s. Thus the economics of the Snowy and Morwell look worse after the event than might have reasonably been foreseen when the decisions were made. And the economics of the Snowy improve with every rise in the real price of fossil fuel. Nevertheless, these two decisions are still targets of legitimate criticism. The initial economic justification put forward for the Snowy has been excoriated by Mathews (1967): a huge sum was committed after some small sums were badly done. Davidson (1969) has difficulty in explaining why the most expensive of the Snowy proposals was chosen, since it was to generate less electricity and less irrigation water. His only suggestion is that New South Wales was able to insist on the proposal that provided most water for the Murrumbidgee (p. 165).

The Morwell mistakes after 1945 echo startlingly those made after 1918, in that two unrepresentative samples were taken and acted upon. After the first brown coal decision was made, it was discovered that the moisture content of the brown coal was 50 per cent higher than had been estimated, necessitating considerable modification of design, and a serious deterioration in financial prospects (Eggleston 1932, pp. 160-73). After the second project was underway, it was discovered that salinity rendered the brown coal unsuitable for the briquetting plant sited at Morwell, so coal was railed from Yallourn to feed the plant. Compounding the difficulties was a serious overestimate of demand for briquettes, which were then forced on government departments and instrumentalities including metropolitan power stations (which had to crush the briquettes) and the Gas and Fuel Corporation for its Lurgi gasification plant near Morwell. Thus were the costs of the mistake partly passed on to consumers of electricity and gas, and to taxpayers.

What is, however, to be appreciated is the probable contrast with private behaviour. There have of course been many instances of private errors of calculation, for reasons similar to or different from those related to these public outlays. What is different is that, unless supported by government, the private enterprises failed and were wound up if they seriously miscalculated. Frequently assets were revalued and activity renewed on this basis. Public decisions appear to lack this flexibility.

10

Monopoly Lost

Government railways 1901 to 1945

Introduction

Several interwoven themes arise in considering the history of the structure, conduct and performance of public transport undertakings: the source, extension, defence and collapse of monopoly power; the various roles of private interests, as more or less favoured customers, as competitive suppliers, as cossetted partners; the extent of politicisation in the decision-making process; the importance of recourse to the general taxing and other coercive powers of government.

Of first importance are the radical changes which have occurred in the monopoly position of government railways. During the 1850s public railway ownership displaced private, due, apparently, to a lack of private entrepreneurial ability and private access to capital. Between 1860 and the 1920s public railways increased in market power but, subsequently, there occurred a drastic erosion of this power. The basis of public transport monopoly had differed in some respects from that in water and sewerage. In each case, however, as also in electricity, there was a significant degree of natural monopoly. That of rail sprang from large indivisibilities of capital, with implications for the shape of railway cost functions. Railways as high-capacity mass-haulage systems offered, until the First World War or later, a service superior to that of the then dominant transport mode, animal power. In the first quarter of this century, they were crucial to the development of transport-dependent rural activities, and what survived of private horse-drawn transport was increasingly adapted to a feeder role in relation to the now dominant mode.

The sharpest contrast between rail and the other reticulated services lies in the regulation of customers and competing suppliers in order to enhance monopoly power. Water, sewerage and drainage authorities compelled the making of connections to properties, and generated most of their revenues by way of taxation rather than by unforced sales. Although the establishment of railway monopoly received no such boost from regulation, its subsequent defence did involve coercion through regulation. Motorised land transport, a product of private technological change, began to compete seriously with public railways in the inter-war years, and after World War II the mass consumption of motor vehicles advanced so rapidly as to shrink dramatically the railway share of transport services. An attempt by the authorities (temporarily and partly successful) to combat this private challenge relied heavily on the regulation of motor transport.

The early establishment of strong market power provided opportunity for commercially respectable financial results for rail; and correspondingly the advent of effective private competition implied an erosion of this profitability. Certainly the downward trend of surpluses was strong, although interrupted by short-term influences, particularly the Second World War. But in interpreting this unfavourable trend, emphasis must be placed on the increasingly politicised nature of decision-making in public transport. From the 1880s investment decisions were increasingly affected by intervention from politicians and local electorates, and adjoining colonies or states competed in the design of their rail systems, and in price, for railway business. Despite this early political intervention financial results were generally satisfactory through the 1910s, reflecting the application of relatively stringent criteria for performance. Subsequently, however, criteria were relaxed drastically in investment planning as well as in output and price policies. In the inter-war years price concessions proliferated in response to the growth of highly organised pressure groups, especially rural. There were internal or cross-subsidies, whereby one set of customers paid more so that another could pay less. In addition the growing importance of income taxation to government revenues increased opportunities to provide external subsidies to the enterprise as a whole.

Besides cross-subsidisation, other factors were important in explaining the decline of railway surpluses, among them the difficulty of countering competition from privately-owned motor trucks and cars. During the inter-war years the railways energetically sought to diminish the consumption of privately supplied motor transport services by routing roads as feeders to rail; by pressing for and obtaining regulation of private motor freight services; by capturing the regulatory control of urban bus systems. Ultimately, however, the natural monopoly of rail proved vulnerable to the competition of very small suppliers offering more attractive alternative services, which helped drive down earnings and surpluses after the Second World War.

Pricing policies were important in the complex stories of the erosion of public monopoly and of rail finances. Parliament forced the railways to grant price concessions to different user groups in response to pressures from those groups. When price discrimination between types of customers is exercised by a private enterprise, it generally results in higher profits for the undertaking. The contrary is more the rule with railways. In particular, the railways had limited power to set rates to defend themselves against external competition: pricing was not flexible in response to competitive modes. After suffering price constraint in face of rising costs and demand in the years immediately after World War II, the railways had to raise rates generally at just the time (the early 1950s) when private motor transport posed its greatest threat. The outcome is revealed in railway accounts, and in government budgets.

Just as railway managements had limited autonomy over pricing, so also they were increasingly restricted in their labour input decisions by arbitration tribunals, and by the power of the transport unions.

A possible response to competition is the incorporation of more and varied transport services. In the nineteenth century, public authorities came to monopolise port and harbour services and the provision of roads (in the latter, extensive private displacement occurred in the 1840s). At the end of the century, steam and subsequently electric tram services were added. In the late 1920s and during the 1930s, public railways assumed control of bus services by regulation and ownership. After the Second World War, public air transport was added. In these circumstances, a major problem of such diverse undertakings is in the form of 'transport co-ordination', a phrase that lends itself to reinterpretation as 'restraint of competition'. The question of co-ordination did indeed become important after 1945. Its resolution requires very complex analysis and, beyond recognising its existence, we have confined attention to the special aspects of air transport.

One of the outstanding characteristics of public enterprise in contrast with private is the ability of public organisations to remain in existence, to resist asset revaluation and, even, to expand in conditions of declining earnings and surpluses. All these responses appear in Australian railways in the twentieth century. The area of control widened to incorporate urban bus systems, adding to and often replacing trams; the regulation of private bus and long-distance private freight services; and the transformation of railway services, during the 1950s and 1960s, by conversion to diesel, replacement of rolling stock, electrification of lines and gauge unification. In the process, some slight asset revaluation occurred.

The economic value of long lived systems like rail is sensitive to changes in relative prices and costs, and to changes in demand. The mineral boom increased the demand for rail services because the freight was suited to rail, and because the energy crisis associated with the boom shifted relative costs in favour of railways. However, not all the increased demand was met by *public* rail. In a great deal of mineral development, there were opportunities for private mining enterprises to internalise most of the benefits of new land transport facilities in remote areas. Hence private transport systems received a stimulus. At the same time, existing public railways were able to offer more effective competition against motorised services. Facilities that had been developed on the basis of natural monopoly and had been relatively unresponsive to lowered earnings were, unexpectedly, placed in a stronger competitive position.

Autonomy versus dependence in railway enterprises

By the standards of their time and place, Australian State railways at Federation were massive undertakings, and great political interest surrounded their operation and control. The railways were begun as private enterprises in the 1850s and subsequently expanded as prime agents for the development of Australia's vast semi-arid pastoral lands.

During the 1850s, the original projects were taken over by government. The chief reasons appear to have been limited private entrepreneurial ability, and the failure of private business either to attract local capital or to establish effective access in the London capital market. Although some experiments with land grant railways were made, they yielded, at best, precarious private enterprises. In the rapid pastoral expansion after 1860, the main railway development depended on action by governments with their ability (a) to capture substantial external economic benefits; (b) to obtain London capital cheaply; (c) to organise managerial skills; and (d) to accept moderate rates of return. The reputation of colonial governments of having been massive borrowers on the London market, particularly in the 1880s, was earned on behalf of the railways; in the early years of this century railway debt made up 60 per cent of total public debt.

The borrowing helped to finance the virtual completion of the trunk (but few branch) lines of southeastern Australia, so that, by 1901, over 19 000 kilometres of track were being operated. One third of public employees were railway workers, and half of public investment was devoted to railways around Federation. Although it is broadly correct to say that the railways were being run so as to cover expenses and interest from receipts (and the same can be said of other State and local enterprises), when trading results were unfavourable there was a significant drain on State finances. For example, in 1902-03, drought contributed to a loss after interest by the combined railway systems of $2.8m, a figure that exceeded the amount spent on police, and was about half that spent on State education.

The numerous changes in *Railway Acts* attest to the difficulty of finding a stable balance between autonomy and control of railways in the various levels of decision making. Both Victoria (1896 to 1903) and New South Wales (1906 to 1916) experimented with single commissioners, with the notable difference that in 1891 Victoria had pioneered the system of confining ministerial writ to general matters of policy, in an attempt to reconcile democratic control with a degree of real autonomy for public corporations. One ideal solution had been to have the great public utilities controlled by disinterested technical experts, generally imported from England, standing outside the local political arena. This approach appears to have been broadly effective until the early 1880s. Then political pressures led to increasing political interference in new line proposals and the process of investment decision-making became highly politicised. In the heyday of British investment in Australia in the 1880s, financial brakes were relaxed encouraging extravagant projects in response to political and local pressures. Ministers could not exercise adequate control over special electoral interests, and bureaucratic commissioners proved able to be swayed by local political pressure. The reasons were not mere temporary lapses from public-spiritedness but, to some extent, were intrinsic to the system of public railway finance in Australia.

Above the freight and fare receipts railway operations generate 'external' economic benefits. In particular, the building and operation of a railway line raises the value of the land in the rail catchment area, causing differential changes in land values. It is difficult for railways to capture these changes by differential pricing, that is, by charging more for the same railway service to customers near the line than to those farther away. It can be profitable, and economically desirable, therefore, to build a railway line that is expected to earn less traffic revenue than its construction, equipment and running costs, as long as there are expected to be sufficiently large offsetting benefits. Under the American land-grant railway system (copied in Australia on several occasions with limited success), a sizable share of the 'external' benefits of land appreciation was captured or 'internalised' by the companies themselves and so was taken into account in investment and pricing decisions.

What distinguished publicly owned from privately owned railways? One important difference was that Government railways rarely receive land grants, and could not capture at all fully the economic benefits they generated. Thus, railway surpluses and deficits conceal wider benefits to the public purse, and other social benefits. However, some benefits 'spilled over' to the Crown as landowner and tax collector, as well as to private landholders on fixed leases or freehold. The private benefits gave rise to pressure, sometimes intense, on the government and the railways to build more lines, and to charge low freight rates.

The benefits to government by way of land revenues (sales and lease rents) and taxes helped lessen the problems of public finance, and provided the rationale for arguments that a developmental function justified operation at a loss. Once it was accepted that an individual developmental line could be built without expectation of railway receipts covering costs, then the way was open for a similar argument to be made about the railway system as a whole, or the State budget as a whole. As the Valuer-General put it, in evidence to the 1924 New South Wales Royal Commission into the Railway and Tramway Services,

> The Income Tax Commissioner, the Land Tax Collector, the Excise Officer, each has his receipts swelled through railway facilities ... No department is entitled to look only at the parochial aspects - sprats must be cast to catch mackeral ... In the long run it is perfectly immaterial whether the Lands Department made a profit, or the Valuer-General's Department made a profit, so long as the State as a whole is able to balance its accounts ... I have always thought the State ought to view their various operations as one big company rather than a segregation of companies.

The State was able to take an attitude that no private railway could have afforded: it is doubtful that private lines could have grown to anything like the scale of 1901 without substantial public aid. After the largely abortive efforts at land-grant railways, political pressure led to the abandonment of 'betterment' taxes or levies on local landholders. State railways could rarely benefit directly from the increases in land values caused by railway operations. As a consequence, the opportunity for railways to secure autonomy was severely limited.

There was, however, a partial remedy and, once again, Victoria led in experimenting with an arrangement with important implications for railway financial responsibility and autonomy. Under 1896 legislation, the Treasury was to compensate the railways for losses caused by directives of Parliament or the Minister. This system of 'recoups' gave the commissioner some financial support but also enhanced the opportunity for political interference and the exercise of private pressures. Under these provisions, Victorian wheat interests were subsidised by specially legislated grain freight charges, and Victorian brown coal given preference in rail consumption. However, in these cases the full recoups were not always paid, and the commissioners agreed to a fifty-fifty split of the losses. Whether this pushed some of the costs of concessions to these private interests from taxpayers onto other rail users is not at all clear, because of the absence of a binding profit-or-loss constraint.

The difficult consequences of the railway financial arrangement were that control over the building of new lines rested with parliament or government, under pressure from interested landholders, often banded together as railway leagues, and that judgements about the value of lines could not be made solely by reference to railway accounts. It would appear that general fiscal constraints limited this process from 1901 to 1914. Income tax provided relatively little of State revenues, the majority of which were closely market-dependent (land revenues and customs returns from the Federal government). Moreover, railway debt obligations were predominantly to British investors and viable railway development depended on severe constraint on freight and passenger rate concessions to customers.

After the war, with greater access to non-enterprise revenues in State budgets, particularly greater income taxation, controls became much looser. Losses could be 'justified' because the general budgets offered fall-back support. Eggleston (1932), contemplating his brief (four-month) experience as Victorian Minister for Railways, came to believe that

> the chief reason against operating railways at a loss is the slackening in efficiency: no service can be efficient unless every worker in it feels some responsibility for its success; the best way for him to measure success is to co-operate towards an achievement which can be seen and realized; the best goal is a balanced profit and loss account [p.122].

There were problems, therefore, of external and internal railway control. The New South Wales Valuer-General, in the statement quoted on p. 264, implied that the financial benefits and costs of railways were more faithfully reflected in State government budgets than in railway accounts. How faithfully, and to what consequence? Through land and tariff receipts, Australian fiscal arrangements 'captured' some of the benefits not otherwise collected as railway receipts. Land sales reflected higher economic values due to rail. More importantly, land rents did so also, but more slowly because they were fixed for varying lengths of time and, with some exceptions (the Western Division of New South Wales included), could not be raised in the interim to reflect the advantages of new public works. In 1905 and 1906, New South Wales allotted land tax to the shires, and in 1910 the Federal government entered the land tax field. Less directly than land tax, customs receipts were also a means of internalising some railway benefits in Federal budgets in so far as railway-stimulated expansion induced increased outputs. Thus the connection between the State budgets and 'spillovers' from railways was attenuated.

What is clear is that, however close the connection between the overall State budget and State railway operations, once decisions about railways were made politically, the way was opened for the granting of political favours at the expense of other rail users, of customers of other state enterprises, or of the taxpayers. This is not to say that *private* railways would have been free of problems of control, but that *public* ownership altered the manner in which these problems presented themselves and, possibly, their magnitudes. Any large enterprise capable of delivering or witholding great benefits is liable to non-market pressures from customers and potential customers, from suppliers of equipment and material and, inside, as it were, from employees. Similarly, all large enterprises, and especially those with monopoly power, present problems of efficient organisation and control. *Given access to non-enterprise budgets*, and particularly to income taxation, publicly-owned enterprises are able to run deficits more freely than private, and the extent of cross-subsidisation or price discrimination (the favouring of one group of customers over another) is likely to be larger within public than private enterprise. These problems appear to have become acutely important after 1918.

There is another important difference between privately owned and publicly owned railways as they operated in Australia. From early days the public undertakings charged freight rates that were 'uniform' in the following sense: the same rate was paid for carriage of a particular commodity over a given distance within a Colony or State, regardless of upon which lines carriage occurred. Lines differ in initial capital costs; average and probably marginal costs vary according to the volume of traffic. Therefore, a State-wide system of 'uniform' freight rates gave rise to the possibility that users of expensive lines were subsidised by users of cheap lines (and by users of lines with lower than average standard of service).

Questions of the influence on railways by groups consuming rail services is discussed below. Here we want briefly to mention the other sources of private pressure - suppliers. Along with most other public enterprises, and in accordance with government policy, railways gave preference, over duty-paid imports, to local private suppliers of equipment and materials. (In part, this was offset by displacing private suppliers when the railways set up their own workshops first for repair, then for renewals, later for new construction. This process was established in the nineteenth century.) The New South Wales government, after calling tenders for engines to be constructed within New South Wales, and after a Royal Commission into the question, awarded the contract to the Clyde Engineering Co. in 1905, beginning a long relationship between this private firm and the railways. In other States unspecified but high rates of preference were granted local firms. (Eggleston (1932, p.137) claimed the margin of preference was 50 or 60 per cent over and above the tariff.)

More dramatic was the reduction in the autonomy exercised by railway managements over decisions about employees. Before 1900, employment in the railways was a matter of political patronage rather than merit. By 1901, however, a more regular system had been evolved internally and railways offered very attractive career employment. After Federation, the power of setting railway wages moved in fits and starts, from the railways, to State wage boards, to the Federal wage fixing system. After the strikes of the 1890s, the colonial legislatures had taken directly into their hands some of the setting of railway wages and salaries, particularly at the upper levels. Once 'company arbitration' was introduced the railway workers were soon unhappy with the State wage fixing boards, and sought to use the Federal Conciliation and Arbitration Court to further their claims. However, by a decision in 1906 (*State Railway Servants' Case*), the High Court ruled that the *Commonwealth Conciliation and Arbitration Act* did not apply to State instrumentalities. This decision was overturned much later in the 1920 *Engineers' Case*, and by 1926 most railway workers were under Federal awards. In October 1930, the Full Arbitration Court set aside Federal railway awards, except for the basic wage and standard hours, so that the State boards (like Victorian Railways Classification Board) shared wage fixing with the Federal Court. The Court restored the Federal awards in late 1934. Along with others the main railway awards were reduced in 1931 by 10 per cent. The general restoration of the cuts in April 1934 excluded the State transport workers, in view of the importance of the railways for State budgets, but the delay was only until November 1934. From 1935-36 until after 1945, the Federal court shared wage fixing with State railway industry boards (acting, however, under provisions of the Commonwealth Act). In 1948, Federal conciliation commissioners were appointed to deal with claims in the railway industry.

Expansion of the rail system 1901 to 1920

There was a very rapid growth in the volume of railway services in the first two decades of this century, completing the nineteenth-century trunk system, amplifying branch networks and extending city transit systems. Freight tonnage doubled and passenger numbers trebled, with the largest growth being in metropolitan services, especially in Melbourne. In the course of supplying this additional output, the financial position of the railways deteriorated for at least two reasons. First, the efficiency of operations did not rise enough to offset the difference between increases in cost and increases in fares and freight rates. A detailed discussion of the financial results is set out below. Here we want to point out that the financial standards by which railways were judged were much more stringent at the start of the century than later. For example, criticisms of overmanning were levied against the Victorian railways in the early 1900s when the ratio of earnings to working expenses fell to around 1.5, a ratio which is about the inverse of that of 1975! The second reason for the falloff in railway returns was that the new business was less attractive than the old, a question also discussed below.

In the years between 1901 and 1920, the length of railway track doubled. Throughout much of this period, new line construction was designed predominantly to support an export-led boom in rural products other than wool. It was, therefore, strongly geared to rural interests, supplying high capacity mass haulage of transport-dependent rural products (and passengers), extensively displacing animal power and widening production possibilities. This was a tremendous investment effort which, because many of the new lines were branches relatively cheap to construct, if not cheap to operate, helped to increase aggregate railway capital stock by half. The pace of building was relatively slow in the first decade, and much faster after 1909 and until the middle years of First World War. In Victoria, there had been a reaction at the turn of the century to the rapid recovery of construction after the depression, and to the run of deficits culminating in that of the worst year of drought. A series of surpluses and the revirval of govenment determination to develop rural districts led to another spurt in line building between 1911-12 and 1915-16; suburban electrification also began in this period.

The branch lines in Victoria built towards the Riverina region (and extended into New South Wales in the 1930s) were designed to complete the capture of the Riverina trade; those into the Mallee, to open it up to wheat growers; the branches into the Western District of Victoria, to speed up the closer settlement of this rich country by graziers and dairy farmers. In New South Wales the pattern of building was somewhat different. Apart from its own branches towards the Murray, New South Wales spread its efforts on the coastal link (uniform gauge) to the north, the connection with Broken Hill in the west, and branch lines in the Central Division for the benefit of wheat growers and sheep graziers. Queensland's system of spurs from coastal ports was greatly added to (especially in the north and west), and progress made in linking the coastal pieces. Significant rail building occurred in South and Western Australia: the Trans-Australian line was completed in 1917; South Australia linked the Western and Murray Mallee districts to its system; Western Australia indulged in an orgy of wheat line construction.

This activity was a continuation of the development strategy of nineteenth-century colonial governments but with an important difference: what was being encouraged, by closer settlement policies and irrigation, was a more intensive rural growth depending primarily on non-wool production. This shift in emphasis had considerable consequences, not the least of which related to railway finance. The 'catchments' of the new branches were generally much smaller than those of the earlier lines, and the form of agriculture was somewhat experimental in terms of climatic zones and type of farmer. On the other hand, capital costs were much lower than in the nineteenth-century trunk lines. Railway earnings were relatively satisfactory until the war, a performance supported by the very limited cross-subsidisation that was provided by way of explicit freight rate and fare concessions. Whether the various railway managements would have decided, had they had the choice, to build these lines is moot because State governments still reserved to themselves (and from railway managements) power to install new capital.

Railway investment between the wars

After having been starved of capital funds for the last few years of the war and the first few of the peace, in the 1920s government railways achieved a rate of capital formation (in price-adjusted terms) approaching that during the investment spurt in the mid-1910s. There were, however, other insistent claimants on public resources, and the railways in the 1920s absorbed an appreciably smaller share of total public investment than in the previous two decades - 28 per cent compared with over 40 per cent. The length of railway track increased at the modest rate of about 1 per cent per year, as long-distance coastal and inland links were completed and branch line networks filled out to serve areas of closer settlement, including settlement by returned soldiers and assisted migrants. Some new lines were recommended and built despite clear evidence that they would be unprofitable, and as the 1920s progressed, larger losses were contemplated. Rather than most weight being given to financial matters, what seemed more important was whether the area through which the new line would pass was already served by rail and, if not, what were the prospects for closer settlement of the land within 16 or 20 kilometres of the rail. The building of new lines was only a part of the capital works undertaken by the railways: in New South Wales, where the length of track increased twice as fast as elsewhere, and where there was a long lull in country line duplications after 1923, new lines absorbed less than one fifth of the capital funds expended during the 1920s on the railways in that State; in addition, there were improvements to existing lines (duplications and relayings), upgrading of rolling stock, installations of devices for faster and safer operations, and electrification of Sydney and suburban lines.

Gross railway investment peaked in 1927, and then fell heavily to reach in 1931 about a third of its 1927 value. The building of new lines slowed and eventually stopped in 1935 when the length of track being operated reached its maximum of 43 660 kilometres.

In the early 1920s, lines were proposed that would yield a revenue sufficient to cover operating costs, but make little contribution to interest charges. In economic terms, the freight rate was the 'price' of the service, and the annual operating costs something like 'marginal cost'. The rule suggested by economists is that the price of a service should, in most instances, be set equal to marginal cost, in order to obtain the most efficient use of a facility once it is built. It is seriously to be doubted that the economic reasoning behind this rule guided governments in their deliberations. Some evidence is provided by the fact that, as the decade of the 1920s progressed, less and less financially sound prospects were found to be acceptable, and the failure of expected revenues to exceed expected working costs was no longer a bar to favourable consideration. For example, a proposed line from Hillston to Roto, completing the link between the Western Line (to Broken Hill) and the South Western Line (to the Murrumbidgee Irrigation Area), at a cost of £ 170 000 was favourably reported upon by the New South Wales Parliamentary Standing Committee on Public Works after a public inquiry in 1929. The line, completed in 1932, was expected to generate revenue of £ 4000, sufficient to cover three quarters of its annual working costs. The Committee thought the revenue estimate was too low because it did not take account of through traffic; it envisaged the transport of produce from the Murrumbidgee Irrigation Area to Broken Hill, as well as passenger traffic between Broken Hill and Melbourne. The annual loss after interest was estimated at over £ 10 000 or £ 224 per kilometre per year. The Railway Commissioner might have been aided in his support by the 1928 New South Wales legislation, similar to that enacted in Victoria in 1896, giving a guarantee from the government of partial recoups of losses on developmental country lines. The Committee was encouraged to its favourable decision by the assurance it received that the line was likely to qualify for an interest subsidy under the provisions of the 1923 migration agreement between the States, the Commonwealth and the British government. Transport investment was seen as an essential component of the policy of closer settlement, and railway costs sometimes exceeded the costs of establishing the farms themselves.

Important as they were, new lines were not the only or even the major source of the relatively poor financial results of the railways in the 1920s. In 1929-30, for example, when the Victorian Railways lost £ 1m after interest payments of £ 3.5m, the Commission was reimbursed for losses resulting from government directives to operate non-paying lines and for various freight concessions to the extent of only £ 0.4m. If the allocation of the losses was appropriate between those caused by government decree and those due to other causes it suggests that the latter were at least as large. In addition, however, the railways in the inter-war years faced substantially one new problem and a dramatic increase in an old one. The new issue was competition from motorised transport, eroding the monopoly position of the railways. With inflexible investment policies and unable to adapt their capital values, railway surpluses suffered. The other matter was the great increase in pressures, exercised with considerable effect, to provide disseminatory benefits to major interest groups - most obviously to rural producers but also to a variety of others including veterans and schoolchildren to whom large-scale fare concessions were made. These pressures represented the full politicising of railway operations in Australia.

Financial results of railway operation 1901 to 1945

There are some special problems in the interpretation of the financial results of the railways, and their comparison with those of private businesses, arising from the accounting treatment of outlays on the renewal and replacement of assets. Very many substantial items of construction and equipment were charged to loan funds when initially built or purchased. A difficulty arose when an asset had to be renewed or replaced. Particularly after the First World War not all the physical deterioration of railway assets was made good by outlays charged to working accounts though a large proportion was replaced through 'maintenance' expenditures. Especially in times of financial stringency and of high demand, assets were allowed to deteriorate temporarily, with deferred maintenance sometimes later charged to loan funds. In addition, when some worn-out assets were renewed or replaced, the railway systems had inadequate depreciation allowances to call upon, so that when replacement or renewal was charged to loan funds, inadequate credits were made to capital account. In effect, there were two debts, and one asset. In both these kinds of cases, the recorded surplus was inflated to the extent that there was underprovision for depreciation in the current accounts, while the net profit was depressed by the interest payments on account of capital that no longer existed. In the 1920s and especially in the 1930s, the interest bills of the railways were adjusted downwards by various direct interest subsidies and by the writing-off of capital debt. In some degree, but haphazardly, the debts and assets were brought closer together, reducing the bias in the annual returns. The most important adjustment in capital liabilities were a £ 28m reduction in Queensland in 1931-32 and a £ 25.7m reduction in Victoria in 1937-38, representing about a third of the respective debts.

As a trend process, there was a long-term degradation of financial results. Prior to 1918, railways performed reasonably well. Although they generated revenue sufficient to pay expenses and interest between 1906 and 1914, performance worsened thereafter. During the 1920s and 1930s the recorded *losses* after interest payments averaged about 1.2 per cent of the capital debt of the railways, with the worst results coming in years of large deferred payments (1925-26 and 1926-27), and in the depression. The losses in the inter-war period placed very severe burdens on State government budgets: the largest inter-war loss was over £ 11m in 1930-31, which equalled about 30 per cent of the taxation collected by the States (a reflection of the large fraction that railway debt made up of total public debt - over one third). The burden was a little reduced by manipulations of railway debt, and more by reductions in interest rates and by some improvements in the railway working results after 1932 (see below). For a few years in the Second World War, with high demand and low maintenance (including replacement) outlays, revenue again exceeded working expenses and interest. (Losses increased greatly after the Second World War: for most of the years after 1950, railway revenue actually fell short of recorded working expenses.)

An examination of the gross (before depreciation) rate of return to capital stock, calculated from annual estimates of gross capital formation, reveals a broadly similar pattern at a different level except that the eleven years after 1934 stand out as the period in which the railways earned more than enough for full depreciation (taken at about 3 per cent) and for interest on the replacement value of their capital stock. After very poor results in the early 1920s, the combined systems earned an average gross rate of return of 3.5 per cent for the 1920s, with relatively small variations between years. From 1930-31 the rate rose until the middle of the 1930s to reach 7 per cent, and there it stayed until the end of the Second World War. (The highest rate of return in this century, over 8 per cent, was achieved in exceptional conditions between 1942 and 1944.) From that peak, until the early 1950s, the rate declined to a level a little below the depreciation rate.

Therefore, according to these calculations, the railways failed after 1918 to earn a 'market' rate of return except for the period 1935 to 1945. Neither the rate of return reported by the railways nor the rate of return as calculated above are ideal measures of the commercial performance of the Australian railway systems. What is needed, as a start, is an estimate of the railway equivalent of the business concept of 'shareholders' funds'. In view of their financial size, business historians might profitably turn their attention to the railways.

The operating ratio

Apart from rates of profit and loss, there are further indications of a deterioration in the financial position of the railways between our first period, 1901 to 1920, and our second, 1920 to 1945 (an even greater decline occurred after 1945). Consider the relationship between revenue and working expenses (not including interest). Working account surpluses declined steadily as a ratio of receipts from 45 per cent in 1907 to 22 per cent in 1920, and then fluctuated around 22 per cent until 1945. This decline in the railway version of the average mark-up resulted from a number of cost and revenue factors, not all of which operated in the same direction or at the same strength.

1. changes in the relationship between the general levels of freight rates and fares on the one hand, and railway wages and material costs on the other (including the growth of discriminatory benefits accorded by railways);

2. shifts in the composition of traffic towards freight and travel with lower mark-up ratios; and

3. a failure of physical operating efficiency to rise sufficiently, due to overstaffing, etc.

That there were changes in the relationships between the general levels of fares and freight rates on the one hand, and railway wages and material costs on the other, is indicated by the following table.

Let us look first at the period 1901 to 1920, during which the mark-up fell by half. The average weekly wage rate paid to adult male workers on railways and tramways rose about 80 per cent, faster than fares and freight rates but slower than industrial wages generally. The price deflator for railway investment, a proxy for maintenance prices, rose even faster than railway wages. Partially offsetting the fall in the ratio between railway input prices and output prices was an improve-

TABLE 10.1 **Indices of railway activity, cost and charges**

	1901	1907	1913	1920	1927	1932	1939
Passenger journeys	34	46	79	100	118	94	116
Freight tonnes	48	64	87	100	127	86	109
Freight tonne–kilometres	n.a.	n.a.	n.a.	100	131	117	141
Metropolitan fares	n.a.	75	70	100	119	132	127
Average earnings per tonne carried	79	77	75	100	127	145	139
Average earnings per tonne–kilometre	n.a.	n.a.	n.a.	100	122	107	107
Wage rates	56	56	n.a.	100	111	87	104
Employment	41	47	90	100	112	93	110
Prices of investment goods	39	41	49	100	88	67	72
Real investment	115	87	270	100	249	91	123

Sources: N.G. Butlin, *Australian Domestic Product*, Cambridge, 1962; *Labour Reports*; Railway *Reports; Transport and Communications Bulletins*; Commonwealth *Year Books*.

ment in physical operating efficiency that was assisted by the spreading of overhead costs as a result of the large increases in traffic (the number of passenger journeys trebled and of tonnes doubled), but retarded by the increase in employment.

The picture is more complicated after 1920. The ratio of working surplus to receipts fluctuated around 22 per cent for the first five years, around 17 per cent between 1926 and 1931, and around 24 per cent for the rest of the decade. These variations corresponded roughly with the movements in the level of railway activity. Passenger numbers and freight tonnages grew relatively slowly in the 1920s until both peaked in 1927. By 1932, passenger numbers had decreased by a quarter and freight tonnes by a third. Neither regained their 1927 peaks before 1939.

A comparison between the second and third lines of the table shows that data for freight tonnage underestimates the growth in freight business, due to an increase in the average length of haul. Railway freight rates had a 'taper', that is, the rate per tonne kilometre fell with distance. In 1924, for example, the average rate for truckloads of agricultural produce fell from 1.06 pence per tonne kilometre for hauls of 80 kilometres, to 0.29 pence for hauls of 800 kilometres. No doubt some tapering was justified on the basis of the spreading of overhead costs like those of ticketing, loading and unloading, and would not have caused a fall in the average railway mark-up. It seems likely, however, that the taper exceeded that dictated by costs and so, as longer lines were built and more distant areas served, the ratio of freight earnings to costs tended to fall.

The fact that many of the newer country lines were 'developmental' reinforced this tendency, in that they were expected for some years to generate less revenue, per dollar of cost, than did the average line. Of course, to the limited extent that 'developmental' expectations were fulfilled, this effect reduced in time. (Developmental lines also contributed relatively little towards their annual interest charges).

There was another factor that already tended to reduce the average mark-up below its pre-1914 levels - the beginnings of the loss of railway monopoly. In the 1920s railway managements began to complain vociferously about competition from road transport, blaming it for both the failure of freight volumes to grow as fast as production, and for the fall in country rail travel (which began in New South Wales in 1924, and earlier in Victoria). Imperfect data indicate tremendous growth in rates in motor registrations between 1923 and 1930: a rise of 350 per cent in car registrations and 700 per cent in commercial vehicle registrations, to reach 470 000 and 100 000 respectively. These, of course, represented growth rates from very low levels: effective competition with the railways came later. This growth was assisted by reductions in the cost of motor vehicles and their operation, and by improvements in vehicle quality and in roads. Non-urban areas were favoured over cities and towns in expenditure on roads, with Federal road grants to the States, starting in 1922, all spent on the country. Although some acted as feeders to rail, many of the new or improved roads parallelled railway lines and drew away business, especially the more highly rated and short-haul traffic. Until the advent of severe road competition, railway freight rates were set not only in an effort to break even or better, but also to extract 'what the traffic will bear': in the words of the 1938 South Australian Royal Commission, 'to secure the lowest possible rates for commodities the production of which would be unduly hampered, or even rendered impossible, if transport charges were as high as those which could be borne by other commodities with a higher selling price'. The difficulty in the 1920s and 1930s was that road transport provided the latter class of commodities a means to avoid high rail freights; shippers of the former class could not (or would not) pay rates high enough to bring rail receipts and outlays into balance.

The railways responded as adversaries of private technological change, protesting that the form of road competition was unfair. Firstly, rail was a common carrier forced to accept unprofitable as well as profitable freight, whereas road hauliers could skim off the cream. Second, railway costs were higher because of the necessity to offer award rates and labour conditions, and to maintain high standards of safety. The third complaint had to do with the meeting of track costs. All important forms of land transport require substantial investment in 'track', and so share common cost characteristics: high fixed costs; marginal costs low in relation to average costs; average costs declining over a substantial range of output. Railway and tramway track are usually owned by the enterprises and used exclusively by them. Meeting the costs of construction and maintenance of track (rail and tram) is, in a natural way, the responsibility of the public enterprises. There was a tendency, in consequence, for the divergence between average and marginal costs of rail or tram to be 'internalised', and for charges to be set to cover average costs including 'track' costs. In contrast, the roads are owned by the State, and not by transport enterprises. Motor vehicles could use roads upon the payment of relatively low fees. The sheeting home to the various road users of the costs of 'track' is not an easy economic (or political) matter, so that road users had a greater opportunity to set 'prices' close to marginal cost. Some form of this argument (along with pleas for safer transport and better working conditions) was used after 1920 to justify control and taxing of private road transport, both in the cities and in the country.

The responses of railway managements to the growth of road transport were more active competition and requests for government regulation of road services. Under the first heading came the cutting of selected rail freights, as well as the running by the Railway Commissioners of their own road services. More importantly, by the middle of the 1930s most States had imposed taxes and licences on road hauliers in order to restrict competition and safeguard the huge public investment in rail; control of private buses in the cities had begun earlier (see below, p. 277). In addition, at the end of the 1920s country roads were being planned as feeders to rail, or as cheap alternatives to new developmental railway lines, and calls were being made for the 'co-ordination' of transport and developmental expenditures.

These changes may have assisted in the improvement in railway operating results after 1932: the 'mark-up' reached 26 per cent in the middle of the decade of the 1930s. Traffic volumes, both passenger journeys and tonne kilometres, increased by about 20 per cent between 1932 and 1939, while fares and rates were largely maintained. Offsetting these was a recovery of railway employment, albeit at a wage level 6 per cent lower than in 1927.

Urban transit

Most urban journeys made in 1901 were 'animal powered': walking or bicycling, or riding horse-drawn trams, buses and cabs. (Already a very large number of rural or long-distance journeys were by rail.) The mechanised urban modes consisted of steam trains and trams, as well as cable and electric trams. Largely representing a segment of the long-distance system, the urban train and tram services fed the central business districts. The close tie between place of residence and place of work was progressively loosened and urban areas were enlarged by transport developments in the first few decades. Workers could escape the crowded inner city for the more salubrious suburbs. There were strong echoes of the cries for rural development in the supplications for the extension of urban transit utilities. Tram services were converted to electric traction and the route length more than doubled between 1905 and 1920, while the number of tram passengers increased threefold. An approximate doubling of suburban train passenger numbers in Melbourne and Sydney was achieved over the same period without the building of new lines, apart from duplications, but aided in Melbourne by electrification starting 1917. (Sydney's electric train services began in 1926, and were associated with ambitious plans, culminating in the opening of the Harbour Bridge in 1932, to improve Sydney's transport).

Apart from Brisbane's (taken over in 1923), by the end of the First World War the electric tram services of the capital cities were in public hands. The form of public ownership varied. The Adelaide Metropolitan Tramways Trust, set up to take over and electrify the trams, began electric traction in 1909. Perth's privately owned electric tram service, operating since 1899, was taken over and run under joint management with the Railways in 1913. In Melbourne, the Railways Commissioners and two municipal trusts already ran electric trams before the Melbourne Tramway and Omnibus Company's lease expired in 1916. The MTOC had been an example of a joint venture, the government providing the initial capital. Sydney trams were run by the Railways Department until 1930; after 1926, the Brisbane trams were controlled by the newly created City Council; in most other places, municipal trusts ran the systems. Previously, when the services had been operated by private companies, considerable government regulation of routes and fares had been involved. The new electric trams, with their associated power generation plants, were 'natural' monopolies that seemed to require or invite that greater degree of regulation afforded by public ownership. The same political questions were still to be answered: where should new lines be placed; who is to gain by the change in property values; what profit criterion should lines meet; what should be the fare structure and level? Now the decisions were being made directly by public bodies rather than by private entrepreneurs under public regulation. (Not that all public decisions were carefully co-ordinated: the Victorian Railways complained that new tram lines were taking business from rail, for example.)

Suburban tram and train passenger numbers continued to grow until the later 1920s, although the fixed-track services began to feel the effects of competition from motor buses after the First World War. Buses improved in comfort and reliability, and their running costs were reduced by the rapid fall in petrol prices. Private bus operation attracted men, including returned soldiers, of modest capital and a willingness to work without the benefits of union membership. The private buses did not ply unprofitable routes or services, and made little or no contribution to the costs of the roads they used. Bus routes were licensed in the 1920s and 1930s, granted a local 'monopoly' in return for regulation of routes and services, and the imposition of various fees. The chief object was to restrict buses to newer areas, and to use them to feed passengers to the government services. Tram managements were also given permission to run their own buses. This 'co-ordination' of urban transit intensified in the 1930s, going furthest in New South Wales under the Lang government, and parallelled the regulation of road trucking in the interests of the railways. Who benefited from the defence of rail or tram? Especially for Labor parties, an important consideration was that unionised workforces in rail and tram were more potent politically than were the unorganised private road operators, and were active in defending their jobs. Some travellers gained at the expense of others, because managements were better able to sustain unprofitable services by 'cross-subsidies' from profitable services. Property owners were keener to have tram services nearby than bus, because the former were less freely relocatable, and the benefits less likely to be removed.

Transport enterprises 1945 to 1975

The decline of public land transport

Since 1945, the public sector has been directly involved in transport in four major ways: ownership of transport enterprises; provision, maintenance and (where relevant) operation of airports, seaports and roads; setting and enforcing safety and environmental standards; regulating intra and intermodal competition. These involvements require public decisions on the level and pattern of public resources devoted to transport and, more generally, on the conditions of cost and availability facing the users of various kinds of transport. Of the many other public policies bearing upon transport, the most important relate to economic growth and development, especially as they influence population increase and its division between urban and rural and, within urban, between city and suburbs. Thus, although this chapter is about public enterprises, we will have to look at a number of other public activities. Similarly, a range of private decisions need to be considered, especially those concerning the location of home in relation to work, shopping and school, and, most important of all for urban transit, the purchase and use of the family car.

We will look chiefly in this section at two aspects of transport history involving public enterprises. The first is the progressive displacement of publicly owned mass transit by the private motor car. The second is the two-airline policy. Repeatedly in this book we give examples of the historical generalisation, which receives some support from a priori economic reasoning, that government regulation, broadly construed, has seemed to bring advantages to the producers of a regulated activity, and often mostly to them rather than to the public at large. Among customers of regulated industries or activities, we have seen regulation tending to favour not final consumers (households) but enterprises using the product as an input of a further productive process. Putting it grandly, a thesis of this book is that both overt and covert redistribution through regulation tend to favour producer interests over those of final consumers, and rural interests over urban. In the two-airline policy both these 'rules' have been obeyed, although there are signs of change. However, the generalisations about covert redistribution do not fit well the case of urban travel. Of course, important producer interests, not the least being GM-H, benefited from the mass consumption of motor cars. Also, restrictions on competition from intermediate forms of transit (e.g. jitneys), to protect pay and conditions of public transport employees, are an important element in the story. Rural interests, too, were able to twist policy in their direction if only for a limited time and to a limited extent. By and large, however, public rail, tram and bus enterprises, their workers and suppliers, have been 'sacrificed' to the interests of final consumers, the urban traveller.

There is an alternative interpretation of the decline in public transit, one which places much more emphasis on the political power of the car producers and oil companies. Bradford Snell (1974) and David St Clair (1980) have argued that General Motors in America deliberately nurtured the mass market for the car by destroying public transit under the pretext of converting electric transit systems to petrol-driven ones. In this alternative, urban car owners, in deserting urban public transit, enjoyed an advantage that has proved or will prove to be temporary - one that they, or their heirs, will come to regret. It is certainly true that some classes of travellers, the poor and the old, have suffered from the deterioration in public transit, and that serious economic distortions - excessive congestion and pollution - have been generated by private motoring so that the individual advantages sought by owners of cars have, collectively, been partly denied them. Nevertheless, we incline towards the rejection of the thesis that the rise of mass private motoring in Australia was primarily the result of interest group pressures from motor car manufacturers, oil companies and transport unions.

Some political factors

A conclusion to be suggested here is that the decline in rail and tram had to do not only with changes in technology and tastes, but also with the different interests and financial strengths of the Federal and State governments. During the Second World War, State railways had moved record tonnages and carried record numbers of passengers, but had been unable to do all the maintenance and renewals that their traffic called for, let alone embark on much new investment. Capital funds were rationed in the immediate post-war years to most public as well as private enterprises with an important exception, discussed below, of the motor vehicle industry. The Liberal-Country Party coalition, elected in 1949, had an ideological commitment to private enterprise, and was not supportive of State government activities in the 1950s, especially State enterprises operated by Labor governments in New South Wales, Queensland and Western Australia. Backed by a prior claim to abundant income tax revenues, and by influence in the Premiers' Conference, Federal interest was in the Snowy Mountains scheme and in its own largest enterprise, the Post Office. While State governments were forced to borrow, on behalf of their instrumentalities, Federal tax surpluses in the form of intergovernmental loans, the Federal Post Office was given interest-free loans for capital works until 1960. Direct competition between the public and private sectors for loan funds was reduced, and the Federal government retained considerable control over the capital works programs of the States. Nevertheless substantial capital funds were diverted to public railway services, particularly during the 'fifties, for conversion to diesel, electrification and gauge unification, though they formed a fraction of total public sector investment well below that of pre-1939 patterns.

In conflict with these policies, Federal governments of all political

Figure 10.1 Australia: Indexes of Prices and Fares Relative to the Consumption Deflator, 1950-1975. (1950 = 100)

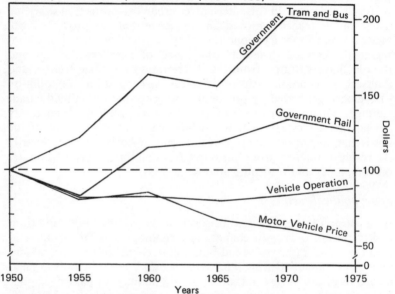

complexions have encouraged the car industry in Australia, as an especially favoured component in our import-replacement strategy of manufacturing development. By 1939, about half the value of motor vehicles and parts sold in Australia were made here, due to natural protection and an escalating tariff. The government tried unsuccessfully in 1940 to increase the Australian component by offering an Australian firm a monopoly of engine manufacture. Four North American companies responded to the Labor Government's 1944 invitation to increase the Australian content, with General Motors-Holden's agreeing to be the first to produce 'Australia's Own Car'. The background to the subsequent growth and Americanising of vehicle manufacture were the dollar-exchange restrictions accepted by

Australia in defence of sterling area dollar reserves, and the fear of an effective exclusion of American-made products from the Australian market. The use of internal combustion engines was encouraged in the 1950s by the exemption of petroleum products from quantitative import restrictions. Although import protection raised the cost of vehicles, car prices rose more slowly than prices generally, much more slowly than public transit fares, and actually fell in the 1960s (Table 10.3 and Figure 10.1).

The Menzies administration continued in the 1950s the policy of favouring road building in country districts to the ultimate detriment of rural rail business. Australians, particularly if living in Labor States, were accustomed to roads far inferior to those, for example, in the United States and, to the extent that opprobrium was received because of poor roads, it was by State and local, not Federal government. By the early 1960s, the situation had altered in that the Federal government came to have political reasons to be concerned with long-distance transport. A gradual change had taken place in manufacturing, with the location of various processes or stages in different cities of Australia, requiring the movement of finished or semi-finished goods between States. The Commonwealth pressed for and helped finance uniform gauge links between capital cities. A more truly national market was being forged, and pressure from manufacturers increased on the Federal government to provide funds for transport improvements. Road hauliers wanted to take fuller advantage of improved technology in road transport, with the advent of the large, fast prime-mover and van. A conflict arose, however, between the road freight hauliers and the lobbying organisations representing the owners of the private car, over congestion of roads and the damage wreaked by heavy trucks.

Urban travel

What we are interested in examining is the decline of public transport, especially passenger transit, and the rise in the private. There were about 1830 million journeys taken in 1944-45 on government train, tram and bus, or 240 per head of population. Thirty years later, the total had fallen to 840 million, or 60 per head. The twenty-five years between 1949-50 and 1974-75 saw a halving in the real or price-deflated fare receipts of government mass land transit, during a period when population doubled, real income trebled, and real travel outlays rose to four and a half times their 1950 level. The government services were capturing a declining amount of a rapidly growing economic activity.

Before 1945, public transit was based firmly on fixed-track systems - trains and trams - which were mostly laid out in a radial pattern, designed to move workers daily in and out of the central business district (CBD). Buses were used, increasingly, as feeders to the rail system. As urban Australians grew richer after 1945, they chose to live further from the CBD. The concentration of jobs in or near the central city declined, as factories and offices moved to the suburbs. Of itself, the decline in the fraction of work trips to and from the CBD caused slower growth of and eventually a decline in the number of train and tram journeys along the spokes of the radial system. The shift from train and tram was, however, greater than that implied by the shift in the pattern of work travel. As they became able to afford a family car, more households preferred its flexibility and privacy to the inflexibility and publicness of train, tram, or bus. The relative decline in public transit over the quarter-century 1950 to 1975 can be measured in a number of ways: the share of publicly owned road transit in total travel outlays fell by 1975 to a quarter of the 1950 share (28.0 down to 7.1 per cent; see Table 10.2); from being a supplier of almost as many kilometres of travel as the motor car in 1950, public land transit declined absolutely to be relegated to only one eleventh as many kilometres in 1975.

There is an important disparity between the social costs of providing various forms of land transport, and the private costs ('prices') facing the users. A result of this disparity has been a more rapid displacement of public by private transport, especially for travel, than would otherwise have occurred. Putting aside temporarily questions of congestion, all forms of land transport have been characterised by high fixed costs of provision of track or road and of vehicles and equipment, and by relatively low running costs. The patterns of

TABLE 10.2 **Distribution of total personal consumption expenditure on travel, by type, in Australia 1950 to 1975**

	1950	1955	1960	1965	1970	1975
			(%)			
Rail, tram and bus fares	28.0	19.1	15.6	11.5	9.0	7.1
Other fares	14.2	14.3	13.3	12.7	14.1	14.6
Total fares	42.2	33.3	28.8	24.2	23.1	21.7
Purchase of motor vehicles	44.5	43.8	41.8	43.5	36.5	35.1
Operation of motor vehicles	13.3	22.8	29.4	32.3	40.4	43.2
Total motor vehicles	57.8	66.7	71.2	75.8	76.9	78.3
			($m)			
Total travel	363	749	1128	1680	2670	4892
Total consumption	3442	6303	8853	12145	19991	34541

Note: Totals and subtotals may not add, due to rounding.
Source: *Australian National Accounts.*

private costs or prices paid by users of land transport has not faithfully reflected these patterns of social cost. For users of rail, tram or bus the cost of travel did not vary much with the amount demanded: there were no fixed user charges analogous to the private costs of purchase, insurance and registration of a private motor vehicle. Public transport tariffs were set at some fraction of average cost, not of marginal cost. By purchasing a car or truck, the private supplier of own road travel or transport purchased the option of having a low private marginal cost of transport, at least with pre-1973 fuel prices. To some extent, therefore, travellers made an all-or-none choice between private motoring and public transport. Travel appears to have been a 'superior' good, the demand for which rose more rapidly than income, in both the quantity and in the quality dimensions. Because of the difference in the configuration of private costs, outlined above, a traveller owning a car has tended to use it, marginally, in preference to public transport because the private marginal cost of motoring was less, quality adjusted, than the private marginal costs of public transport. From the point of view of social costs, however, the reverse could be true: the marginal social cost of public transport could be less than the marginal social cost of private transport, especially where the roads are congested. Certainly, the disparity in pricing structure hastened the decline of public transport.

Movements in relative prices also favoured motoring as cars became cheaper and better (the price index in Table 10.3 is quality-adjusted) and more reliable, whilst fares, especially bus fares, rose much faster than prices generally, and the quality of service on public transit tended to deteriorate.

The central business district, which was well served by rail and, to a less extent, tram, was badly served by competition for road space between private and public vehicles. In the 1950s, the building of wider or better urban roads was not yet on the agenda. Trams were cursed by motorists for delaying and obstructing private vehicles; the tramways protested that the reverse was true. In Sydney in the 1950s, and later

TABLE 10.3 **Price indices of consumption and travel, Australia, 1950 to 1975**

	1950	1955	1960	1965	1970	1975
Motoring	1000	1301	1541	1500	1662	2517
Vehicle prices	1000	1299	1543	1352	1433	1995
Vehicle operation	1000	1304	1538	1589	1942	3196
Government fares	1000	1496	2341	2596	3618	5475
Rail	1000	1312	2058	2360	3115	4634
Tram and bus	1000	1896	2958	3139	4718	7231
Travel	1000	1366	1710	1747	2013	2961
Consumption (CPI)	1000	1566	1799	2007	2344	3680

Sources: ABS correspondence; *Australian National Accounts*; M.W. Butlin, *A Preliminary Database 1900/01 to 1973/74*, Reserve Bank Discussion Paper 7701, May 1977; NSW *Yearbooks*; Railway *Reports*.

elsewhere (though Melbourne, in particular, retained tram services), the private motorist won the battle for the city streets, and trams were progressively removed to be replaced only partially by buses. The loss of tram service in the CBD made the loss elsewhere in Sydney more likely.

What of trips not involving the CBD? To build new cross-suburban rail links was mostly out of the question, due to the high costs of resuming right-of-way. The new, more diffused pattern of travel that accompanied suburban development, with its decentralised workplaces and, later, shopping centres, was not easily served by tram except where, as in Melbourne, streets were wide, straight and flat. Buses, improving in comfort, reliability and cost, seemed the most sensible way of meeting the changing demand for public transit. With no track to be laid, buses have the advantage of lower initial cost and flexibility - routes and service volumes could be altered fairly cheaply in response to demand. These very advantages, however, came eventually to contribute to a more rapid decline in bus services when, due to the rise in motoring and other factors, bus operating losses began to mount. From a strictly business point of view, a service should continue as long as fare receipts exceed running or recurrent costs: there is no use crying over fixed costs. Because the running costs of bus services bore a higher proportion of total cost than for tram or train, a decline in bus revenue in relation to total cost could not go as far before it became 'unprofitable' to continue operation on that route, if at all. The characteristics of low fixed cost and flexibility made bus services more vulnerable to threats of abandonment on account of losses.

Brief contrast with freight

Whereas the relative sizes of the various passenger services changed greatly between 1950 and 1975, variations in freight shares have been

TABLE 10.4 **Estimated distribution of freight tonne-kilometres, by mode, Australia 1950 to 1975**

	1950	1960	1965	1970	1975
Road (%)	23	23	22	20	20
Public rail (%)	31	23	23	19	18
Private rail (%)	1	1	1	7	16
Sea (%)	45	55	54	53	46
Total (tonne-km x 10^8)	362	581	789	1248	1621

Note: Air freight was estimated at 0.1 x 10^8 tonne-km in both 1970 and 1975.
Source: Commonwealth Bureau of Roads, Roads in Australia, 1973 and Roads in Australia, 1975.

comparatively slight; see Table 10.4. Coastal shipping was badly disrupted during the Second World War, and has since been held back by the exclusion of foreign vessels, by the protection of the Australian National Line from Australian competition, and by union practices. It has moved about half the freight carried between Australian points, with an increasing emphasis on bulk commodities like minerals, and containerised shipments. Road transport, in contrast to its rapid domination of travel, has held a relatively steady share of about one fifth. Both coastal shipping and road tended to 'displace' rail in the 1950s, although rail more than regained its 1950 freight share by 1975.

Financial results

Because of the substantial restructuring of railway debt, comparisons cannot readily be made of pre-1939 surplus and deficits after interest payments with those since 1945. Therefore we look at the relationship between earnings, exclusive of government subsidies, and working expenses. The combined railway systems of Australia made operating losses before interest and depreciation for the first time from 1951 to 1953. Until the early 1970s, these deficits were small in relation to working expenses, a matter of a few per cent; small contributions were made towards interest charges. Railway finances deteriorated sharply in the 1970s. The 1975 working account deficit of $336m was equal to about 30 per cent of working expenses: in other words, users met only 70 per cent of operating costs. The contrast with the beginning of the century is striking: earnings of government rail were then over 180 per cent of working expenses. Capital charges added another quarter to 1974-75 costs, so that rail in that year covered only 59 per cent of its total costs from fare and freight receipts (see Table 10.5), a poorer record than those of road (89), air (72), but better than that of coastal shipping (56 per cent).

The financial difficulties of the 1970s were the result of a cost-price squeeze that accentuated trends established earlier. In the 1950s and 1960s, possibly because of the rapid rise in rail fares, passenger business declined (for reasons discussed above), more so in the city than in the country. Despite hikes in fares, passenger business became more and more unprofitable until by 1974-75 only 40 per cent of costs were being covered - see Table 10.5. The remarkable divergence between freight rate and fare increases, evidenced by Table 10.6, calls for some comment. The railways of Australia were begun as a means of providing cheap carriage of export commodities to ports, and cheap return of imported goods to the rural districts. Country passenger business was substantial from early days, while city passenger traffic became important in the first two decades of the century. Since 1950, metropolitan rail fares have increased twice as fast as freight rates. Have the costs of carrying the city rail traveller increased twice as fast as the cost of carrying freight? Or was the 1950 relationship between freight rates and freight costs very different from that between fares and passenger costs?

State railways were struck a double blow in the 1950s. Improvements in roads and vehicles and a fall in the relative cost of private motoring assisted the drift of passengers from rail. Efforts to protect rail freight traffic from road competition were undermined by a series of legal decisions, starting with the Hughes and Vale judgement of 1954, declaring the force of section 92 of the Australian Constitution against regulation of 'interstate' road transport. A restoration of rail business prospects would have required improvements in service quality and cuts in costs and prices. Some progress was made, but it was limited by the inability of rail to undertake large investment programs - railways did not generate any profits which could be ploughed back. Some substantial development occurred through capital outlays in the introduction of diesel engines and new rolling stock. Despite technical and managerial advances, achieved with the co-operation of large private freight forwarding companies, rail suffered a decrease in the 'quality' of freight carried. This deterioration was particularly important because public rail has looked increasingly to freight for its earnings: for every dollar from passengers in 1950, two were earned from freight; by 1975, the figure was four from freight.

TABLE 10.5 **Cost recovery, domestic transport 1974–75**

		Passengers Cost	Passengers Recovery	Freight Cost	Freight Recovery	Total Cost	Total Recovery
		($m)	(%)	($m)	(%)	($m)	(%)
Air		670.3	72	—	—	670.3	72
Sea		—	—	604.9	56	604.9	56
Road	urban	807.6	144	1673.9	79	2481.5	100
	non-urban	793.9	69	1065.2	80	1859.1	75
	Total	1601.5	107	2738.1	79	4340.6	89
Rail	urban	300.0	40	—	—	300.0	40
	non-urban	170.9	46	913.6	67	1084.5	64
	Total	470.9	42	—	—	1384.5	59
Total		2742.7	87	4257.5	73	7000.2	79

Note: Where no figures are entered, the absence is due to data difficulties or irrelevance.
Source: Bureau of Transport Economics, *Cost Recovery in Australian Transport 1974–75*, AGPS, Canberra, 1977, p. 227.

TABLE 10.6 **Indices of government railway activity, charges and costs 1939 to 1975**

	1939	1945	1950	1955	1960	1965	1970	1975
Passenger kilometres	n.a.	n.a.	100	n.a.	98	94	92	91
Freight tonne–kilometres	66	n.a.	100	118	129	180	236	298
Employment	76	90	100	103	99	91	84	81
Investment in prices of 1938–39	58	65	100	131	123	126	139	148
Metropolitan fares	80	80	100	135	211	239	314	463
Coaching earnings per passenger kilometre	n.a.	n.a.	100	n.a.	165	184	217	278
Freight rates (NSW)	58	58	100	177	183	185	206	236[a]
Freight earnings per tonne–kilometre	69	n.a.	100	193	192	178	163	183
Minimum award wage rates	44	62	100	149	177	204	262	556
Average earnings per rail employee	51	67	100	172	203	253	347	790
Prices of investment goods	49	72	100	153	181	205	247	400

[a] With freight concessions, index in 1975 is 225.

Sources: Railway Reports; *Rail, Bus and Air Transport; Labour Statistics; Australian National Accounts.*

The eighth row of Table 10.6 shows that government railway earnings per tonne kilometre actually fell between 1955 and 1975. A change in the commodity composition of freight was one of the causes, with a relative shift occurring from highly rated to lower rated items. The extent of this shift is difficult to estimate, but it must have had a substantial effect, some of it beneficial to rail, however.

As the Bland Report on Victoria's transport pointed out, the freight rate schedules of railways were, even in the 1970s, based on classifications devised before the advent of serious road competition. Commodities were charged different rates according, among other things, to the market value of the commodity, with higher rates for expensive goods. Naturally enough, some differentiation would be justified on account of the different costs of handling and carrying types of freight, but the real basis for rates was not cost, but rather attempts to cross-subsidise. For example, the rates include a taper whereby rates for long hauls are cheaper, per tonne kilometre, than for short. It is widely believed that the magnitude of the taper is more than what is justified by the presence of once-for-all terminal costs. Similarly, long-distance travel is cheaper per kilometre than metropolitan travel (country fares have risen more slowly than metropolitan fares since 1955). Where the rates differ on account of the value of the commodity, it is very likely that the cause is not differences in rail costs, but attempts to force some shippers to subsidise others. It is indeed price discrimination, but not of a type that increases profit. Whilst there was no cheap and convenient alternative to rail, then the cross-subsidisation could succeed. Road increasingly provided that alternative. Rail charges on highly rated commodities either fell, or rose very slowly. Despite price competition, however, rail lost to road short hauls and the carriage of expensive goods for which time was important.

There is another characteristic of rail charges, already mentioned (p. 266): with limited exceptions, freight rates are set according to freight type and distance carried, regardless of upon which lines the freight is to be carried. Australian railways still carry most of their traffic at Statewide, published rates, whereas only 2 per cent of British freight now goes at national, published rates. When a service is making large losses, railway management may try either to cut costs by cutting or even eliminating the service, or it may try to attract more business. The possibility of altering prices selectively, an option used by private road carriers in similar circumstances, is largely denied rail. And if the service is one being supplied to a politically strong group, then railway management often finds it impossible to cut or eliminate the service.

A rise in the average freight rate would produce an increase in earnings per tonne kilometre of about the same proportion (that is, 30 per cent between 1950 and 1975, if New South Wales experience is a reliable guide). In fact, average earnings per freight tonne kilometre 1955 to 1975 fell 5 per cent. Thus, changes in commodity composition and changes in relative freight rates combined to reduce average freight earnings by about 35 per cent. The 'quality' of passenger and parcel traffic also deteriorated: comparison of lines 5 and 6 of Table 10.6 shows that average coaching receipts (fares plus parcels) per passenger rose very much more slowly than metropolitan fares.

Which groups would gain from a shift of rail traffic to road due, say, to increases in rail charges? Suppliers of road services, road constructors, and other groups producing goods and services connected with road use would gain in demand. The data of table 10.5, referring to averages and not margins, do not rule out the possibility that the taxpayer could be made worse off by a shift in traffic to road. First, although the table does not show it, the taxpayer subsidises the bus passenger at least as much as the rail passenger. So let bus fares be raised to cover costs. More cars in the cities means more pollution and more congestion - someone pays. Congestion could ' lead to the building of very expensive urban roads, the use of which is not charged highly enough to recover taxpayers' costs. Again, heavy road transports caused some $230m of damage to roads in 1975-76, (Bureau of Transport Economics, 1979) besides requiring much higher initial construction costs. Only $44m of this was recovered by way of road maintenance taxes (which are being abolished). Extra road freight, therefore, could have very high marginal costs, costs being recovered not from users, but from taxpayers.

Speculations like these do not help much in explaining the extent of the rail subsidy. How then did the level of taxpayer subsidy to rail come about? Unless one expects the energy crisis to pull rail into profit, and credits rail decision-makers with magnificent foresight, then past investment decisions are at fault, especially those deliberately designed to make losses. Making a contribution was the leakage from railway finances of external benefits associated especially with enhanced land values. Inadequate pricing techniques were also involved, as was the inability of rail managements to close down lines or, at least, offer loss-minimising combinations of price and frequency. Behind these financial features lay the political power of user groups to hold onto rail services without paying the full cost, and of railway unions to hold onto jobs, conditions and labour practices no longer appropriate to the pattern of rail demand and to current technology.

Domestic air transport

Regulation of air transport and public ownership of TAA and Qantas are closely connected. As air policy developed, it coddled suppliers of air transport services at the expense of customers and taxpayers. Although the two-airline policy has secured its avowed goal of financial stability of trunk airlines, and has ensured high use of airline capacity (high 'load factors'), these advantages have been won dearly. Neither TAA nor Ansett-ANA have had enough incentive to cut cost, or to provide the appropriate mixture of service quality and fares. Fares have been high; costs have been high. Apart from mails, air freight has languished in a land to which one would have guessed it ideally suited. Rather than being a crucible in which to assay the comparative fineness of private and public enterprise, the two-airline policy became the alchemist's nightmare: it turned both enterprises to lead.

With its demand stimulated by great improvements in speed and comfort, air travel was the fastest growing form of travel between 1950 and 1975. Growth was fairly steady at an average rate of over 8 per cent per year in domestic passenger kilometres flown, and over 14 per cent in international. TAA introduced pressurised airliners, cruising at 480 km/h, in 1948. Viscount and Electra propjets were in service here from the late 1950s, Boeing 727s from the mid-1960s, and DC9s later in that decade. Technological improvements allowed fare increase to lag behind the CPI (at least since 1960), although by less than did costs of motoring. Air freight grew very rapidly from the later 1940s until the mid-1950s, but then fell by about a third, due to competition from newly deregulated road transport, from road-rail freight forwarding, and from coastal shipping. Since the early 1960s, air freight volume has grown at about the same rate as domestic freight generally, 7.5 per cent per year. Although Ansett-ANA has had some specialist air freighters, TAA has mostly used passenger liners for freight, regarding it as very subsidiary to the business of carrying passengers.

The regulation of air transport has two aspects, safety and competition. Within Australia the Commonwealth government has regulated safety as, in effect, an agent for the States: the Constitution was framed without precognition of air travel, and the States have not referred their implied powers to the Federal government. The original basis for Federal regulation was on agreement between the two levels of government to implement the 1919 Paris International Convention on Air Navigation. Actual regulations came to exceed that function, and some were successfully challenged in 1937. Subsequently, by passing uniform legislation the States empowered the Commonwealth civil aviation administration to collect fees and once again control air navigation. We will not comment on air safety regulations, except to say that Australia has very stringent flying rules, a geography and meteorology very favourable to safe flying, an excellent safety record on scheduled routes, and a poor record for general aviation.

Besides TAA, the Federal government owns the international carrier, Qantas, having bought out BOAC and others in 1947 and having purchased in 1954 the shares of the New Zealand and British governments in British Commonwealth Pacific Airlines. That government also builds and maintains major airports, and provides navigation aids. Decisions have been taken to increase the rate of recovery of the costs of airports and air navigation services and so, from some points of view, their provision and operation is a more enterprise-like activity than, for example, the running of buses.

Regulation of competition relates to competition between air and other transport modes, and competition between airlines; only the latter is discussed here.

Trans-Australia Airlines

During the early years of flying, the Federal government assisted a pioneering, infant industry by direct subsidies for carriage of mail and by other means. Most of the infant airlines had failed or merged by the end of the 1930s, when the advent of superior American planes had allowed profitable, unsubsidised business, especially on the trunk routes dominated by ANA (Australian National Airways Pty Ltd, not to be confused with the Australian National Airlines Commission, created in 1945 to run TAA). Shipping interests had developed ANA so that it was not dependent on government subsidies. However, during World War II, ANA prospered on profitable government work, including air engineering and mails. By the end of the war, ANA flew 80 per cent of total passenger kilometres, up from 53 per cent in 1940 (Brogden 1968, p. 47).

Having twice failed in referenda to obtain increased powers, including air transport powers; fearing Holyman of ANA and hating the shipping interests he represented; wishing to have government own what taxpayers had paid for; and desirous of a showpiece of public enterprise, the wartime ALP government attempted to nationalise the airlines. The reasoning was that if there were to be a natural monopoly (and ANA's merger record gave rise to this conclusion), it was preferable that it be a government monopoly that could be forced to engage in cross-subsidisation, with passengers travelling between capital cities subsidising those on less popular routes (Brogden 1968, p. 42). Those parts of the *Australian National Airlines Act* 1945 which restricted interstate airline operations were found to be invalid by the High Court. The Commonwealth, however, could legally engage in interstate operations through its own airline, TAA, and could grant TAA a monopoly of services to and from Commonwealth territories. The ALP government did these things, and gave Federal government business exclusively to TAA.

Due to this preferment, to poor business decisions, and to competition from Ansett, ANA ran into financial trouble. The incoming coalition government could not disregard the popularity of TAA or ignore its climb towards a profit. By the early 1950s, the question was not whether TAA would be allowed to survive, but whether ANA could survive without positive government action. The *National Airlines Act* 1947 was amended to make TAA liable to income and sales taxes; it still remained free of interest obligations on Treasury debt. The *Civil Aviation Agreements Act* 1952 provided for government-guaranteed loans to ANA for equipment, for equal access to Federal government business and for the avoidance of 'wasteful competition'. This last was achieved by 'rationalisation' of routes, schedules and prices, that is, by a government-enforced co-operative duopoly. The third operator, Ansett, not party to the agreement, prospered while ANA continued to decline, and in 1957 Ansett took over ANA. Rationalisation was made more mechanical by the *Airlines Equipment Act* 1958. Under it, the capacities of both trunk operators were restricted to be equal on competitive routes, with an overall requirement that the prospective 'load factor' be 65 per cent. The 1961 Act extended the agreement to 1977, and specified more detailed and complete 'rationalisation', including the requirement that new planes be introduced simultaneously, and that TAA pay a 'dividend' to the Treasury. Under 1958 and 1961 Acts, financial assistance was given both airlines for equipment purchases. Some relaxation was allowed by the 1972 Agreement in that parallel scheduling was to be referred to the Co-ordinator of the rationalisation committee, and the possibility of specialist freight lines was envisaged (permission to import aircraft remained an ultimate means of Federal control of air transport). The 1972 Act also specified that the lines were to continue any rural routes as long as receipts covered direct costs. The year 1974 saw the adoption of a formula, followed since, that specified the fare between any two points as equal to a 'flagfall' plus a constant rate per kilometre, enshrining price discrimination against longer routes and more heavily loaded flights.

In its more restrictive form, the two-airline policy allowed for competition only in terms of service qualities like friendliness, reliability and reputation. The type of equipment, fares, and capacity were equal. We then have to wonder what room remained for competitive effort and what incentive remained to economic efficiency.

It has been argued that Ansett Transport Industries has an incentive to increase profits by economical cost-cutting. Details of the regulatory framework weaken the a priori agreement that a private, profit-making firm will be more efficient than a public firm. Consider the difficulties of cost cutting. If it involves making the Ansett workers work harder, accept less pay, or generally, to vary work terms and conditions from those enjoyed by their TAA counterparts, industrial strife is likely. Now, fares have been set so as to cover changes in *industry* costs, not the costs of one firm. If Ansett does succeed in cutting costs without losing custom, then half that cost reduction is lost, as it were, in the next fare adjustment. If Ansett does succeed in making extra profits, there are political dangers to be faced. Even though the accounts of Ansett Transport Industries do not allow a completely accurate assessment of the profitability of Ansett's air transport operations to be made by outsiders, increases in Ansett profits could lead to a public outcry which, among other possibilities, could force the government to allow new entrants into air freight, where Ansett has much more business than TAA.

Whether these factors operate on Ansett or not, the results of the two-airline policy has been to encourage a high level of staffing in both airlines, low levels of technical efficiency, and poor catering to consumer tastes. Mackay has a statistical analysis of airline costs which indicates that TAA and Ansett's costs per available tonne kilometre are respectively 16 and 13 per cent higher than the unit cost norm, and as much as 35 per cent higher than the best performers in Mackay's wide sample. However, at 65 per cent the load factors of TAA and Ansett-ANA exceed those of many lower cost airlines, so that our fare levels may not differ much from the norm. Using standard economic formulae, one can show that a 14 per cent fare rise would cost Australian consumers about $80m   in 1976-77, or about the amount by which taxpayers subsidised trunk air routes.

Did public ownership make any difference? A private natural monopoly or near monopoly of trunk-line services seems to have been a likely possibility in the 1940s, because of the cost savings available from the co-ordinated use of common facilities serving similar routes, as well as from the familiar economies of scale on any particular route. No doubt any monopoly would have been regulated as to fares, routes, cross-subsidies etc. If serving the trunk routes was then potentially a natural monopoly, any private entry during the late 1940s or early 1950s would have either collapsed or have driven out ANA, unless prevented by regulation: in the fullness of time a trunk route duopoly would have been possible only if imposed by regulation or subsidy. In its early days it was TAA that needed protection; in the 1950s, ANA. The fact that TAA was publicly owned and that the government in power was antipathetic to public enterprise meant that the ailing ANA was taken over not by TAA but by Ansett. Government intervention was therefore necessary for the survival of a duopoly, and government ownership the means. Having regard to TAA's superior business decisions in the 1950s, customers benefited from the presence of more than one firm. However, if TAA had not existed, it is likely that Ansett would have taken over ANA earlier than it eventually did. After that takeover, regulation ensured that the two airlines, one public, one private, were virtually indistinguishable. Public policy once again assured that competition should be kept under tight rein.

11

Service at Any Cost: PMG

In contrast with the case of public railways, it was technological change within the public sector (indeed, within the PMG's own sphere of operation) that mainly affected the nature and extent of public monopoly in communications. We have seen how technological change in the private sector eroded and to a large extent destroyed the public monopoly in land transport. Public authorities in railways acted against growing private competition, but private interests eventually predominated. When airways were added to the transport system, the public and private institutions concerned co-operated to defeat competition, jointly forming a tightly regulated industry. In post and telecommunications, a different experience of the character and degree of monopoly evolved. Only to a relatively small extent and indirectly did technological change in the private sector, in transport and in communications, reduce the market power of the public communications undertakings.

The transmission of letters and the telegraph system were vital modes of communication in 1900. Progressively, their importance was reduced by telephone, radio and television; and in their turn radio supplied many of the services provided by telephone, and television displaced radio. In fact, private development reinforced this progressive obsolescence of one part of the public communications service by other parts. But in Australian conditions, it appears to have been technological application and development within the public sector that principally influenced the competitive viability of older services.

One of the striking features of Australian experience in post and telecommunications was the comparatively rapid response of the Postmaster-General's service to new technological possibilities. As technological change in communications accelerated in the course of the twentieth century, it is possible that public enterprise in this area may have reacted by delivery of services that were too large, too quickly supplied and too cheap. We cannot, at this stage, judge this matter. But such an inference would be consistent with the essentially engineering approach adopted - an approach maximising the quality of the service supplied with little regard to the cost. This attitude appears to have underlain public policy towards post and telecommunications before 1900. The consequences would need further detailed exploration to include, we believe, an investigation of the hypothesis that bureaucratic standards not responsive to market tests might end in oversupply in quantity or quality. However, these issues emerged gradually at first and then, after 1945, with increasing speed. To understand them, we need to look at the historical process.

Other questions intervene in this historical process, relating to internal and external subsidisation. On the first, there are questions of the extent of and reasons for discriminatory treatment in favour of rural and remote customers and a range of specific business interests. On the second, it is relevant to remark that unlike all other public enterprises discussed, the post and telecommunications services were under direct Federal authority. As the fiscal and monetary dominance of the Federal Government grew, the opportunity for all public enterprises to be subject to centralised policy direction was strengthened. This change led to public enterprises acting more and more like private ones, exercising their monopoly power to improve earnings and surpluses. (However, for fifteen years after World War II the Post Office had a favoured position in the struggle for capital funds, obtaining them free of interest from Treasury cash surpluses: taxpayers subsidised Post Office customers generally.) The stronger use of monopoly power to enhance earnings, as well as the consistent cross-subsidisation are both in sharp contrast with the emphasis, early in the century, on sweetheart arrangements for labour when the Post Office accounted for as much as 90 per cent of all Federal Government employees.

Setting the pattern, 1901 to 1920

Apart from defence, the young Commonwealth government of the 1900s did scarcely more than collect customs duties to be remitted to the States, and run the Post Office. The Postmaster-General's Department employed as many workers as the New South Wales railway system, about 16 000, making it one of the two largest employers in the economy. Expenditure of the Postmaster-General's Department (which excluded interest) equalled nearly two thirds of the cost of all Federal government departments in the early 1900s. On the other side of the ledger, receipts from post and telegraph (which were about equal to expenditures on them) were 20 per cent of the Commonwealth government's total receipts, the large difference between

Commonwealth receipts and total departmental expenses being distributed to the States in accordance with constitutional requirements.

Three questions dominated the operations of the Postmaster-General's Department up to 1920. First, because of the financial terms of the Constitution, Federal departments were initially starved of funds: the States had direct interests in monitoring Federal spending. Second, within the Federal sphere, dispute arose about the degree of political control that should be exercised over the enterprise: whether the Post Office should be run by an independent board, or as a department; and whether run as a commercial undertaking, or a source of taxation or, as Coghlan said in 1887 (p. 453), so that the public was served at any cost to revenue. The final question was of control over labour conditions: what was to be the role of the Commonwealth Conciliation and Arbitration Court *vis-a-vis* the Public Service Commissioner?

Between 1901 and 1920, the output and resources of the PMG grew rapidly. The number of postal articles carried doubled, as did employment. In a development that was significant because the service required considerable technical ability and capital equipment, the number of telephones per thousand persons increased fourfold as they became increasingly common not only in business but also in wealthier residences. Not all this growth occurred smoothly. When PMG business picked up in the middle of the first decade, spare capacity was not large. The colonies had deliberately curtailed works in the depression of the 1890s and, in anticipation of Federation, had not made up the difference as conditions improved. For reasons detailed below, the PMG was starved of capital funds and labour. Only after 1906 did employment start to rise rapidly, with a 40 per cent growth to 1911.

The Constitution provided (section 87) that Commonwealth expenditure be severely limited for the first ten years of Federation to one quarter of net revenue from customs and excise (net, that is, of costs of collection, refunds and drawbacks). In addition, section 93, the 'Braddon clause', prescribed that for at least five years after the imposition of uniform customs duties, the Commonwealth return to each State the difference between all revenues collected in the State, and the outlays made in that State on account of 'transferred' departments plus a per capita share of 'other' Commonwealth expenditures. This 'bookkeeping system' lasted until the Fisher government had enacted the *Commonwealth Surplus Revenue Act* 1910 by which annual payment to the States was set at 25s per head, with special grants to Western Australia (and later to other small States).

Even though there was some loan financing of telephone works after 1913, the Department still was, in the words of William Webster (PMG from 1915 to 1920), subject to a policy of systematic starvation, of suicidal parsimony: 'So long as the Treasury is unable to trust this Department with the expenditure necessary to keep it going it will be impossible to conduct its activities on efficient or economical lines' (PMG *Report* 1918-19, p. 21).

It was in this context of financial constraint that a variety of efforts was made to consider the objectives of the Post Office and possible modes of operation. A Royal Commission reported in 1910 in terms most critical of the administration of the services, but also blamed rationing of funds for some of the problems with staffing and efficiency. It recommended that the Department be placed under a board of management, and that staff be removed from the jurisdiction of the Public Service Commissioner. The services were to be run so as to cover costs on an all-up basis, that is, losses in one line or one State could be cross-subsidised by profits from another line or State. It said that the Posts and Telegraph Department was neither a purely commercial proposition, nor a taxing department (though it was used as a taxing department during the First World War), but that every effort should be made to conduct the services on business lines. None of the radical suggestions was adopted.

A second report, this time by a businessman rather than by politicians, was highly critical of the Department in 1915 but again the main recommendations were not adopted. However, just as the Royal Commission had seemed to spark the Public Service Commissioner into reform, so the 1915 report may have pushed senior Department officers to recommend new telephone charges and economies to bring that branch, in 1917, into profit. The 'Economies Commission' reported on the PMG and other departments during 1919-1921. It found important differences in the costs of earning revenue in the various States and attributed much of these differences to laxity in administration. Acknowledging a vast improvement in finances between 1913-14 and 1918-19, this commission refused to credit Webster's efforts at cost-cutting, but attributed the turnaround to abnormal revenue due to war, and to the deferral of replacement and renewals. It warned the new government against undertaking more loss-generating services, advice which was promptly ignored. Like the two previous inquiries, it also recommended a three-man board of management, and displacement of the Public Service Commissioner from his position in control of staffing matters.

Failure to change the status and structure of the Post Office and to formalise its objectives left it in an ambiguous position that was not finally clarified until 1975. The Postmaster-General's Department was expected to operate in a businesslike way, in general making neither profit nor loss (though this proscription was far from clear cut) and providing some services at loss rather than cost. At the same time, being a government department headed by a Minister, its finances and staffing were subject to the same procedures as any other department. Funds required for all its expenditures, current and capital, were provided by Parliament through annual appropriations specifying in detail (until 1968) how the money was to be spent. All receipts were paid into Consolidated Revenue. There was no direct or necessary link between profit or loss and investment plans. Many Post Office staff were employed under conditions determined by the Public Service Commissioner who was responsible for maintaining uniformity across the Service. In addition, basic postal and telegram charges could be varied only by an Act of Parliament.

Unprofitable services

Despite financial constraints, there was already a tendency to allow certain types of preferential services with the result that the Department depended not only on cross-subsidies between customers but also on subsidies from the general budget. For some time, the mode of operation was obscure. The 1910 Royal Commission called the annual financial statement issued by the Department 'absolutely useless for the purpose of supplying the requisite information to determine the financial position of its several branches' (para. 70). In its judgement, the telegraph branch was very unprofitable, the telephone branch unprofitable, and what profits the postal branch made were insufficient to balance losses elsewhere.

The telegraph losses were due, according to the Royal Commissioners, to the too drastic rate reductions made in 1902. Losses on telephones had a number of causes, including the poor condition into which the colonies had allowed their systems to fall, as well as the change to the 'compound' system, part annual rent, part measured rate, introduced in 1907. (The previous flat rate system had benefited subscribers using the telephone more frequently. Many of these mainly commercial users chose to remain on a flat rate.) The postal profits were made despite losses on mail services to isolated country settlements which the Commission was unable to calculate exactly, but which appear to have exceeded all other sources of loss.

No data were published until 1913 of the finances of the individual branches. Between then and 1917-18 - the first year in which all branches reported profits and the first overall profit was made - the telegraph branch was again very unprofitable, the telephone branch unprofitable to 1917, and the postal branch showed a mixture of profits and losses.

In the second decade, significant concessions were made to rural customers. Postal profits were seriously eroded by the introduction of universal penny postage in May 1911: surcharges on country letters, previously charged in all States except Victoria and South Australia, were eliminated; postage in South Australia was halved. (Table 11.1

TABLE 11.1 **Basic postal, telegram and telephone charges 1911 to 1980**

Date of Change	Basic Letter Postage (pence/ cents)	Bulk Newspaper Postage (pence/ cents per 10 oz.)[a]	Ordinary Local Telegram (pence/ cents per word)	Local Telephone Call (pence/ cents)[b]	Annual Telephone Rental ($)[c]	Telephone Service Connection ($)
1911[d]	1d					
Sep. 1915					8.00	
Oct. 1920[e]	2d	0.75d	0.5625d	1d	10.00	
Oct. 1923	1.5d	1d				
Dec. 1929					11.00	
Aug. 1930	2d	0.75d				
Jan. 1934				1.5d		
Sep. 1934				1.25d		
June 1940			0.6428d			
Nov. 1941				1.5d	12.50	
Dec. 1941	2.5d	1d				
July 1949	1.56d	1.071d	2d			
Aug. 1949					15.00	
Dec. 1950	3d		1.5d		18.50	
June 1951				3d		
July 1951	3.5d	3.12d	1.9285d		24.50	
Oct. 1956	4d		2.75d		26.50	20.00[f]
Oct. 1959	5d	4.17d		4d	34.50	
Oct. 1964			3d		40.00	30.00
Feb. 1966	4¢	3.3¢	2.5¢			
Oct. 1967	5¢	4.16¢	3¢	4¢	47.00	40.00
Oct. 1970	6¢	5¢	4¢			
Oct. 1971	7¢	7¢		4.75¢	55.00	
Oct. 1972						50.00
Oct. 1973					60.00	
Oct. 1974	10¢	48¢	6¢	6¢	85.00	80.00
Sep. 1975	18¢	60¢				
Oct. 1975			9¢	9¢	120.00	120.00
Oct. 1976			12¢			
Oct. 1977			15¢[g]			
July 1978	20¢	70¢				
Mar. 1980	22¢	80¢				

Notes: [a] From October 1974, non-standard articles 250–500 g.
[b] For largest exchanges and widest network areas.
[c] Exclusive, business rental in largest exchange areas.
[d] Previously, town letters were one penny and country letters two pence in all States except Victoria and South Australia, where rates were uniform at one penny and two pence respectively.
[e] An additional 0.5 pence was charged in 1918 as a war tax; repealed in 1920. Prior to October 1920, bulk newspaper postage and telegram rates were 0.5 pence and 0.375 pence respectively.
[f] No charge previously.
[g] Telegram delivery and minimum charges introduced from October 1976.
Source: Telecom correspondence; PMG *Reports.*

lists the changes in basic postal, telephone and telegraph rates, 1911 to 1980.) Postage revenue fell 12 per cent between 1910-11 and 1911-12, and the loss due to penny postage was put at £ 470 000. A new and 'very liberal' policy for non-paying country mail services was introduced during 1910, whereby those being served had to pay only half the loss. Similarly, conditions for the provision of country telephone services that were unlikely to prove 'financially sound' were relaxed in 1910 (PMG responsible for 50 per cent of the loss; 'local call' areas were increased to 13 or 16 kilometres), and again in 1920 (applicants to cover 25 per cent of the loss by contributions in cash, labour or material). Although the first annual report, that of 1910-11, stated that separate accounting would be made of country finances, no systematic information was published in this period of the value of these concessions.

Labour conditions

In the transfer of colonial departments of posts and telegraph to Federal control, difficulties were involved of the kind experienced after the merger of private companies, but of a complexity rarely to be faced privately. Each of the six departments had its own organisational structure and rules, its own ways of doing things, its own labour relations. Some colonies had granted their civil servants more generous terms and conditions than others: South Australia had long offered superannuation. Some had rushed to saddle the new Commonwealth with costly labour conditions they had been unwilling to carry themselves. Western Australia, for example, had given its postal officers a parting gift of generous long-service leave which, in the event, Commonwealth Public Service Commissioner McLachlan refused to honour.

McLachlan held to the view that public employment was a privilege and an honour, carrying greater security of tenure than did private employment (at least for white-collar staff), but with offsetting disadvantages by way of reduced political rights, no right to strike, and inferior wages and conditions (Caiden 1966, pp. 70 ff). The opposing view, held by the Labor Party and trade union movement but not by them alone (see Mansfield 1958), was that public employment should be a vehicle by which the general conditions of labour were to be improved. It was McLachlan's attempts strictly to apply the loose provisions of the *Commonwealth Public Service Act* of 1902, in the interests of economy, which largely sparked the Labor and worker protests in the middle of the first decade that led to the Royal Commission on the PMG.

Members of the Commonwealth Public Service were given access to the Commonwealth Conciliation and Arbitration Court in 1911, despite the opposition of the majority of the staff associations, some of which preferred the idea of a Board of Management, as proposed by the Royal Commission (Caiden 1966, ch. 7). Antagonism between the Public Service Commissioner, the government and the associations did not abate. Resignations abounded. When Mr Justice Higgins made his first very liberal award to postal unionists, McLachlan publicly voiced his criticism. Higgins discounted the special privileges of public servants, and applied the principles he had used in private awards. The Postmaster-General's Department was then in the position of having two bodies determining its labour costs, with the workers being able to choose the more generous. Not too surprisingly Webster, as Postmaster-General, was very critical of the court's generous awards for worsening the Department's financial troubles although, with the appointment of Mr Justice Powers to Commonwealth Public Service matters in 1914, a less open-handed approach had been taken.

Another labour question was preference in employment, a matter that generated considerable political conflict. The Fisher Labor Government granted limited preference to unionists in 1911. In 1915, amendments to the *Commonwealth Public Service Act* allowed full leave of absence for the duration of the war (a quarter of the eligible Post Office employees actually enlisted), and absolute preference in appointments to veterans. This greatly damaged the competitive quality of the Post Office labour force. These and other problems caused the Commonwealth Public Service to be described in 1917 by Professor William Harrison Moore as a statutory monopoly of the uneducated and a haven for the mediocre (Caiden 1965, p. 125).

Inter-war emphases

During the inter-war period the PMG Department was operated predominantly by Country Party Ministers and by Labor or Liberal Ministers from rural constituencies. Rural subsidies became an enduring part of its activities. The Department, in this period, also adopted and furthered technical developments in wireless transmission, long-distance telephone and wire telegraph services, and air transport. To cater to increased telephone demand, most importantly in the country, and to other demands, it made in some years up to 5 per cent of the economy's gross investment, much of it from loan funds. Partly due to pricing policies, the profit records of the various branches deteriorated in the 1920s, postal services alone consistently returning profits though often insufficient to offset losses elsewhere. Performance improved in the 1930s.

The Postmaster-General's Department came out of the war suffering financial stringency. Although postal business grew slowly between 1913-14 and 1918-19, telecommunications traffic rose substantially, with the number of telephones increasing by 40 per cent and the number of telegrams by 13 per cent. Employment in the Department, including mail contractors, had fallen slightly between 1914 and 1919; it was to rise 10 per cent over the financial year 1919-20 as ex-soldier employees returned to their jobs and not all their temporary replacements dismissed. During the 1920s output and employment, as well as investment, grew very rapidly as some of the constraints were eased.

In 1918-19, the Treasurer had agreed to less than half the £ 1.27m requested for new works to meet the backlog of telephone orders (4000 in 1919, 11 000 in 1920), modernise post offices and develop wireless telegraphy. The Postmaster-General, who had been a member of the 1910 Royal Commission on the postal services, argued to little avail that, because the Post Office had a monopoly on telephones, there was an obligation to meet demand especially as the branch had been profitable since 1916-17.

The government's initial response in 1920 was to increase charges in order to assist Commonwealth finances generally, and to help meet the costs of providing services. Postage on an ordinary letter doubled to 2d. (The simultaneous abolition of the halfpenny wartime tax meant that while Post Office revenues per letter doubled, customers noticed only a one-third increase in what they paid.) No increases applied to trunk calls or to telephones connected with small (that is, rural) exchanges. At 25 per cent, the maximum increase in telephone rentals was modest: consumer prices generally had risen about 40 per cent since the previous change in telephone rentals in 1915. The new telephone charges remained unchanged until December 1929. The basic letter rate was reduced to 1½d in 1923. Telephone rentals and letter rates were increased again in 1929 and 1930 respectively, in response to government budgetary needs, and local charges in 1934. The infrequency of price changes and the apparent unimportance of Post Office performance in their determination had important implications for the historical pattern of profitability.

Despite PMG Department surpluses of £ 2.2m in 1921-22, (equal to about 4 per cent of Commonwealth consolidated revenue from non-PMG sources) predominantly in the postal branch, loan funding of PMG works became imperative if the backlog of telephone orders was to be met, rather than to be reduced by further increases in rentals. A three-year capital program, largely loan financed, was begun in 1921-22 and later increased, so that capital formation by the PMG Department rose to £ 6m in 1923-24 (compared with £ 1.7m in 1913-14, the previous largest figure), and did not fall appreciably below £ 6m until 1930-31. During the depression years investment dropped to scarcely more than £ 1m and exceeded £ 3m only in 1939. About 90 per cent of the outlays were for telecommunications, including wireless. At its peak, this investment represented about 10 per cent of public gross capital formation, or 5 per cent of all capital formation, public and private.

The depression and increased charges at the end of the 1920s reduced demand for postal and telephone services only in 1931 and 1932. From 1934 output resumed an upward trend, though at growth rates lower than those achieved in the 1920s. Employment, however, was cut back sharply. After rising by a third during the 1920s, so that in 1929 it accounted for three quarters of Commonwealth government civilian employment, it fell by 16 per cent between 1929 and 1932 and regained its 1929 level only in 1937. In that year, Post Office output, measured crudely as letters carried and telephone calls made, was very considerably higher than it had been in 1929. Lower wage and salary commitments were an important element in the profits recorded during the 1930s.

Rural subsidies

The introduction of penny postage in 1911, and the special conditions for country customers mentioned earlier, already provided preferential treatment. In 1920, the criteria for the operation of non-paying country mail deliveries were liberalised. Previously the Department bore 60 per cent of the loss. The new policy was for the Department to bear any 'reasonable' cost for once-a-week delivery of less than 120 kilometres to five or more residences; all of the cost of services if revenue exceeded two thirds of cost; or generous shares of the deficiency, up to 75 per cent, if revenue fell below two thirds of cost. In 1923-24, 1450 non-paying mail delivery services lost a total of £ 63 000, or up to £ 10 per person served.

Telephones were the chief objects in the 1920s of the policy to provide communication services to country people below cost; the exemption of rural users from the rises in telephone rentals in 1920 was a part of the policy. New directives were announced in 1921-22 to bring telephone services 'well within the reach of the majority of residents in country districts'. There was a weakening of the financial test of continuous operation of exchanges and their late closing. Without requiring any contribution from subscribers, the Department would establish country exchanges 'wherever practicable, and provided it is in the interests of subscribers to do so'. Much more liberal terms were offered to isolated rural subscribers who, unlike others, were required to contribute directly to the cost of erecting telephone lines. For example, contribution or guarantee was required of subscribers if the cost of a line did not exceed £ 1500, or was expected to prove financial within seven years; otherwise, a contribution in cost, labour or material was required of no greater than a quarter of the estimated annual deficiency, capitalised at 10 per cent. As much of the work as possible was to be carried out by contract or local labour, in order to cut costs. Further liberalisations occurred in the next year, 1922-23, the first under a Country Party Postmaster-General. In order to place country residents in a favourable position compared with those in densely populated areas, 'prospective development' was to be taken into account in decisions on the erection of subscribers' lines, ensuring that the Department would bear all of the cost in most cases. Also, a local call fee, rather than a trunk fee, was to be paid for calls between exchanges within 8 kilometres of each other, and the system of charging trunk calls was altered from one depending on the length of circuit involved (that is, cost) to a radial or 'as the crow flies' system. Rentals on long lines were reduced.

A remarkable boom in country telephone services resulted. The number of country telephone lines grew by 17 per cent in 1924-25 to reach 112 000 or about 34 for each thousand persons living outside the metropolitan areas; the growth rate in the city was about half that, to reach 166 000 or 61 for each thousand city dwellers. Whilst acknowledging that country services were unprofitable, Postmaster-General Gibson stated there could be little doubt that the substantial national benefits from expansion of country services vastly exceeded the financial losses. Unfortunately, he provided no estimate of the losses like those reported for country mail deliveries, claiming that financial assessment was impossible. However, in 1924-25 came the first in a series of ten years of losses by the telephone branch. The components of that loss were as follows ('+' profit; '-' loss).

	± '000
Metropolitan exchanges	+ 197
Non-exchange lines	+ 17
Non-metropolitan exchanges	− 277
Interstate trunk services	+ 29
Non-interstate trunk services	− 225
Total telephone	− 259

It is admittedly difficult to allocate revenue and costs to various parts of a network; the method used by the PMG Department was to credit revenue to the exchange where the call originated. On this basis, and depending how the loss on intra-state trunk calls is apportioned between country and city, the subsidy to country subscribers may have been between £ 225 000 and £ 500 000 in that year. Charging for trunk calls was altered in 1925-26 by the addition of a unit call fee to the radial distance charge, in order to cover some of the 'local' costs of calls.

Between 1924-25 and 1932-33 the telephone branch made losses averaging £ 290 000 annually, of which the trunk services contributed £ 250 000 a year. These losses did not deter investment. Considerable attention was given during the later 1920s to improvements in long-distance telephone services and there was a continuing program to convert all exchanges to automatic switching, a program that concentrated on rural exchanges after 1936-37.

Improving the service

Possibly the chief improvement in postal services during the inter-war period was due to the introduction of airmail. During World War I, flying schools had been established in Australia; subsequently, grants were made to flying clubs to further the development of air transport. In 1919, the Commonwealth offered a prize, won by Ross Smith, for the first flight from England to Australia in less than thirty days. The Commonwealth took control of the regulation of air navigation under powers granted by the States in 1920, and set about acquiring and constructing aerodromes and establishing air routes. A contract was let in 1921 by the Department of Defence for a route between Geraldton and Derby in Western Australia. The conditions of the contract specified the space to be set aside for the carriage of mails and set the scale of charges for the carriage of freight and passengers. Similar conditions applied for the other services begun soon afterwards: Sydney-Adelaide, Sydney-Brisbane, Charleville-Cloncurry (by QAN-TAS Ltd). Not all these services survived and progress was fairly slow, so that by March 1928 only five regular airmail services were operating, and none between capital cities. The Commonwealth appropriated £ 200 000 for further development, and during the next two years, more air routes were opened, including Adelaide-Perth, Sydney-Brisbane, and Sydney-Melbourne, the last two operating without explicit subsidies. More internal airmail services were organised later in the 1930s, and by the outbreak of war there were over thirty scheduled services. About half of these received no subsidies other than those arising from the government provision of aerodromes and air navigation aids, including radio directional beacons.

In order to speed interstate mail, plans were made in the mid-1930s to develop a fast network of night flights to link all capital cities. Overseas airmail services were also established. After experimental flights in 1931, a tender was accepted from Qantas Empire Airways to make regular airmail flights from Darwin to Singapore, where the mails were transferred onto aeroplanes bound for England. The growth of overseas airmail traffic was greatly accelerated by the 1938 extension to Australia of the Empire Airmail Service, offering very cheap postage to and from most parts of the Empire. Outward postage was 5½d per half ounce (14g). The weight of overseas airmail from Australia was 120 per cent greater in 1938-39 than in 1937-38, while inward airmail increased over 600 per cent. This service was interrupted by the war; the Auckland to Sydney route, however, was opened in 1940.

Technical developments in telephonic communication, typically involving long time-horizons, dominated strategic investment programs in this branch of the Post Office. As early as 1913, it was an objective of PMG engineers to replace manual exchanges by automatic exchanges because of the increased speed of connection and reduced direct labour input. Continued through the inter-war period, concentrated primarily first on metropolitan and later on rural exchanges, by the outbreak of war the program had connected more than half of Australia's telephones to automatic exchanges. Long-distance services were an essential element in the telephone system. Trunk-line facilities between country towns and between country towns and metropolis were continually upgraded but the major thrust of investment was to increase and improve direct inter-capital city links. The use of the 'carrier' wave system of transmission from 1925, its subsequent improvement, and the reconstruction of the Sydney to Melbourne line (first opened in 1907) encouraged a deliberate provision in those links of capacity sufficient to satisfy future needs. By the opening in 1930 of the Adelaide to Perth link, using existing telegraph lines, a telephone call was possible from Cairns in Queensland to Geraldton in Western Australia. In the 1930s, further connections were made: Tasmania to the mainland by cable (1936); England to Australia (1930) and Australia to North America (1938) by radio telephone. Used primarily by private business, these provisions helped to create a national market.

The origins of the other great technical development - wireless communications - lay in the early days of the century. The Commonwealth took complete control of wireless telegraphy in 1905, the year the Marconi company demonstrated the feasibility of wireless communications between Tasmania and the mainland. Apart from wartime and for a short period in the early 1920s, technical development and control was with the PMG Department and much of the equipment used was manufactured here. But unlike telephony, radio broadcasting did not remain a public monopoly, becoming subject to partly public, partly private operation.

Nevertheless, a great deal of the development that occurred in radio depended on a close relationship between public and private sectors, with the public sector using the services of private enterprise in a variety of ways. Efforts before the 1920s were mainly concerned with the establishment of stations around the coast for purposes of defence and to aid shipping. Even before 1914, some private companies in Sydney were licensed to communicate with ships at sea. In addition, private stations were to be encouraged in remote regions to aid outback communications.

In the 1920s we have to distinguish developments in radio broadcasting from wireless telegraphy and telephony. Amalgamated Wireless (Australia) Ltd was engaged in both kinds of use. Majority ownership of this company was purchased by the Commonwealth government in 1922. AWA owned various patents, and had taken over the wireless stations established after 1912. Under the 1922 *Wireless Agreement Act*, AWA established high-power wireless links with England and Canada. Once the 'beam' method of wireless transmission was improved and operating (1927), wireless telegraphy threatened the financial position of the partly private seabed cable companies. The cable offered some advantage, especially for defence - secrecy and continuous operation - but had great initial (sunk) capital costs. A decision was made, after consultation with various governments, to merge the wireless and cable interests within the UK into one private company. The government in 1929 refused a similar merger here. After the Second World War, an agreement was reached to transfer overseas telecommunications within the British Commonwealth to public hands.

In broadcasting, a short experiment was made in 1923 with sealed receivers, capable of tuning to a restricted number of frequencies. The PMG Department collected licence fees from the dealers, paying part to AWA for use of patents, and part to the broadcasters. In the next year, the system of licensing was altered to a zonal one, with receivers within 400 kilometres of the capital cities paying higher fees. Again, part of the fees were paid to a limited number of 'A' class stations (in the capitals), with the 'B' class stations relying on advertising revenue. When the National Broadcasting Service was formed in 1928 to take up expired 'A' class licences, following the Royal Commission on wireless, the PMG became responsible for the technical operation of the Service's stations in addition to a relatively few stations it had continued to run. Programs were supplied on tender to the Service by private companies until 1932, when the newly established Australian Broadcasting Commission took over. Licence fees were then divided between the Commission and the Department. (The Department research laboratory developed a superior transmitting mast in the mid-1930s.) Just as overseas wireless telegraphy threatened the cable business, so the development of broadcasting had a detrimental effect on PMG Department finances by cutting into its telegram business, especially for sporting results. The public and private interests affected by this evolving pattern of industry control and the ways in which they were represented have not been fully and carefully studied. Research would be revealing.

Monopoly transformed, 1945 to 1975

Large enterprises behave differently from small ones, monopolies differently from competitive enterprises. Australian public utilities are large and often have considerable natural monopoly power; as well, they frequently have market power bestowed by legislation or regulation. If we are to sort out the effects of ownership of these enterprises from the effects of size and natural monopoly, we need to recognise that governments do interfere in large monopolies, whether public or private, and that public ownership is a variety of public regulation, with its own distinctive effects. Some of the features of behaviour of public enterprises arise from ownership, some from size and natural monopoly, and some from unnatural monopoly.

Public ownership in communications did have its effects. Putting it crudely, since 1945 the Australian Post Office and its successor organisations, Overseas Telecommunications Commission (OTC), Telecom and Australia Post, have been transformed from enterprises providing a service partly financed by taxpayers, to enterprises neither drawing upon nor contributing net to the current Federal budget, to enterprises used as a means of indirect taxation. No private business of its size would have survived as long as did the Post Office when it drew upon taxpayers (1945 to 1959). As well as potential access to government subsidies, exemption from income tax (a privilege afforded only charities and pension funds) gave the Post Office an edge in competition for resources. This exemption was a consequence of public ownership, as well as of the lack of major, private competitors (contrast TAA).

The actual profit performance, as recorded in the Post Office's own commercial accounts, do not fully reflect the implications of ownership. What they omit is taken up below (p. 315). At their face value, however, the accounts show a picture of losses by the enterprise as a whole at the end of the forties and beginning of the fifties, on average a balance of profits and losses from 1952 to 1956, profits from 1957 to 1961, losses generally between 1962 and 1968 and profits, generally, from 1969 to 1975. The earnings behaviour of Post Office branches changed dramatically from its pre-war pattern. Postal services returned repeated profits only in the first half of the 1960s. Whether Post Office operations as a whole made a profit depended critically on the net earnings of telephony. Sustained profits from telecommunications, sometimes insufficient to outweigh losses on telegraphic and postal services were recorded (by measures used) between 1953 and 1961 and between 1968 and 1975. Only from 1969 to 1975, to emphasise the point again, were large and sustained profits shown for the operation of the Post Office as a whole.

Possessing some natural and some artificial monopoly, why did not the Post Office make obvious monopoly profits throughout more of the post-1945 period? The question raises complex issues deserving more investigation. Part of the answer lies in the political nature of prices. (Table 11.1 lists changes in basic postal, telegram and telephone rates since 1911.) Post Office charges have always been political as well as business matters, and remain so despite the metamorphosis, almost complete by 1975, of that organisation into two private corporations, publicly owned. Even today, Telecom and Australia Post need Ministerial approval of changes in basic prices and, no doubt, take informal political advice, or bow to pressure, on other prices. Large private firms, too, were subject to extra-market pressures on prices, which were increased by the establishment of the Prices Justification Tribunal in 1974. The Australian Postal Commission (APC) and Telecom have escaped, however, the purview of the PJT, and of the Trade Practices Commission.

Monopoly power can be manifest in ways other than as profits. First, the Post Office monopoly enabled a persistent, systematic and substantial degree of cross-subsidisation to occur: postal services were subsidised by telephone users; rural and remote customers were subsidised by urban customers; certain business interests were subsidised by other interests. Second, at least in telecommunications, enjoying as they did relatively rapid growth in demand, economic errors were not punished by the appearance of losses; aggressive, uneconomic pursuit of technical excellence was feasible. Third, monopoly also brought certain advantages to the workforce and to equipment suppliers in Australia, again especially in telecommunications. Apportioning these effects to natural or to artificial monopoly is problematic at this stage.

Output, technology and productivity

Until its division into two separate organisations in 1975 (OTC was split off in 1946), the Australian Post Office combined the postal service - labour-intensive, technically unprogressive - with the telephone or telecommunications services - capital-intensive, bursting with technical possibilities. These contrasts had wide consequences. The telecommunications branch was able to improve the quality and variety of service without large increases in price. Because its task, especially in the first decade after 1945, was to satisfy strong demand, it enjoyed a degree of flexibility. In contrast, the postal services found it difficult to maintain quality, let alone improve it, without incurring large increases in cost. As postal charges rose relative to prices generally and telephone charges particularly, postal output grew relatively slowly and eventually peaked in the 1970s. The postal services were forced to pay more attention to the tailoring of their output to the pattern of demand. They were caught in the 1960s and 1970s in the same kind of bind first experienced by public transport enterprises, comprising a loss of custom to newer means of communications, limits set on price increases by political considerations as well as by the fear of losing even more business, rising input prices, and slow productivity growth. Table 11.2 displays, in index number form, data about trends in Post Office output, inputs, prices and costs, since 1939.

The output of postal services, crudely measured by the number of articles delivered, has grown since 1945 at an average rate of about 3 per cent annually, a rate about half that of simple measures of the quantity of telephone services. Since the mid-1960s, this difference has increased: the growth in postal output has been very slow. A comparison of the price and productivity experiences of post and telecommunications for the decade 1962-3 to 1972-3, presented in Table 11.3, shows that postal total factor productivity grew at less then 1 per cent per year, whereas telecommunications output rose, in real terms, 4 per cent a year faster than input. The Post Office was able, despite rising input prices, to keep average telephone charges tied closely to the CPI; postal charges, in contrast, rose appreciably faster than the CPI (5.1 per cent per annum compared with 3.7).

TABLE 11.2 **Selected Post Office Indices, 1939 to 1975**

| | Index Numbers (1950 = 100) | | | | | | | | (Level in 1975) |
	1939	1945	1950	1955	1960	1965	1970	1975	
Postal articles	74	79	100	113	133	167	190	183	(2682 million)
Local calls	67	79	100	124	166	230[a]	299	400	(3560 million)
Basic letter postage (December)	67	83	100	117	167	167	240	720	(18¢)
Local call charge (December)	63	75	100	150	150	150	240	360	(6¢)
Employment (December)	54	75	100	107	117	110	129	146	(121,000)
Investment, deflated to 1966–67 prices	38	31	100	114	160	224	350	410	($358 million)
Wage rate, communications (December)	46	55	100	148	181	223	323	664	($1.4167/hour)
Working expenses/ earnings: postal	65	72	100	101	88	94	100	109	(1.168)
Working expenses/ earnings: telephone (+ telegraph 1965 on)	72	68	100	99	88	85	83	82	(0.748)

Note:[a] Extended local service areas in May 1960 diverted former trunk traffic to local calls traffic.
Sources: Transport and Communications Bulletins; PMG Reports; Labour Reports.

TABLE 11.3 **Average annual compound rates of increase in earnings and expenses, 1962-63 to 1972-73**

	Postal % p.a.	Telecommunications % p.a.
Actual earnings, current dollars	8.5	13.3
Due to:		
Growth of business at constant tariff	3.2	9.5
Increases in tariffs	5.1	3.5
Actual expenses, current dollars	9.6	12.3
Due to:		
Growth of expenses at constant prices	2.3	5.4
Increases in input prices[a]	7.1	6.5

[a] Labour, materials, services.

Source: *Report of Commission of Inquiry into the Australian Post Office* (Canberra, Government Printer, 1975), p. 40.

The technical basis of the present telephone service was laid in the middle of the 1950s, with the almost simultaneous introduction of improvements to the carrier wave system of transmission (enabling more messages to be carried on one line); a superior form of cable, co-axial, which was 'broadbanded' in the 1960s; improved automatic switching equipment; and, some years later, a new metering technique. To all the major elements - transmission, switching, metering, billing - considerable technical improvements were subsequently made: cheap, reliable transistors in the 1960s, and reliable, computer-controlled exchanges in the 1970s. The telephone connections, especially over very long distances were improved by the development of microwave (radio) technology in the 1960s and 1970s, while overseas cable links were supplemented by satellite links after 1967.

The postal services could not increase the number of letters in a given space in the same way that the telephone system could increase the number of messages being sent along one line simultaneously. However, the speed of postal 'transmission' was increased by transferring internal letter carriage to aircraft, by faster trucks on better roads, by motor bikes for postmen. Efforts at curbing the costs of mail handling were not as successful as efforts at cutting those of telephone switching. Electronic mail-handling, started in Redfern in the mid-1960s, required a centralisation of mail processing and was by and large a failure. An improvement in efficiency was obtained with the introduction of the postcode system (which put some of the costs of mail sorting on the sender), but the expected benefit was not fully realised. Generally speaking, advances in postal services were mostly non-technical: standard articles by air, 1959; postcode, 1967; priority paid system, 1970; most recently, courier service. Meanwhile, offsetting rationalisation in the postal service *was* taking place, with a progressive decline in the quality of service - in the number of post boxes, in the frequency of clearing and of delivery. The output of the more labour-intensive services, therefore, grew relatively slowly for reasons of cost: slow rates of increase in labour productivity combined with rising wage rates.

It is likely also that the demand for postal services grew slowly for reasons other than relative prices and costs. The rise in incomes, changes in social custom and in tastes, cheaper private motoring, changes in technology elsewhere in the economy, conspired to hold back the growth in the postal services. (Contrast the decline in telegrams, firstly due to radio broadcasting of race results, then to the telephone and, later, telex.) The habit of writing letters to friends was largely lost - it was more sociable and not merely relatively cheaper to telephone or to visit. Businesses, too, economised on paperwork, although this trend was much more visible in the 1970s than earlier.

Inputs

Plans were made by the Post Office in the final years of the war for a major post-war capital works program, calling for a lift in outlays from the 1938-39 level of £ 3.8m to an average of £ 6.7m for three years. Shortages of money, skilled workers and materials forced delays and reformulations, and by 1946-47 the revised program was £ 14m for three years. This was achieved in the years 1947-48 to 1949-50, but, costs having risen meantime, only in the last year was the desired real level of investment achieved. Unsatisfied telephone applications rose from 54 000 at the end of 1945-46 to 114 000 two years later, and remained at about that level until after 1951-52. Line 6 of Table 11.2 indicates the growth path of real capital outlays. The 1960s saw real investment more than double as the Post Office implemented its plan, announced in 1959, eventually to provide subscriber-to-subscriber dialling nation-wide, and not just to the profitable intra-metropolitan and inter-capital traffic. (Telecommunications plant and equipment typically absorbed 80 to 90 per cent of total Post Office capital expenditures.) This policy required the installation of automatic exchange equipment, multi-metering, and a great increase in the carrying capacity of lines.

To undertake this vast investment program, and to maintain the telecommunications service, the recruitment of a skilled labour force was required. After 1945 many temporary workers, mostly female, were sacked to make way for servicemen returning to their old positions; and preference in new recruitment was given to ex-servicemen. The share of permanent, full-time employees had fallen by 1950 to 53 per cent, from the 71 per cent reached in 1939, and a policy was adopted to raise it. Such employees were not vulnerable to the sackings which occurred in 1951-52 after the PMG staff quota was reduced by 4000: the majority sacked were 'new Australian' construction workers. Public service rules hampering the Department were relaxed progressively, and a special connection developed between the Department and its employees involving, in effect, a special arbitration system. The Department recruited when possible from its temporary staff; built up its own training schools, numbering twenty in the late 1960s; granted paid leave for full-time training; recruited student engineers at home and qualified engineers abroad. Partly in consequence of this special relationship, the wage level in communications, dominated by PMG workers, rose faster than that in other industries, reflecting an upgrading of skills as well as a cosy relationship between employer and unions.

Another cosy relationship was established between the PMG and Australian suppliers of equipment. Throughout the 1950s and 1960s, Federal purchasing policy was *not* to provide import protection over and above the tariff, but to obtain the best value for money, subject to exceptions for reasons of defence and security of supply. PMG purchases were exempted from the general rule: Department policy was to grant an unspecified margin of preference to Australian products over imported. Indeed, from 1948 it deliberately set out to encourage a private manufacturing industry to supply its needs. About half of supplies were purchased abroad in 1949-50; about 20 per cent in 1953-54; 8 per cent in 1972-73. Switching equipment and telephone cables are now local industries. However, suppliers also wished to install and maintain the equipment they supplied, which was against Department policy. Important concessions were made, nevertheless, on installation of PABX in 1956-57; of cross-bar switching equipment in 1963-64; of private cables in 1970-71. Maintenance was reserved to the PMG.

Rate of return

There has been a remarkable progression since 1945 in the financial frameworks set by Government and Treasury for the post and telecommunications enterprises, particularly as regards capital funds and interest. From 1945 until the end of the 1950s, Post Office capital works were financed largely through interest-free loans from the Consolidated Revenue Fund, during a period when State government instrumentalities were forced to pay interest on loans from the same fund. Past expenditures from the Commonwealth Loan Fund, on which interest was payable, consequently fell to very low levels in relation to Post Office assets. In late 1959, a new policy was announced. Telephone charges (and the telephone service was by far the largest user of capital) were to be sufficient to recoup operating and maintenance costs as well as to make a reasonable annual return on *new* capital. This was a step towards the principle that the user should pay. Indeed, the new policy went further towards that principle than its announcement suggested, because the government also raised the debt upon which interest was to be paid from less than £ 82m to £ 340m at the start of the year 1959-60. Interest charges on *all* capital debt rose from 0.8 per cent of revenue in 1958-59 to 12 per cent in the next year. (How close the Department came towards paying the interest bill is discussed below; here we are concerned with the formal arrangements.) The third change occurred in 1968, when amendments to the *Post and Telegraph Act* gave a degree of financial flexibility to the enterprise by altering its appropriation from an itemised, departmental form to a single-line, trust account form. Parliament approved the total but not, as in the past, the detail of outlays. Resting with the Postmaster-General, with the concurrence of the Treasurer, were powers to determine the financial goals of the Post Office, its charges, and the disposition of any surplus. The next change to take place was in 1975, when Telecom Australia and the Australian Postal Commission were formed as distinct trading enterprises, separately charged with finding at least half of their capital requirements from retained profits. The relevant Minister had power to disapprove changes in basic charges; the enterprises, however, were to be compensated for any losses this involved. Again, surpluses were to be used as directed by the Minister.

There is one further step which, if taken, would complete the transformation of these postal and telecommunications services into businesses almost indistinguishable from private monopolies. Unlike TAA, Qantas and the Commonwealth Bank, Telecom and APC are still free of the obligation to pay income taxes. It is possible that the political outcry raised by recent large Telecom surpluses could be muffled if the surpluses were diminished by the payment of company tax. A remaining step is much less likely to be taken: to free the enterprises, as much as is possible, from the requirement of providing some of their services at a loss; in other words, to eliminate cross-subsidisation. Telecom and APC pricing is a reflection of the political power of various user groups, a power exercised over private as well as public enterprises, and unlikely to fade even if the two organisations were stripped of their legal monopolies.

The overall financial results of the operation of the postal and telecommunications enterprises reflect these changes in the formal relationships between the Post Office, the Treasury and the Government. As a rough approximation it can be said that, between 1945 and 1960, receipts covered all costs debited to the Post Office, including the minimal interest charges. Taxpayers, therefore, were subsidising consumers of Post Office services during these years to the amount of interest not charged on grants from Consolidated Revenue Fund for capital purposes. Between 1960 and 1975, a period when interest was charged on an enlarged debt, revenues again almost equalled all costs charged; additions to capital were financed by interest-bearing loans. The taxpayers of 1960 to 1975 neither gained nor lost much from Post Office operations. In 1975, the assets and debt of the Post Office were apportioned with both Telecom and APC beginning life with balance sheets recording zero net worth: APC was forgiven past losses of the postal services, and Telecom allowed to disguise past profits of the telephone service. Taking the two enterprises together, in their first years of trading, capital programs were wholly financed through retained earnings; substantial surpluses were generated which were applied by the Minister towards the reduction of debt to the Treasury. In effect, the Treasury was taking a dividend, and customers of the enterprises were contributing towards the financing of the Federal budget deficit. The relationship that existed in the first fifteen years after 1945 between taxpayers and Post Office customers was reversed after 1975. The internal rate of return was first negative, then zero, and subsequently positive.

These judgements rely upon Post Office accounting. But the size of the net financial advantage obtained from the Treasury (that is, the sum on which interest was paid from 1960), asset valuations, rates of depreciation, provisions for pensions, long-service leave and holidays - these and more have been in dispute. Consider pensions. With the passage of the 1922 *Superannuation Act* the Treasury became responsible for the payment of new pensions. Confusion and dispute arose over the appropriate 'premium' the Post Office should pay annually to the Treasury as 'insurer'. By and large, the Post Office did not make provision to meet the extra costs arising from the repeated improvements in pensions made, since 1947, by the government on its own initiative.[1] At the end of 1958-59, the Commonwealth Actuary estimated an outstanding liability of over $140m because of pensions, most of which was 'forgiven' the Post Office when its capital account was reorganized in 1959-60 and its debt set at $680m. During the 1960s and early 1970s the Post Office built up a hidden liability, due to pension increases, assessed at $380m in 1974 (*Report of Commission of Inquiry*, 1974, p. 162); again it was mostly forgiven when the APC was formed in 1975. A private employer would have had the option of acting as its own 'insurer', as did TAA, charging profit and loss account for pensions only when they were actually paid. No private employer, however, would have been able to pass onto another body

---

[1] 'There is undoubtedly a "social service" element in pensions payable to public servants. The average business would not provide a pension scheme as liberal as that now in operation for the employees of the Post Office.' (Minority Report, *Ad Hoc* Committee, 1961, p. 65)

some of the present value of future pension liabilities in the way the Post Office did.

There is a much more serious matter which can only be touched lightly here. It is strongly argued in Chapter 2 that the accounting methods of most of the important public enterprises and statutory authorities, particularly railways, have been defective because they seriously undercount gross investment, due to the substantial omission of internally financed gross capital formation. The consequence is that working expenses are overstated, and working account surpluses understated. It is not possible to make appropriate re-estimates of the Post Office from published accounts. Some rough adjustments may be suggested. In 1959-60, for example, the commercial accounts of the Post Office record working expenses of £ 109.8m and revenues of £ 125.6m, leaving a 'profit' of £ 15.8m. Reserve and capital provisions and some internal funding of actual capital outlays within the Post Office recorded in 'working expenses' could perhaps double this surplus figure if we wish to obtain consistent social accounting measures. Comparable adjustments in other enterprises would sometimes be less, sometimes very much larger, implying significantly different experience of comparative performance. We are not here reporting complete recalculations of the financial results of the Post Office and other enterprises. The example given, by no means untypical, shows that answers to the questions of which enterprises paid their way, when, and by how much, cannot be given solely on the basis of authority accounts.

Cross-subsidisation

More difficult than arriving at an accurate assessment of the overall financial results of Post Office operations and their implications for subsidies to and from taxpayers and customers is the task of allocating costs and revenues to various branches of the enterprise or to various classes of customers, in order to estimate subsidies. In discussing these, we are considering the differential benefits that some groups of consumers received in relation either to other consumers of the same service (that is, cross-subsidies), or to consumers of different services or to the general taxpayer (that is, external subsidies). There are two common definitions of cross-subsidisation. The first of these states that it occurs to the extent that a class of users is charged less than the 'normal' rate for a service. This approach applies solely to cases in which there are no differences in costs of supplying various classes of users, or when such cost differences as do exist are ignored on the grounds that, although they are not known with any high degree of accuracy, they are believed to be small. The second approach relies explicitly on differences between costs and prices: a group is obtaining a subsidy equal to the amount by which the revenue received by the enterprise from sales to the group falls short of the costs to the enterprise of supplying those customers.[2]

In a multi-commodity enterprise like the Post Office, the cost of supplying a particular set of customers is a disputed concept, and we are forced to accept here the methods used, but rarely spelled out, by the Post Office to distribute overhead or common charges between various services.

Broadly speaking, postal and telegraph customers were subsidised by telephone customers after 1945, according to Post Office accounting. Working expenses of all branches rose rapidly in relation to revenue during the first five post-war years. After 1950, however, the experiences of the two chief branches, post and telephones, diverged. Postal working expenses exceeded earnings by an average of 5 per cent between 1950 and 1975; only in the years 1960 to 1965 and in 1972 did earnings exceed expenses. Contrasting with the flat trend in the postal branch was the fairly steady fall of telephone expenses, as charged, in relation to earnings. Telephone expenses never exceeded earnings, and fell from about 95 per cent of earnings in the early 1950s to about 75 per cent in the early 1970s. Of course, in view of the capital-using character of telephone technology, that branch had to make surpluses on working account if it were to meet interest obligations, which it succeeded in doing in all but a few years, those immediately following the great increase in interest-bearing debt in 1959-60. The great rise of Australian Postal Commission receipts in 1975-76 from agency services provided other government departments (including Telecom), throws some doubt on the accuracy of the earlier allocation of revenues and costs between the postal and telecommunications branches.

In its examination of uneconomic services provided by the Post Office since 1901, the 1961 Ad Hoc Committee based its estimates of the value of subsidies on the differences between concessional charges and those *normally applicable*, the results having been checked by way of a sample of 'direct costs' (*Report*, p. 75). Between 1945 and 1959, the concession on bulk postage rates was the largest single source of 'loss', averaging over £ 1.6m a year, closely followed by 'losses' on rural

---

[2] Strictly speaking, a group of customers is said to be subsidising others when the group could supply its own needs more cheaply by 'going it alone' (that is, by arranging independent supply), than by paying the prices charged by the monopoly enterprise. When the enterprise is constrained to zero profits, the subsidies are to other customers, and hence are called cross-subsidies (Faulhaber 1975, p. 966). However, if the enterprise is making profits, then the 'subsidies' are paid to the owners (e.g. to taxpayers via the Treasury) or to other customers or to both. Because 'stand-alone' costs are difficult to estimate, most calculations of the extent of cross-subsidisation rely on conceptually different definitions, like those in the text, ones closer to notions of price discrimination than to cross-subsidisation.

TABLE 11.4 **Losses on certain Post Office services, 1945–46 to 1972–73**

| | ($m) Average Losses | | | |
	1945–46 to 1949–50	1950–51 to 1954–55	1955–56 to 1958–59	1972–73
Bulk postage	2.20	3.37	3.80	9.9
Rural telephone services	1.48	4.83	5.35	88.9
Press/public telegraph	0.53	0.42	0.47	18.7
Other identified services	0.30	0.51	0.50	44.9
Total	4.51	9.13	10.12	162.4
Overall Post Office Loss (−) or Profit (+)[a]	+4.10	−1.17	+6.37	+41.22

[a] After interest.

Source: 1945–46 to 1958–59: *Ad Hoc Committee of Inquiry into the Commercial Accounts of the Post Office* (Canberra, 1961), pp. 75–79. 1972–73: *Report of Commission of Inquiry into the Australian Post Office* (Canberra, 1975), Tables 2.10 and 2.11.

telephone line rentals, at £ 1.5m. In fact, the vast majority of 'losses' shown were due to rural and remote services, accentuating the pattern well established before 1939 of subsidies flowing from urban to non-urban customers. (Exactly who is being subsidised is a bit more complicated than this allows. For example, some urban businesses and households might gain directly from the provision of uneconomic postal and telephone connections with their rural customers or friends. However, the political pressure from the rural population was what was effective in obtaining the concessions.) A similar pattern of losses was recorded for the year 1971-72 (Table 11.4). Of the $20.9m 'loss' on mails, half was due to concessions on periodicals and newspapers. The 'profit' on metropolitan telephones and on telex ($84.8m) was closely matched by the 'losses' on country telephone services ($89.9m); we might also assume that the large 'profit' on trunk calls ($113.8m) was mainly due to calls between metropolitan areas. Whereas in 1971-72 telecommunications services earned an overall average of $112 for every $100 of expenses, rural services earned a mere $44. So far as this evidence goes it suggests that the main customers accorded discriminatory advantage were rural population and urban businesses involved in bulk distribution and advertising.

Part Five

Summary Interpretation

12

Summary Interpretation

The outline of seventy-five years of public-private interaction displays a tortuous path. There is no single trend of government action or the private use of government. The 'decline of colonial socialism' or of direct public participation in the market is counterbalanced by the growth of allocative and regulatory intervention and by rising public expenditures on social (welfare) policies. In turn, social policy measures disclose a profound shift from concern with poverty to non-redistributive provisions of 'welfare for all' and from direct public intervention to increasing reliance on the (guided) market. Similarly, the performance of public enterprises follows particular paths, with conflicting experience in which some intensified and others lost 'monopoly' characteristics, yet with a common tendency of public enterprises increasingly (after 1945) to use their 'monopoly' or market power. Moreover, as public enterprises lost their leading role as investors and producers, many, as statutory authorities, gained regulatory authority over private decision-making.

Few would doubt the increasing importance of or dependence on government. But these conflicts in trends make it impossible to draw any overall conclusion. This is partly because of conflicting tendencies in government policy, and partly also because of changing private pressures on government, and the nature and operations of private interests.

The decline of 'colonial socialism'

Traditionally, Australian colonial governments during the second half of the nineteenth century performed what was, in effect, a general management role in the economies. In its essence, 'colonial socialism' entailed direct action by governments to attract foreign (British) resources of capital and labour through public borrowing overseas and large-scale programs of publicly assisted migration, the investment of British capital in publicly owned fixed assets in Australia, the concentration of this investment in public business undertakings primarily in transport and communications, and the delivery of marketed services by these public enterprises. In the process, therefore, the various governments were responsible directly for enlarging the flow of factor inputs and marketed services into the Australian economy, beyond levels that the private market could deliver, through accessing foreign resources and through business activity by government in the domestic market.

This pattern of nineteenth-century behaviour was strongly established at the beginning of the twentieth century and is the primary reason for the high Australian ratio, in 1901, of public expenditure to gross product and of public employment to total workforce. During the twentieth century, this set of public activities became progressively less significant in the total array of public functions and in relation to the activities of the private sector. One important theme in the relations between public and private behaviour is, therefore, the decline, relative to other public functions and to the private sector, of this nineteenth-century style of public intervention. This relative decline, conflicting markedly with many other tendencies, is fundamental to an understanding of Australian use of public means in the twentieth century.

Central to this accession of foreign resources was the generally accepted *domestic* Australian aim of rapid population expansion - an aim based on the assumption that local defence and local economic development required a rapid population build-up to a larger nucleus. The acquisition of foreign capital through government action was a correlative of this population aim: to combine increasing inputs of overseas capital and migrant labour with domestic natural resources in order to establish the conditions for enlarged foreign trade and domestic activity. Public action therefore supplemented rather than displaced private decision-making *in leading sectors of the economy*, greatly amplifying capital and labour flows to Australia.

In the main, the publicly supported flows of labour were not retained in the public sector but were made available to the private market and were responsive to local private pressures to accelerate or retard rates of migration. Public support in the second half of the nineteenth century occurred in circumstances of very high real income levels relative to the rest of the world and public intervention could then be limited primarily to reducing information and transfer costs. As Australian real standards relative to the outside world fell after 1890, the scale and scope of public intervention increased progressively until it penetrated almost every area of private decision-making in the process of population movement and resettlement.

Access to foreign capital in the nineteenth century and until 1930 was basic to government action in the domestic economy in the direct public provision of productive assets - in infrastructure of transport and communications enterprises and water and sewerage and more generally in roads, electricity and gas and a miscellany of minor activities. In the first thirty years of the twentieth century, public investment ran at a level roughly equal to aggregate private investment, and in this investment activity, public enterprise assets predominated. The injection of capital assets through government therefore greatly increased the rate of growth of Australian capital stock and its embodied technology. But, in addition, the delivery of marketed services by government significantly increased other inputs of intermediate goods and services consumed by private business and also increased the production of a limited but important array of final goods and services.

The year 1930 marks a crucial turning point for this mode of intervention. For public action in relation to immigration, that date had only medium-term significance. Public and private commitment to the goal of artificially expanded population growth was too strong. Public support of immigration was resumed after the Second World War and brought government into a highly detailed manipulation of private choice. The underlying aim of population expansion was not effectively questioned until the early 1960s and thereafter public action adjusted to its present reduced levels.

But in all other respects, the rationale of public intervention in respect of these inputs into the economy was strongly challenged from 1930. Thereafter, the effective rejection, publicly and privately, of foreign borrowing by governments severely limited the scope of further public intervention. Public capital outlays fell below private (omitting war years) and their share tended to decline steadily to the present level to just over one third of total capital formation in the 'seventies. In the process, public outlays on enterprise account fell progressively as a fraction of total public investment. Moreover this decline occurred despite the assumption of some new public activities such as air transport and civil aviation, the extension of public electricity supply and the modernisation of a great deal of public infrastructure. This relative decline was a major factor holding in check all public expenditures relative to gross product and public employment relative to total workforce.

It appears that 1930 is the crucial turning point in the *relative* withdrawal of public intervention supplementing private inputs and productive activity in these particular ways. The most immediate issue sparking that change was the fact that the burden of adjustment to fixed public debt obligations overseas, in a situation of deep external imbalance, was thrown on the private sector. This might be seen as an antagonistic public act. Certainly, in its effect, it contrasted sharply with the long-established tradition of a supportive partnership relation of government towards private business. In reality, of course, the actual and perceived sources of external imbalance arose in other sources such as wage costs as well as public behaviour. Nevertheless the matter is relevant in this context partly because of prior long-established relationships between public and private behaviour, and partly because it was largely private pressure on public actors that forced the private readjustments to public debt obligations. The Australian response to the depression problems has some significant contrasts with experience in other countries. The so-called 'mass market failure' of the 1930s is seen traditionally in Western countries as greatly stimulating public intervention, including public ownership of assets. In Australia there was, in this particular and important area of public action, a marked withdrawal relative to private counterparts.

There was, however, another and more fundamental consideration. The depression of the 1930s with its widespread shake-out in private business led to a deeper reappraisal of the conditions of private economic growth. Two central points are worth noting. First, the concept of Australian capacity to absorb foreign resources, particularly labour, in the rural sector was largely laid to rest. Although governments had intervened to enlarge capital and service inputs in urban activity, the case for mass public activity rested to a large extent on rural claims. The diversion of activity towards manufacturing as recovery proceeded narrowed the area in which public infrastructure was an important contribution to Australian growth. Post-war manufacturing expansion confirmed that reassessment. The second point is more specific. At the very end of the 1920s and throughout the 1930s, motor vehicle use and particularly truck use escalated. Technological change and the beginning of mass consumption of motor vehicles cut deeply into the core of government intervention through railway investment and enterprise and eroded the transport 'monopoly' of the public sector. In the process a second exceptional act, this time explicitly adversary, towards private choice occurred through public efforts to constrain private vehicle use.

Depression crisis, technical change in transport and reappraisal of labour absorptive potential appear as dominant in forcing a new evaluation of the developmental role of public inputs. One might suggest that thereafter public attention turned progressively from physical capital inputs to an increasing concern with human capital - growing preoccupation with education at progressively higher levels and with immigration. These concerns were clearly leading ones after 1945 and until the late 1960s. Then these also were open to severe doubt. That doubt turned on the capacity to absorb large numbers of humans in *any* Australian activity (not merely rural) and led, in the seventies, to a substantial reduction in efforts towards artificially expanded population that had been the essential aim determining much of the pattern of public and private relations over the past 150 years.

It is necessary to appreciate at least the broad outlines of this fairly complicated shift in the relative importance and composition of public action in participating directly in market activity. There are two questions related to this experience that need particularly to be addressed. The first is: what was the general nature of the relationships between public and private aims and behaviour and did this change with changing relative levels and composition of public activity? The second is closely related: why was this public intervention undertaken and did the reasons change in fundamental terms?

The two questions can largely be dealt with simultaneously. The nineteenth century experience, including both sustained growth of the economy and depression in the final decade, left little option but the assumption of direct government responsibility for large-scale investment and foreign borrowing and large-scale public intervention in migrant flows. Nominally, private efforts were displaced and to that extent a crowding-out process may seem to have occurred. But it occurred within clearly defined limits and with the increasing support of dominant business interest groups. The hypothesis that intervention was prompted by market imperfections will not work. Basically one might suggest that specific business interests sought to limit their capital commitments in the generation of private growth by distributing widely, through public intervention, the costs of borrowing, of infrastructure and of immigration and by minimising foreign interest obligations. A substantial price was paid in the creation of a powerful bureaucracy and in private dependence on competing colonial governments introducing strong public oligopolistic elements into decision making. Nevertheless, on both public and private 'sides', the expectation and intent was to introduce a strong supportive role of government aiding the development of private business. Direct public participation in the market provided the means to this end. But it also eliminated the specific pressures that developed in other countries to regulate private 'monopolies' carrying out activities comparable to those of Australian governments. From both points of view, adversary relations between public and private interests were therefore greatly constrained. This fact is vital to the whole understanding of Australian public-private relations.

A strongly supportive relationship of government towards major business interests related to pastoral development was clearly established during the second half of the nineteenth century. Given the conditions of rapid economic growth to 1890 and a relatively specialised economy, there was little pressure or incentive for public allocative intervention imposing clearly recognisable costs on some sections.

These conditions changed in the nineties and increasingly so between 1900 and 1930. One might suggest that relative bargaining strengths between the public and private sector were significantly altered given the new emphasis on the development of relatively small-scale farming and manufacturing. Direct government intervention, particularly from 1900 to 1914, appeared as more significantly and autonomously an engine of development, in important respects directing private growth. Given their small scale of activity, financial insecurity, limited political cohesion and lack of industrial organisation, the private interests of 1900 to 1914 depended heavily on public support. We cannot possibly try to explain this experience in terms of private maximisation or private group pressures.

That public support continued after 1900 to be directed towards the encouragement of organised interests is one of the most important features of twentieth century economic history in Australia. Partly, of course, developing external markets and growing domestic population and markets provided the economic conditions for private recovery up to 1914. But there were also important characteristics of the public sector that reinforced its support of private growth. The first of these was the fact that the still dominant State governments were perhaps essentially large-scale producers of marketed services. They depended on the market and hence on the encouragement of that market, especially in rural activity. Secondly, as large landowners they depended on the recovery of the rural real estate market. Thirdly, they were constrained in charging policies for public inputs by obligations to foreign creditors. Fourthly their dominant revenues were essentially dependent on the private market. The limited income taxation of pre-1914 made only a relatively small qualification to this statement.

These conditions broke down rapidly in the 1920s. Farm, manufacturing and trade union groups were much more powerfully established and organised both politically and industrially. Private activity faced disrupted world trading conditions and different interests pressed more strongly and effectively for *specific* discriminatory support from government. Within government itself, growth of the more obviously coercive income taxation opened greater opportunities for discriminatory charging systems and discriminatory allocation of infrastructure services.

In effect, the relationship between two partners - public and private - changed, with private interests now able much more effectively than during the period 1900 to 1914 to use the coercive powers of government for discriminatory private purposes and with less constraint than before. Moreover competition between them accentuated allocative issues. The effects on the levels of public inputs were enhanced because of the conflict of claims from separate urban and rural interests; and the eventual instability of public activity was made considerably worse because of the failure of private business to develop on the one hand sufficient export growth and on the other sufficient import replacement to service rapidly growing public debt obligations abroad. Then the leadership of manufacturing in recovery from the depression and the subsequent manufacturing development during and after the war radically altered the private pressures for public charged services and their underlying assets. At the same time the development of the motor vehicle undercut the degree of monopoly of transport services by the public sector and indeed introduced a new and for the first time much more consumer-oriented private interest affecting public and private relationships in the supply of physical assets and transport services.

Though there was a falling trend of public capital inputs relative to private after 1930 and more particularly after 1950, it would be wrong to conclude that the mutual public and private assumption of a supportive role of government was ended during the 1930s. For a period immediately after the Second World War, the peacetime recovery of private activity and particularly private manufacturing depended on a prior restoration and expansion of public assets and services. But from 1950 the pattern (still to some extent selective) of a definite relative withdrawal by government is displayed. Public investment in physical assets and related public infra-services became less prominent as compared with the strong supportive and developmental role traditional over the preceding century. As a result, the scale and quality of Australian infrastructure declined considerably, above all in transport and communications and in water and sewerage.

A number of reasons might be suggested. Not all of them represent a reverse crowding out of public by private interest. Public action remained accepted within clearly defined areas and might even step over these limits as it did with air transport. The mass consumption of the motor vehicle was clearly a factor, constraining the willingness of government to invest in mass transport and transit infrastructure and enhancing private pressures for alternative transport assets. Even so, roads did not establish high priority in public investment. Political ideologies may have influenced the outcome. The unwillingness of the private sector to accept competition in the domestic capital market from a government virtually prohibited from long-term borrowing overseas may also have played a part.

Curiously, until the mineral boom, the most obvious explanations appear to lie in government rather than the private sector. Uniform taxation and Federal constraints on States' capital outlays and domestic borrowings provided a financial and administrative structure for centralised limitation of activity by the levels of government (States) that had dominated public capital outlays and public enterprises before 1939. But one of the most intriguing questions arises directly in the basic information available to both the public and private sectors on the composition and level of public capital outlays during the first twenty-four years after the Second World War. Until 1969, official estimates represented public investment as running very slowly down at around one-third of aggregate capital formation. There was no adequate indication of the long-term public decline relative to private that did, in fact, occur from the mid-fifties. Secondly, until 1969, the components of public investment, as estimated, suggested that a much greater priority had been accorded to road construction and maintenance than had in fact occurred. At the same time, these estimates gave a very muted representation of the greatly enhanced claims of telecommunications, and they suggested that railway investment had been much more severely pruned than was in fact the case.

Given the role of these estimates in budget preparation, it must be a possibility that both public and private policy and public and private attitudes to public investment and enterprises were founded on serious misapprehensions. The fact that some of these misapprehensions were corrected by 1969 and the estimates then extended back in time did not correct the evolving calculus up to 1969. By that time, a pattern and a trend relationship were established, progressively reducing the overall role of government in providing basic infrastructure inputs into the economy.

Subsequently, the mineral boom accentuated this withdrawal. Mineral prospects altered public attitudes to the provision of infrastructure. But in a great many cases, a new element emerged. This was in the fact that a great deal of the new mining ventures were geographically isolated and in remote unpopulated areas. The private enterprises could, in these cases, expect to internalise a great deal of the benefits, directly or indirectly, occurring from private provision of infrastructure. The continued provision of public assets and services related primarily to cases where this condition did not apply.

Allocative policy and regulation

Background: before 1900

Nineteenth-century colonial socialism was concerned only slightly, other than through direct market activity of government, with regulatory or allocative intervention in the decision-making of the major Australian interest groups represented by pastoral, financial and trading activities.

Assisted immigration, public overseas borrowing and public (transport) capital formation, approximately half, respectively, of total immigration, total foreign borrowing and total gross capital formation, represented a large-scale government intervention in Australian economic development. In the (perhaps) wealthiest country of the nineteenth-century world, the government task was to achieve these transfers, not to meddle in domestic relativities or arrange reception conditions. The circumstances of access were affected; the rest was mainly private decision-making within the 'rules of the game' imported from Britain. Simplification as this may be, it provides the crucial departure point for an understanding of twentieth-century evolution of public-private sector relationships within Australia. Increasingly, general economic management after 1900 demanded allocative intervention.

Basic relationships 1900 to 1914

The destruction of many pastoral fortunes by depression and foreclosure and the termination of some pastoral enterprises by deaths of pioneers radically altered the environment of public and private decision-making and the objectives of public policy after 1900. State governments, replacing the old colonial governments, retained most of their dominance, despite Federation. Ambitions to attract foreign (British) immigrants and overseas capital remained. Above all, public and private objectives of artificial population growth remained. But the direction of growth shifted, internally, towards non-pastoral activity and, above all, to smaller and less powerful or resourceful private decision-making entities, first in non-pastoral land use and secondly in small-scale manufacturing enterprise. Moreover, in determining transfer conditions of capital and labour, government was required, in pursuit of expansionist objectives, to adapt itself to circumstances in which per capita standards were shrinking towards competitive world levels and in which scope for absorption of resources from outside was narrowing. In these conditions, artificial rates of increase of factors from abroad largely compelled attention to much more allocative measures. From this stemmed the dominant twentieth-century trend in economic management.

Arrangement of factor transfers remained a major issue in public policy from 1900 to 1914. But it had become more important to arrange, by conscious public action, the reception conditions for additions to the Australian population and hence to be more concerned with domestic income distribution. This emphasis was strongly welcomed by nascent but politically significant Labor parties seeking to strengthen the bargaining powers of trade unions and to restore wage standards by use of the coercive powers of government. A coalescence of the interest of employers and trade unions in the encouragement of manufacturing and the attraction of an enlarged manufacturing workforce allowed extensive intervention in the labour market. The primary functions of arbitration, before 1914, were to support the bargaining power of trade unions, to protect employed union labour by raising wage standards towards judicially declared minimum levels (a floor under wage incomes) and to encourage the re-formation of union organisation and the development of Federal unions.

Government relations with new or expanding business interests from 1900 to 1914 were radically different from those that existed before 1890. Production possibilities in both rural and manufacturing activity were uncertain, though rural development was taken still to offer the greater opportunities - but in non-pastoral land use. In both rural and manufacturing activities, however, expansion was sought by individuals with far less wealth, with more limited access to finance, with business expectations on a relatively small scale and with far less ability to compete in or against world markets than nineteenth-century pastoralists. Public policy remained predominantly supportive. But a basic shift in power was implied and a critical change in the scope and nature of intervention occurred. Public intervention in private decision-making was greatly extended - the intervention going beyond the Federal determination of the conditions of competition with the outside market (tariffs, bounties) to the predominantly State Govern-ment intrusion in decisions on location, entry, financing, scale and in-put purchases. Little intervention in output decisions occurred except indirectly through large-scale public capital outlays and preference to local suppliers. This intrusion was primarily designed to encourage ex-pansion of new activities. It was not restrictive. In so far as restrictive conditions developed, it was government support of private restrictive practices that was dominant. One of the intriguing historical issues ap-pears to be the willingness of government to legislate for restrictive practices (not all of which can be explained by capture processes), not of private firms, but of private trade associations predominantly related to manufacturing and trade (but not, yet, rural activities). The development of 'monopoly' and 'restraint of competition' are recurr-ing themes in this book.

Experience 1919 to 1939

Considerations of distribution rather than efficiency were at the core of inter-war public policy, of public approach to private decision-making and of private appeal to public action. Ambitions to ac-celerate growth through factor transfers from abroad persisted. But external factor increments, compared to the Australian nucleus with which they were being joined, were now significantly less than they had been. New rural industries had attained greater technical security and substantial size. But they depended for growth on large-scale entry into world markets in which increasingly restrictive and uncertain conditions applied. Dwindling expansion prospects in rural activities encouraged greater attention to manufacturing import substitution and 'new' industries of the First World War were now subject to more severe external competition. Nevertheless, these new manufacturing enterprises and older, simpler processing industries had attained a significant presence in the Australian economy.

Given these conditions, the circumstances of depression apart, the character of public-private sector relationships in the inter-war years yielded an intricate coalescence of public and private action and decision making, with a more complex interpenetration on each side than existed before (or, possibly, since). The slogan of 'protection all round' reflected an increased awareness (however uneasy) of a symbiotic relationship between manufacturers, rural producers and wage earners and a consciousness of the need for political accommodation of these groups. Complex off-setting public policies, devious and haphazard as they may have been in practice, served to a large degree to preserve or to seem to preserve the relativities of the major interest groups in the face of considerable alteration in world trading conditions. Accordingly, in pursuing a public growth strategy through artificial encouragement to exports by non-pastoral rural activity and import replacement by manufacturing, what was perceived as the appropriate (last best?) growth path was pursued.

A significant step towards a nation-wide (and nationalistic) market interference was implied by the concern with export encouragement and highly protected import replacement. This meant the somewhat greater intervention by the Federal Government (i.e. greater centralisation) in regulatory processes to arrange the conditions of Australian competition with the outside world through import restrictions on manufactured goods and organised and subsidised rural production and marketing. Behind these arrangements lay the internal support for or acquiescence in monopolistic and quasi-monopolistic practices, arrangements in which Commonwealth and State governments, local authorities and rural producers were all implicated.

Australian per capita real income relative to leading trading countries shrank markedly in the inter-war years. The pursuit of assisted immigration policy was represented as subject to the maintenance of real wages. Arbitration authorities, backed by Federal and State powers, interfered more pervasively and intricately in labour markets. In the process, there was a significant shift of importance towards the Federal system, though arbitration did not become, in the inter-war years, highly centralised.

Real wages were protected by the provision of basic wages and regular cost-of-living adjustments. This protection was an essential condition of trade union acceptance of publicly assisted immigration.

But just as manufacturing and rural enterprises had acquired a more secure and organised position, so too had trade unions. They were able to manipulate the arbitration system to secure the ends of employed unionists in preserving and improving working conditions, including wage rates. The basic wages that were set became platforms on which highly detailed margins for skill were built, achieving a quite intricate segmentation of wage earners by occupation and skill. Thanks to cost-of-living adjustments and the proliferation of margins, money wage rates rose rapidly during the twenties (particularly relatively to British wage rates); their rise was accompanied by a progressive increase in tariff protection and an increasing support of rural export dumping.

Though there were significant centralising tendencies, even in the twenties, towards greater Federal intervention in the regulatory supportive process, it was the demands of macro-regulation during the depression beginning in the second half of the twenties that brought more definitely centralised Federal action.

Slow and incomplete recovery combined with the attempts to encourage the upswing preserved a prominent role for Federal authorities. Basically, however, the mode of 'protection all round', adopted throughout the twenties, was resumed and continued until 1939 - with its mix of Federal and State intervention as described.

Intervention after 1945

The war projected the Federal Government into a dominant position and, in the post-war period, Federal policies and regulatory measures acquired the leading role in the process of peacetime decision-making.

Centralisation of regulation, enhanced bureaucratic autonomy, increasing general constraint for macro-management purposes, the increased concentration of regulation in Federal hands, increased speed of application and increased nation-wide effects of public policy appear to become special characteristics of the Australian civilian economy after 1945. In certain major areas, it may be possible to detect a withdrawal from specific, direct regulatory measures and the application of more general and simpler rules. This does not necessarily mean a less significant influence on private decision-making. General rules may be more powerful, and general rules also apply to changing circumstances and have differential impact on particular interests and institutions. In any event, there were other important areas in which greater specificity of public action and more strongly discriminatory regulation appear to have developed. The concept of 'big government' is particularly difficult to capture in regulatory terms.

Apart from the periods of Federal Labor Government after the war and from 1972 to 1975, equity considerations played only a small part in the formulation of public policy. This was not merely a matter of political ideology. The Australian economy expanded rapidly after 1949, became structurally more complex and per capita standards rose considerably. Governments and private interests were more concerned with the encouragement of growth and the sharing of increments in output. This contrasted most obviously with inter-war experience.

The demands for full employment were not alone responsible for centralisation and the generally constraining regulation after 1945. The elimination, under the Uniform Tax Agreement of 1942, of State rights to levy personal and company income taxation, combined with a decade of Federal dominance under wartime and extended defence powers until 1949, provided basic conditions for effective full employment measures. The prestige and authority of the Federal government were enormously enhanced by the experience of managing the war economy and the re-conversion to peace.

Below the level of macro-regulation, other major structural changes moved regulation progressively from State influence and transferred it within the ambit of Federal constitutional authority. Manufacturing development depended on private decisions, chiefly by foreigners, to provide capital, technology and managerial skills. As they moved across the Australian protective wall of import quotas and tariffs, these firms still depended on discriminating or discretionary treatment in the movement of funds, the right to enter, the import of necessary materials and equipment, protection against the finished imports of other foreigners and the transfer of surpluses abroad. The State Governments were left to compete for fragments of foreign concerns and to share with the Commonwealth the public influences on the dispersal of establishments and the restriction of scale. The nature of private economic development in the context of the Australian Constitution was an important contributor to centralisation.

Until 1960, the dominant Federal mode of intervention was by direct and specific import restrictions (quota controls). This intervention led the Federal Government into detailed supervision of activity and intervention in a wide range of decision making. The substitution of high protective tariffs for quota controls after 1960 was by no means complete. Nevertheless, although tariff protection provided a less detailed intervention and allowed greater scope for market influences, the actual consequences of restoring the role of the tariff appear to have been relatively slight in terms of decentralising regulation, of government pressure on domestic content or of restructuring. It was not until the Whitlam Government that some attempts were made to achieve restructuring (though with very limited effect), through proposals for across-the-board tariff cuts and support for the gradual transfer of factors out of reducing activities.

In the rural sector, a comparable centralisation occurred. In part this was for different reasons than those in manufacturing. The Federal Government played a key role in research and development, of prime significance in expanding rural output potential. But in addition, the effects of the war, combined with the establishment of major statutory authorities on which national rather than State growers' representatives were members, made Federal rather than State-organised marketing schemes more important than before 1939. The greater export orientation of rural industries gave larger scope for Federal trade intervention. The role of Federal authorities was clinched by the underlying financial and monetary powers of the Commonwealth Government, a matter of acute importance in managing, after 1950, the process of rural price equalisation and export subsidies.

In the rural industries, also, the problems of restructuring gradually developed in the sixties. As in the case of manufacturing, there was a great deal of shilly-shallying as to appropriate action - by the Federal Government. Some slight efforts by government were made to manage a restructuring process. Again, it was not until the Whitlam Government that efforts were made to withdraw supports and expose farming to competitive forces. This approach was reversed after 1975.

We have traced in this volume, with different considerations intervening, a growing centralisation in the regulation of the labour market and with similar distortion. In a less obvious manner, a story of increased centralisation, loss of control and recovery of centralisation applied in the case of banking. In both cases, the tendencies were towards a combination of public sector changes and alterations in the structure and activity of the private sector. In both cases, the private interests concerned became increasingly or extensively subject to the priorities of macro-management and to a public policy with limited susceptibility to the pressures of particular major interest groups. In the end, despite the contrary efforts of the Whitlam Government, even the highly centralised labour organisations were subjected to this control - and, perhaps because of delays in constraint, labour may have been affected more severely than most other private interests. But here, evaluation depends on one's expectations of the prospects of containing inflation or of avoiding other deep social problems of continued high and rising unemployment.

Some of the structural changes in the private sector operated, in part, as a counter to increasing centralisation and autonomy. It is essential to recognise divergent tendencies. Thus the growth of large-scale enterprise in manufacturing, the increased role of rural producers' representation at the national level, the increased concentration of trade union power, and the development of more centralised trade associations implied that, as these activities moved into the Federal regulatory sphere, they became much more powerful pressure groups. The legal support for monopolistic or oligopolistic structures offered by all governments contributed to this increase in private influence. From this development flowed the extension of monopolistic practices of almost every sort, with greater or less active assistance but almost always with legal permission given by the Federal and State Governments.

Even in these cases, however, pressures for public control and restriction developed, partly because of the sheer size and significance of these private institutions. Growing concern with monopolistic practices, with consumer protection and with market failure in environmental protection led to an interest in the restraint on monopolistic practices. The reinterpretation of the powers over corporations eventually placed the Commonwealth in the leading role to exercise - very limited but significant - restraints on some monopolistic practices. Even in environmental protection, where State Government activity grew steadily from the early fifties, the Federal Government held and exercised the major powers by its control of trade and import of technology.

One fundamental change provides an appropriate conclusion, because it raises a major question mark over the interpretation of regulatory trends. The mineral boom induced massive inflow of foreign capital, multinational enterprises and foreign technology. These enterprises represented a private 'interest group' novel in scale and significance if not in type. Primarily concerned with export activity, they escaped many of the conventional controlling approaches and methods of the Federal Government. They were powerful enough to offer strong resistance to the exercise of Federal trade powers. Exploiting natural resources, they were deployed in activities over which State Governments had primary constitutional rights. Concentrated particularly in two outlying States, the entry of these concerns disturbed the Australian 'arrangements' between States and Commonwealth and between the public and private sectors built up over the preceding fifty years. It would be rash to try to predict the implications of these activities for the future of the relationship between the public and private sectors.

Social policy: welfare

Most existing theoretical approaches tend to lead to the conclusion that twentieth-century welfare policies have introduced ameliorative and redistributive provisions in society. These theoretical preconceptions appear to be based on one or more of three possible hypotheses.

One is that the spread of voting franchise to progressively lower income levels opened access to public authority to groups seeking redistribution in their favour and less concerned about the fundamental philosophies of capitalism and private enterprise.

A second lies in a hypothesis by Adolph Wagner, reputedly confirmed by empirical test, that the income elasticity of demand for public services and especially welfare services exceeds unity. This hypothesis is a much more complex one than appears at first sight. What is relevant here is that there is a close connection between this and the first hypothesis - that the *effective* demand for certain types of publicly delivered goods depended on access to political and governing authority.

The third hypothesis relates not to private but rather to public motivation and is perhaps more relevant to later stages of public intervention. Given the limitation of market constraint on bureaucratic behaviour, public solutions to welfare problems might be expected to stress the quality of welfare services without close attention to cost-benefit calculus. The presumption, again, is that the probable outcome is redistributive in favour of the disadvantaged.

Australian experience challenges the redistributive implications of all three hypotheses.

Underlying Australian attitudes there was comparatively little concern with equity. This attitude may have been a major factor both in the severe limitation of benefits and, more importantly, in the post-1949 tendency to transfer the task of providing protection to publicly guided private institutions rather than relying on public programs. After its early innovations by and immediately following 1900, there are three dominant characteristics of the Australian welfare system. One is the very low rates of public protection that were and are offered. The second is the increasing dependence on the private market (or to a much less extent on private non-market behaviour) after the Second World War. Finally, there is the shift of emphasis from concern to protect categories of individuals from severe poverty to the identification of and support for a large variety of 'disadvantaged' groups with less regard for their general economic status.

Early this century, with non-contributory age and invalid pensions and maternity allowances, Australia was comparatively innovative and, *in an international context*, generous in the public delivery of social security. Centralised State public school systems provided primary (elementary) education services at little or no direct charge to the 80 per cent of the school-age population that used them. This too was a significant departure from British (and American) precedent. Privately organised and operated non-profit hospitals and voluntary charitable concerns, both serving the poor, were heavily subsidised by government. Through the next seventy-five years, Australia followed, in a broad way, the Western pattern of increasing public expenditures on these welfare services, whether publicly delivered services or cash transfers.

After the social security innovations in the first decade, public commitments expanded partly from multiplication of benefits and partly from increasing longevity (itself a product, to a substantial degree, of public health services). In the process, private welfare was crowded out or surrendered part of its role. The claims of veterans of the First World War and of the unemployed in the depression of the 1930s enlarged demands on public welfare services. During the Second World War the public commitment to a 'cradle-to-the-grave' concept of welfare was adopted in Australia in conformity with general western (especially British) experience. This led to a vast extension of the kinds of income support payments made and of the groups receiving them.

Public delivery of education services became more complex. Maintaining their share of total school enrolments, State systems extended to include secondary and technical education. Governments impinged increasingly on the provision of tertiary education services, culminating in full Federal funding in the 1970s. Access to education services was progressively widened, as it was throughout Western countries, so that by 1975 the number of full-time students of working age formed a large and very significant social group. By the end of the period the long-standing separation of religiously based schools from public funding was broken and the government role was extended to include direct support of private production of education services. These developments resulted in part from the changing, more sophisticated requirements of employers, in part from parents' perceptions of individuals' private returns from education, each mediated by an increasingly influential public education bureaucracy.

Preventive public health services, such as quarantine, vaccination and the supervision of standards of hygiene in food preparation, expanded slowly though importantly through the seventy-five years. Developments in the production of health services within hospitals, however, determined the major pattern of inter-relationships between public and private choice. As hospitals became first safe places of treatment and then the location of capital-intensive diagnostic and surgical technologies, pressures mounted to ensure that everyone, not merely the poor, had access to them. The medical profession was advantaged by public provision of facilities; consumers and hospital administrators were unwilling to have hospital charges set to cover all costs. Governments continued to subsidise both capital and running expenses, at the same time exerting closer and closer regulation of hospital administrations, extending the principle of 'user pays' and reducing the role of voluntary charity in hospital funding. The development of the medical profession's ability to treat ill health successfully led increasingly to the invocation of coercive public authority to reduce financial barriers to 'needed' consumption. On this was erected the vast, at times universalistic, National Health Scheme of post-1945 Australia. Government health expenditures, like social security and education expenditures, were increasingly determined by Federal government policies after the Second World War. Unlike those other two welfare areas, however, health services saw the early development of effective private (producer) pressure groups. Apart from veterans, welfare recipients have rarely organised and, except at the very local level affecting individual politicians, welfare policies did not become important specific electoral issues until the post-war years.

This potted version begs several vital questions central to the relevant chapters of this book. On the one side, there is the issue of the significance for private choice between cash transfers and public delivery of goods and services in kind. On the other is a set of questions relating to redistributive consequences. One of these questions is whether the public provision of welfare services in Australia was actually redistributive. A second is whether Australia kept pace with world-wide tendencies towards the public provision of welfare. The third is whether there were, in Australia, significant readjustments over the three quarters of a century between public and private provision of welfare or between processes of public or private provision in meeting actual or potential welfare claims.

The question of the redistributive implications of welfare services is a complex one. It is possible to debate the differential redistributive consequences of, for example, old-age pensions as compared with publicly-provided education. In much of current discussion of the evolution of welfare services there is a basic confusion about the redistributive effects of welfare (i.e. the coerced alteration of market outcomes) in terms of classes of individuals as distinct from levels of incomes of actual welfare recipients.

One remarkable achievement in Australian history was the establishment, early in the century, of separate floors under the incomes of certain classes of individuals. Most obviously, the basic wage, introduced in 1907 and made substantially universal by the beginning of the 1920s, was an almost unique achievement. Similarly, the adoption of old-age pensions in Victoria and New South Wales and the spread of these, with maternity and invalid pensions, throughout Australia from 1908 quite properly made Australia something of a social laboratory in the Western world.

The provision of these floors for categories of persons in and outside the workforce implied public action to alleviate poverty, regardless of the funding process. In this sense, these measures were redistributive, protecting the very poor who remained within the specified categories but whose incomes were non-existent or very low.

Nevertheless, the question remains whether persons otherwise exposed to the risk of impoverished old age, unemployment, invalidity or maternity secured support through public funding processes from categories of individuals who were exposed to similar risk or from others who were cushioned, by personal affluence, from these risks. We would hesitate to define the problem in terms of conventional Marxist concepts. Nevertheless, the issue is fundamentally to be phrased, realistically, as a question whether it was wage earners who funded members of their 'class' in protection against lifetime risks; or whether other wealthier groups, not dependent on wage incomes, provided funding support.

In this more ambiguous sense, Australian welfare services appear to have developed slowly and subject to severe restrictions until about the Second World War essentially by a self-supporting system, organised through coercive taxation, of wage-earner provision of protection for their kind. Obviously, in the process, particular individual mishaps were swept up in the process regardless of wage-earner status. Curiously, a mythology and a rhetoric developed based on the assumption that a substantial redistributive process was involved. So long as funding processes developed based on indirect taxation (until the First World War), this mythology may have had some if little justification. The spread of income taxation up to but before the adoption of Uniform Taxation in 1942 may have added a little more substance and not merely empty rhetoric. With virtually universal taxation at substantial rates for all income levels from 1942, rhetoric and mythology were reconciled with reality: welfare benefits were available to coerced contributors. From this recognition flowed the proliferation and universal accessibility of Australian welfare, with all income levels making substantial tax provision for their own protection against lifetime risks.

Obviously, it is possible that, combining both public and private 'welfare', Australian coverage of lifetime risks may be as effective as those in other countries. Comparative measurement based only on a public delivery of cash transfers and benefits in kind fail grossly in assessing the protection offered institutionally by any society. Nevertheless, it appears to be the case that, having acted to displace private efforts in the early years of this century, Australian governments subsequently acted, after 1949, to encourage and support increasing private action in the welfare field.

In this process there appear to have lain two conflicting issues: one was the widespread willingness to protect the unfortunate given that they had shared in past tax burdens. The other was the strong public commitment, subject to coercive guidance and support, to the private market and individual enterprise. In practice, Australian development and per capita income had, by 1950, passed beyond the point at which the unfortunate were prominent numerically. It appears to have been the commitment to the philosophy of private enterprise that predominated. Nevertheless this commitment did not extend to free market behaviour in supplying services. On the contrary, it was powerful public intervention that led progressively, in particular in health, education and housing and less directly but no less importantly in age pension (cf. also actions in relation to superannuation), to the publicly guided private delivery of an increasing proportion of these services based essentially on insurance benefits. At the same time and consistently, public provision in terms of benefit rate per person tended to become increasingly constrained relative to other income levels. An experiment that had begun with strong emphasis on direct public action was progressively developed towards private delivery dependent on public distortion of market incentives. In almost every sense, Australian welfare experience was contrary to most of Western behaviour.

The conduct of public enterprises

Very little has been written about the conditions and mode of operation of public enterprises in Australia. Given their importance in the Australian economy, in 1901 and now, and given the belief in their significance in Australian economic growth, it is surprising that they have not attracted greater attention by both business historians and economists (or by persons interested in public administration). The chapters in this volume dealing with particular important types of public business undertakings are intended to re-open historical inquiry into the operation of these businesses. Rather than pursue a single type of public undertaking, we have used a broad comparative canvas to indicate the variety of characteristics and behaviour in public businesses and in comparison with private enterprise.

An outstanding issue in dealing with the conduct of public businesses is the degree of 'monopoly' or market power that they possessed. There was a large range of these undertakings that were established (chiefly by Labor governments in the years before and immediately after the First World War) explicitly to compete with private enterprises. These 'petty socialist' undertakings are largely disregarded in this volume though they had some (passing) significance. The major undertakings all had or acquired a natural or artificial monopoly. Railways, water and sewerage, post and telecommunications, port and harbour undertakings and gas enterprises all were established with a high degree of monopoly at the beginning of the century. In some cases, this 'monopoly' position was greatly eroded by technological change and changed tastes in the private sector.

The railways are the leading example and the threat to their 'monopoly' for a time led to important adversary responses by public bodies towards the growth of private competition. In other cases, market power actually increased - most obviously, until the 1970s, in electricity. Here - a relatively exceptional circumstance - there was a large-scale displacement of private by public enterprise, particularly between 1900 and 1940.

In all cases and at all times, public 'monopoly' was subject in varying degrees to the presence or threat of substitutes. Successively, the horse, the cycle, the motor vehicle and aircraft offered private alternatives to the public carriage of people and goods by rail. In these changes lay an evolving interaction between private and public interest. Yet it was not merely changing competition between the public and private sector that altered the functions and operations of public undertakings. Important forms of 'competition' within the public sector also led to changes in public behaviour. This was most noticeable in the field of post and telecommunications, where communication through letters faced competition successively from the telegraph, telegram, telephone and radio, along with the efficiency and speed of transport. In these changes lay an interplay between sections of given public undertakings and between different public enterprises. In addition, however, there was the complex interaction of private pressures inducing public responses to technological possibilities - pressures from producers of equipment, from consumers and from political representatives.

Petty socialism apart it was perhaps only the railways that have been the obvious market losers in this process. Public business undertakings have shown various forms of vitality in responding to change to a degree that has often belied the frequent ideological criticisms of their behaviour. In part, responses have been channelled in directions that have led to other criticisms. This has perhaps been most notably the case in the ability of public air transport to share with competing private enterprise in an accommodation that has stifled competition and led to artificial market sharing. But it may be suggested that the responsiveness of public enterprise to change (a comment qualified by railway experience) may be accounted for in part by the acceptance by the private sector of the important supportive role played by public undertakings - supportive through enhanced service volumes, reduced service charges or reduced capital claims on private business through the substitution of public for private enterprise.

The acceptance of this supportive relationship is an underlying characteristic of Australian experience. Had the natural or artificial monopolies not been conducted as public enterprises, they would, on overseas experience, have been regulated private businesses. In other words, large-scale public undertakings in Australia to a large extent eliminated an important source of conflict between public and private interest through the public regulation of private businesses. Moreover, progressively through the twentieth century, a variety of private interests were able to attract discriminatory benefits from public business in a way and to a degree that would not have been possible had these undertakings been conducted privately.

In many respects, the growth of discrimination in favour of particular competing private interests by public undertakings is among the most interesting and important features of public business undertakings. There is little in this trend that is unique to Australia. It is important, however, to observe the degree and circumstances of these discriminatory practices (and at the same time to explore the 'poor-mouthing' to which some private interests subjected public business in the process). What is striking in comparing experience before 1920 with that subsequently is the comparatively high standards of non-discrimination with which the century began and the related strictness of the tests of financial performance by the main undertakings. A variety of explanatory possibilities are open: the dependence of these public enterprises on foreign capital, the degree of commitment of the public sector as a whole to market operations, limited fiscal resources (limited coercive power) of the public sector from which subsidies might be forthcoming and comparatively weak political and industrial organisation of private interests. The decline in the ability of public undertakings to resist either private pressures or public inclinations to engage in cross-subsidisation follows, at least in part, the course of events changing these circumstances of public undertakings - the decline of external dependence, increasing political and organisational strength of private interests combined with their market problems and possibilities, the proliferation of fiscal sources and most importantly the growth of income taxation as a subsidy source.

These changes form part of the story. But there is another part. Public enterprises have typically not used their market power to achieve profit maximisation that is conventionally supposed to characterise private enterprise. At least until the last decade or so of the period covered, public business was typically prepared to accept a low rate of return on capital. Increasingly some, like railways, have been allowed to tolerate losses and to continue operations and even to re-equip and expand assets despite poor financial performance.

In this characteristic lies an important feature of public enterprise in contrast with private business: the ability to disregard, at least within quite wide limits, market performance. In turn, this rests on the coercive powers of government. But coercion may take a variety of forms and this variety has prompted some of the divisions in the chapters 9-11 of this volume. Some undertakings (transport most obviously) offered services sold at price per unit consumed. For these, survival despite poor market performance rested ultimately on fiscal resources of government and government's ability to restrain some expenditure programs; symptomatically, the growth of income taxation particularly since the First World War (and more so since the depression) has been accompanied by worsening transport performance. But other enterprises, such as water and sewerage or electricity, only partially operated through unit price charging. Underlying their operations has been the progressive enlargement of a largely captive market subject to rating systems that are to a limited degree related to consumption and that are backed by the enforcement authority of the State. These modes of charging distort decision-making processes, both in the supply of services and in their consumption.

One of the problems that plagues any investigation of the sort attempted in this volume is that rates of return to public capital are of relatively limited value as indicators of performance in these conditions. Hence it is difficult to assess whether public enterprise has performed 'better' or 'worse' than some hypothetical private alternative. In turn, however, this casts a good deal of doubt on any prejudicial assessment of the quality of public enterprise performance.

In chapters 9-11, little attempt has been made for this reason to use these performance tests. There is, however, a related problem. This is the extent to which public undertakings may or may not be able to internalise the external benefits that they generate. Many of these advantages were captured either by the private sector or by other parts of the public sector. Thus public business undertakings may enhance land values to the benefit of private owners, or they may indirectly enlarge other sources of public revenue. The 'burden' on public budgets implied by low internal 'profitability' or small surpluses of receipts over expenses may then be - and possibly typically are - considerably less than would be indicated by a broader social evaluation. Any attempt to undertake an assessment of these external benefits is a very large task that warrants a great deal more research. Most importantly, it would be necessary to trace the historical trends in social rates of return and to calculate the distribution of benefits between the public and private sectors. In chapters 9-11, some indication of the types of external benefits of major public undertakings is given, suggesting that in many cases their social net benefit may be considerably larger than their own rates of return.

Despite these problems, it is suggested that for many public undertakings, the enterprise surpluses or losses as experienced over time are a useful beginning point for a study of the interplay of private interest and public action. In very general terms, the time series of surpluses in relation to the volume of activity of public business shows very long swings from relatively respectable yields into declining returns (and losses) and back into more recently restored surpluses, land transport apart. Clearly there are several issues to be explored in any attempt to explain this time sequence - changing efficiency, changing demand, possible misallocation of resources, pressures on factor prices and the like. Nevertheless, there are two other important possibilities. One is the changing public attitude to pricing policy and service volumes, representing in part a public willingness to vary the exploitation of market power over time. The other is the intervention of private pressures to induce changing degrees of cross-subsidisation by public pricing and service delivery - i.e. to discriminate in favour of particular private interests. Obviously the two issues are closely interdependent and this interdependence forms an important part of the story of public and private choice in this context.

Reading List

The subsections of this list echo those of the chapters in the main text, so that sources of particular statements can be checked. More importantly, the list is designed as an aid to further study of the matters discussed in the book.

Each part of the reading list is self-contained, with internal cross references only. Cross-references are of the style of entry like 'J. Roe (ed.): see 6.1', which indicates that the full bibliographical details of the work edited by J. Roe can be found in the subsection 6.1 of the list. If the '6.1' did not appear, then 'Roe' is an entry in the subsection in which the cross-reference itself arises. The following are the special abbreviations used.

AGPS   Australian Government Publishing Service
ANU   Australian National University
ANUP   Australian National University Press
CUP   Cambridge University Press
MUP   Melbourne University Press
NBER   National Bureau of Economic Research
NSW   New South Wales
OECD   Organization for Economic Cooperation and Development
OUP   Oxford University Press
PP   Parliamentary Paper
SUP   Sydney University Press
UQP   University of Queensland Press
V & P   Votes and Proceedings

It should be noted that there is a vast mass of relevant material, either literary or statistical, in official publications, covering all policy aspects dealt with in this book. Where these official series are specialised (as, e.g., in the *Labour Reports*), they have been listed in the appropriate section. The more general ones, valuable for studies over time, are listed immediately below; they are mostly annual issues.

Australia. *Official Year Book of the Commonwealth of Australia*, 1908 to date.

New South Wales. *Official Year Book of New South Wales*, 1904-05 to date.

New South Wales. *Statistical Register* 1900 to 1955-56 (thereafter divided into specialised parts).

Queensland. *The Queensland Official Year Book*, 1901.
Queensland. *The A.B.C. of Queensland Statistics*, 1905 to 1936.
Queensland. *Queensland Year Book*, 1937 to 1956.
Queensland. *Official Year Book of Queensland*, 1957 to date.
Queensland. *Statistics of the State of Queensland*, 1901 to 1966-67, (issued in separate parts 1940-41 to 1952-53).
South Australia. *Official Year Book of South Australia*, 1912, 1913.
South Australia. *South Australian Year Book*, 1966 to date.
South Australia. *Statistical Register of South Australia*, 1901 to 1965-66.
Tasmania. *Statistics of the State of Tasmania*, 1901 to 1966-67.
(Note. In its statistical publications, Tasmania at times relied on the publications of Commonwealth of Australia and one must look there.)
Western Australia. *Western Australian Year Book*, 1900-01 to 1905.
Western Australia. *Official Year Book of Western Australia*, 1957 to 1965.
Western Australia. *Western Australian Year Book*, 1967 to date.
Western Australia. *Statistical Register of Western Australia*, 1901 to 1960-61 (thereafter in separate parts).
Victoria. *Victorian Year Book*, 1900 to date.
Victoria. *Statistical Register of the State of Victoria*, 1901 to 1916.
(Note: A copy of the *unpublished* sections of the *Register* 1917 to 1955 is in the possession of the Horrie Brown Library, Research School of Social Sciences, ANU.)
For a more complete listing, see
Finlayson, Jennifer, *Historical Statistics of Australia. A select list of official sources*, ANU, Department of Economic History, Canberra, 1970.

1 Methods and Themes

Borcherding, T. (ed.), *Budgets and Bureaucrats: The Origins of Government Growth*, Duke University Press, Durham, 1975.
Buchanan, J.M. and Flowers, M.R., *The Public Finances: An Introductory Textbook*, Irwin, Homestead, 4th ed., 1975.
Fabricant, S., *The Trend of Government Activity in the United States Since 1900*, NBER, New York, 1952.
Kendrick, M.S., *A Century and a Half of Federal Expenditures*, NBER, Occasional Paper No. 48, New York, 1958.
Mueller, D.C., *Public Choice*, CUP, Cambridge, 1979.
Niskanen, W., *Bureaucracy and Representative Government*, Aldine-Atherton, Chicago, 1971.
OECD, *Studies in Resource Allocation No. 5: Public Expenditure Trends*, Paris, 1978.
Peacock, A.T. and Wiseman, J., *The Growth of Public Expenditures in the United Kingdom*, NBER, New York, 1961.
Samuelson, P.A., 'The pure theory of public expenditure', *Review of Economic Studies*, XXXVI, Nov. 1959, pp. 387-389.
Samuelson, P.A., 'Diagrammatic exposition of a theory of public expenditure', *Review of Economic Studies*, XXXVII, Nov. 1955, pp. 350-356.

2 The Decline of Colonial Socialism

Barnard, A., and Butlin, N.G., 'Australian public and private capital formation, 1901-1975', *Economic Record* (forthcoming, 1981 or 1982).

Butlin, N.G., 'Colonial socialism in Australia 1860-1900', in Hugh G.J. Aitken (ed.), *The State and Economic Growth*, Social Science Research Council, New York, 1959.

Butlin, N.G., *Australian Domestic Product Investment and Foreign Borrowing 1861-1938/39*, CUP, Cambridge, 1962.

New South Wales. Royal Commission on Charges against The Minister for Public Works, 'Report etc.', *V & P* 1912, vol. 3, p. 489.

Robertson, J.R., 'The Foundations of state socialism in Western Australia', *Historical Studies*, X, 39, Nov. 1962.

Sinclair, W.A., 'Capital formation', in C. Forster (ed.), *Australian Economic Development in the Twentieth Century*, George Allen & Unwin, London, 1970.

3 Managing Diversified Recovery

3.1 Economic Conditions

Butlin, N.G., 'Some perspectives of Australian economic development 1890-1965', in C. Forster (ed.), *Australian Economic Development in the Twentieth Century*, George Allen & Unwin, London, 1970.

Coghlan, T.A., *A Statistical Account of the Seven Colonies of Australasia 1899-1900* ff, Government Printer, Sydney, 1900 ff.

New South Wales. Royal Commission on the Administration of the Lands Department, 'Report etc.', *V & P* 1906, vol. 2, p. 1.

Sawer, G., *Australian Federal Politics and Law 1901-1929*, Cheshire, Melbourne, 1956.

Sawer, G., *Australian Federal Policy and Law 1929-1960*, Cheshire, Melbourne, 1963.

South Australia. Royal Commission on the Public Service, *First* and *Second Progress Reports* and *Final Report etc.*, PP Nos 20, 1899; 20, 1901.

3.2 Rural

Australia. Royal Commission on the Butter Industry, *Final Report*, PP No. 11, 1905.

Australia. Royal Commission on the Fruit Industry, *Progress Report* and *Minority Report*, PP No. 9, 1913. *Minutes of Evidence and Appendices*, PP No. 59 1913. *Final Majority Report*, PP No. 32, 1914. *Final Minority Report*, PP No. 24, 1914-1917.

Australia. Royal Commission on the Meat Export Trade, *Report*, PP No. 33, 1914-1917.

Australia. Royal Commission on the Sugar Industry, *Report* and *Minutes of Evidence & Appendices*, PP Nos 59, 1912; 64, 1913.

Dunsdorfs, E., *The Australian Wheat Growing Industry 1788-1948*, MUP, Melbourne, 1956.

Easterby, H.T., *The Queensland Sugar Industry: An Historical Review*, Queensland Government Printer, Brisbane n.d.

King, C.J., *An Outline of Closer Settlement in New South Wales*, NSW Department of Agriculture, Sydney, 1957.

New South Wales. Royal Commission to Inquire into the Condition of the Crown Tenants of the Western Division, 'Report etc.', *V & P* 1901, vol. 4, pp. 131 and 323.

New South Wales. Royal Commission on Forestry, 'Interim Report', *V & P* 1907 (second sess.), vol. 1, p. 191; 'Final Report etc.' and 'Evidence and Appendices', *V & P* 1908 (second sess.), vol. 1, pp. 191 and 343.

New South Wales. Royal Commission on Rural, Pastoral, Agricultural & Dairying Interests, 'Report', *V & P* 1917-18, vol. 1, p. 157.

Queensland. Royal Commission on the Desirability of the Establishing by the Government of More Central Sugar Mills, *Report etc.*, PP, CA 6, 1911-12.

Queensland. Royal Commission on the Supply and Distribution of Wheat and Flour, *Progress Report and Report etc.*, PP, CA 53, 1915.

South Australia. Royal Commission upon the Charges against Produce Merchants, *Report etc.*, PP No. 20, 1907.

South Australia. Royal Commission on the Marketing of Wheat, *Progress and Final Reports*, PP Nos 20, 1908; 23, 1909.

Victoria. Royal Commission on Handling Grain in Bulk, *Report etc.*, PP No. 29, 1902-1903.

Victoria. Royal Commission on The Butter Industry, *Progress* and *Final Reports etc.*, PP Nos 43, 1904; 3, 10 and 10*, 1905.

3.3 Manufacturing

Australia. Royal Commission on the Commonwealth Tariff, *Report etc.*, PP Nos 8, 1905; 3, 4, 5, 6, 11, 12, 13, 53, 56, 57, 58, 113, 114, 115 and 116, 1906.

Australia. Royal Commission on the Tobacco Industry Monopoly, *Report etc.*, PP No. 26, 1906.

New South Wales. Royal Commission on the Alleged Shortage of Labour, 'Interim Report etc.', *V & P* 1911-12, vol. 2, p. 665.

New South Wales. Royal Commission on Construction of Locomotives, 'Precis of Papers and Facts Relating to the Proposed Local Manufacture of Locomotives', *V & P* 1905, vol. 3, p. 39.

Wilkinson, H.L., *The Trust Movement in Australia*, Critchley, Melbourne, 1914.

3.4 Services

Australia. Royal Commission on Insurance, *Progress* and *Final Reports etc.*, PP Nos 10, 1909; 6, 66, 1910.

Butlin, S.J., *Australian and New Zealand Bank*, Longmans, London, 1961.

Gollan, R., *The Commonwealth Bank of Australia. Origins and Early History*, ANUP, Canberra, 1968.

Holder, R.F., *Bank of New South Wales. A History*, 2 vols, Angus & Robertson, Sydney, 1970.

New South Wales. Royal Commission on Uniform Standards for Food and Drugs in the States of the Commonwealth of Australia, 'Report etc.', *V & P* 1913, vol. 4, p. 769.

Queensland. Royal Commission on Local Government, *Report etc.*, PP No. CA 45, 1896.

Victoria. Royal Commission on Local Government Laws, *Report*, PP No. 2, 1902.

Victoria. Royal Commission on Uniform Standards for Foods and Drugs in the States of the Commonwealth of Australia, *Report etc.*, PP No. 11, 1913-14.

3.5 Labour

Commonwealth Bureau of Census and Statistics, *Labour Bulletin* (quarterly), No. 1, May 1913, ff, Melbourne.

Commonwealth Bureau of Census and Statistics, *Labour and Industrial Branch Reports*, Nos 1-11, Melbourne.

McCarthy, P.D., 'The Harvester Judgement', unpublished Ph.D. Thesis, ANU, 1968.

New South Wales. Royal Commission on Strikes, *Report etc.*, Government Printer, Sydney, 1891.

New South Wales. Royal Commission into the Working of Compulsory Conciliation and Arbitration Laws, 'Report', *V & P* 1901, vol. 6, p. 747.

New South Wales. Royal Commission on Industrial Arbitration in the State of New South Wales, 'Interim Report etc.', *V & P* 1913, vol. 2, p. 268; 'Final Report', *V & P* 1913 (second sess.), vol. 2, p. 297.

New South Wales. Royal Commission into the Formation, Constitution and Working of the Machine Shearers' and Shed Employees' Union, Industrial Union of Employees, 'Report etc.', *V & P* 1905, vol. 3, p. 1097.

Sutcliffe, J.T., *A History of Trade Unionism in Australia*, Macmillan, Melbourne, 1921.

South Australia. Royal Commission on the Shortage of Labour in the Clothing and Boot Trades, *First Progress Report etc.*, PP No. 12, 1912.

Victoria. Royal Commission on the Operation of the Factories and Shop Law of Victoria, *Report etc.*, PP Nos 30 and 31, 1902-3.

4 Protection All Round

4.1 Economic Conditions

Aitkin, D., *The Country Party in New South Wales*, ANUP, Canberra, 1972.

Crisp, F.L., *The Australian Federal Labor Party*, Longmans Green, London, 1966.

Ellis, U., *The Country Party. A Political and Social History of the Party in New South Wales*, Cheshire, Melbourne, 1958.

Hancock, W.K., *Australia*, E. Benn, London, 1930.

Scott, Ernest, *Australia During the War*, vol. XI of *Official History of Australia in the War of 1914-18*, Angus & Robertson, Sydney, 1938.

4.2 Rural

Australia. Royal Commission on the Wheat, Flour and Bread Industries, *Reports etc. Nos 1-5*, PP Nos 234, 1932-34; 10, 85, 233, 234 and 235, 1934-37.

British Australian Wool Realisation Association Ltd., *Annual Reports* 1921-26.

Graham, B.D., *The Formation of the Australian Country Parties*, ANUP, Canberra, 1966.

Queensland. Royal Commission on the Fund Raised from Wheat Growers, *Report*, PP No. A 68, 1922.

New South Wales. Royal Commission into the Administration of the Returned Soldiers' Settlement Branch, Department of Lands, 'Report', *V & P* 1921, vol. 1, p. 805.

South Australia. Royal Commission on the Pastoral Industry, *Report etc.*, PP No. 62, 1927.

South Australia. Royal Commission on Rural Settlement, *1st - 8th Progress Reports*, PP Nos 70, 71, 1925; 55, 60, 61, 63, 64, 64a, 1926.

Smith, W.M., *The Marketing of Australian and New Zealand Primary Products*, Pitman, London, 1936.

Victoria. Royal Commission on Soldier Settlement, *Report etc.*, PP No. 32, 1925.

4.3 Manufacturing

Allin, C.D., *Australasian Preferential Tariffs and Imperial Free Trade*, Univ. of Minnesota, 1929.

Australia. Royal Commission on Bonuses for Manufactures Bill, *Report etc.*, PP No. 2, 1904.

Australia. Tariff Board, *Annual Reports*, 1923-1972/73, Government Printer.

Brigden, J.B. et al., *The Australian Tariff: An Economic Inquiry*, MUP & Macmillan, Melbourne, 1929.

Forster, C., *Industrial Development in Australia 1920-1930*, ANU, Canberra, 1964.

Hall, G., 'The Australian Tariff Board 1922-1956', unpublished M.Comm. thesis, Melbourne University, 1958.

Hughes, Helen, *The Australian Iron and Steel Industry 1848-1962*, Cheshire, Melbourne, 1964.

McColl, C.D., 'The tariff: A century of debate', in R. Preston (ed.), *Contemporary Australia*, Duke University Press, Durham, 1969.

Mills, R.C., 'The Tariff Board of Australia', *Economic Record*, III, May 1927.

Scott: see 4.1.

4.4 Services

Australia. Royal Commission on the Monetary and Banking Systems, *Report etc.*, PP No. 74, 1937.

New South Wales. Royal Commission on the Administration of the Dental Board and the Conduct of its Registrar, 'Report', *V & P* 1915-16, vol. 5, p. 217.

Queensland. Royal Commission on the Control and Management of Horse Racing and Race Courses in and around Brisbane and Ipswich, *Report etc.*, PP No. A.2, 1930.

4.5 Labour

Australia. Royal Commission on the Basic Wage, *Report and Memoranda* and *Supplementary Report*, PP Nos 80 and 94, 1920-21.

Commonwealth Bureau of Census and Statistics, *Labour Bulletin* : see 3.5.

Commonwealth Bureau of Census and Statistics, *Labour and Industrial Branch Reports*: see 3.5.

Commonwealth Bureau of Census and Statistics, *Labour Report*, annual, Melbourne.

Foenander, O de R., *Solving Labour Problems in Australia*, MUP, Melbourne, 1941.

Foenander, O de R., *Towards Industrial Peace in Australia*, MUP, Melbourne, 1937.

New South Wales. Royal Commission into the Proposed Reduction of the

Standard Working Week from 48 to 44 Hours, 'Report', *V & P* 1920, vol. 2, p. 1221.

Oxnam, D.W., 'The relation of unskilled to skilled wage rates in Australia', *Economic Record*, XXVI, June 1950.

Sawkins, D.T., 'The effect of the living wage policy on wages for skill', *Economic Record*, VI, Nov. 1930.

4.6 General Economic Management

Australia. Development and Migration Commission, *Report on Unemployment and Business Stability in Australia 1928*, PP No. 252, 1925-29.

Australia. Royal Commission on Taxation, *Reports etc.*, PP Nos 147, 1920-21; 1, 35, 1922; 15, 16, 1923-24.

Benham, F.C., *The Prosperity of Australia*, P.S. King, London, 1928.

Copland, D.B., *Australia in the World Crisis 1929-33*, CUP, Cambridge, 1935.

Copland, D.B., *The Crisis in Australian Finance*, Angus & Robertson, Sydney, 1931.

Gilbert, R.S., *The Australian Loan Council in Federal Fiscal Adjustments 1890-1965*, ANUP, Canberra 1973.

Mathews, R.L., and Jay, W.R.C., *Federal Finance. Intergovernmental financial relations in Australia since Federation*, Nelson, Melbourne, 1972.

Ratchford, B.U., *Public Expenditures in Australia*, Duke University Press, Durham, 1959.

Schedvin, C.B., *Australia and the Great Depression. A Study of Economic Development and Policy in the 1920s and 1930s*, SUP, Sydney, 1970.

Walker, E.R., *Australia in the World Depression*, P.S. King, London, 1933.

5 All the Restrictive Practices Known to Man

5.1 Economic Conditions

Butlin, S.J., *War Economy 1939-42*, The Australian War Memorial, Canberra, 1955.

Butlin, S.J., and Schedvin, C.B., *War Economy 1942-45*, The Australian War Memorial, Canberra, 1979.

Dixon, J. (ed.), *The Public Sector*, Pelican, 1972.

Gruen, F.H. (ed.), *Surveys of Australian Economics*, George Allen & Unwin, Sydney, vol. I, 1978; vol. II, 1979; vol. III, forthcoming.

Pincus, J.J. and Withers, G.A., 'The economics of regulation', in F.H. Gruen (ed.), Vol. III.

Smith, Ben, 'The economics of resources', in F.H. Gruen (ed.), vol. III.

5.2 General Economic Management

Arndt, H.W. and Corden, W.M. (eds), *The Australian Economy. A Volume of Readings*, Cheshire, Melbourne, 1963.

Auld, D.A.L., *Australian Fiscal Policy*, UQP, St Lucia, 1973.

Australia. *Report of the Committee of Economic Enquiry* (mimeo), 1965 (reviewed in whole volume *Economic Record* March 1966).

Australia. *Interim Report from the Senate Select Committee on Securities and Exchange* with minutes and evidence, AGPS, Canberra, 1974.

Australia. *Australian Financial System. Interim Report*, PP No. 167, 1980.

Cameron, B., *Federal Economic Policy*, Cheshire, Melbourne, 1968.
Davis, K. and Lewis, M., 'Monetary policy', in F.H. Gruen (ed.), vol. I: see 5.1.
Downing, R.I. (et al.), *Taxation in Australia. Agenda for Reform*, CUP, Cambridge, 1964.
Groenwegen, P.D., 'Taxation', in F.H. Gruen (ed.), vol. III: see 5.1.
Hagger, A.J., 'Inflation' in F.H. Gruen (ed.), vol. I: see 5.1.
Hirst, R.R. and Wallace, R.H., *Studies in the Australian Capital Market*, Cheshire, Melbourne, 1967.
McFarlane, B.J., *Economic Policy in Australia: The Case for Reform*, Cheshire, Melbourne, 1968.
Mathews, R.L., *Public Investment in Australia*, Cheshire, Melbourne, 1967.
Merry, D.H., 'The changing role of trading banks in the Australian national economy', *Economic Record*, XXXV, April 1959.
Nieuwenhuysen, J.P. and Drake, P.J. (eds), *Australian Economic Policy*, MUP, Melbourne, 1977.
Norton, W.E. (ed.), *Conference in Applied Economic Research*, Reserve Bank of Australia, Sydney, 1979.
Waterman, A.M.C., *Economic Fluctuations in Australia, 1948 to 1968*, ANUP, Canberra, 1973.

5.3 Labour

Australia. Treasury Economic Paper No. 4, *Job Markets, Economic and Statistical Aspects of Australian Markets for Labour*, AGPS, Canberra, 1979.
Gregory, R.G. and Duncan, R.C., 'The labour market in the seventies', in *Conference in Applied Economic Research*, Reserve Bank of Australia, Sydney, 1979.
Nieuwenhuysen, J.P. and Sloan, J., 'Wages policy', in F.H. Gruen (ed.), vol. I: see 5.1.

5.4 Rural

Australia. The Rural Reconstruction Commission, *Reports* Nos 1-10, Government Printer, Canberra, 1944-1946.
Australia. *Rural Policy in Australia. Report to the Prime Minister by a Working Group* (mimeo), 1974.
Crawford, J.G., *Australian Trade Policy 1942-1966. A Documentary History*, ANUP, Canberra, 1968.
Edwards, G.W. and Watson, A.S., 'Agricultural policy', in F.H. Gruen (ed.), vol. I: see 5.1.
Williams, D.B. (ed.), *Agriculture in the Australian Economy*, SUP, Sydney, 1967.

5.5 Manufacturing

Australia. *Policies for Development of Manufacturing Industry, A Green Paper*, PP No. 292, 1975-6.
Australia. *Study Group on Structural Adjustment*, PP No. 59, 1979.
Australia. Industries Assistance Commission, *Annual Reports*, especially 1973-4, AGPS, Canberra, 1974.
Brash, D.T., *American Investment in Australian Industry*, ANU, Canberra, 1966.

Bushnell, J.A., *Australian Company Mergers 1946-1959*, MUP, Melbourne, 1961.

Butlin, N.G., *Sydney's Environmental Amenity 1970-75*, ANUP, Canberra, 1976.

Harris, S.F., 'The Control of Imports into Australia 1952-60', unpublished Ph.D. thesis, ANU, 1964.

Hoover, C.B. (ed.), *Economic Systems of the Commonwealth*, Duke University Press, Durham, 1962.

Hunter, A. (ed.), *The Economics of Australian Industry. Studies in Environment and Structure*, MUP, Melbourne, 1963.

Kasper, W. and Parry, T.G. (eds), *Growth, Trade and Structural Change in an Open Australian Economy*, Department of Economics, Research School of Social Sciences, ANU, 1978.

Lloyd, P.J., 'Protection policy', in F.H. Gruen (ed.), vol. II: see 5.1.

Moffatt, G.G., *Import Control and Industrialization*, MUP, Melbourne, 1970.

Rattigan, G.A., 'The Tariff Board: some reflections', *Economic Record*, 45, March 1969, p. 17.

6 The Poor and Needy

General Note on Social Policy
Mendelsohn (1954, 1979) and Kewley (1973) are the only authors to have studied developments, over the first seventy-five years of the century, in all or a substantial number of those areas of social policy dealt with in chapters 6 to 8. Historians are immensely indebted to them. Mendelsohn (1979) contains the estimates made by Andrew Podger of annual expenditure by each Australian government on social security, health and education from 1900-01 to 1969-70. All three books, as well as Roe (1976), include extensive and largely complementary bibliographies. What follows is therefore highly selective.

General sources, additional to those listed below, that repay consultation on specific issues include the *Official Year Books* of the Commonwealth, New South Wales and Victoria, the *Statistical Registers* of the various States and annual *Reports* of State Ministers of Education or Public Instruction.

6.1 Social Security

Australia. Royal Commission on Old-Age Pensions, *Report, together with proceedings, minutes of evidence, etc.*, PP No. 31, 1906.

Coghlan, T.A., *Labour and Industry in Australia*, OUP, 1918.

Dickey, B., 'Charity in N.S.W. 1850-1914. A study of public, private and state provisions for the poor', unpublished Ph.D. thesis, ANU, 1966.

Gollan, Robin, 'Nationalism, the labour movement and the Commonwealth, 1880-1900', in Gordon Greenwood (ed.), *Australia*.

Gollan, Robin, *Radical and Working Class Politics*, ANU/MUP, Melbourne, 1960.

Greenwood, Gordon, 'National development and social experimentation, 1901-14', in Gordon Greenwood (ed.), *Australia, A Social and Political History*, Angus & Robertson, Sydney, 1955.

Kewley, T.H. (ed.), *Australia's Welfare State*, Macmillan, Melbourne, 1969.

Kewley, T.H., *Social Security in Australia, 1900-72*, SUP, Sydney, revised edition, 1973.

Macarthy, P.G., 'Employers, the tariff, and legal wage determination in Australia, 1890-1910', *Journal of Industrial Relations*, 12, 1970, p. 68.

Macarthy, P.G., 'Justice Higgins and the Harvester judgement', *Australian Economic History Review*, XI(1), March 1969, p. 17 (reprinted in Roe (ed.)).

Macarthy, P.G., 'Labour and the living wage, 1890-1910', *Australian Journal of History and Politics*, vol. 13, April 1967, p. 16.

Macarthy, P.G., 'The living wage in Australia - the role of government', *Labour History*, No. 18, May 1970, p. 3.

Mendelsohn, Ronald, *The Condition of the People: Social Welfare in Australia, 1900-1975*, George Allen & Unwin, Sydney, 1979.

Mendelsohn, Ronald, *Social Security in the British Commonwealth*, Athlone Press, London, 1954.

Nairn, N.B., *Civilising Capitalism*, ANUP, Canberra, 1975.

New South Wales. Royal Commission on Public Charities, [Five] 'Reports, minutes of evidence,etc.', *Journal Legis. Council* 1898, vol. 1, p. 173; 1898 (second sess.), vol. 1, p. 1203; 1899 (second sess.), vol. 1, pp. 67, 523 and 779.

Reeves, W. Pember, *State Experiments in Australia and New Zealand*, Grant Ritchards, London, 1902.

Rickard, John, *Class and Politics*, ANUP, Canberra, 1976.

Roe, Jill (ed.), *Social Policy in Australia: Some Perspectives 1901-1975*, Cassell, Sydney, 1976.

South Australia. Royal Commission on the Aged Poor, *Report, minutes of evidence, etc.*, PP No. 21, 1898-99.

Victoria. Royal Commission on Old-Age Pensions, *First Progress Report, Report with minutes of evidence*, PP Nos 32, 1897; 28, 1898.

6.2 Education

Austin, A.G., and Selleck, R.J.W., *The Australian Government School 1830-1914*, Pitman Pacific Books, Melbourne, 1975.

Barcan, Alan, *A Short History of Education in New South Wales*, Martindale Press, Sydney, 1965.

Crane, A.R., and Walker, W.G., *Peter Board*, Australian Council for Educational Research, Melbourne, 1957.

Fogarty, Ronald, *Catholic Education in Australia 1806-1950*, MUP, Melbourne, 1959.

New South Wales. Royal Commission on the Hours and General Conditions of Employment of Female and Juvenile Labour in Factories and Shops, 'Report and minutes of evidence', *V&P*, 1911-12, vol. 2, p. 1137 (especially sectional report on apprenticeships).

New South Wales. Commission on Primary, Secondary, Technical and Other Branches of Education, 'Interim Report', *Legislative Assembly Papers* 1904, vol. 1, p. 29 and 'Report', *V&P* 1904 (second sess.), vol. 2, p. 453.

Victoria. Department of Education, *Vision and Realization: A Centenary History of State Education in Victoria*, Melbourne, 1973.

Victoria. Royal Commission on Technical Education, [Five] *Progress and Final Reports and minutes of evidence*, PP Nos 34, 51, 1899-1900; 11, 19, 1900; 23, 29, 36, 1901.

6.3 Health

Dickey, Brian, 'The Labour government and medical services in N.S.W., 1910-1914', *Historical Studies*, April 1967, p. 541 (reprinted in J. Roe (ed.): see 6.1).

Inglis, K.S., *Hospital and Community: A History of the Royal Melbourne Hospital*, MUP, Melbourne, 1958.

Thame, Claudia, 'Health and the state: The development of collective responsibility for health care in Australia in the first half of the twentieth century', unpublished Ph.D. thesis, ANU, 1974.

7 The Heroes and the Hungry

7.1 Social Security

Australia. Department of Repatriation, *The Civil Re-establishment of the A.I.F.*, PP No. 67, 1920-21.

Australia. Repatriation Commission, annual *Reports*.

Australia. Royal Commission on the Basic Wage, *Report, and Memoranda* and *Supplementary Report*, PP Nos 80 and 94, 1920-21.

Australia. Royal Commission on Child Endowment or Family Allowances, *Report*, PP No. 20, 1929.

Australia. Royal Commission on National Insurance, [Four] *Reports*, PP Nos 12, 1925; 78, 79 and 120, 1926-28.

Barnard, A., Butlin, N.G., and Pincus, J.J., 'Public and private sector employment in Australia, 1901-74', *Australian Economic Review*, 1st quarter 1977, p. 43.

Bland, F.A., 'Unemployment relief in Australia', *International Labour Review*, July 1934, p. 23 (reprinted in J. Roe (ed.): see 6.1).

Charteris, A.H., 'Family endowment in New South Wales', *Australian Journal of Psychology and Philosophy*, June 1927, p. 94 (reprinted in J. Roe (ed.): see 6.1).

Chenoweth, R.W., *Income and Unemployment Relief Taxes*, The Public Accountants and Students' Society of Victoria, Melbourne, 1935.

Commonwealth Bureau of Census and Statistics, *Labour Bulletin*, annual, Melbourne. Issues in the 1930s have convenient accounts of unemployment taxes and unemployment relief.

Development and Migration Commission, *Report on Unemployment and Business Stability in Australia*, Commonwealth PP No. 252, 1926-28

Greenwood: see 6.1.

Kewley (1969, 1972): see 6.1.

Kristianson, G.L., *The Politics of Patriotism: The Pressure Group Activities of the Returned Soldiers' League*, ANUP, Canberra, 1966.

McDonald, D.I., 'The Australian Soldiers' Repatriation Fund. An experiment in social legislation', *Royal Australian Historical Journal*, 49,5 (1964), p. 376 (reprinted in J. Roe (ed.): see 6.1).

Mendelsohn (1954, 1979): see 6.1.

New South Wales. *Official Year Books* are essential sources of information about child endowment, changes in definitions of the living wage and widows' pensions.

Roe (ed.): see 6.1.

Scott, Ernest, *Australia during the War*, Angus & Robertson, Sydney, 1941 (ch.XXIV).

7.2 Education

Barcan: see 6.2.
Goodman, R., *Secondary Education in Queensland, 1860-1960*, ANUP, Canberra, 1968.
Mitchell, Bruce, *Teachers, Education, and Politics. A History of Organizations of Public School Teachers in New South Wales*, UQP, St Lucia, 1975.
Victoria. Department of Education: see 6.2.

7.3 Health

Inglis: see 6.3.
New South Wales Hospitals Commission, annual *Report*, 1929 to 1939.
Page, Sir Earle, *Truant Surgeon*, Angus & Robertson, Sydney, 1963.
Thame: see 6.3.
Victorian Hospitals and Charities Board, annual *Report*, 1923 to 1939.

8 Welfare for All

8.1 Social Security

Australia. Commission of Inquiry into Poverty, *Outline to First Main Report*, *First Main Report* (vols 1 and 2), *Second Main Report*, *Third Main Report*, *Fifth Main Report*, PP Nos 189, 210, 1975; 80, 1976; 294, 1975; 145 and 368, 1976.
Australia. Department of Social Security, *Annual Report*, 1972-73--.
Australia. Director-General of Social Services, *Report*, 1942 to 1971-71.
Australia. Joint Parliamentary Committee on Social Security, [Nine] *Progress Reports*, PP Nos 48, 71, 72, 77, 88, 104, 1940-43; 11, 1943-44; 21, 71, 1945-46.
Australia. Priorities Review Staff, *Possibilities for Social Welfare in Australia*, PP No. 163, 1975.
Australian Bureau of Statistics, *Income Distribution 1968-69. Consolidated and Revised Edition*, Canberra, 1975. Ref.No. 17.17.
Australian Bureau of Statistics, *Income Distribution 1973-74, Part 1, Part 2* and *Part 3*, Canberra, 1976, 1977 and 1978. Ref. nos 17.6 and 17.8 and Catalogue no. 6504.0.
Bentley, Philip, Collins, D.J., and Drane, N.T., 'The incidence of Australian taxation', *Economic Record*, December 1974, p. 489.
Hancock, K.J., 'The economics of social welfare in the 1970s', in H. Weir (ed.), *Social Welfare in the Seventies*, Australian Council of Social Service, Sydney, 1971.
Henderson, Ronald F., 'Social welfare expenditure', in R.B. Scotton and Helen Ferber (eds).
Jones, M.A., *The Australian Welfare State*, George Allen & Unwin, Sydney, 1980.
Kewley (1969, 1972): see 6.1.
Kewley, T.H., 'Social security: legislative and policy changes', in R.B. Scotton and Helen Ferber (eds).
Mendelsohn (1954, 1979): see 6.1.

OECD, *Public Expenditure on Income Maintenance Programmes*, Paris, 1976.

Podder, N., 'Distribution of household income in Australia', *Economic Record*, June 1972, p. 181.

Podder, N., and Kakwani, N.C., 'Distribution and redistribution of household income in Australia', in Taxation Review Committee, *Commissioned Studies*, Canberra, 1975.

Richardson, S., 'Income distribution, poverty and redistributive policies', in F.H. Gruen (ed.), *Surveys of Australian Economics*, vol. II, George Allen & Unwin, Sydney, 1979.

Roe (ed.): see 6.1.

Scotton, R.B., and Ferber, Helen (eds), *Public Expenditures and Social Policy in Australia*, vol. 1, *The Whitlam Years, 1972-75*, Longman Cheshire, Melbourne, 1978.

Tulloch, Patricia, *Poor Policies: Australian Income Security 1972-77*, Croom Helm, London, 1979.

Warren, N.A., 'Australian tax incidence in 1975-76: some preliminary results', *Australian Economic Review*, 3rd quarter 1979, p. 19.

8.2 Education

Australia. Committee on Technical and Further Education, *Reports*, PP Nos 203, 1974 and 102, 1975.

Australia. Commission of Inquiry into Poverty, *Fifth Main Report*, PP No. 368, 1976.

Australia. Committee on Australian Universities, *Report*, PP No. 12, 1958.

Australia. Committee on the Future of Tertiary Education in Australia, *Report to the Australian Universities Commission* (3 vols), PP Nos 132, 133 and 222, 1964-65.

Australia. Interim Committee for the Australian Schools Commission, *Schools in Australia*, PP No. 55, 1973.

Beighton, F.C.L., and Gallagher, A.P., 'Socio-economic differences between University and C.A.E. students', *The Australian University*, September 1976.

Davey, Patricia, 'Financing of education', in R.B. Scotton and Helen Ferber (eds): see 8.1.

Hogan, Michael Charles, *The Catholic Campaign for State Aid: A Study of a Pressure Group Campaign...1950-72*, Sydney Catholic Theological Faculty, Manly (N.S.W.), 1978.

Mitchell: see 7.2.

Mithen, W.J., 'What is happening in primary education today?', in Peter Gill (ed.), *Catholic Education: Where is it Going*, Cassell, Melbourne, 1972.

Slamowicz, R., Smurthwaite, A.M. and West, L.H.T., 'Trends and biases in university entrance: Monash, 1970-75', *Vestes* XIX(2), 1976, p. 16.

Williams, Bruce, 'Universities and the Universities Commission', in I.K.F. Birch and D. Smart (eds), *The Commonwealth Government and Education 1964-76: Political Initiatives and Developments*, Drummond, Richmond (Victoria), 1977.

8.3 Health

Australia. Committee of Enquiry into Health Insurance, *Report*, PP No. 2, 1969.

Australia. Hospitals and Health Services Commission, *Hospitals in Australia*, PP No. 218, 1974.

Australia. Joint Parliamentary Committee on Social Security, *Sixth, Seventh* and *Eighth Progress Reports*: see 8.1.

Australia. Senate Select Committee on Medical and Hospital Costs, *Report*, PP No. 82, 1970.

Australian Bureau of Statistics, *Australian Health Survey 1977-78*, Catalogue Nos 4309.0, 4310.0, 4311.0.

Barnard, Alan, 'Equity and health policies', in P.N. Troy (ed.), *A Just Society*, George Allen & Unwin, Sydney, 1981.

Deeble, J.S., and Scotton, R.B., 'Compulsory health insurance for Australia', *Australian Economic Review*, 4th quarter 1968, p. 9.

Hunter, Thelma, 'Planning national health policy in Australia, 1941-45', *Public Administration* (London), Autumn 1966, p. 315.

Palmer, G.R., 'Health', in Roy Forward (ed.), *Public Policy in Australia*, Cheshire, Melbourne, 1974.

Scotton, R.B., 'Health services and the public sector', in R.B. Scotton and Helen Ferber (eds): see 8.1.

Scotton, R.B., 'Membership of voluntary health insurance', *Economic Record*, March 1969, p. 69.

Scotton, R.B., 'Voluntary insurance and the incidence of health costs', *Australian Economic Papers*, Dec. 1967, p. 171.

8.4 Housing

Australia. Priorities Review Staff, *Report on Housing*, PP No. 26, 1975.

Hill, M.R., *Housing Finance in Australia*, MUP, Melbourne, 1957.

Jones, M.A., *Housing and Poverty in Australia*, MUP, Melbourne, 1972.

Mendelsohn: see 6.1.

Neutze, M., *Urban Development in Australia*, George Allen & Unwin, Sydney, 1977.

Pugh, C., *Intergovernmental Relations in the Development of Australian Housing Policies*, Centre for Research on Federal Financial Relations, ANU, Canberra, 1976.

9 Statutory Profits

9.1 General Historical

Brigden, J.B., 'State enterprises in Australia', *International Labor Review* XVI, 1, 1927, pp. 26-49.

Eggleston, F.W., *State Socialism in Victoria*, P.S. King & Son, London, 1932.

Fitzpatrick, B., *Public Enterprise Does Pay, a Story of Sucessful Government Industrial and Financial Enterprises in Australia 1911-1944*, Rawson's Book Shop, Melbourne, 1945.

Karmel, P.H. and Brunt, M., *The Structure of the Australian Economy*, F.W. Cheshire, Melbourne, 1963.

Mathews, R.L., *Public Investment in Australia*, F.W. Cheshire, Melbourne, 1967.

McFarlane, B., *Economic Policy in Australia. The Case for Reform*, F.W. Cheshire, Melbourne, 1968.

Neutze, M., *Urban Development in Australia. A Descriptive Analysis*, George Allen & Unwin, Sydney, 1977.

Sharkey, L.L., and Campbell, E.W., *The Story of Government Enterprise in Australia. The Real History of the Commonwealth Bank, the Commonwealth Shipping Line, State Brickworks, etc*, Australian Communist Party, Sydney, 1945.

Wiltshire, K., 'Public enterprises in Australia', in A. Gelinas (ed.), *Public Enterprise and the Public Interest. Proceedings of an International Seminar*, The Institute of Public Administration of Canada, Toronto, 1978.

9.2 General Theoretical

Baumol, W.J., 'On the proper cost tests of natural monopoly in a multiproduct industry', *American Economic Review*, 67, 5, 1977, pp. 809-822.

Demsetz, H., 'Why regulate utilities?', *Journal of Law and Economics*, 11, 1968, pp. 55-65.

Faulhaber, G.R., 'Cross-subsidization: pricing in public enterprise', *American Economic Review*, 65, 1975, pp. 966-977.

Lindsay, C.M., 'A theory of government enterprise', *Journal of Political Economy*, 84.5, 1976, pp. 1061-1077.

Stigler, G.J., *The Citizen and the State. Essays on Regulation*, The University of Chicago Press, Chicago, 1975.

9.3 Organization of Water and Sewerage

Annual Reports of the various regional or State authorities, especially Metropolitan Water, Sewerage and Drainage Board (Sydney); the Hunter District Water Board (New South Wales); the Melbourne and Metropolitan Board of Works; Brisbane City Council; South Australian Engineering and Water Supply Department.

Aird, W.V., *The Water Supply, Sewerage and Drainage of Sydney*, Metropolitan Water, Sewerage and Drainage Board, Sydney, 1961.

Goodsell, J.W., 'The Metropolitan Water, Sewerage and Drainage Board', *Public Administration*, 16, 1957.

Henry, F.J.J., *The Water Supply and Sewerage of Sydney*, Halstead Press, Sydney, 1939.

Larcombe, F.A., *The Advancement of Local Government in New South Wales 1906 to the Present. A History of Local Government in New South Wales*, vol. 3, SUP, Sydney, 1978.

New South Wales. Royal Commission into Rating, Valuation and Local Government Finance, 'Report', *V&P* 1967, vol. 6, p. 785.

Pickett J.C. (ed.), *Public Authorities and Development in Melbourne*, Urban Research Unit, ANU, Canberra, 1973.

Rees, R., *Public Enterprise Economics*, Weidenfeld & Nicolson, 1976.

Scott, R.H., 'Government Enterprise in Australia. Water and Sewerage Management', unpublished ms., Economic History Department, Research School of Social Sciences, ANU, 1981.

9.4 Electricity Industry

Annual Reports of the various Federal, State and regional Electricity Authorities, Boards, Commissions and Trusts.

Boehm, E., 'Ownership and control of the electricity supply industry in Australia', *Economic Record*, 32, 1956, pp. 257-272.

Davidson, B., *Australia Wet or Dry? The Physical and Economic Limits to the Expansion of Irrigation*, MUP, Melbourne, 1969.

Electricity Supply Association of Australia and New Zealand, *Statistics of the Electric Supply Industry in Australia*, Melbourne, annual.

Forward, R., *Public Policy in Australia*, F.W. Cheshire, Melbourne, 1974.

Hardman, D.J., *The Snowy Scheme: Management and Administration*, West Publishing Corp., Sydney, 1970.

Hawkins, R.G., 'The market for energy services' in K.A. Tucker (ed.), *The Economics of the Australian Service Sector*, Croom Helm, London, 1977.

Joint Coal Board, *Reports*, Government Printer, Sydney, 1947 to 1974-75.

Longfield, C.M., *The Past, Present and Future of Australian Power Supplies*, Economic Society of Australia and New Zealand, Melbourne, 1947.

McColl, G.D., *The Economics of Electricity Supply in Australia*, MUP, Melbourne, 1976.

Prest, W., 'The electricity supply industry', in A. Hunter (ed.), *The Economics of Australian Industry. Studies in Environment and Structure*, MUP, Melbourne, 1963.

Queensland. Royal Commission on Electricity, *Report*, PP No. A48, 1936.

Victoria. Royal Commission on Railway and Tramway Systems of Melbourne and Suburbs, *Report*, PP No. 39, 1911.

Swan, P.L., 'Pricing of electricity to Alcoa at Portland, Victoria,' unpublished ms., Department of Economics, The Faculties, ANU, Canberra, March 1981.

Taits Electrical Directory of Australia and New Zealand, Tait Publishing Co., Sydney and Melbourne, 1929.

10 Monopoly Lost

10.1 Basic Official Materials

Considerable institutional and statistical information is to be found in official *Year Books* of the Commonwealth and States, and *Statistical Registers*. The most convenient statistical sources are the *Transport and Communications Bulletins* of the Commonwealth Bureau of Census and Statistics, later called *Rail, Sea and Air Transport* and put out by the Australian Bureau of Statistics. The annual *Reports* of the various government railway authorities present, at least until more recent decades, statistical data as well as arguments and pleas about transport policy; similarly, for the authorities operating the trams and buses: in Victoria, see the *Reports and Statement of Accounts* of the Melbourne and Metropolitan Tramway Board; in New South Wales, the annual *Reports* of Commissioner of Road Transport and Tramways (1931 to 1952), of Government Transport (1953 to 1972) and of Public Transport (1973 to 1975). Besides the royal commissions and other official documents, (see below), the reports on proposed railways and tramways by parliamentary standing committees on public works, especially in New South Wales, provide much useful information.

10.2 Introduction

Blainey, G., *The Tyranny of Distance. How Distance Shaped Australia's History*, Sun Books, Melbourne, 1966.

Butlin, N.G., 'Colonial socialism in Australia, 1860-1900', in H.G.J. Aitken (ed.), *The State and Economic Growth*, Social Science Research Council, New York, 1959.

Hensher, D.A. (ed.), *Urban Transport Economics*, CUP, Cambridge, 1977.

Hirst, R.R., 'The transport industry' in A. Hunter (ed.), *The Economics of Australian Industry. Studies in Environment and Structure*, MUP, Melbourne, 1963.

Webb, G.R. and McMaster, J.C. (eds), *Australian Transport Economics. A Reader*, Australia & New Zealand Book Co., Sydney, 1975.

10.3 Autonomy versus Dependence

New South Wales Railway Department, *The Railways of New South Wales 1855-1955*, Sydney, 1955.

Pratt, E.A., *The State Railway Muddle in Australia*, John Murray, London, 1912.

Victoria. Legislative Assembly. Parliamentary Standing Committee on Railways, *Report on Special Railway Rates*, PP No. 5, 1900; *Land in the Fumina District*, PP No. 1, 1902; *Loading Lands for Public Works in the Beech Forest District*, PP No. C.3, 1904.

Victoria. Royal Commission on the Management of the Railways Department, *Progress Report. Freights and Fares*, PP No. 17, 1902.

Wettenhall, R.L., *Railway Management and Politics in Victoria 1856-1906. Report of a Case Study in the Origins of the Public Corporation*, Royal Institute of Public Administration, Canberra, 1961.

10.4 Expansion 1901 to 1920

Australia. House of Representatives, Select Committee on Australian Overseas and Inter-State Sea Carriage, *Final Report*, PP No. 4, 1920.

Glynn, S., *Government Policy and Agricultural Development. A Study of the Role of Government in the Development of the Western Australian Wheat Belt 1900-1930*, University of Western Australia Press, Nedlands, 1975.

New South Wales. Legislative Assembly. Parliamentary Standing Committee on Public Works, 'Report together with Minutes of Evidence and Plan relating to the Proposed Railway from Hermidale to Nymagee', *V&P* 1910, vol. 2, p. 465; 'Muswellbrook to Mirriwa', *V&P* 1910, vol. 2, p. 631; 'Canowindra to Eugowra', *V&P* 1913, vol. 3, p. 333; 'Coonabarabran to Burren Junction', *V&P* 1913, vol. 3, p. 553.

South Australia. Royal Commission on the Murray Lands Railways, *Progress Reports,* PP Nos 31 and 31a, 1909; 30, 1911-12; 33 and 37, 1912.

Victoria. Royal Commission on Railway Freights and Fares, *Progress* and *Final Reports,* PP Nos 5 and 11, 1902.

Victoria. Royal Commission on the Working as a Business Undertaking of the Victorian Railways, *Interim* and *Final Reports*, PP Nos 8 and 9, 1917.

10.5 Railway Investment between the Wars

Australia. Commonwealth Transport Committee, *Report on the Coordination of Transport in Australia*, PP No. 70, 1929-30.

Copland, D.B., et al., *The Economics of Australian Transport*, Supplement to *The Economic Record*, August 1930.

New South Wales. Legislative Assembly. Parliamentary Standing Committee on Public Works, 'Report, etc.,... Proposed Railway from Cooma to Adaminaby', *V&P* 1925, vol. 1, p. 412; 'Grafton to Killarney', *V&P* 1925

(2), vol. 1, p. 121; 'Hillston to Roto', *V&P* 1928-29, vol. 4, p. 187; 'Combaning to Grong Grong', *V&P* 1930-32, vol. 4, p. 1181.

New South Wales. Royal Commission on the Railway and Tramway Services 'Report etc.', *V&P* 1924, vol. 3, p. 141.

Queensland. The Bureau of Economics and Statistics [J.B. Brigden], *Railway Economics. A General Survey of the Principles and Developments in Australia and Abroad, with an analysis of the Distribution and Causes of Railway Losses in Queensland*, Government Printer, Brisbane, 1931.

Sinclair, W.A., 'Capital formation' in C. Forster (ed.), *Australian Economic Development in the Twentieth Century*, George Allen & Unwin, London, 1970.

South Australia. Royal Commission upon the Control, Administration, and Financial Position of the South Australian Railways, *Progress* and *Final Reports,* PP Nos 5, 1930; 55, 56, 57, 1931.

South Australia. Royal Commission on Traffic Control, *Progress* and *Final Reports,* PP Nos 50, 1926; 56, 1928.

South Australia. Royal Commission on Transport, *Report*, PP No. 20, 1938.

Victoria. Royal Commission upon the Control, Management, Working, and Financial Position of the Victorian Railways, *Report*, PP No. 32, 1928.

Victoria. Royal Commission on Victorian Outer Ports, *Progress Reports*, PP Nos 25, 1925; 41, 1925; 14, 1927.

10.6 Urban Transit

Forster, C., *Industrial Development in Australia 1920-1930*, ANUP, Canberra, 1964.

New South Wales. Legislative Assembly. Parliamentary Standing Committee on Public Works, 'Report etc. Proposed Electric Tramway from Darley Road, Randwick, to Little Coogee', *V&P* 1910 (2), vol. 2, p. 517; 'Curl Curl to Freshwater', *V&P* 1923, vol. 3, p. 833; 'Narrabeen to Mona Vale', *V&P* 1924, vol. 3, p. 813.

St. Clair, D.J., 'Enterpreneurship and the American automobile industry', *Journal of Economic History*, XL, 1, March 1980, pp. 177-179.

10.7 Decline of Public Land Transport 1945 to 1975

Australian Transport Advisory Council. Committee of Transport Economic Research relating to Road and Rail Transport, *Report*, Part 1, *Road Transport Costs, etc.*; Part 2, *Railway Costs and Coordinating Summary*, mimeos, September 1956 and February 1958.

Dodgson, J.S., *The Economics of Australian Railway Deficits*, Centre for Research in Federal Financial Relations, Canberra, 1979.

Ebasco Services Inc., 'Report upon a Study of Department of Railway and Department of Government Transport', New South Wales *V&P* 1962-3-4, vol. 3, p. 357.

Kolsen, H.M., *The Economics and Control of Road-Rail Competition: A Critical Study of Theory and Practice in the United States of America, Great Britain and Australia*, SUP, Sydney, 1968.

Nash, C.A., *Public versus Private Transport*, Macmillan, London, 1976.

Rimmer, P.J., 'Transport' in D.N. Jeans (ed.), *Australia a Geography*, SUP, Sydney, 1977.

Victoria. Legislative Assembly, *Report of the Board of Inquiry into the Victorian Land Transport System* ['The Bland Report'], PP No. 29, 1972.

10.8 Some Political Factors
Maxcy, G., 'The motor industry' in A. Hunter (ed.), *The Economics of Australian Industry. Studies in Environment and Structure*, MUP, Melbourne, 1963.
Nelson, J.C., 'The economic effects of transport deregulation in Australia', *Transportation Journal*, Winter 1976, pp. 48-71.

10.9 Urban Travel 1945 to 1975
Manning, I., *The Journey to Work*, George Allen & Unwin, Sydney, 1978.

10.10 Financial Results 1945 to 1975
Australia. Bureau of Transport Economics, *Long Distance Road Haulage Industry*, AGPS, Canberra, 1979.
Rimmer, P.J., 'Freight-forwarding: changes in structure, conduct and performance', in K.A. Tucker (ed.), *The Economics of the Australian Service Sector*, Croom Helm, London, 1977.

10.11 Domestic Air Transport
Australia. Department of Transport, *Domestic Air Transport Policy Review*, Canberra, 1979.
Brogden, S., *Australia's Two Airline Policy*, MUP, Melbourne, 1968.
Corbett, D., *Politics and Airlines*, George Allen & Unwin, London, 1965.
Davies, D.G., 'The efficiency of public versus private firms: the case of Australia's two airlines', *Journal of Law and Economics* XIV, 1, April 1971, pp. 149-65.
Forsyth, P.J. and Hocking, R.D., 'Property rights and efficiency in a regulated environment: the case of Australian airlines', *Economic Record*, 56, 153, June 1980, pp. 182-185.
Kirby, M.G., *Domestic Airline Regulation. The Australian Debate*, The Centre for Independent Studies, St. Leonards (NSW), 1981.
Mackay, K.R., 'A comparison of the relative efficiency of Australian domestic airlines and foreign airlines', Appendix A6.1 in Australia. Department of Transport, *Domestic Air Transport Policy Review*, vol. 2, AGPS, Canberra, 1979.

11 Service at Any Cost
Annual *Reports* of the Postmaster-General's Department (from 1910) and The Overseas Telecommunications Commission (from 1947).
Australia. Ad Hoc Committee of Inquiry into the Commercial Accounts of the Post Office, *Report of the Majority, Report of the Minority, etc.*, PP No. 12, 1961.
Australia. Anderson, R.McC., *Report on the Business Management of the Postmaster-General's Department of the Commonwealth of Australia*, PP No. 205, 1914-15.
Australia. Commission of Inquiry into the Australian Post Office, vol. 1: *Commission Report*; vol. 2: *Consultants Reports*, PP No. 123, 1975.
Australia. Commonwealth Public Service Commissioner, *Memorandum Relating to Recommendations of the Royal Commission on Postal Services*, PP No. 15, 1911.
Australia. Joint Committee of Public Accounts, *Twelfth Report: Postmaster General's Department*, PP No. 14, 1954; *Nineteenth Report: Treasury*

Minute and Comments of Postmaster-General's Department on the Twelfth Report, etc., PP No. 97, 1954-55.

Australia. *Progress Report of Inquiry in relation to the Post Office*, PP No. 195, 1907-08.

Australia. Royal Commission on Postal Service, *Report, etc.*, PP Nos 50, 52, 53, and 54, 1910.

Australia. Royal Commission on Public Expenditure of the Commonwealth with a view to effecting Economies, *First Progress Report, etc.*, PP Nos 176, 179 and 181, 1917-19; 47, 64 and 84, 1920-21.

Barnard, A., 'Cui Bono?: The Post Office at Work', *unpublished ms.*, Economic History Department, Research School of Social Sciences, ANU, 1978.

Caiden, G.E., *The A.C.P.T.A.: a Study of White Collar Public Service Unionism in the Commonwealth of Australia, 1885-1922*, Department of Political Science, Research School of Social Sciences, ANU, Canberra, 1966.

Caiden, G.E., *Career Service: An Introduction to the History of Personnel Administration in the Commonwealth Public Service of Australia 1901-1961*, MUP, Melbourne, 1965.

Coghlan, T.A., *The Wealth and Progress of New South Wales*, W.A. Gullick, Sydney, 1887.

Index

Agricultural education and extension services, 87–8

Agricultural protection, 135, *see also* Rural

Aid to private industry: airlines, 289, 291, 295, 305; electricity, 252–3; manufacturing, 250, 281; motor vehicle industry, 278–9, 281; road hauliers, 281, *see also* Manufacturing, Rural

Airlines, 126–7

Anti-monopolistic legislation, 125–7

Arbitration, 61, 71–3, 75, 99, 100, 102, 150, 152–4, 180, 331; labour input decisions, PMG, 300–1; labour input decisions, railways, 261, 267, *see also* Basic wages, Labour, Wages

Banks and finance companies regulation, 65–6, 97–8, 121–4

Basic wage, 72, 128, 150–5, 173, 179–80

Bounties, 91

British preferential tariff, 89–91

Centralisation of regulation, 331, 333–43

Charities: private, 155–6, 163, 173–4, 181, 203–4; public funding, 157, 162–3, 194; and veterans benefits, 173–4

Child endowment, 179, 184–5, 198–201

Child welfare, 157, 162, 184–5, 188

Closer settlement, 138

Colonial socialism: and Australian public securities in London, 16; concept of, 320–1; decline of, 320–7; and direct market intervention by government, 11–12; and effects of the depression, 12; and expansion of private sector, 12; general, 11–18; and immigration policy, 14–15; influence of market failure on, 322; and nature of indirect intervention, 11; and private dependence on public action 1890's recession, 17–18; and public foreign borrowing and capital formation, 15–16; and public ownership of large business enterprises, 13–14; and role public service, 16; and scale of public intervention by 1900, 16–17; and shift from direct to indirect public intervention, 10; and supportive relations between private and public sector, 11, 13, 19; and transfer of overseas capital, labour, technology, 13–14; and yields on public assets, 15

Commonwealth bank, 67, 121–2

Comparative wage justice, 130

Construction industry, 69–70, 96

Cross subsidisation, 341; airlines, 291–2; electricity, 252–3; general, 237–8; PMG, 241, 295, 297, 309, 314, 316–18; railways, 260, 266, 269, 274, 277, 286–8; water supply, 250–1

Crowding out or displacement, 326

Developmentalism: electricity, 238, 254–7; PMG, 303–4; railways, 261, 264, 268–9, 274, 278

Direct import restrictions, *see* quotas

Economic and political change 1900–1914 summary outline, 50–5; and Federal powers, 51–2; and Labor party, 51, 54–5; and construction, 54; and diversification rural exports, 53;